Maharshi Dayanand Saraswati Book Series-1

The Yogadarśana

(The Science of Psycho-engineering)

Sanskrit Text, Roman Transliteration and Scientific English
Translation according to Vyāsa Bhāṣya and Bhoja Vṛtti

Prof. Ravi Prakash Arya

Chair Professor
Maharshi Dayanand Saraswati Chair (UGC)
Maharshi Dayanand University, Rohtak, Haryana (India)

Assisted by

Dr. Claudia Wanessa Poletto

Director
YOGA e CIÊNCIA Online Courses, Brazil

Amazon Books, USA

In Association with

Indian Foundation for Vedic Science

1051, Sector-1, Rohtak, Haryana, India; Ph. 9313033917
Email: vedicscience@rediffmail.com; vedicscience@gmail.com
website: https://vedic-sciences.com

First Edition
Kali era 5122 (c. 2021)
Kalpa era 1,97,29,49,122
Brahma era 15,55,21,97,29,49,122

ISBN: 9788194759317

© Author

Printed by

Indian Foundation for Vedic Science, 1051, Sector-1, Rohtak-124001, Haryana

Contents

Preface

Diwan Bahadur Harbilas Sarda (2007:252) says, "Philosophy is the real ruler of the globe. It lays down principles that guide the world. Philosophy shows how a transcendent genius exacts homage consciously or unconsciously from lower intellects. It is philosophy that blows the trumpet blast, and it is philosophy that blunts the edge of the sword. Philosophy reigns supreme, undisputed, and absolute. It conquers the conqueror and subdues the subduer".

If it is true that a great nation alone can produce great philosophers or a complete system of philosophy, the ancient Indians may, without hesitation, be proclaimed as the greatest nation. 'Philosophers,' says Professor Max Müller (1859:564-565) 'arise after the security of a State has been established, after wealth has been acquired and accumulated in certain families, after schools and universities have been founded and taste created for those literary pursuits which even in the most advanced state of civilization must necessarily be confined to but a small portion of an ever toiling community.'

To what high pinnacle of civilization, then, must the ancient Indians have reached, says Professor Max Müller (1859:31) further on that 'the Hindus were a nation of philosophers'

The philosophy of the Vedic people is another proof of their superiority in civilization and intellect to the moderns as well as the ancients. Mrs. Manning (1869:

vol. 1, p. 114) says, 'The Hindus had the widest range of mind of which man is capable.'

Schlegel (1818) speaks of the noble, clear, and severely grand accents of Indian thought and says, 'Even the loftiest philosophy of the Europeans, the idealism of reason, as is set forth by Greek philosophers, appears in comparison with the abundant light and vigour of Oriental idealism like a feeble promethean spark in the full flood of heavenly glory of the noon day sun–faltering and feeble and ever ready to be extinguished.' (Sarda, 2007:253)

Professor Weber (1878:27), speaking of Hindu philosophy says, 'It is in this field and that of grammar that the Indian mind attained the highest pitch of its marvellous fertility.' 'The Hindus,' says Max Müller (1859:565), 'were a people remarkably gifted for philosophical abstraction.' Schlegel (1818:126) says, 'India is pre-eminently distinguished for the many traits of original grandeur of thought and of the wonderful remains of immediate knowledge.'

Like all other things in India, the Hindu philosophy, too, is on a gigantic scale. Every shade of opinion, every mode of thought, every school of philosophy has found its expression in the philosophical writings of the Hindus and received its full development. (Sarda, 2007:253). Sir W. Hunter (1881:213-214) says, 'The problems of thought and being of mind and matter and soul apart from both, of the origin of evil, of the sommum bonum of life, of necessity and freewill, and of the relations of the creator to the creature, and the intellectual problems, such as the compatibility of evil with the goodness of God and the unequal distribution of happiness and misery in this life, are endlessly discussed. Brahmin Philosophy exhausted the possible solutions of these difficulties and of most of the other great problems which have since perplexed Greeks, Romans, Mediaeval school men and modern men of science.'

Speaking of the comprehensiveness of Indian philosophy, Dr. Alexander Duff is reported to have said in a speech delivered in Scotland, that 'Hindu philosophy was so comprehensive that counterparts of all systems of European philosophy were to be found in it.' (Sarda, 2007:254).

Professor Goldstucker finds in the Upaniṣads, 'the germs of all the philosophies' (Mrs.Manning, 1869: Vol.1, 149). Count Bjornstjerna (1844:29-30) says, 'In a metaphysical point of view we find among the Hindus all the fundamental ideas of those vast systems which, regarded merely as the offspring of fantasy, nevertheless, inspire admiration on account of the boldness of flight and of the faculty of the human mind to elevate itself to such remote ethereal regions. We find among them all the principles of Pantheism, Spinozism, and Hegelianism, of God as being one with the universe; of the eternal spirit descended on earth in the whole spiritual life of mankind; of the return of the emanative sparks after death to their divine origin; of the uninterrupted alternation between life and death, which is nothing else but a transition between different modes of existence. All this we find again among the philosophers of the Hindus exhibited as clearly as by our modern philosophers more than three thousand years since'.

Here we cannot afford to avoid the prejudiced view of James Mill who was all out to give the most stupid statement that can ever be given by a learned person on this globe. He ventures to say that Hindus were extremely barbarous, for they cultivated metaphysics so largely. Prof. Wilson had to come out to take exception of it. He (1845:74, ft.) said, 'With regard to the writer's theory that the cultivation of metaphysics is a proof rather of civilization than of barbarism, it may be asked if Locke, Descartes, Leibnitz, Kant, Schelling were barbarous'. According to Harbilas Sarda (2007: 255 fn.), Mr. James Mill is a conspicuous instance of a man whose mind becomes completely wrapped by prejudice. Mill's mind could conceive the most absurd impossibilities. 'Mr. Mill', says Wilson, 'seems inclined to think that it was not impossible that the Pyramids had dropped from the clouds or sprung out of the soil.' How this perverted intellect could educate one of the greatest English thinkers is a problem of some psychological interest.

Even with the limited knowledge of Hindu philosophy and science that could be obtained at the time, Sir William Jones could say, 'I can venture to affirm without meaning to pluck a leaf from the never-fading laurels of our immortal Newton, that the whole of his theology, and part of his philosophy, may be found in the Vedas, and even in the works of the Sufis. The most subtle spirit which he suspected to pervade natural bodies, and lying concealed in them, to cause attraction and repulsion; the emission; reflection and refraction of light; electricity; sensation and muscular motion; is described by the Hindus as the fifth element, endued with those very powers.'(Sarda, 2007: 255)

Mrs. Besant while delivering a lecture at National University in India (Calcutta) in January 1906 says,

'Indian psychology is far more perfect a Science than European psychology'. (Sarda, 2007: 255)

Professor Max Müller has observed, 'the Hindus talk philosophy in the streets,' and to this reason is due to the thoroughly practical character of their philosophy.' (Sarda, 2007:255) 'In this respect,' says Bjornstjerna (1844:27), 'the Hindus were far in advance of the philosophers of Greece and Rome, who considered the immortality of the soul as problematical.'

'Socrates and Plato with all their longings could only feel assured that the soul had more of immortality than anything else.' In India, however, the doctrine has not been accepted in theory only, it moulds the conduct of the whole nation. This is true of philosophy. And it is due to its practical character that Hindu philosophy has extended its sway over so wide an area of the globe. Hindu philosophy even now holds undisputed sway over the minds of nearly half the inhabitants of the world, whilst its partial influence is no doubt universal. (Sarda, 2007:255-256).

In ancient times people came to India from distant lands to acquire learning and gain wisdom, and Hindu philosophy thus worked silently for centuries. That the Egyptians derived their religion, mythology, and philosophy from the Hindus has been clearly established by Count Bjornstjerna; and that the Greek philosophy, too, was indebted almost wholly to the Hindu philosophy for its cardinal doctrines has also been shown by eminent Orientalists. The resemblance 'between the Hindu and the Greek philosophy is too close to be accidental. The Hindus being far more advanced, must be the teachers, and the Greeks, the disciples. Mr.

Colebrooke (1827:579), the eminent antiquarian, decides in favour of Hindu originality and says, 'The Hindus were, in this respect, the teachers and not the learners.'

Dr. Enfield (1791:49) says, 'From whatever quarter India, the country which, as adjacent to Persia, next comes under our notice, received its wisdom, there can be no doubt that its wise men very early obtained a high degree of reputation. We find that it (India) was visited for the purpose of acquiring knowledge by Pythagoras, Annaxarchus, Pyrrho, and others who afterwards became eminent philosophers in Greece.'

Discussing the question as to what constitutes human nature according to the Hindus, the Swedish Count (Bjornstjerna, 1844:77) says, 'Pythagoras and Plato hold the same doctrine, that of Pythagoras being probably derived from India, whither he travelled to complete his philosophical studies.' Mr. Pococke (Ravi Prakash Arya, 2003:340) says, 'Certain it is that he (Pythagoras) visited India, which I trust it shall make self-evident.'

Schlegel (1818:109) says, 'The doctrine of the transmigration of souls. was indigenous to India and was brought into Greece by Pythagoras.'

Mr. Princep says, 'The fact, however, that he (Pythagoras) derived his doctrines from an Indian source is very generally admitted. Under the name of Mythraic, the faith of Buddha had also a wide extension.' (Ravi Prakash Arya, 2003:347).

Monier Williams (1879:68) says that Pythagoras and Plato both believed in this doctrine, and that they were indebted for it to Hindu writers.

'Pyrrhon', according to Alexander Polyhistor, 'went

with Alexander the Great to India, and hence the skepticism of Pyrrhon is connected with the Buddhist philosophy of India' (Max Müller, 1866:86).

According to Greek tradition, Thales, Empedocles, Anaxagoras, Democritus, and others undertook journeys to Oriental countries in order to study philosophy (Praphulla Chandra, 1902:2).

Professor H. H. Wilson (1864:Preface XIV) says, 'We know that there was an active communication between India and the Red Sea in the early ages of the Christian era, and that doctrines, as well as article of merchandise, were brought to Alexandria from the former. Epiphanius and Eusebius accuse Scythianus of having imported from India in the second century, books on magic and heretical notions leading to Manichaeism; and it was at the same period that Ammonius Saccas instituted the sect of the New Platonists at Alexandria. The basis of the heresy was that true philosophy derived its origin from the Eastern nations.'

Mr. Davies (1907:196) says, "Scythianus was a contemporary of the Apostles, and was engaged as a merchant in the Indian trade. In the course of his traffic, he often visited India and made himself acquainted with Hindu philosophy. Having amassed a considerable fortune, he settled at length in Alexandria, and here, according to Epiphanius and Cyril, he wrote a book in four parts, which they affirm to be the source from which the Manichaean doctrines were derived."

It is thus clear that the Hindu philosophy is the fountain head of the Greek philosophy with regard to some of its cardinal points. True philosophy in fact originated with the Hindus. Man first distinguished the

Eternal from the perishable, and next he perceived within himself the germ of the Eternal (Sarda, 2007:258).

'This discovery,' says Professor Max Müller (1859:20), "Was an epoch in the history of the human mind, and the name of the discoverer has not been forgotten. It was Śāṇḍilya who declared that the self within the heart was Brahmā."

Excluding the extensive atheistic and agnostic systems of philosophy propounded by Chārvaka and others, and those by the Jain and Buddhistic philosophers, the principal Hindu schools of philosophy are known as the *Darśanas*. But much of the philosophical literature of the Hindus is lost. Professor Goldstucker, too, thinks that 'probably besides the *Upaniṣads,* there were philosophical works which were more original than those now preserved, and which served as the common source of the works which have come down to us as the six Darśanas. (Sarda, 2007:259).

The six Darśanas are: *Nyāya* and *Vaiśeṣika; Sāṅkhya* and *Yoga*; and *Pūrva* and *Uttara Mimānsās.* Since the present work is devoted to the *Yogadarśana*, so it would not be out of context to say a few words on Yoga.

Yoga is the psycho-engineering that elaborates upon the procedure of disembodiment of the soul. Without the knowledge of Yoga,[1] one cannot reach the real depths of human nature, and can never fathom the hidden mysteries and the realities of the heart, and know the nature of the soul and of God. True metaphysics is impossible without Yoga, and so is mental philosophy.

---

[1] Al-Baruni translated Sāṅkhya and *Yoga* into Arabic in the reign of Khalifa Al-Mammum (Max Müller, 1866:165).

Pata¤jali divides his work into four chapters. The first chapter, after discussing the nature of the soul and of Yoga, enumerates eight means or stages in the process by which Yoga can be accomplished.

The second chapter describes in detail the ways and means to perform Samādhi. The third chapter describes the powers developed in a Yogī, when he has reached the last stage of Yoga. Sañyama (when three dhāraṇā, dhyāna and samādhi are together focussed on different objects imparts different divine powers to the Yogī). Sañyama on the sun gives one particular power, on the Jupiter another and so on. The fourth, chapter treats Mokṣa. Patañjali declares that when a man becomes an adept at Samādhi, he gains a knowledge of the past and the future, a knowledge of the sounds of animals, of the thoughts of others, the time of his own death, etc.

In an instance recorded by Prof. Wilson (1861:209-210), a Brahmaṇa appeared to sit in the air wholly unsupported and to remain so sitting on one occasion for twelve minutes and on another for forty minutes.

Colonel Olcott (1885: 141-142) records an account of a Yogī described to him by Dr. Rajendralal Mitra, "It is not known when this Yogī went into Samādhi, but his body was found about 45 years ago quite lifeless in Sunderbunds by woodchoppers. All manner of tortures were used by the Hindu Rājā and the Englishman to bring him back to consciousness, but all to no purpose. People were not able to arouse him by shouting, pushing, beating, putting fire into his hands, plunging him into deep waters into the Ganges with a rope in his as if he were a ship's anchor and twice keeping him there all night. They pried his tetanus jaws apart, put beef into his mouth and poured brandy down his throat. He was then touched by the hand of a female and he instantly came back to his senses, but died shortly after sometime due to the effect of food poison they had forced into him."

Dr. McGregor (1846) says in his *History of the Sikhs*, "A novel scene occurred at one of these garden houses in 1837. A faqeer who arrived at Lahore engaged to bury himself for any length of time shut up in a box without either food or drink! Runjeet disbelieved his assertions, and determined to put them to proof; for this purpose, the man was shut up in a wooden box, which was placed in a small apartment below the level of the ground. There was a folding door to the box which was secured by a lock and key. Surrounding this apartment there was the garden house, the door of which was likewise locked: and outside of this a high wall having the door built up with bricks and mud. Outside the hole, there was placed a line of *santries* (guards), so that no one could approach the building. The strictest watch was kept for the space of forty days and forty nights, at the expiration of which period the Mahārājā, attended by his grandson and several of his Sirdars, as well as General Ventum, Captain Wade, and myself, proceeded to disinter the fakeer.' After describing the condition of the fakeer after disinterment, in a few words, the author says, 'When the fakeer was able to converse, the completion of the feat was announced by the discharge of guns and other demonstrations of joy; while a rich chain of gold was placed round his neck by Runjeet himself.'

Another gentleman of unimpeachable veracity

describes the wonderful feat of a Lama who became his guest in September 1887 at Darjeeling. After describing his postures, etc., the eye-witness proceeds: 'Suddenly he, still retaining his sitting posture, rose perpendicularly into the air to the height of, I should say, two cubits (one yard), and then floated without a tremor or motion of a single muscle, like a cork in still water. The above are two out of numberless similar cases. In India not only these things but feats of a far more extraordinary nature are so common that they fail to evoke surprise at all. "

Fryer was quite astonished to see Yogīs who fixed their eyes towards the sun without losing their sight.

The Yoga philosophy is peculiar to the Vedic people, and no trace of it is found in any other nation, ancient or modern. It was the fruit of the highest intellectual and spiritual development. The existence of this system is another proof of the intellectual superiority of the ancient Vedic people over all other peoples.

It may be informed that there is no dearth of editions, small and voluminous alike, on Yogadarśana with English and Hindi translations in the market, but none of the editions have been able to give the actual and factual estimate of Patañjali's Yogasūtras based upon Vedic ethos and philosophy. These days, yoga has become the most popular subject throughout the world and there have emerged innumerable schools of yoga which try to read methods of yoga propounded by them in the Patañjali's Yogadarśana, so the various editions of Yogadarśana present in the shelves of modern libraries are not able to pluck out the actual intended sense of Yogasūtras. Keeping in view of the desideratum of a scientific edition of Yogasdarśana based upon the ancient commentaries of

Vyāsa and king Bhoja, the author of the present lines has come forward to present the Vedic philosophy of yoga handed down to us by a great seer Patañjali in the most modern scientific terms. Through this edition, the readers and seekers will find an opportunity to learn more clearly about the work of Patañjali.

Here I must not fail to acknowledge the selfless help rendered by Dr. Claudia Wanessa Poletto, a popular Yoga teacher and scholar of Yoga philosophy in the west for sparing her valuable time in going through the present manuscript of Yogadarśana. She tried to explain some of the intricate issues of Yogadarśana through graphic-designs thus adding to the beauty of the book. After finishing the work on this edition, she observed as follows:

"In this work, it can be observed that in a brilliant, concise, and descriptive way, Patañjali used words to express one of the legacies of Yoga. After millennia of his angular work is still reverberating majestically. The term engineering can be understood as a set of technical and scientific knowledge that aims at its application and implementation so that a certain function or objective can be realized. That is why, the understanding of Patañjali's work as a "Science of Psycho-engineering", because it is a methodology that leads to human liberation. Another fundamental factor of his work is perpetuity, only the Truth has this power of survival over time and space, as it sustains itself. The genius of Patañjali and his commentators lies in a profoundly experienced wisdom, that is, not only words from intellectuality, but also by the real verification of the proposed path."

The above observations are self-explanatory and no further elaboration is required.

Last but not the least, it gives me immense pleasure to inform you that this valuable first-ever scientific English rendering of the Yogadarśana based upon Vyāsa-bhāṣya and Bhoja-vṛtti is the first work to be released and published on my appointment (post-retirement) as a Chair Professor on Maharshi Dayanand Chair (UGC) in Maharshi Dayanand University, Rohtak. Here it may be pointed out that Maharshi Dayanand Saraswati (1824-1883 A.D) was the first Vedic scholar, social reformer and the foremost leader of the first Indian renaissance who highlighted the importance of the revival of the Vedas, Pāṇini's Grammar and Patañjali's Yogadarśana for the upliftment of the Indian society in particular and humanity at large in general. He was a great embodiment of Vedic life and thought. The clarion call 'Back to the Vedas' given by him still reverberates in the minds of the Indian masses. This work is a humble tribute to such a great 'Renaissance Rishi'.

Prof. Dr. Ravi Prakash Arya
Chicago, USA

Introduction

Six philosophical thoughts, most often called as Ṣaḍ Darśanas of ancient India are the help books to understand the different aspects of the comprehensive knowledge enshrined in the Vedas. These six Darśanas are not different from Vedas, but the part and parcel of the long Vedic tradition of India. That is why, these books are called as Āstika (theist) Darśanas as they are pro-Vedas or say follow the guidelines of the Vedas. The philosophical thoughts developed other than these were called as Nāstika Darśanas or the philosophical thoughts developed disregarding the guidelines of the Vedas. The terms Āstika and Nāstika denote respectively pro-Vedas and anti-Vedas. Yogadarśana deals with the spiritual/metaphysical aspect of creation and achievement of liberation. Its main objective is to help human beings to develop themselves to the extent as to realise the Supreme Power/God.

All the six philosophical schools supplement each other. They deal with separate aspects of knowledge and creation. For instance, Mīmānsā of Jaminī deals with karmakāṇḍa. The Karmakāṇḍa represents karmas to be done by human beings for their pāmārthika (spiritual) elevation and laukika (material) upliftment and advancement. Thus karmakāṇḍa of Mimānsā at one side deals with karmas that produce sāttvika sanskāras leading an individual towards divinity, on the other hand, it talks about the sankāras of material things for devising eco-friendly technology for upliftment and advancement of human life at the laukika level.

Thus, according to the Vedic philosophy, the purpose of karmakāṇḍa is the Sanskāra of dravyas (matter and soul) for their spiritual and material upliftment and advancement of human beings. Mimānsā philosopher, Jaimini (3100 BC), defines karma as under:

द्रव्यसंस्कार कर्मसु परार्थत्वात् फलश्रुतिरर्थवादः स्यात् ॥ 4.3.1

Karma is the sanskāra of the matter (made of five gross elements) for developing technology for the benefit of humanity so that the technology may provide desired results.

Further defining the purpose of the karma, Jaimini says:

द्रव्याणां तु क्रियार्थानां संस्कारः क्रतुधर्मः स्यात् ॥ 4.3.8

The main objective of the क्रतुधर्मः (karma) is the sanskāra (processing) of the material things for developing various technologies.

Here it may be known that the modern technique of refinement, modification, purification, and processing the material things is known in Vedic science as sanskāra. The main thrust of modern science has been the sanskāra of material things of the external world and to develop a technology to promote the convenience and comfort of human beings. Here there is a basic difference in the concept of Vedic Science and modern science. Vedic science stresses upon the sanskāra of human beings primarily before going for the sanskāra of material things. According to Vedic science, a human being who has not gone through the certain process of sanskāras remains in his crude form and is recognized as no better than an animal. As such, a human being is not considered to be the actual social being. Just as the material things cannot be used efficiently so long as they are used in their crude form, similarly, a human being without undergoing the process of sanskāras, cannot become a social, cultural, and civilised being. As for the practical application, the material things are subjected to undergo a particular process of refinement or sanskāra, like an oil in its crude form cannot be used, but after undergoing the process of refinement it becomes usable. Thus, the conversion of oil from its crude form to the refined form is known as kratudharma (engineering). Similarly, the processing of other material things for the use of human beings is also known as kratudharma (engineering). In the race for developing technology, modern science has totally ignored the need for sanskāra of humans. It is worth mentioning that the paradigm of modern science is based on rationality supremacy over any metaphysical approach. That is why, today in the age of machinery, human beings are also considered as good as machines. They are equated with lifeless things and so there is always a talk of human resource development and never as human development. The concept of human resource development is embedded in the very philosophy that gives human beings no better value than other natural resources, which are often exploited for the benefit of the exploiter and so are human beings. However, there is a basic difference between the exploitation of natural sources and the exploitation of human resources. The exploitation of natural resources takes place uniformly for the benefit of humanity at large. But so far as human beings are concerned, the poor and weak are exploited by the powerful and rich creating a systemic and complex power relation.

So, Vedas are equally concerned about the sanskāra of human beings as well as material things for developing technologies beneficial to humankind. Vedic seers never considered human beings as the resource or means, but as ends. Everything is directed towards the development and elevation of human beings.

The Vaiśeṣika of Kaṇāda deals with the physics and metaphysics of the existing universe in an elegant way. It explains and describes the guṇa-dharmas (properties) of the nine constituents of the existing universe called dravyas. Accordingly,

पृथिव्यापस्तेजो वायुराकाशं कालो दिगात्मा मन इति द्रव्याणि ।

Pṛthivī (solid), Āpaḥ (liquid), Teja (heat and light), Vāyu (air, vitality), Ākāśa (spatiality), Kāla (time), Dik (Space), Ātmā (soul) and Mana (mind) are called Dravyas (substance).

Nyāya of Gautama deals with the research methodology. It teaches us all methods and techniques through which a human being can attain knowledge of material things, cosmos, and Brahman.

Vedānta of Vyasa deals with the supreme entity called Brahman who is the nimitta kāraṇa (efficient cause) of the whole creation and the Governor of the universe in the manifest as well as the unmanifest state. This whole universe is governed by certain rules which are nothing but the will of Brahman. This will of Brahman is also called a unified law or Ṛta which is at work in the existing universe in diverse forms.

Sāṅkhaya of Kapila deals with the embodiment and

disembodiment of an individual soul. It also deals with the process of creation of the material and immaterial world.

Lastly, yoga is a science of psycho-engineering. It provides all tools and techniques as to how to engineer the human mind so that an individual being may be elevated towards divinity. It reveals the secrets of life, death, and mokṣa. Just as physical sciences and technologies involve kinetic and potential energies for their operation, similarly science of psycho-engineering and māntrika technology developed in ancient India was based on Bhāvanā Sanskāra or psychic energy, which modern science has never acknowledged as 'real' in human nature. Yogadarśana teaches us how to pool the psychic energy and utilize it in achieving various siddhis or divine powers without attachment. Yoga enables one to command over one's mental functions by knowing its processes and developing the full potential. A long journey of discipline and commitment with no shortcut to achieving enlightenment or self-realization.

The Yoga-tradition

The Yoga and Sāṅkhya are the twin Śāstras, as it is known from the Bhagvadgitā. If one is the theory, another is the practical aspect of the same. The tradition of Yoga and Sāṅkhya is very old. It started from the Vedas and developed as a separate school by the end of Upaniṣads. In Bhagvadgitā we find the mention of the antiquity of this tradition. Accordingly, Sāṅkhya-tradition was prevalent by the end of the Satyayuga of Vaivasvantara Manvantara. I quote here the śloka from Bhagvadgitā shedding light on the antiquity of Sāṅkhya-tradition as under:

पंचेमानि महाबाहो कारणानि निबोध मे ।

सांख्ये कृतान्ते प्रोक्तानि सिद्धये सर्वकर्मणाम् ।। 18.13

pañchemāni mahābāho kāraṇāni nibodha me.

Sāṅkhye kṛtānte proktāni siddhaye sarva-karmaṇām.

Learn from Me, O Arjuna, the five causative factors for the birth of anything, as described in the Sāṅkhya doctrine by the end of Satyayuga. They play a lead role in the accomplishment of all actions/works. This means thereby any action cannot be accomplished if any one of the five causative factors is missing.

The above verse of the Bhagvadgītā, tells clearly that the Sāṅkhya system was prevalent by the end of Satyayuga of Vaivasvata Manvantara. If it is taken as the first Satyayuga of Vaivasvata Manvantara, the time period of this tradition works out to be 117485122 years; if the same is considered as the 28th Satyayuga this tradition can be assigned an epoch as old as 216,5108 years ago.

Here it may also be informed that Maharṣi Patañjali is the last propagator of this tradition and not the first as is often speculated. Here it may also be reminded that Maharṣi Patañjali associated with the tradition of yoga is different from the Patañjali who wrote Mahābhāṣya. Patañjali of yoga tradition is much-much older than the Mahābhārata (3102 B.C.). Even the bhaṣyakāra Vyāsa appears to be older than the period of Mahābhārata. Vyāsa's commentary on the Veda shows that he was a great yogī who himself practically realised the entire yogaśāstra.

As mentioned above, Yoga is intimately allied to Sāṅkhya philosophy. Yoga is practical and Saṅkhya is theory. Thus Sāṅkhya and yoga may be treated as the theoretical and the practical sides of the same system. Sāṅkhya deals with the science of the birth or embodiment of the soul and yoga is a science of engineering to transform the embodied soul back to its original disembodied nature like a reverse engineering.

The Yogasūtras of Patañjali are divided into four parts traditionally known as 'Pādas'. The first chapter called as 'Samādhi pāda' deals with the preparations for self-realization. The second chapter called Sādhana pāda deals with the means to realization. The third chapter called 'Vibhuti pāda' deals with the divine powers to be acquired by the practice of earlier stages of the yoga and the last chapter is 'Kaivalya pāda' which explains the nature of liberation and the reality of the transcendental self.

Yoga is ādhyātmic Science that teaches the method of joining the human spirit with Brahman. Yoga is the Science that guides the Jīva (embodied soul) on how to disentangle from the phenomenal world of sensory objects and links him with the absolute, whose inherent attributes are 'Paramānanda', infinite knowledge, unbroken joy, and eternal life.

Maharṣi Patañjali in the second sūtra of 'Samādhipāda' defines yoga as:-

योगश्चित्तवृत्ति निरोधः ।

That is yoga is the withdrawal of the mind from objects of the external world.

It's worth it to mention that if we understand this sūtra correctly, especially what 'mind' signifies, we will be able to comprehend the meaning of Yoga itself throughout Patañjali's work. Etymologically, the word yoga is derived from the Sanskrit root √yuj *'samādhau'* which means 'to join'. The two things which are sought to be joined by the practice of yoga is already explained in the above passages. As we already know yoga is defined as the withdrawal of the mind from the external world. This withdrawal is through the practice of yogic methods and detachment from the objects of the visible world. This is important because the attachment to materiality is a direct result of ignorance. Yoga enables us to acknowledge the Ultimate Reality which is beyond physicality.

The word 'Chitta' (चित्त) is also derived from sanskrit root √cit or citi (चिति). Here chitta is the mind full of information of the visible world. This information is stored in the mind in the form of sanskāras. The mind has many dimensions variously known as mana, buddhi, and ahankāra. Chitta being full of information from the external world is always fickle and volatile. The objective of yoga is to empty the chitta of the information of the external world so that it may settle down and stop identifying itself with the physical body, the part of the material world. Or say, chitta is the conditioned mind and the objective of the yoga is to decondition the mind. Efforts are required for allowing the light of puruṣa to be reflected on chitta, but for that, its modifications must be restrained. The mind with the information from the external world modifies itself in various ways. These modifications are called vṛttis. The modifications of chitta are of five kinds - "प्रमाणविपर्ययविकल्पनिद्रास्मृतयः" (fig.1).

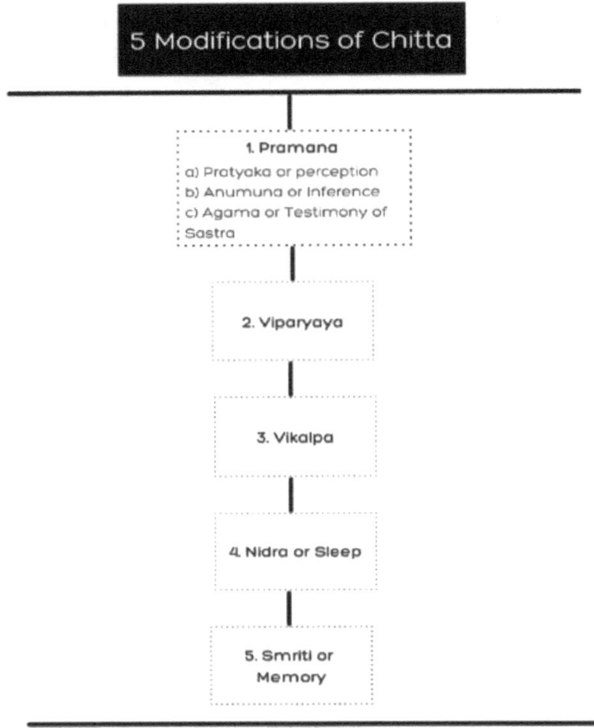

Figure 1: Five modifications of Chitta

1. Pramāṇa is right cognition.

2. Viparyaya is wrong cognition.

3. Vikalpa is verbal cognition of imagination.

4. Nidrā is sleep or absence of cognition.

5. Smṛti is memory.

1. **Pramāṇa vṛtti** is again of three kinds:

(a) **Pratyakṣa** or perception —Pratyakṣa vṛtti or perception takes place when chitta, through the sense organs, comes into contact with the external object.

(b) **Anumāna** or Inference — Inference is knowledge produced by a previous knowledge of the object and its attributes. If you have seen the fire and smoke together previously and currently you watch the smoke emitting from any place, you can immediately have an inference of the fire.

(c) **Āgama** or Testimony of a Śāstra (text composed by a Ṛṣi) —'Aptavākya' is the testimony. A Ṛṣi is an Apta (आप्त पुरुष). The Vedas and Śāstras are the highest testimony.

2. Viparyaya — Viparyaya vṛtti of mind develops due to false information, or information not corresponding to the thing as it is or information unable to explain the true nature of a concept, thing, or object of an external object. The viparyaya is defined in the Yogadarśana as "विपर्ययोमिथ्याज्ञानमतद्रूपप्रतिष्ठतम्"

3. Vikalpa — Vikalpa vṛtti develops on the basis of verbal information when its actual content is not known (शब्दज्ञानानुपाती वस्तुशून्योविकल्पः) for example, 'horns of a hare', 'son of a barren woman', 'lotus in the sky', etc.

4. Nidrā or Sleep - The Absence of awareness in mind is known as nidrā vṛtti (sleeping state of mind). Patañjali says - 'अभावप्रत्ययालम्बानावृत्तिर्निद्रा'.

5. Smriti or Memory — Patañjali defines Smṛti (memory) as - 'अनुभूतविषयासंप्रमोषः स्मृतिः ', i.e Non-forgetfulness of the perceived, experienced or realized fact or thing is called as smṛti vṛtti (memory state of mind). Memory is non-forgetting the perceived/experienced/or realized objects. Here the word non-forgetting is important. It points to the desirability of a selective memory. Yoga philosopher Patañjali's definition of memory, i.e. non-forgetting an experienced knowledge or fact clearly shows that memory consists of recalling a past experience which has been retained in the mind encoded as sanskāra. It involves retention and recall.

To ensure that the mind stops modifying itself, it is necessary that the mind is withdrawn from the objects of the material world. According to Patañjali, through Abhyāsa (constant efforts) and vairāgya (detachment to the object of the mundane world (external world), the mind can be withdrawn from the visible world. 'अभ्यासवैसन्याभ्यां तन्निरोधः'.

Efforts to stabilize the mind are called abhyāsa.

Vairāgya is of two types. The first one is called vaśīkāra type of vairāgya. Free from a desire for the worldly objects directly seen or enjoyed and or for those heard from others or known from Śāstras, is called vaśīkāra type of vairāgya. Vaśīkāra type of vairāgya is a lower level vairāgya. 'दृष्टानुश्रविकविषयवितृष्णस्य वशीकारसंज्ञा वैराग्यम्'

The second type of vairāgya is called 'para' vairāgya'. Para vairāgya, which is higher than vaśīkāra type of lower-level vairāgya, is attained by the realization of the true nature of the self. It is called Guṇa vaitṛṣṇya vairāgya. तत्परं पुरुषख्यातेर्गुणवैतृष्ण्यम् ॥ 16 ॥

Obstacles in Yoga: Distractions of the mind

Yoga is the inhibition of the modifications of the mind, when the inhibition of modifications of the mind is achieved then the seeker identifies with his/her true nature. When the modification of mind are not inhibited the seeker is not to identify with his/her true nature. He/she identifies with a particular vṛtti (modification). The modification of the mind is fivefold which may be painful or not.

Maharṣi Patañjali Says, ततः प्रत्यवचेतनाधिगमो ऽप्यन्तरायाभावश्च। The obstacles will not allow the practitioner to go forward in his practice. The nine obstacles which causes distraction of mind are disease, languor, doubt, carelessness, laziness, worldly-mindedness, delusion, non-achievement of a stage, and instability (fig. 2).

'व्याधिरत्यानसंशयप्रमादालस्याविरतिभ्रान्तिदर्शनलब्धभूमिकत्वानवस्थितत्वानि चित्तविक्षेपास्तेऽन्तरायाः।'

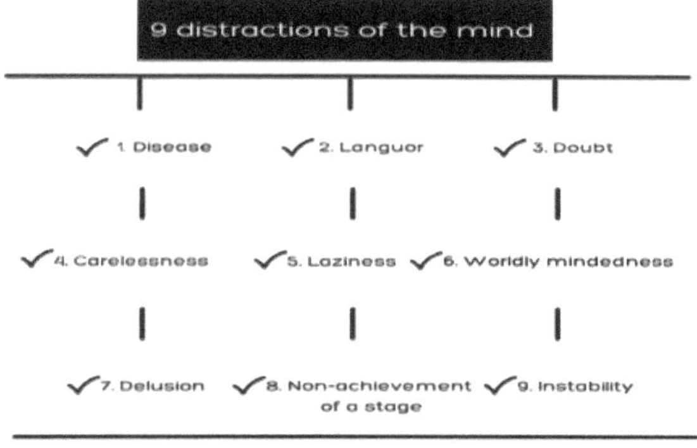

Figure 2: Obstacles in Yoga

Now let us discuss each obstacle step by step.

व्याधिः (Sickness): Physical sickness arises through the disturbance in the three doṣas viz., vāta, pitta, and kapha, mental diseases arise due to imbalance in the three Guṇas — Sattva, Rajas and Tamas (fig.1). Diseases make it the seeker difficult to continue in his Sādhanā. So perfect health is essential in the path of yoga. This hindrance may be due to irregularity in taking food, malnutrition, and late sleep, loss of seminal energy, etc. This hindrance can be removed by the practice of Āsanas, Prāṇāyama, Meditation, Kriyas, Bandhas, Dietetic adjustment,

Fasting, sun-bath, sufficient rest, etc.

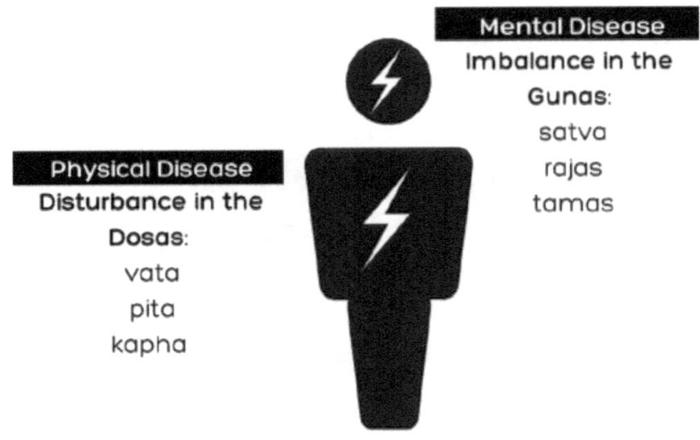

Figure 3: Causes of sickness

स्त्यान (Sloth/dullness): In this stage, the Sādhaka is unfit to do any practice on account of some defect in the prāṇamaya kośa, which results in an inadequate supply of vital force to the physical body. This is also an obstacle which brings disposition of mind in the progress of Sadhana, this hindrance can be removed by the practice of Āsanas, Prāṇāyama.

संशयः (doubt). Whether it is this or that, various doubts arise in the Sādhaka's mind i.e., If there really is any reality to be realized or is he/she merely pursuing a miracle? Are the methods he/she is using really effective? Has he/she the capacity to go through all the obstacles and reach the goal? etc. Yes, such indecisive notion is a doubt which can be eradicated or dispelled by right knowledge, viveka, vichara, study of scriptures and by Satsaṅga with Mahātmas.

प्रमाद (Casualness): - This is another obstacle that does not allow many aspirants for the yogic life. It has the effect of relaxing the mind and thus undermines its concentration. In the field of yoga, this carelessness is not only an obstacle but also a great danger. This obstacle can be removed by paying attention to the right knowledge, study of Śāstras, Viveka, and spending valuable time with noble scholars, etc.

आलस्य (Laziness): - This hindrance also distracts the condition of mind. This is a bad mental habit of showing love towards comfort and a tendency to avoid exertion. Languor is a purely physical defect while this laziness is generally a purely psychological condition. This laziness can be dispelled by developing good habits; prolonged discipline based on the execution of hard and difficult tasks is the means of coming out of this dangerous situation.

अविरतिः (Worldly-mindedness/Indulgence): - This obstacle is a serious cause of distraction of mind. Avirati is that tendency of the mind which unceasingly longs keenly for one or the other kind of sensual enjoyment on account of attachment. This is destroyed by Vairāgya (detachment), looking into the faults of worldly objects and worldly life, such as impermanence, diseases, old age, miseries, death, etc., This hindrance also can be avoided by constant Satsaṅga with dispassionate Mahātmas and study of books on Vairāgya (detachment).

भ्रान्तिदर्शनम् (Confusion): This is mistaking an undesirable state as the most desirable one due to illusion. This hindrance is due to a lack of intelligence and discrimination.

अलब्धभूमिकत्व (Deprivation/Non-attainment of yogic state): - This leads the seeker away from the right path,

Samādhi. The attractions of divine power will bar the seeker from achieving the yogic state. This obstacle can be removed by developing more and more detachment, doing constant and intense practice in seclusion, etc.

अनवस्थितत्वम् (Instability): - Instability is that fickleness of the mind which does not allow the yogi to remain in the state of Samādhi, even though he has reached it with great difficulty. Yes, indulgence in the visible world is a powerful inherent of the fickleness of the mind that brings instability.

Pain, despair, nervousness, and irregular breathing are the symptoms of a distracted condition of mind. Maharṣi Patañjali (1.31) says :-

दुःखदौर्मानस्याङ्गमेजयत्वश्वासप्रश्वासाविक्षेपसहभुवः

Pain provides uneasiness of body and mind. Pain with the consciousness of impotence or incapacity leads to despair, despair leads to nervousness. Despair is the unsteadiness of the mind caused by the non-fulfillment of some desires. When the mind is distracted, the inhalation and exhalation are not in a normal condition because of disharmony in the flow of pranic currents.

For removing these obstacles one should practice meditation on the one Principle or Reality.

Maharṣi Patañjali (1.32) says: तत्प्रतिषेधार्थमेकतत्त्वाभ्यासः ।

Intense concentration on the one Reality will obviate the above accompaniments of distraction. The object is obviously the reversal of the tendency of the mind to run constantly after a multitude of objects in the outer world and to develop the capacity to pursue constantly one objective inside within the realm of consciousness.

Perfect control of mind and Indriyas (senses) is required to completely destroy the distractions. The practice of Trāṭaka Kriya - steady gazing at a particular point (fig.4), is an effective practice to remove Vikṣepa — distractions of the mind.

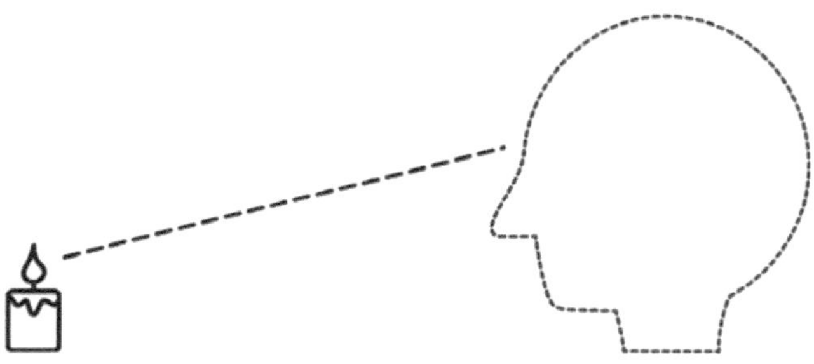

Figure 4: Example of Trataka Kriya

When slight difficulties appear do not stop the practice. Find out suitable means to eradicate the obstacle. Plod on till you get the highest Asaṁprajñāta Samādhi. Success is bound to come if you are sincere and steady in Sādhanā (practice). Have perfect Trust in God and be steady in your Sādhanā. When a seer identifies his own nature, there cannot arise such obstacles. The obstacles soon pass off by repetition of AUM, (प्रणवः) (fig. 5) self-surrender to God and repeated practice in concentration and Meditation.

Figure 5: AUM/OM

Concept of Iśvara in Yoga Philosophy

Maharṣi Patañjali is the last person in the tradition of the yoga system. Yoga is intimately allied to Sāṅkhya philosophy. Yoga means karma (spiritual action for the liberation of an embodied soul) and Sāṅkhya means jñāna (knowledge or information about the embodied soul). Sāṅkhya is theory and yoga is practice (fi. 6). Sāṅkhya and yoga may be treated as the theoretical and the practical sides of the same system. It shows the practical path by following which one may attain Viveka-khyāti (true identity of the soul) which alone leads to liberation. Yoga is defined as the withdrawal of the chitta (योगश्चित्तवृत्तिनिरोधः)

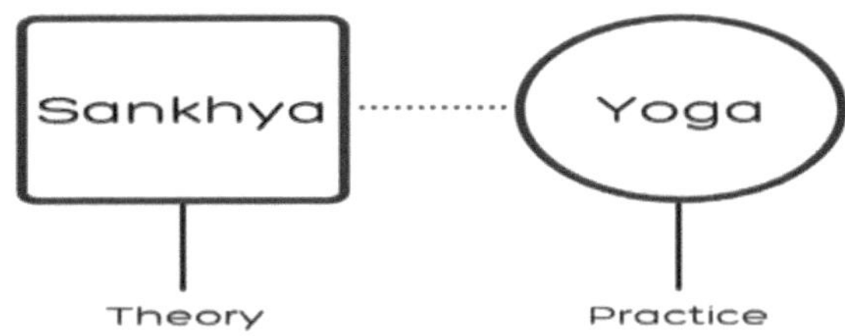

Figure 6: The theoretical and the practical sides of the same system.

The suppression of modifications can be brought by constant practice and non-attachment (अभ्यासवैराग्याभ्यां तन्निरोधः). This withdrawal of the mind from the objects of the external world through meditation or concentration is also called yoga. (योगः समाधिः) In Samādhi Pāda while explaining about Samādhi Maharṣi Patañjali quoted 'ईश्वरप्रणिधानाद्वा', withdrawal of mind and the attainment of Samādhi is also possible by following another path i.e., by self-surrender or resignation to God. Here Iśvara is the Supreme Ruler of Brahmāṇḍa'. It is in Him that the Brahmāṇḍa lives, moves, and has its being. The different planets, the universe are His bodies and the powers working on the machinery of the universe. In short, he is the reality whom we generally refer to as God. Here Iśvara is a particular centre of Divine consciousness who is untouched by the afflictions of life, actions and their result and the impressions produced by these actions. Maharṣi Patañjali (1.24) says - 'क्लेशकर्मविपाकाशयैरपरामृष्टःपुरूषविशेष ईश्वरः'. There is in Him the infinite source of knowledge (तत्र निरतिशयं सर्वज्ञबीजम-योग. 1.25) This Iśvara is Ādi-Guru (First Teacher), who is not subject to time. But our ancient teachers were subject to time. The magazine of knowledge and power is within Iśvara. No spiritual progress is possible without the aid of a Guru. A Guru is necessary to awaken spiritual power. That Guru who removes the veil of aspirants and obstacles and throws light on their path, who is omniscient, who exists transcending the past, present, and future, who is independent. The syllable 'OM' refers to Him (Iśvara). Patañjali (1.27) said 'तस्य वाचकः प्रणवः'. The physical vibration of 'OM' is the original vibration of creation. 'OM' is everything. The syllable 'OM' is the most appropriate name of the Supreme Self. Just as a man is pleased when addressed by a name dear to him, so also God is pleased when this name 'OM' is used. Praṇava is unchanging, eternal, and always new, 'OM' is the highest flower or offering for God. The aspirant gets a one-pointed mind by the repletion of 'OM'. Through the grace of Iśvara, the yogi will not get any disease. The divine grace will come when one repeats 'OM' and meditates on Him (it's meaning) with concentration. Japa on 'OM' makes the mind inward and removes all physical to mental obstacles. By 'OM' the cognition of the individual soul arises. As 'OM' and Iśvara are inseparable, meditating the mind on 'OM' means meditating the mind on Iśvara. Doing Japa on 'OM' is the remembrance of Iśvara.

To sum up, the Supreme power mentioned in Yoga is a creator, preserver, or destroyer of this world. He is not a soul in general, but a specific entity called 'Puruṣa Viśeṣa'. Directly Iśvara has nothing to do with the bondage and Liberation of the 'Puruṣas', as they are free to act as per their own discretion. Attraction to the visible world binds them and identification of true nature liberates them. The end of human life is the separation of Puruṣa from Prakṛti followed by the union with God.

Methods recommended by Maharṣi Patañjali to bring steadiness of the Mind

Although the Mind is one, it could be understood as a complex system that has different dimensions as we saw before like Chitta or Ahaṅkāra. It passes into many conditions or states, as it is made of three qualities (Guṇas) viz., Sattva, Rajas, and Tamas. All these qualities enter into a variety of combinations. So, the modifications or Vṛttis of the mind are also various. Peace of mind (śānta-vṛtti) is sāttvika vṛtti. Lust is rājasika vṛtti. Laziness is a tāmasika vṛtti. Anger is a ghora vṛtti. The internal fight is ever going on between guṇas, between good vṛttis and evil vṛttis. This is the internal war-field between Suras and Asuras. Only when the mind is absolutely free from attachment of all sorts that true knowledge begins to dawn. The yoga system represented by Patañjali is an ancient Indian doctrine of concentration of mind by breaking its resistant patterns such as distraction or confusion. Patañajali knowing the need for a calm, peaceful, and steady mind, he recommended some techniques which stabilise the mind. Now let us know what are the techniques discussed by Maharṣi Patañjali.

The Mind becomes clarified, peaceful and stable by cultivating attitudes of friendliness, compassion, gladness, and indifference respectively towards happiness, misery, virtue and vice and is known as a sāttvika mind. Major sources of disturbed mind are uncontrolled reactions to our human environment, the problem of adjustment, etc., concentration cannot come in the mind that is filled with hatred, jealously, anger, etc. Friendliness and mercy will eradicate hatred. Gladness will remove jealousy.

Mercy softens the hard heart and removes the cruel, harsh nature. By this practice, anger, egoism, hatred, the envy of various sorts will vanish. Rajas and Tamas will be removed. The mind will be filled with Sattva. The fickleness of the mind will disappear. The mind becomes pure and concentration will come. It is said in Yogadarśana (1.33):

मैत्रीकरुणामुदितोपेक्षाणां सुखदुःखपुण्यापुण्यविषयाणां भावनातश्चित्तप्रसादनम् ।

When the mind is not clarified then the nervous system weakens which again leads to an unstable central organ. Various kinds of nervous disturbances are due to the disturbed flow of Prāṇa-vitality in the Prāṇamayakoṣa. These disturbances provide physical and mental restlessness which causes Vikṣepa (distraction). Hence Patanjali recommended that by the expiration and retention of breath the steadiness of the mind can be gained. Unstable condition of the mind can be removed by practicing one of the well-known breathing exercises for the purification of the nāḍis i.e. Nāḍi-śuddhi etc.

In the 34th Sūtra of Samādhipāda says the same "प्रच्छर्दनविधारणाभ्यां वा प्राणस्य". All Vṛttis are restrained by the practice of Prāṇayama. Rajas and Tamas will be removed and Sattva will take place entirely. The mind will become one-pointed. The body becomes light. The mind will become calm. Another method recommended by Maharṣi Patañjali to bring a stable mind is the practice of concentration (fig. 7) on higher sense perceptions brought about by the enjoyment of senses. By concentrating on the tip of the nose, the yogi experiences 'divya gandha'; by concentrating on the tip of the tongue, he tastes 'Divya essence'; by concentrating on the palate, the yogi experiences 'Divya colour'; by concentrating on the middle of the tongue, he experiences 'divya touch'; by concentrating at the root of the tongue, he experiences 'divya Sound'. By concentrating on these Super- sensual perceptions. he gets a steadiness of mind.

Types of Concentration

Divya Gandha	Concentration on the tip of the nose
Divya essence	Concentration on the tip of the tongue
Divya colours	Concentration on the palate
Divya touch	Concentration on the middle of the tongue
Divya sound	Concentration on the root of the tongue

↓

Steadiness of mind

Figure 7: Types of concentration

These experiences give him definite encouragement, he gets faith in Yoga. As a result of such practice, the Sādhaka may begin to see unusual light within him or feel an utter sense of peace and tranquility. These experiences, while of no great significance in themselves can hold the mind by their attractive power and gradually bring about the required condition of steadiness. It is said - "विशोका वा जयोतिष्मती" (Yogadarśana, 1.36). Another method to bring steadiness of the mind to make it free from worldly attachments. Maharṣi Patañjali says- "वीतरागविषयं वा चित्तम्". A mind free from passions and attachment attains steadiness.

Concentrating on the knowledge of dream and sound sleep also brings steadiness of the mind and Samādhi. The same said- "स्वप्ननिद्राज्ञानालम्बनं वा". In the sleep state, the jīvātmā leaves the physical body and begins to function in the next subtler vehicle. Very partial contact is maintained with the body to enable it to carry on its normal physiological activities, but the conscious mind is really functioning in the subtler vehicle. Through special training, it is possible and practice to bring down into the physical brain a memory of experiences undergone in these subtler worlds corresponding to svapna (dream) and Nidrā (sleep) states. Under these conditions the brain is able to transmit the mental images without any distortion and the knowledge obtained under these circumstances is reliable. By concentrating on such experiences will surely bring the steadiness of the mind.

Kriya-Yoga or Preparatory Yoga

Aspirants to Yoga may be divided into three classes:

1. Ārurukṣu (Mandas)   — One aspiring to climb

2. Yuñjāna (Madhyamas) — One actually engaged in the Practice.

3. Yogarūḍha (Uttamas) — One who has attained Yoga.

Yogarūḍha will attain Yoga through Abhyāsa and Vairāgya (Practice and attachment) where as Yuñjānas will attain Yoga through Kriyāyoga (preparatory Yoga)

In the Second chapter of Yoga darśana of Patañjali, there is a discussion on Kriyāyoga.

It is said, " तपः स्वाध्यायेश्वरप्रणिधानानि क्रियायोगः" (Yoga, 2.1) means 'Tapas' (austerity), 'Svadhyaya' (study of scriptures) and 'Iśvara-Praṇidhāna' (meditation on God).

Of the eight parts of Yoga (Aṣṭāṅga Yoga), the second part is Niyama. The five practices enumerated under the title of 'Niyama' are 'Śaucha' and 'Santoṣa', besides the three 'Tapas' 'Svādhyāya' and 'Iśvara-Praṇidhāna', which will be discussed below.

There are two benefits of this Kriya-yoga: 1.) To

enable the Yogī to proceed towards the attainment of Samādhi; 2.) Do away completely with troubles or to minimize them, technically known as the Kleśas. It is said in Yogadarśana (2.2):- 'समाधिभावनार्थः क्लेशतनूकरणार्थश्च'

Let us discuss each step of Kriya-yoga:-

i.   Tapas

ii. Svādhyāya

iii. Iśvara Praṇidhāna

1. Tapas (austerity)

The tapas (austerity) is the entire preparation necessary for the accomplishment of dharma (moral and ethical values and attainment of knowledge). By Tapas (austerity), the mind, speech, and Indriyas are purified. Yamas and Niyamas, Āsana, Prāṇāyāma, etc., come under Tapas. By the performance of Tapas, all Kleṣas (afflictions) and impurities can be destroyed. According to the Gita, Tapas is of three types:

1. शारीरिकतप 2. वाक् तप 3. मानसतप

1.   शरीरिकतप (Austerity of the body): This type of Tapas consists in giving respect to and care of the scholars, learned people, Gurus (Āchārya, Mother and Father), maintenance of cleanliness, simplicity, celibacy and non-violence. It is said:

देवद्विजगुरुप्राज्ञपूजनं शौचमार्जवम् ।

ब्रह्मचर्यमहिंसा च शारीरं तप उच्यते ॥

वाक्तप (Austerity of speech): This tapas consists in speaking words that are truthful, pleasing, beneficial and not agitating to others and also in regularly reciting Vedic hymns. The same is said:

अनुद्वेगकरं वाक्यं सत्यं प्रियं हितं च यत् ।

स्वाध्यायाभ्यसनं चैव वाङ्मयं तप उच्यते ॥

मानसतपः (Austerity of Mind):- This kind of apas consists in the serenity of mind, gentleness, silence, self-restraint, and the purity of thought.

मनः प्रसाद सौम्यत्वं मौनमात्मविनिग्रहः ।

भावसंशुद्धिरित्येतत् तपो मानसमुच्यते ॥

Tapas is to tolerate the pairs of opposites — 'तपो द्वन्द्वसहनम्' The pairs of opposites are hunger and thirst heat and cold etc. Maharṣi Patañjali said all the impurities can be removed by penance, so the perfection of the body and the senses can be achieved. 'कायेन्द्रियसिद्धिरशुद्धिक्षयात्तपसः' Kena Upaniṣad describes the three pillars of the entire structure of Brahmavidyā (fig. 8) or Spiritual Science as Tapas (austerity), Dama (self-restraint), Karma (Action).

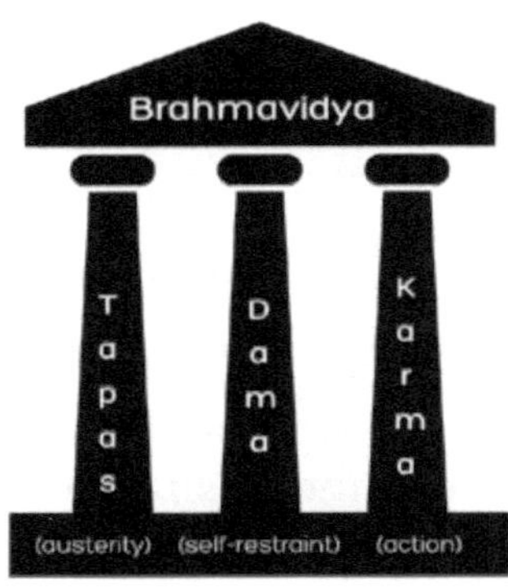

Figure 8: Brahmavidya by Kena Upanisad

The trio of Tapas, Brahmacharya, and Satya has been repeatedly emphasized in Praśnopaniṣad (5.3) and other Upaniṣads.

So, Tapas is one of the necessary elements to attain

perfection.

2). Svādhyāya

The study and practice of Vedas, Śāstras, and spirituality is Svādhyāya. Self-contemplation is also known as Japa. Japa consists in reciting the sacred syllable 'AUM', the name of the Brahman.

'स्वाध्यायः मोक्षशास्त्राणामध्ययनं प्रणवजपोवा'

The study of the Śāstras, the Vedas, and the Upaniṣads including the other literature associated with these influences' thoughts, takes away the fickleness of the mind, ennobles the soul, and removes malice and evils.

A Kriyāyogī is neither worried about his past nor cares about the future. He is a creature of the present. He doesn't permit others to assess him. He is ever progressive. He knows his weakness and he is also conscious of the hurdles that he is likely to face on his path.

3). Iśvara Praṇidhāna

Iśvara-Praṇidhāna means to dedicate all actions to the Supreme soul. 'ईश्वरप्रणिधानं तस्मिन्परमगुरौ सर्वकर्मार्पणम्'.

Iśvara-Praṇidhāna is one of the alternate means of attaining Samādhi. It is said in Yogadarśana - 'ईश्वरप्रणिधानाद्वा'

Iśvara is distinguishable from us, so he is called as Puruṣa Viśeṣa (Special Puruṣa) who remains unbound and unclung to pains and sufferings, to actions, to the fruits of actions, and to the tendencies left there after. Iśvara is Omniscient; the depth of his knowledge is unfathomable. He is the teacher of the ṛṣis. AUM (praṇava) is the designation of Iśvara. Iśvara, is the surest way of obtaining concentration and there by liberation. Iśvarapranidana is the means to Samādhi. The same is said: 'समाधिसिद्धिरीश्वरप्रणिधानात् ॥'

Those who are unable to attain Yoga through Practice and Non-attachment (Abhyāsa and Vairāgya) can also attain Yoga through the practice of Kriyā-Yoga, discussed above. It is true to say that the different methodologies for achieving Yoga are valid according to the nature of the practitioner.

Kleśas or Afflictions of Mind

In the second aphorism of Patañjali Yogadarśana, there is a discussion on Kriyāyoga or Preparatory Yoga. There are two benefits of Kriyayoga, one is the attainment of Samādhi and another one is the minimization of troubles, technically known as

Kleṣas:

The same is said: 'समाधिभावनार्थः क्लेशतनूकरणार्थश्च '

The afflictions (Kleṣas) are of five kinds. They are 'अविद्यास्मितारागद्वेषाभिनिवेशाः क्लेशाः ' tendency towards the knowledge of the material world, egoism, attachment, hatred-ness, clinging to life are afflictions of the mind.

Avidyā is the breeding ground of the succeeding ones, i.e., asmitā, rāga, dveṣa, and abhiniveśa whether they are in a dormant (प्रसुप्त) thinned out (तनु) overpowered (विच्छिन्न) or expanded (उदार) condition. 'अविद्या क्षेत्रामुत्तरेषां प्रसुप्ततनुविच्छिन्नोदाराणाम् ।'

Avidyā is the field or source for the four kleśas, viz. asmitā, rāga, dveṣa and abhiniveśa. These four afflictions are only modifications or varieties of āvidya only. These kleśas have four stages:-

1. Dormant (प्रसुप्तावस्था): This is the stage in which they are (Kleśas) are hidden or occluded like the tree in the seed. Videhas and Prakritilayas have got this stage.

2. Thinned out (तनु): In this stage, they are (Kleśas) in an attenuated condition like a thin thread. Yogīs who have got this stage through practice. They thin-out one evil vāsanā (sanskāra) by developing a good vāsanā to counter it. Anger can be thinned out by developing mercy, love, and forgiveness, etc.

3. Overpowered (विच्छिन्न): In this stage, kleśas are overpowered for the time being in the fight between wife and husband. At first, we find out hatred vṛtti between them and after sometime as soon as the fight is over, we find love vṛtti.

4. Expanded (उदार): In this stage, the kleśas are very powerful. Their operation will be in force.

There is another avasthā called dagdha avasthā wherein the kleśas are fried out like burnt seeds. This we can find in Yogīs who reached 'Asamprajñāta Samādhi'.

Avidyā

Avidyā is a sense of permanence in the transient, of purity in impure, of pleasure in pain, of soul in the body 'अनित्याशुचिदुःखानात्मसु नित्यशुचिसुखात्मख्यातिरविद्या'

By undisturbed discriminative knowledge, we can remove avidyā.

Material-as-eternal: Thinking that earth is eternal, the sky with the moon and stars is eternal. Some of the sādhakas do sādhanā (practice) for such things due to Avidyā.

Impure as pure: The wise know for certain the body

to be impure an account of its source seed, sustenance, perspiration, destruction, and the necessity of keeping it constantly clean with mud, herbs water, etc.

स्थानाध्बीजाट्टपषृम्भात्रिस्यन्दन्निधनादपि ।

कायमाधेयशौचत्वात्पण्डिताह्यशुचि विदु ॥

But due to avidyā, some think that the body is pure instead of impure.

Pain as pleasure: All mundane world experiences are full of misery for the enlightened.'परिणामतापसंस्कार-दुःखैर्गुणवृत्तिविरोधाच्च दुःखमेवसर्वंविवेकिनः ।' But many, who indulge in the material world (avidyā) say that this jagat (universe) is both pleasure and pain.

Body as Soul: Believing the body, mind as Atma (self) is due to Avidyā.

Asmitā

'दृग्दर्शनशक्त्योरेकात्मतेवास्मिता'

Asmitā is the identification of the seer with the power of the seeing.

The soul is the seer and eyes are the power of seeing, so considering eyes as a seer is asmitā (ahaṅkāra).

Rāga

सुखानुशयी राग

Seeking pleasure is rāga (attachment).

For example, we seek money. We are attached to money, because we can get various objects that can give us pleasure, through money. This is due to previous experience regarding such enjoyments.

Dveṣa

दुःखानुशयी द्वेषः ।

Aversion is (hate द्वेष) that which dwells on pain. Dveṣa is the root cause of human suffering. Wars, splits, quarrels, murders, etc. are due to dveṣa. Jealousy is the intimate companion of dveṣa.

Abhiniveśa

स्वरसवाही विदुषोऽपि तथारूढोऽभिनिवेशः ।

Abhiniveśa is the strong desire for living. The fear of death exists in both learned and laity. The past experience of the pain of death is there in our chitta. Therefore, we are afraid of death in this life. This is the reason for the strong desire for being alive.

How we can destroy these Afflictions?

It is said 'ध्यानहेयास्तद्वृत्तयः' Through Meditation, we can destroy the modifications (five Kleśas) of the mind. By following Kriya-yoga contents, Tapas (austerity), Svādhyaya (self-study), and Iśvarapraṇidhāna (dedicating all acts to God) one can minimize these kleśas but by meditation, all the kleśas can be destroyed. Good and bad actions are born of lust, avarice, forgetfulness, and anger. It is to be experienced in the present birth or in the future births.

क्लेशमूलः कर्माशयो दृष्टादृष्टजन्मवेदनीयः ।

The Kleśas, if not completely uprooted would lead to three consequences - Jāti (yoni or species), Āyu (life span) and Bhoga (rewards of karmas)-'सतिमूले तद्विपाको जात्यायुर्भोगाः' Āyu (life span), the Jāti (the species or yoni in which a person is to be born is decided according to his/her kārmika sanskāras) and not for the particular person. For man, the normal expectancy of life is a hundred years or so. For Dog, the expectancy of life would be eight to ten years and a cow may live for 20 years, etc., Regarding Jati, it is understood that Ayu is fixed. So also, Bhoga - rewards of karmas is also fixed based on Jāti. Bhoga depends on the limitations placed on organs of perception and enjoyment. Bhoga or the carnal satisfaction depends on the type of sense organs given to you in a particular species. The organs of perception and carnal satisfaction in a bat or a cat are different from those given to a man, cow, or a horse. A Sheep does not enjoy the music in the same sense as a man does. Bats are capable of hearing and transmitting those wavelengths of sound which normally are beyond the reach of the human ear. Cats and owls have very sensitive eyes which enable them to see quite a lot in the range that we call darkness. Dogs have a remarkable sense of smell, which makes them fine police dogs. In that sense, the range of satisfaction is fixed up when it happens to be born in a particular living species. Jati, Ayu. Bhoga is possessed of the fruits of pleasure and pain on account of their origination in virtue and vice.

Viveka-khyāti

Sānkhya tradition deals with the embodiment of the soul. It gives in detail the description of the embodiment process of the soul. It also accepts as other systems of Indian philosophy plurality of the Puruṣas (souls). In Sānkhya, the soul is called Puruṣa, because of its embodiment, it gets the body as its pura (residence). Generally, the scholar argues that Sānkya is silent about God. But they don't understand that God is not the subject matter of Sāṅkhya, the same being exclusively dealt with in Vedānta. The Sāṅkhya tradition was very well aware of its limitations and the scope and nature of their philosophy. Moreover, in '*Iśavarāsiddhe*', Sāṅkhya has clearly accepted that the non-existence of God is not proved. The System is purely and predominantly and theoretical science. Right knowledge is the knowledge of the separation of the puruṣa from the body (Prakṛti).

According to Sāṅkhya, the embodiment of soul is the play of 24 principles. When the soul due to its sanskāras of the visible world undergoes embodiment (identify itself with prakṛti which is a unified state of sattva (intelligence), rajas (motion), and tamas (inertia), the first product is mahat (intelligence). This is distinct from Puruṣa (soul) which is pure consciousness, buddhi (intelligence) being the evolute of prakṛti, which is material. It is followed by the birth of the notion of Ahaṅkāra (a sense of individuality or discrete identity of an individual soul). From ahaṅkāra proceeds the mind, five sense organs, five tanmāras, and five motor organs. Buddhi's functions are said to be ascertainment and decision. buddhi is called mahat (general intelligence), Ahaṅkāra is often identified with 'I' and 'Mine'. Manas or mind is the internal and central sense organ called antaḥkaraṇa. It comes into contact with the five sense organs to receive information about the outside visible world. Sāṅkhya assigns to manas the important function of synthesising the sensory data into determinate perceptions, passing them on to the ahaṅkāra, and carrying out the orders of the ahaṅkāra through the motor organs.

Five Tanmātras of sensory organs in the body are:

1). Rūpa (luminosity)

2). Gandha (odour)

3). Rasa (taste)

4). Sparśa (touch)

5). Śabda (sound)

Five sensory organs in the body are:

1). Eyes,

2). Nose

3). Tongue

4). Skin

5). Ears

Five Motor organs in the body are:

1). Mouth (organ of speech)

2). Feet (organ of movement)

3). Hands (organ of grasp)

4). Anus (organ of excretion)

5). Genitals (organ of reproduction)

Five Mahābutas in the body are:

1). Flesh product of carbon (Earth)

2). Blood product of liquid (water)

3). Body temperature product of Fire

4). Breathings and other vital airs product of air

5). Cavities product of Ākāśa.

Puruṣa needs prakṛti (body) for enjoyment (bhoga) as

well as for liberation. Liberation means complete cessation of all sufferings and three pains:

1. Ādhyātmika sufferings- It is due to intra-organic psychological causes- these include mental and bodily sufferings.

2. Ādhibhautika — It is caused by men, beasts, birds, thorns, etc., and physical objects like sword, knife, gun shot etc.

3. Ādhidaivika — It is due to natural causes like earthquakes, rains, famines, etc.

Having understood the process of embodiment and Karma Siddānta Vivekī (enlightened one) concludes that all is pain and tries to escape the pain that is yet to come through "Yoga Mārga". 'अनागतं दुःखं भयम्।'

In this connection, Patañjali said that due to Sañyoga of draṣṭā and dṛśya this duḥkha arises. 'द्रष्टृदृश्ययोः संयोगो हेयहेतुः' Here drāṣṭā (seer, the soul) and dṛśya (visible world) is distinguished from each other. The correlation of seer and the object of sight (visible world) is the cause of misery and bondage. Here the object of sight exists for the sake of the experience and the liberation of the self. dṛśya is composed of प्रकाशक्रियास्थितिशीलम्- intelligence (light), motion and inertia, भूतेन्द्रियात्मकम् -gross evolutes of prakṛti and senses. This object of sight is भोगापवर्गार्थम् - for the enjoyment and for the liberation of seer drāṣṭā-seer is द्रष्टा -दृशिमात्रः शुद्धोऽपि प्रत्यायानुपश्यः. Puruṣa is the soul, the self, the spirit, the subject, the knower. It is neither senses nor brain nor mind nor ego. It is itself pure consciousness, the peaceful, eternal. It is beyond time, space, change, and activity. It is uncaused, eternal, all-pervading. So it is called- निस्त्रैगुण्य, कर्ता, द्रष्टा, ज्ञाता, etc.

The very purpose of dṛśya (object of sight) is only for the sake of the self (seer). 'तदर्थ एव दृश्यस्यात्मा ' If the seer gets liberated, though the object of sight never deteriorates because it is common to other those who have not yet liberated - 'कृतार्थं प्रति नष्टमप्यनष्टं तदन्यसाधारणत्वात्'

Avidyā (visible world) is the reason for this correlation (संयोग). Uninterrupted discriminative knowledge is the means of attaining escape from miseries- 'विवेकख्यातिरविप्लवा हानोपायः'.

Aṣṭāṅga yoga is one of the ways to attain discriminative knowledge between Puruṣa and Prakṛti, a specific discernment that leads to liberation. By following Aṣṭāṅga yoga, destruction of mental, physical and intellectual impurities arises a light of wisdom and shines which leads to discriminative knowledge between Puruṣa (soul) and Prakṛti (body) which is very essential to attain Samādhi. Maharṣi Patañjali said the same:- 'योगाङ्गानुष्ठानादशुद्धिक्षयेज्ञानदीप्तिराविवेकख्यातेः ।'

Aṣṭāṅga Yoga

Maharṣi Patañjali in the Yogasūtra's second chapter, Sādhanapāda explained about Aṣṭāṅga Yoga. By Practising Kriyayoga one can attain Samādhi and can minimize kleśas and through dhyāna afflictions (kleśas) can be removed. If kleśas are not completely uprooted. they would lead to three consequences:

Jāti (yonī or species) (2) Āyu (life span in a particular yonī) (3) Bhoga (the reward of karmas). These Jāti, Āyu, and Bhoga are determined on the basis of kārmic sanskāras. So Vivekī (yogī) knowing about Karma Siddhanta concludes that "All is pain" and tries to escape through "Yoga Mārga" the pain that is yet to come. Here this pain (duḥkha) is due to the union of Puruṣa and Prakṛti- द्रष्टृदृश्ययोः संयोगो हेयहेतुः. So, uninterrupted discriminative knowledge between Puruṣa and Prakṛti is hānopāya- a way to attain Isolation or Liberation- 'विवेकख्यातिरविप्लवा हानोपायः । '. According to Sāṅkhya philosophy, the union of Puruṣa and Prakṛti is birth, and the separation of Prakṛti and Puruṣa is liberation (fig.9).

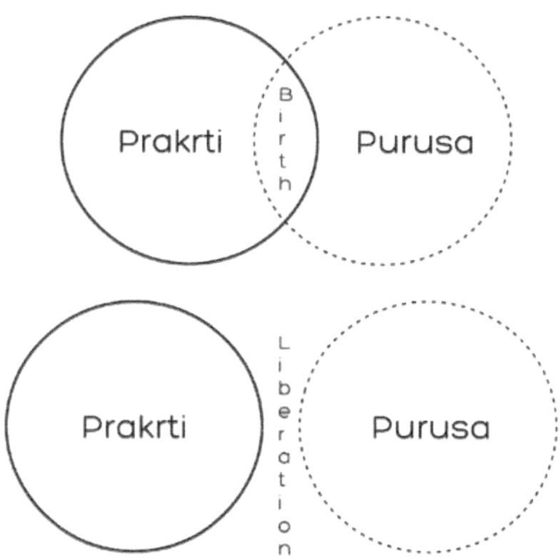

Figure 9, Union and separation of Purusa and Prakrti

This kind of Vivekakhyāti (discriminative Knowledge) can be gained by following Aṣṭāṅga yoga. In the reference Maharṣi Patañjali explained Aṣṭāṅga yoga and said that by following Aṣṭāṅga yoga all the impurities that relate to mind, body, and intellect can be removed through which the discriminative knowledge between Puruṣa and Prakṛti can be achieved. It is said:

'योगाङ्गानुष्ठनादशुद्धिक्षये ज्ञानदीप्तिराविवेकख्यातेः ।'

The eight accessories of yoga are:

1. Yama - (social discipline)

2. Niyama - (personal discipline)

3. Āsana - Posture

4. Prāṇāyāma - Control of Breath

5. Pratyāhāra - (Withdrawl of the Senses)

6. Dhāraṇā - Concentration

7. Dhyāna - Meditation/Contemplation

8. Samādhi - Settling in one's own self

Maharṣi Patañjali said-'यमनियमासनप्राणायामप्रत्याहार-धारणाध्यानसमाधयोऽष्टवङ्गानि'. Here the first five steps are called 'Bahiraṅga Yoga' and the last three steps are called 'Antaraṅga Yoga'. The eight accessories of yoga described above are like the eight steps in the path of Rāja Yoga. They all should be practiced in the order given. One will not be benefited if he takes to the practice of Āsanas, Prāṇāyāma without practising Yama, Niyama, and other steps which are the very foundation of yoga. It is a sequence that instrumentalizes an order to the practitioner gradually. So, by following Aṣṭāṅga yoga destruction of mental, physical and intellectual impurities take place and the light of wisdom shines which leads to discriminative knowledge between Puruṣa and Prakṛti (body), which is very essential to attain liberation. So, in Yoga-darśana, Aṣṭāṅga yoga plays a major role.

Let us discuss each step:

1. Yama -Social discipline: Yama contains five steps:

(a) Ahinsā - Non violence

(b) Satya - Truthfulness

(c) Asteya - Non-Stealing

(d) Brahmacharya - Celibacy

(e) Aparigraha - Non-hoarding

(a) Ahinsā (Non-violence) - Ahinsā is not just to kill or to wound. Scriptures say that not to kill or even hurt any living being in any way by speech-thought-action. Ahinsā is the mainstay for all others yamas and niyamas, it is said: 'तत्राहिंसा सर्वदा सर्वभूतानामनभिद्रोह ।' one who is firmly (strongly) established in Ahinsā even rivals also becomes friends. The same said - 'अहिंसाप्रतिष्ठायां तत्सन्निधौ वैरत्यागः'.

(b) Satya (Truthfulness) - Vyāsa said 'सत्यं यथार्थे वाङ्मनसे यथा दृष्टं यथा श्रुतं तथा वाङ्मनश्चेति ' Whatever seen-heard must be followed in mind and speech. The words one speaks should not harm any creature and has to produce happiness and joy to all. The words should be pleasing, beneficial, and not agitating. One who is established in Truthfulness of all actions of the Sādhaka will be fruitful. 'सत्यप्रतिष्ठायां क्रियाफलाश्रयत्वम्'

(c) Asteya (non-stealing)— 'स्तेयमशास्त्रपूर्वकं द्रव्याणां परतः स्वीकरणम् तत्प्रतिषेधः पुनरस्पृहारूपम् अस्तेयमिति ' - due to desires the idea of stealing arises. So, one who is firmly established in non-stealing all the gems and wealth comes to him. अस्तेयप्रतिष्ठायां सर्वरत्नोपस्थानम्'

(d) Brahmacharya (celibacy)- 'ब्रह्ममचर्यं गुप्तेन्द्रियाणां संयमः ' means if a man saves seminal fluid his body becomes brilliant and fragrant and takes Brahmachārī near to Brahman. One who is firmly established in Brahmacharya, he can gain vigour. The same is said here ' ब्रह्मचर्य प्रतिष्ठायां वीर्यलाभः । '

(e) Aparigraha (Non-hoarding)— It is said-

'विषयाणामार्जनरक्षण-क्षयसंगहिंसादोषदर्शनादिस्वीकरणमपरिग्रहः ।' So, परिग्रह is a process of hoarding the objects more than required (one's necessity). Non-hoarding can be attained easily by developing detachment to all. By doing so the Sādhaka acquires the knowledge of past-present and future. 'अपरिग्रहस्थैर्ये जन्मकथन्तासम्बोधः'.

Some people say "I will not kill a human being, I will not kill in a holy place, I will not kill on the fourteenth day (chaturdasi, etc.,) and I will not kill anybody anywhere except in battles". But yamas (social disciplines) are great observances. They are to be observed beyond the limits of yonis, time, and place. It is said- 'जातिदेशकालसमयानवच्छिन्नः सार्वभौमामहाव्रतम् ।'

2. Niyamas - Niyamas (self-discipline) are also of five kinds.

(a) Śaucha - Cleanliness

(b) Santoṣa - Contentment

(c) Tapas - Austerity

(d) Svādhyāya - Study

(e) Iśvarapraṇidhāna - Dedication to God.

(a) Sauca (Cleanliness)- This śauca is of two types:

1. External

2. Internal

External purity will be achieved by mud-water etc, internal purity by purifying the mind with सत्य, ज्ञान, etc., by doing this external śaucha, the Sādhaka shows detachment to his own body without comparing with others. The same is said- 'शौचात्स्वाङ्गजुगुप्सा परैरसंसर्गः । ' By internal purity a pure mind, concentration, control of organs, and self-realization can be attained. 'सत्वशुद्धिसौमनस्यैकाग्र्येन्द्रियजयात्मदर्शनयोग्यत्वानि च' ।

(b) Santoṣa (Contentment) — 'सन्तोषः सन्निहितसाधनादधिकस्यानुपादिता' contentment means not wanting to earn more than what is needed. It also involves a profound level of acceptance and appreciation. It is a state in which the aspirant satisfies with what he/she is having by developing detachment to material objects 'सन्तोषादनुत्तमसुखलाभः ।'

(c) Tapas (Austerity) — 'तपो द्वन्द्वसहनम् द्वन्द्वश्च जिघत्सापिपासे , शीतोष्णे, स्थानासने' means austerity is the power to tolerate opposite feelings like hunger-thirst, cold-hot, happiness-unhappiness, etc., equally. By practising austerity all the impurities of body and senses can be removed. 'कायेन्द्रियसिद्धिरशुद्धिक्षयात्तपसः ।'

(d) Svādhyāya (Study) — 'स्वाध्यायः मोक्षशास्त्राणामध्ययनं प्रणवजपो वा '. Svādhyāya means, studying and following Śāstras or chanting of "AUM"-"Praṇava" which shows us the path of liberation. By perfectly following the Svādhyaya the sādhaka realizes the desired subject. 'स्वाध्यायादिष्टदेवतासम्प्रयोगः ।'

(e) Iśvara praṇidhāna (dedication to God) — It is said, 'ईश्वरपप्रणिधानं तस्मिन्परमगुरो सर्वकर्मार्पणम् '. That is Iśvara praṇidhāna means to dedicate himself/herself and his/her actions to God. By doing so सम्प्रज्ञातसमाधि can be attained. Patañjali said :- 'समाधिसिद्धिरीश्वरप्रणिधानात् ।'

3. Āsana — After acquiring perfection in Yama and Niyama, the yoga-sādhaka has to enter into the third phase i.e., Āsana. It is said a steady and comfortable posture is the Āsana-' स्थिरसुखमासनम्'. These are as follows-padmāsana, svastikāsana, bhadrāsana, siddāsana, etc. Yogī

always sits in siddhāsana, i.e posture perfected by him/her. Patañjali is not fastidious in respect to these postures. In his opinion, any pose that is conductive to stabilize the mind, which is not strenuous to the body limbs, and in which a yogī can sit for a sufficient time is the posture prescribed to him. Accepting these conditions, a yogī can choose a suitable posture for his purpose. When efforts cease the posture is completed so that there is no agitation of the body or the mind comes into a balanced state. It is said, 'प्रयत्नशैथिल्यानन्तसमापत्तिभ्याम्'. As a result of mastering the postures he (yogī) is not affected by the extremes of cold-heat, etc. 'ततो द्वन्द्वानभिघातः ।'

4. Prāṇayāma—Prāṇa means breath-respiration. Āyāma means expansion. Prāṇāyāma helps to regulate the breath. It is true that one can have control of sensualities on the one hand and on mental perturbations on the other hand by practising breathing controls. Inspiration-Expiration-Restraint are three processes involved in Prāṇāyāma. Inspiration is the inhalation of the outer-wind; the expiration is the expulsion of the internal air of the lungs. Restraint of the breath is the cutting off of the flow of these two, the absence of both kinds (Inspiration and Expiration). According to Patañjali-Prāṇāyāma means-"Suspension of the inspiration and expiration is prāṇāyāma". Patañjali enumerated our types of prāṇāyāmas:

1. Bāhya — External

2. Ābhyantara —Internal

3. Stamba — Suspended or stilled as it is, without motion either way.

4. Kumbhaka is of three kinds

    a. Kevala Kumbhaka-Holding up without motion

    b. Outer Kumbhaka-Holding up outside

    c. Internal Kumbhaka- Holding up inside

The first three - External, Internal, and Suspended are regulated by space, time, and number so that breath-control becomes long and subtle.

The sutras of Patañjali regarding prāṇāyāma are:-

1- तस्मिन्सति श्वास प्रश्वासयोर्गतिविच्छेदः प्राणायामः

2- बाह्याभ्यन्तरस्तम्भवृत्तिर्देशकालसंख्याभिः परिदृष्टो दीर्घसूक्ष्मः

3- बाह्याभ्यन्तर विषयाक्षेपी चतुर्थः

By practicing prāṇayāma the veil of darkness caused by rajas and tamas is removed and the light of knowledge shines fully. It is said- 'ततः क्षीयते प्रकशावरणम्'. Breath-control itself is the greatest penance. Which destroys impurities so that the brilliancy of knowledge is manifested. By the practice of prāṇāyāma, the capability of the mind for concentration is secured — 'धारणासु च मनसः योग्यता '. Manu also (6. 72) says, "By restraints of breath one should burn up effects". Prāṇa and mind are inter-linked. Fluctuation of Prāṇa leads to fluctuation of the mind. So, whenever prāṇa moves then chitta also moves. When prāṇa does not move then chitta stays still. So, by restraining the Vayu-air, the yogī attains steadiness. This is also accepted by Haṭhayoga as follows-

चले वाते चलं चित्तं, निश्चले निश्चलं भवेत।

योगी स्थाणुमवाप्रोति ततो वायुं निरोधयेत ॥

The breathing process is directly connected to the brain and CNS (Central Nervous System) and it is one of

the most vital processes in the body system. The voluntary control of respiration by Pranayamas interferes with the autonomic nervous system that bifurcates into sympathetic and parasympathetic antagonistic to their functions, so the yoga techniques provide a dynamic balance in this dichotomy. It has also some connection with the hypothalamus (fig.10), the brain centre which controls emotional responses. The hypothalamus is responsible for transforming perception into a cognitive experience. Erratic breathing sends erratic impulses to this centre and thus creates a disturbing response. If the nāḍis are impure the vital air does not pass in the middle channels of nāḍis which are capillary structures or subtle veins through which prana circulates. So, the attainment of perfection becomes difficult. By getting victory over prāṇa the nāḍis work properly. When nervous impulses are steady and rhythmic, the brain functions are regulated and the brain waves become synchronized. So, Prāṇa plays an important role in yoga.

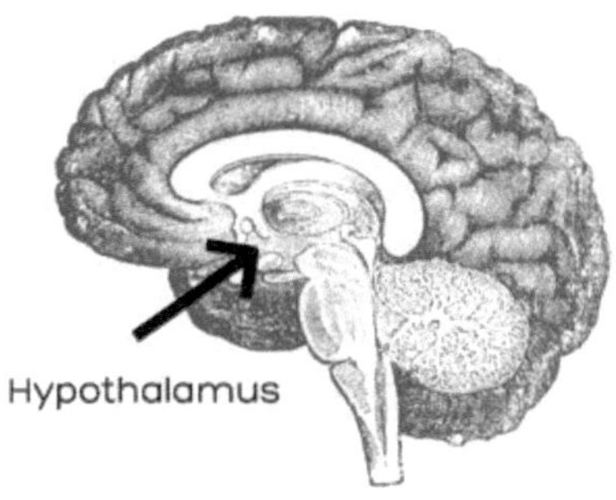

Figure 10: Hypothalamus

5. Pratyāhāra—The word pratyāhāra literally means "taking back" or "reversing". According to Patañjali, pratyāhāra is referred to the sense organs or 'Indriyas';

they have a natural tendency to rush to their sensualities (viṣayas); the eye rushes to the enjoyment of colour and form; the ear rushes to enjoy melodies and tones: tongue craves to enjoy tastes and flavours; the nose rushes towards smells and perfumes; and the organ of touch towards soft and sweet embraces. Each has a duty to perform, but each is attached to a sensuality characteristic of its own. Pratyāhāra consists in distracting the sense organs from their sensualities:

स्वविषयासंप्रयोगे चित्तस्य स्वरूपानुकार इवेन्द्रियाणां प्रत्याहारः ।

Viṣṇu Purāṇa (6.7.43) says, "A man skilled in yoga, having restrained the organs attached to, the various things, sound and so forth, should make there initiate the mind-stuff, in that he is intent upon the withdrawal of the senses".

Patañjali in relation to pratyāhāra said that the sense organs or Indriyas in respect to the control over sensualities become very well aligned with the activity of the citta or mind in its essential form. Swirling of citta or mind is not Svarupa or essential form: a mind free from perturbations is the mind in its essential form. Whatever is pleasant is the sensuality (viṣaya) it leaves behind a shadow of vāsanā (sanskāras) which finally becomes the cause of bondage.

A man who has practiced prāṇāyāma would find it easier to accomplish pratyāhāra. Pratyāhāra leads to "śreyas" or "Vidyā" or "spiritual science"; and the other that leads to "Preyas" is "avidya" or "material science".

The Kaṭhopaniṣad (2.4) says that by Practising pratyāhāra one can acquire complete control over the sense organs 'ततः परमावश्यतेन्द्रियाणाम् ।'

6. Dhāraṇa — Fixing the citta or mind at one place is dhāraṇa or concentration - 'देशबन्धश्चित्तस्यधारणा' concentration is the confinement of the mind in a place. The confinement of the mind by each operation in such places as the navel sphere, the lotus of the heart, the head, the shining part, the forepart of the nose the forepart of the tongue, etc., or in any external object which leads to Samādhi; is the concentration. In yoga Sūtras, first chapter, Patañjali, explained methods for the steadiness of the mind from the 32nd sūtra to the 40th sūtra. By following such methods Dhāraṇā can be attained.

7. Dhyāna — the continuous flow of mind towards the pratyaya or goal is dhyāna or meditation. Just as a river continuously flows into a sea, similarly the entire consciousness of the self starts continuously flowing towards God, the Higher Self. When so happens, it is dhyāna. Sāṅkhya sūtra (3. 30) defined dhyāna as:- "Removal of attachment is Dhyāna". Probably the same thing meant-dhyāna consists in rendering the mind free from attachments.

In Dhāraṇā disturbances may take place, but in Dhyāna no disturbance takes place. It is said - 'तत्र प्रत्ययैकतानता ध्यानम्' Continuous presence of one object is meditation.

8. Samādhi- There is an essential difference between dhyāna and Samādhi. In the state of dhyāna the mind of the contemplator (dhyātā), the act of contemplation (Dhyāna), and the object to which the contemplation is directed (dhyeya)-all these three remain distinct, whereas, in the state of Samādhi, all the three merge into one.

Just as a ball of iron placed in a red hot furnace

becomes red at the final stage that it becomes indistinguishable from the red hot appearance of the furnace, similarly, in the state of Samādhi, the yogī forgets himself, he forgets even where he is, he becomes completely absorbed in Brahman. Here in Samādhi, the object of Meditation vanishes and the subject (truth) alone shines - 'तदेवार्थमात्रानिर्भास स्वरूपशून्यमिव समाधिः'

That dhyāna, verily, is Samādhi, in which artha (the meaning of the object) alone shines and the intrinsic form or svarūpa disappears. In this transcendental state, the thinker gets absorbed in the thought, and the activity of the mind ceases, as if it has become one with the object of meditation. Then this stage is called Spiritual Absorption.

The eight steps of the yoga discussed in the above first five steps are known as Bahiraṅga Yoga - external and the last three are known as Antaraṅga Yoga - Internal.

Externals (Bahiraṅgas)	Internals (Antaraṅgas) and also Sañyama
1) Yama	6) Dhāraṇā
2) Niyama	7) Dhyāna
3) Āsana	8) Samādhi
4) Prāṇāyāma	
5) Pratyāhāra	

The internals are to be given preference over the externals, though the externals cannot be avoided; Bahiraṅga or externals constitute the earlier stage, whilst the antaraṅga or internals constitute the next higher stage, the superior are Dhāraṇa, Dhyāna, and Samādhi. The three together constitute Sañyama or co-conciliation (त्रयमेकत्र संयमः). Having practiced this sort of Sañyama, one very easily acquires prajñā or divine intellect (eternal truth).

प्रथमोऽध्यायः
समाधि-पादः
Samādhi-pāda

(Transcendental Meditation)

अथ योगानुशासनम् ॥ 1 ॥

atha yogānuśāsanam

1. यहाँ से योग का अनुशासन शुरू होता है।

1. Here begins the discipline of *Yoga*.

व्यास भाष्य-अथेत्ययमधिकारार्थः । योगानुशासनं शास्त्रमधिकृतं वेदितव्यम् । योगः समाधिः । स च सार्वभौमश्चित्तस्य धर्मः । क्षिप्तं मूढं विक्षिप्तमेकाग्रं निरुद्धमिति चित्तभूमयः । तत्र विक्षिप्ते चेतसि विक्षेपोपसर्जनीभूतः समाधिर्न योगपक्षे वर्तते । यस्त्वेकाग्रे चेतसि सद्भूतमर्थं प्रद्योतयति क्षिणोति च क्लेशान्कर्मबन्धनानि श्लथयति निरोधमभिमुखं करोति स संप्रज्ञातो योग इत्याख्यायते । स च वितर्कानुगतो विचारानुगत आनन्दानुगतोऽस्मितानुगत इत्युपरिष्टात्प्रवेदयिष्यामः । सर्ववृत्तिनिरोधे त्वसंप्रज्ञातः समाधिः । तस्य लक्षणाभिधित्सयेदं सूत्रं प्रवर्तते

भोजवृत्ति-अनेन सूत्रेण शास्त्रस्य सम्बन्धाभिधेयप्रयोजनान्याख्यायन्ते । अथ शब्दोऽधिकारद्योतको मङ्गलार्थकश्च । योगो युक्तिः समाधनम् । युज् समाधौ अनुशिष्यते व्याख्यायते लक्षणभेदोपायफलैर्येन तदनुशासनम् । योगस्यानुशासनं योगानुशासनम् । तदा शास्त्रपरिसमाप्तेरधिकृतं बोद्धव्यमित्यर्थः । तत्र शास्त्रस्य व्युत्पाद्यतया योगः ससाधनः सफलोऽभिधेयः । तदव्युत्पादनञ्च फलम् । व्युत्पादितस्य योगस्य कैवल्यं फलम् । शास्त्राभिधेययोः प्रतिपाद्यप्रतिपादकभावलक्षणः सम्बन्धः । अभिधेयस्य योगस्य तत्फलस्य च कैवल्यस्य साध्यसाधनभावः । एतदुक्तं भवति व्युत्पाद्यस्य योगस्य साधनानि शास्त्रेण प्रदर्श्यन्ते तत्साधनसिद्धो योगः कैवल्याख्यं फलमुत्पादयति । तत्र को योगः इत्याह

योगश्चित्तवृत्तिनिरोधः ॥ 2 ॥

Yogaścittavṛttinirodhaḥ

2. बाहरी दुनिया से मन को हटा लेना ही योग है।

2. Yoga is the withdrawal of the mind from the external world.

Modern science identifies consciousness with the mind and the mind with the brain. This identification has resulted in seeking to improve our mental and emotional functioning through altering brain chemistry with pharmaceutical preparations or psychological interventions. Mainstream science usually does not recognize consciousness as a spiritual or cosmic principle apart from the mind, though some trends in the new physics like quantum mechanics are beginning to suggest this. It is still a largely physical view of the mind that we find in medicine today. The yogic view of the mind, however, is very different. It is based on meditation and inner experience, rather than outer experimentation. It tries to understand the mind through introspection or turning our awareness within, rather than by analyzing outer mental patterns. It encourages us to observe the mind rather than to follow its reactions. It teaches us to understand the process of perception and how it conditions us, rather than to merely examine our memories. The Yoga tradition also classifies the mind in a different manner. It defines the mind in the broadest sense, what is called chitta in Sanskrit, as the mind with sanskāras of the visible world. Under the concept of chitta is included reason, emotion, sensation, memory, the instinctual part of the mind, and the ego, in other words, chitta is a complex system with several components with their functionalities and interactions; all that we ordinarily consider possessing some degree of consciousness within us.

Yoga radically distinguishes between mind and consciousness, which it regards as two separate but related powers. Yoga regards consciousness, called 'chit' as the mind devoid of sanskāras of information from material world which is something other than the mind or 'chitta' (mind full of sanskāras or information from material world). This is very different than modern science but also most of the world's philosophies, which generally identify as a mental apparatus, consciousness. The mind is an instrument of thinking and sensing on various levels. Mind is called the 'inner instrument' or antaḥkaraṇa in Sanskrit, related to the body which is our outer instrument. The mind is looked upon as the sixth sense after the five bodily senses and is regarded as an organ, not our true being or the basis of our sense of self.

Chit is the mind devoid of sanskāras (information from the material world) or called pure consciousness or unmodified mind whereas Chitta is mind coloured with sanskāras of the material world.

Yoga similarly regards the mind and brain as different though related. The brain is the physical vehicle for the mind, but not the mind itself.

The Puruṣa is our inner-self while the mind, we could say, is like our computer and the body is like the car we drive. Mind and body are our internal and external instruments but not our real identity. Just as you are not your computer, so, too, your true Soul and Being is not the mind. The light that allows the mind to function comes from the Puruṣa. The mind does not have any light of its own. Your sense of self-being, that you are a unique, whole, and continuous centre of awareness, derives from the soul, not from the mind.

In Yoga, realization of one's true nature or knowledge alone is said to bring about the liberation of soul, specifically self-knowledge or the knowledge of the true nature of self within or Puruṣa. When we speak of self-knowledge for the personal mind, we are mainly referring to knowledge of one's personal history, habits, and inclinations. Self-knowledge for the inner Being, however, consists of understanding the essence of awareness beyond thought and personal history. Though our thoughts are constantly changing, our inner Being remains the same.

True Self-knowledge is a matter of being, not of thought or emotion. It is a state of being, not of events, experiences, or ideas known. Our inner Being has no conceptual content, nor is it conditioned by time, space and action. It is a state of openness, surrender, and presence like a steady thread through all our experiences. Contacting it brings us into a state of peace in which the mind and its psychology are naturally put to rest. To reach our inner Being requires a different orientation of our consciousness, a willingness to let go of our history of the visible world and dive within which will reveal your personal history beginning from the creation.

Usually, we think of Self-realization as the realization of our hidden personal potentials, some special abilities or talents we might not have yet developed. However, yogic Self-realization is the understanding that our true Self is beyond body and mind, which also means beyond psychology, culture, and conditioning. It is the dissolution of the personal, psychological self or mind into the soul that is not born and does not die.

True consciousness is the mind (chit) devoid of sanskāras which is not chitta, which is a conditioned consciousness, a mere collection of tendencies and activities from our various births. The mind (chit) devoid of material world information can at best reflect it, which requires that the mind be still, subtle and sensitive within, this is what Yoga does with the mind. We must learn to move from the embodiedment to disembodiment; in which we transcend our personal self to the universal Self. This occurs when we go to the root of the mind and discover the light of awareness that radiates through it.

Mind and Self-realization

For such higher Self-realization, the mind plays a crucial role. The mind can be the instrument for bondage or liberation, ignorance or enlightenment. If we turn the mind towards the external world as the reality, it becomes a force of attachment and sorrow. If we turn the mind within to the inner being as the reality, it slows down and comes to reflect that higher reality. The mind becomes a mirror for the light of the Self to shine. Making an analogy, the mind works on the same principle as a telescope like Hubble. It only reflects images of the universe through its sophisticated mirroring mechanism. So, turning the mind within is the essence of Yoga and meditation. For this, the mind must be first brought to a one-pointed state. A fragmented or distracted mind cannot turn within. This inward turning process can be looked upon very simply as immersing the mind in the deeper consciousness of the inner Being that dwells within the heart.

The mind's knowledge is conceptual or thought-based. It results in facts, data, information, ideals, theories, opinions, concepts, or formulas. Our inner Being has a higher kind of knowledge, which is radically different from what the mind can know. Our inner being has a special "knowledge by identity', which is not coloured by thought and its preconceptions. Through one's inner-being one can merge into the inner being of all that one comes in contact with through the body and senses. For most of us, this is a very difficult condition to imagine. But whenever the mind becomes totally concentrated, it experiences a quantum leap in awareness and a special knowledge arises through the inner unity of the seer and the seen. This inner knowledge through identity is the real yogic knowledge that frees us from all bondage and suffering. All that the mind knows is simply thought, which is name and form, and but a modification of the mind. True knowledge is knowledge of the Being, which arises through pure consciousness (chit) when mental activity comes to rest, when the mind becomes cool, calm, and silent.

From Chitta (mind) to Chit (pure consciousness)

We must learn to move beyond the mind (chitta) to Chit (pure consciousness), which is to return to our true nature, our inner Being. It is to rest in the silence and peace within that no thought, opinion, belief, or conclusion can touch. It is to enter into the realm of being and direct experience, where no words can go, which leaves no outer trace, where one becomes everything and nothing.

The mind is an excellent tool and instrument for the soul. It has a wonderful capacity for action, expression, memory, and coordination of our outer actions. But if we try to understand the soul through the mind, we fall into spiritual ignorance and confusion. We wrongly identify our true Self and Being with our outerbeing. However, if we abide in chit (pure consciousness), then the mind (chitta) has its place to help us function in life. Learn to witness the mind (chitta). Dwell as the seer of the mind (chitta) and its modifications (vṛttis). This is the Yoga that empties the mind of its conditioning (sanskāras) and allows us to rest in our true nature, to see Reality.

व्यासभाष्य- सर्वशब्दाग्रहणात्संप्रज्ञातोऽपि योग इत्याख्यायते । चित्तं हि प्रख्याप्रवृत्तिस्थितिशीलत्वात् त्रिगुणम् । प्रख्यारूपं हि चित्तसत्त्वं रजस्तमोभ्यां संसृष्टमैश्वर्यविषयप्रियं भवति । तदेव तमसाऽनुविद्धमधर्माज्ञानवैराग्यानैश्वर्योपगं भवति । तदेव प्रक्षीणमोहावरणं सर्वतः प्रद्योतमानमनुविद्धरजोमात्रया धर्मज्ञानवैराग्यैश्वर्योपगं भवति । तदेव रजोलेशमलापेतं स्वरूपप्रतिष्ठं सत्त्वपुरुषान्यताख्यातिमात्रं धर्ममेघध्यानोपगं भवति । तत्परं प्रसंख्यानमित्याचक्षते ध्यायिनः । चितिशक्तिपरिणामिन्यप्रतिसंक्रमा दर्शितविषया शुद्धा चानन्ता च सत्त्वगुणात्मिका चेयमतो विपरीता विवेकख्यातिरिति । अतस्तस्यां विरक्तं चित्तं तामपि ख्यातिं निरुणद्धि । तदवस्थं संस्कारोपगं भवति । स निर्बीजः समाधिः । न तत्र किंचित्संप्रज्ञायत इत्यसंप्रज्ञातः । द्विविधः स योगश्चित्तवृत्तिनिरोध इति ।
तदवस्थे चेतसि विषयाभावाद् बुद्धिबोधात्मा पुरुषः किंस्वभाव इति

भोजवृत्ति- चित्तस्य निर्मलसत्त्वपरिणामरूपस्य या वृत्तयोऽङ्गाङ्गिभावपरिणामरूपास्तासां निरोधो बहिर्मुखतया परिणतिविच्छेदादन्तर्मुखतया प्रतिलोमपरिणामेन स्वकारणे लयो योग इत्याख्यायते । स च निरोधः सर्वासां चित्तभूमीनां सर्वप्राणिनां धर्मः कदाचित् कस्याञ्चित् बुद्धिभूमावाविर्भवति । ताश्च क्षिप्तं मूढं विक्षिप्तमेकाग्रं निरुद्धमिति चित्तस्य भूमयश्चित्तस्यावस्थाविशेषाः । तत्र क्षिप्तं रजस उद्रेकादस्थिरं बहिर्मुखतया सुखदुःखादिविषयेषु विकल्पितेषु व्यवहितेषु संनिहितेषु वा रजसा प्रेरितं । तच्च सदैव दैत्यदानववादीनाम् । मूढं तमस उद्रेकाकृत्याकृत्य विभागमन्तरेण क्रोधादिभिः विरुद्धकृत्येष्वेव नियमितं तच्च सदैव रक्षः पिशाचादीनाम् । विक्षिप्तं तु सत्त्वोद्रेकाद्वैशिष्ट्येन परिहृत्य दुःखसाधनं सुखसाधनेष्वेव शब्दादिषु प्रवृत्तं तच्च सदैव देवानाम् । एतदुक्तं भवति रजसा प्रवृत्तिरूपं तमसा परापकारनियतं सत्त्वेन सुखमयं चित्तं भवति । एतास्तिस्रश्चित्तावस्थाः समाधावनुपयोगिन्यः । एकाग्रनिरुद्धरूपे द्वे च सत्त्वोत्कर्षाद्यथोत्तरमवस्थितत्वात् समाधावुपयोगं भजेते । सत्त्वादिक्रमव्युत्क्रमे तु अयमभिप्रायः द्वयोरपि रजस्तमसोरत्यन्तहेयत्वेऽप्येतदर्थं रजसः प्रथममुपादानं यावन्न प्रवृत्तिदर्शिता तावन्निवृत्तिं शक्यते दर्शयितुमिति द्वयोर्व्यत्ययेन प्रदर्शनम् । सत्त्वस्य चेतदर्थं पश्चात्प्रदर्शनं यत्तस्योत्कर्षेणोत्तरे द्वे भूमी योगोपयोगिन्याविति ।
अनयोर्द्वयोरेकाग्रनिरुद्धयोर्भूम्योर्यश्चित्तस्यैकाग्रतारूपः परिणामः स योग इत्युक्तं भवति । एकाग्रे बहिर्वृत्तिनिरोधः । निरुद्धे च सर्ववृत्तीनां संस्काराणां च प्रविलय इत्यनयोरेव भूम्योर्योगस्य सम्भवः ।
इदानीं सूत्रकारश्चित्तवृत्तिनिरोधपदानि व्याख्यातुकामः प्रथमं चित्तपदं व्याचष्टे

तदा द्रष्टुः स्वरूपेऽवस्थानम् ॥ 3 ॥

tadā draṣṭuḥ svarūpe'vasthānam

3. जब बाहरी दुनिया से मन हट जाता है, तब साधक अपने वास्तविक स्वरूप में स्वयं को स्थापित कर लेता है ।

3. When the mind is withdrawn from the external world, then the seeker establishes himself in his true nature.

व्यासभाष्य-स्वरूपप्रतिष्ठा तदानीं चितिशक्तिर्यथा कैवल्ये। व्युत्थानचित्ते तु सति तथाऽपि भवन्ति न तथा। कथं तर्हिं दर्शितविषयत्वात्

भोजवृत्ति- द्रष्टुः पुरुषस्य तस्मिन्काले स्वरूपे चिन्मात्रतायामवस्थानं स्थितिर्भवति । अयमर्थः उत्पन्नविवेकख्यातेश्चित्संक्रमाभावात् कर्तृत्वाभिमाननिवृत्तौ प्रोच्छन्नपरिणामायां बुद्धौ चाऽत्मानः स्वरूपेणावस्थानं स्थितिर्भवति । व्युत्थानदशायान्तु तस्य किं रूपम् इत्याह

वृत्तिसारूप्यमितरत्र ॥ 4 ॥

vṛttisārupyam itaratra

4. अन्यथा साधक स्वयं को मन और उसकी वृत्तियों (प्रवृत्तियों) से पहचानता है ।

4. Otherwise the seeker identifies himself with the mind and its vṛttis (tendencies).

If a person is not able to exercise control over his mind, his mind overpowers him and carries him towards worldly allurements as its (mind's) nature is. Our Body and Mind are the parts of Prakṛti (nature), so it is but natural that they are attracted towards outside nature until and unless a reasonable control is exercised over them. The Yoga of meditation empties the mind of its conditioning of the outside world and allows us to rest in our true nature, to see Reality.

व्यासभाष्य- व्युत्थाने याश्चित्तवृत्तयस्तदविशिष्टवृत्तिः पुरुषः । तथा च सूत्रम् एकमेव दर्शनं ख्यातिरेव दर्शनम् इति । चित्तमयस्कान्तमणिकल्पं संनिधिमात्रोपकारि दृश्यत्वे स्वं भवति पुरुषस्य

स्वामिनः । तस्माच्चित्तवृत्तिबोधे पुरुषस्यानादिः संबन्धो हेतुः ।   ताः पुनर्निरोद्धव्या बहुत्वे सति चित्तस्य ।

भोजवृत्ति- इतरत्र योगादन्यस्मिन्काले वृत्तयो या वक्ष्यमाणलक्षणास्ताभिः सारूप्यं तद्रूपत्वम् । अयमर्थः याट्टश्यो वृत्तयो दुःखमोहसुखाद्यात्मिकाः प्रादुर्भवन्ति ताट्टग्रूप एव संवेद्यते व्यवहर्तृभिः पुरुषः । तदेवं यस्मिन्नेकाग्रतया परिणते चित्तिशक्तेः स्वस्मिन् स्वरूपे प्रतिष्ठानं भवति यस्मिंश्चेन्द्रियवृत्तिद्वारेण विषयाकारेण परिणते पुरुषस्तद्रपाकार एव परिभाव्यते यथा जलतरङ्गेषु चलत्सु चन्द्रश्चलन्निव प्रतिभासते सच्चित्तम् । वृत्तिपदं व्याख्यातुमाह

वृत्तयः पञ्चतय्यः क्लिष्टाऽक्लिष्टाः ॥ 5 ॥

vṛttayaḥ pañcatayyaḥ kliṣṭā'kliṣṭāḥ

5. जब मन बाहरी दुनिया की वस्तुओं के संपर्क में आता है, तो पाँच वृत्तियाँ (प्रवृत्तियाँ) विकसित होती हैं । वे दुःखद या सुखद हो सकती हैं ।

5. When the mind is exposed to objects of the external world, five vṛttis (tendencies) develop. They may be painful or pleasurable.

व्यासभाष्य-   क्लेशहेतुकाः कर्माशयप्रचये क्षेत्रीभूताः क्लिष्टाः । ख्यातिविषया गुणाधिकारविरोधिन्योऽक्लिष्टाः । क्लिष्टप्रवाहपतिता अप्यक्लिष्टाः । क्लिष्टच्छिद्रेष्वप्यक्लिष्टा भवन्ति । अक्लिष्टच्छिद्रेषु क्लिष्टा इति । तथाजातीयकाः संस्कारा वृत्तिभिरेव क्रियन्ते संस्कारैश्च वृत्तय इति । एवं वृत्तिसंस्कारचक्रमनिशमावर्तते । तदेवंभूतं चित्तमवसिताधिकारमात्मकल्पेन व्यवतिष्ठते प्रलयं वा गच्छतीति । ताः क्लिष्टाश्चाक्लिष्टाश्च पञ्चधा वृत्तयः ।

भोजवृत्ति-वृत्तयश्चित्तपरिणामविशेषाः वृत्तिसमुदायलक्षणस्यावयविनो या अवयवभूता वृत्तयस्तदपेक्षया तदप्यप्रत्ययः । एतदुक्तं भवति पञ्च वृत्तयः कीट्टश्यः क्लिष्टा अक्लिष्टा क्लेशैर्वक्ष्यमाणलक्षणैराक्रान्ताः क्लिष्टाः । तद्विपरीता अक्लिष्टाः । एता एव पञ्च वृत्तयः संक्षिप्योद्दिश्यन्ते

प्रमाणविपर्ययविकल्पनिद्रास्मृतयः ॥ 6 ॥

pramāṇa viparyaya vikalpa nidrāsmṛtayaḥ

6. वे हैं: प्रमाण, विपर्यय, विकल्प, निद्रा और स्मृति

विशेषः प्रमाण किसी चीज को जानना या जानना है । योग मनोविज्ञान इसे प्रमाण कहता है । हालाँकि न्याय दर्शन इसे केवल प्रमा कहता है, और जिस

माध्यम से प्रमा की प्रक्रिया को पूरा किया जाता है उसे न्याय में प्रमाण के रूप में जाना जाता है। प्रमाकरणं प्रमाणम्। 'प्रमा के साधन को प्रमाण के रूप में जाना जाता है।'

6. They are:

1. Cognition (प्रमाण)

2. False knowledge (विपर्यय)

3. Fiction (विकल्प)

4. Sleep (निद्रा)

5. Memory (स्मृति)

Note: Cognition consists in knowing or knowledge of something. Yoga psychology calls it pramāṇa. Though Nyāya Darśana simply calls it pramā and the means through which the process of pramā (cognition) is accomplished is known in Nyāya as prāmaṇa. Pramākaraṇam pramāṇam. 'Means of pramā is known as pramāṇa.'

भोजवृत्ति—आसां क्रमेण लक्षणमाह

प्रत्यक्षानुमानागमाः प्रमाणानि ॥7॥

pratyakṣānumānāgamāḥ pramāṇāni

7. मन की प्रमाण वृत्ति (बाहरी वस्तु की जानकारी को प्रामाणिक मानने की प्रवृत्ति) तब विकसित होती है जब बाहरी दुनिया की कोई वस्तु इंद्रियों के माध्यम से देखी जाती है, या पहले से ही उपलब्ध जानकारी के आधार पर अनुमान लगाया जाता है या ऋषियों द्वारा कहा जाता है या शास्त्रों में लिखा जाता है।

1. इन्द्रियों द्वारा अनुभव करना

2. स्मृति संग्रह में सूचना के आधार पर अनुमान

3. ऋषि या शास्त्र का कथन

तीनों प्रकार के प्रमाण की प्रकृति और परिभाषा का विस्तृत विवरण देने से पहले, यहाँ यह बताना आवश्यक है कि न्याय-दर्शन उपमान को मिलाकर प्रमाण

के चार साधन मानते हैं ।

प्रत्यक्षानुमानोपमानाप्तोपदेशाः प्रमाणानि ।

7. Pramāṇa vṛtti (tendency to accept information of external object as authentic) of mind develops when an object of the external world is perceived through sense organs, or inferred on the basis of information already available to mind or stated by seniors or written in Śāstras.

1. Perceiving through sense organs

2. Inference on the basis of information in store

3. Statement of a seer or Śāstra

Before giving a detailed break up of the nature and definition of all three types of cognition, it is necessary to point out here that the Nyāya-philosopher also enumerates upamāna (comparison) as the fourth means of cognition in addition to those mentioned by Patañjali.

प्रत्यक्षानुमानोपमानाप्तोपदेशाः प्रमाणानि

pratyakṣānumānopamān-āptopadeśāḥ pramāṇāni)

1. Perception (pratyakṣa): This takes place in the presence of sense organs and a stimulus outside (Indriyārtha sannikarṣa). The other way round, it can be said that perception presupposes a sensation. Nyāya philosopher defines perception as इन्द्रियार्थ सन्निकर्षजन्यं ज्ञानं प्रत्यक्षम् (*indriyārtha sannikarṣa janyaṁ jñānaṁ pratyakṣam*).

'The proximity of sensory organs with a stimulus leads to the process of perception.'

So, perception is the first type of cognition based on sensation. Modern psychologists, however, consider sensation also as one kind of cognition. On the other hand, ancient Indian scholars do not take sensation as a form of cognition. Rather they consider it as a basic factor or a priory to the perception or say as an element in perception.

2. Inference (anumāna): Inference has been considered as one type of cognition or means of cognition. For instance, if one sees smoke, one can infer the presence of fire also. यत्र यत्र धूमः तत्र-तत्र वह्निः *yatra yatra dhūmaḥ tatra tatra vahniḥ*)

'Where there is smoke there is fire.' This type of reasoning also leads to the cognition. Hence inference can also be taken as a type of cognition or a means of cognition. In cognition by inference, the mental function of imagination is also involved.

3. Authority (āgama): Another type of cognition is authority or testimony of a person who is senior in knowledge. Cognition of everything can never take place directly or by direct experience. For the cognition of most of the things, one has to depend upon one's seniors who have already gained it from their seniors in tradition. So cognition is also mostly gained in tradition from seniors by juniors. That is why we are able to make advancements in our knowledge. Had we not gained it from the authority or testimony of seniors, there would have been no advancement as everyone would have to begin with the same beginning. Thus the knowledge would be repeated and duplicated, but it would not have advanced. It would rather have stagnated. Thus it is crystal clear from the foregoing discussion that the authority (āgama) is also one of the vital factors leading to cognition. In fact, testimony is the cognition of

historical facts.

Earlier psychologists had no idea of this factor, but now the Indian philosophy is widely and extensively studied abroad, modern psychologists are hard-pressed to talk about inference and testimony while dealing with the concepts of cognition.

4. Comparison (Upamāna): Fourth factor helpful in cognition is comparison. Cognition is sometimes gained through the comparison of one object with another. For instance, when one sees a Nīla-gāya (blue bull) in the jungle, he is able to recognize it on the comparison of the experience of a cow already had by him in his vicinity.

In the cognition, by comparison, the mental function of memory is also keenly involved, as for example, it is the reproduction of the past experience of a cow that helps one in the cognition of Nīla-gāya (blue bull) in the jungle.

Simply because of the involvement of some mental function or another, the involved function cannot be termed as a form of that function. This is what has been done by modern psychologists in the case of the mental functions of memory and imagination on account of their involvement in the mental function of cognition by way of inference and comparison. However ancient Indian psychologists did not include these into the forms of cognition.

The above said kinds of cognition are attained in the normal course of life by individuals. Cognition of a large number of objects or things is not possible. For instance, we can have the sensation of only those objects or things that are within the sensory range of our sense-organs, so their perception is also possible. But sometimes, the objects or things due to their location or size do not come within the range of our sensation or sensory power of our sense-organs, e.g. our eye can see objects within a particular range, our ears can hear up to a particular range, our nose can smell up to a limited distance, our skin can have sensation only of the objects that are closeted with it; we can taste only the things that are inserted into our mouth.

In other words, one can say, an individual has no power of extra-sensory perception. Here it is necessary to point out that the scope of Yoga starts where the range of sensory perception ends. Yoga deals with extra-sensory perception. It explains a technique as to how to develop the power of extra-sensory perception. It explains how an individual can have an extra-sensory perception of the things located at far-off places or intervened by some other object or objects having an atomic size and ultimately the extra-sensory perception (or realization) of self or individuated consciousness in the form of universal consciousness.

Yoga endows the practitioner with the divine sight, divine audition, divine olfaction, divine skin-sensation, and divine taste. It tells one how an individual endowed with divine sight sees the objects intervened by some bigger object and objects located far off places or the objects which are atomic in size. It tells one as to how an individual endowed with divine audition, hears the sound from far off places; endowed with divine olfaction, smells odours of objects located at far off places; endowed with divine skin-sensation, feels the objects located at far off places; endowed with divine taste, receives tastes of the distant things.

Perception is the realization of the presence of a stimulus, but it may also be remembered that as per Vedic scholiasts realization of the absence of a stimulus already perceived is also a perception. For example, if a glass is not on the table or glass is missing is also a perception that arose on account of the realization of the absence of stimulus.

व्यासभाष्य-इन्द्रियप्रणालिकया चित्तस्य बाह्यवस्तूपरागात्तद्विषया सामान्यविशेषात्मनोऽर्थस्य विशेषावधारणप्रधाना वृत्तिः प्रत्यक्षं प्रमाणम्। फलमविशिष्टः पौरुषेयश्चित्तवृत्तिबोधः। प्रतिसंवेदी पुरुष इत्युपरिष्टादुपपादयिष्यामः। अनुमेयस्य तुल्यजातीयेष्वनुवृत्तो भिन्नजातीयेभ्यो व्यावृत्तः संबन्धो यस्तद्विषया सामान्यावधारणप्रधाना वृत्तिरनुमानम्। यथा देशान्तरप्राप्तेर्गतिमच्चन्द्रतारकं चैत्रवत् विन्ध्यश्चाप्राप्तिरगतिः। आप्तेन दृष्टोऽनुमितो वाऽर्थः परत्र स्वबोधसंक्रान्तये शब्देनोपदिश्यते शब्दात्तदर्थविषया वृत्तिः श्रोतुरागमः। यस्याश्रद्धेयार्थो वक्ता न दृष्टानुमितार्थः। स आगमः प्लवते। मूलवक्तरि तु दृष्टानुमितार्थे निर्विप्लवः स्यात्।

भोजवृत्ति-अत्रातिप्रसिद्धत्वात् प्रमाणानां शास्त्रकारेण भेदलक्षणेनैव गतत्वात् लक्षणस्य पृथक्कल्लक्षणं न कृतम्। प्रमाणलक्षणन्तु अविसंवादिज्ञानं प्रमाणमिति। इन्द्रियद्वारेण बाह्यवस्तूपरागाच्चित्तस्य तद्विषयसामान्यविशेषात्मनोऽर्थस्य विशेषावधारणप्रधाना वृत्तिः प्रत्यक्षम्। गृहीतसम्बन्धाल्लिङ्गात् लिङ्गिनि सामान्यात्मनाऽध्यवसायोऽनुमानम्। आप्तवचनं आगमः। एवं प्रमाणरूपां वृत्तिं व्याख्याय विपर्य्यरूपामाह

2. False Cognition

प्रमाण वृत्ति का स्वरूप परिभाषित करने के बाद यहाँ 'विपर्यय वृत्ति' का स्वरूप परिभाषित किया गया है:

After defining the nature of 'pramāṇa vṛtti', the nature of '*viparyaya vṛtti*' is defined here:

विपर्ययो मिथ्याज्ञानमतद्रूपप्रतिष्ठितम् ॥ 8 ॥

viparyayo mithyājñānamatadrūpapratiṣṭhitam

8. मन की विपर्यय वृत्ति मिथ्या सूचना, या वस्तु जैसी है उससे मेल न खाने वाली सूचना, या वस्तु के वास्तविक स्वरूप की व्याख्या करने में असमर्थ सूचना के कारण विकसित होती है।

8. Viparyaya vṛtti of mind develops due to false information, or information not corresponding to the thing as it is, or information unable to explain the true nature of a concept, thing, or object of an external object.

व्यासभाष्य-स कस्मान्न प्रमाणम्। यतः प्रमाणेन बाध्यते। भूतार्थविषयत्वात्प्रमाणस्य। तत्र प्रमाणेन बाधनमप्रमाणस्य दृष्टम्। तद्यथा द्विचन्द्रदर्शनं सद्विषयेणैकचन्द्रदर्शनेन बाध्यत इति। सेयं पञ्चपर्वा भवत्यविद्या अविद्यास्मितारागद्वेषाभिनिवेशाः क्लेशा इति। एत एव स्वसंज्ञाभिस्तमो मोहो महामोहस्तामिस्रोऽन्धतामिस्र इति। एते चित्तमलप्रसङ्गेनाभिधास्यन्ते।

भोजवृत्ति-अतथाभूतेऽर्थे तथोत्पद्यमानं ज्ञानं विपर्ययः। यथा शुक्तिकायां रजतज्ञानम्। अतद्रूपप्रतिष्ठमिति। तस्यार्थस्य यद्रूयं तस्मिन्रूपे न प्रतितिष्ठति तस्यार्थस्य यत्पारमार्थिकं रूपं न तत्प्रतिभासयतीति यावत्। संशयोऽप्यतद्रूपप्रतिष्ठत्वान्मिथ्याज्ञानम्। यथा स्थाणुर्वा पुरुषो वेति। विकल्पवृत्तिं व्याख्यातुमाह

3. Fiction

'मिथ्या ज्ञान' की प्रकृति को परिभाषित करने के बाद, मन की तीसरी वृत्ति जिसे विकल्प (काल्पनिक कथा) के रूप में जाना जाता है, को निम्नानुसार परिभाषित किया गया है:

After defining the nature of 'false cognition', the third vṛtti of mind known as Vikalpa (fiction) is defined as under:

शब्दज्ञानानुपाती वस्तुशून्यो विकल्पः ॥ 9 ॥

śabdajñānānupāti vastuśūnyo vikalpaḥ

9.[विकल्पः] मौखिक जानकारी के आधार पर मन की विकल्प वृत्ति [शब्दज्ञानानुपति] विकसित होती है जब इसकी वास्तविक सामग्री ज्ञात नहीं होती है या कहें जब मौखिक जानकारी से जुड़ी बाहरी दुनिया से कोई भौतिक जानकारी नहीं होती है।

नोट: जब एक शब्द सुना जाता है , मन उसे ज्ञात बाहरी दुनिया की किसी वस्तु या वस्तु के साथ जोड़ने की ओर प्रवृत्त होता है, भले ही वह ध्वनि या शब्द से सम्बन्धित बाह्य जगत के पदार्थ की जानकारी से रहित हो।

यहाँ विकल्प मन की वह अवस्था है जिसमें बाहरी दुनियां से कोई जानकारी नहीं होती है। संकल्प मन की वह अवस्था है जहाँ यह बाहरी दुनिया की

जानकारी से भरा होता है। दोनों टीकाकार व्यास और भोज विकल्प की मनः स्थिति को स्पष्ट करने के लिए एक ही उदाहरण का हवाला देते हैं। उदाहरण के लिए, यदि कोई कहता है कि 'चेतना पुरुष का स्वभाव है' तो यह कथन विकल्प की श्रेणी में आता है। उपर्युक्त कथन में पुरुष और चेतना को दो भिन्न वस्तुओं के रूप में दिखाया गया है, जबकि वास्तविकता यह है कि चेतना पुरुष से भिन्न नहीं है। लेकिन विकल्प की मनः स्थिति में एक व्यक्ति इसे तथ्य की पुष्टि किए बिना इसे स्वीकार कर लेता है। जिस तरह स्कूल जाने वाले बच्चे अक्सर अपने शिक्षकों पर बिना उनकी प्रामाणिकता पर सवाल उठाए आंख मूंदकर विश्वास कर लेते हैं।

9.[Vikalpaḥ] Vikalpa vṛtti of mind develops [śabdajñānānupātī] on the basis of verbal information when its actual content is not known or say when there is no material information from the outside world associated with verbal information.

Note: When a word is heard, the mind has a tendency to associate it with some object or thing of the external world known to him, even when it is devoid of material information from outside the sound or word is concerned with.

Here vikalpa is a state of mind where there is no material information from the outside world. Saṅkalpa is a state of mind where it is full of information from the outside world. Both the commentators Vyāsa and Bhoja cites the same example to illustrate the Vikalpa state of mind. For instance, if one says 'consciousness is the nature of Puruṣa' this statement falls under the category of Vikalpa. In the above statement, Puruṣa and consciousness have been shown as two different things, whereas the reality is that consciousness is not different from Puruṣa. But an individual in vikalpa state of mind accepts it as it is without verifying the fact. Just as school-going children often believe their teachers blindly without questioning their authority.

व्यासभाष्य-स न प्रमाणोपारोही । न विपर्ययोपारोही च । वस्तुशून्यत्वेऽपि
शब्दज्ञानमाहात्म्यनिबन्धनो व्यवहारो दृश्यते । तद्यथा चैतन्यं पुरुषस्य स्वरूपमिति । यदा चितिरेव
पुरुषस्तदा किमत्र केन व्यपदिश्यते । भवति च व्यपदेशे वृत्तिः । यथा चैत्रस्य गौरिति । तथा
प्रतिषिद्धवस्तुधर्मो निष्क्रियः पुरुषः तिष्ठति बाणः स्थास्यति स्थित इति यतिनिवृत्तौ धात्वर्थमात्रं
गम्यते । तथाऽनुत्पत्तिधर्मा पुरुष इति

उत्पत्तिधर्मस्याभावमात्रमवगम्यते न पुरुषान्वयी धर्मः ।
तस्माद्विकल्पितः स धर्मस्तेन चास्ति व्यवहार इति ।।   9 ।।

भोजवृत्ति-शब्दजनितं ज्ञानं शब्दज्ञानं तदनु पतितुं शीलं यस्य स शब्दज्ञानानुपाती ।
वस्तुनस्तथात्वमनपेक्षमाणो योऽध्यवसायः स विकल्प इत्युच्यते । यथा पुरुषस्य चैतन्यं स्वरूपमिति ।
अत्र देवत्तस्य कम्बल इति शब्दजनिते ज्ञाने षष्ठ्या योऽध्यवसितो भेदस्तमिहाविद्यमानमपि समारोप्य
प्रवृत्तेऽध्यवसायः । वस्तुतस्तु चैतन्यमेव पुरुषः । निद्रां व्याख्यातुमाह

4. Sleep

निद्रा वृत्ति के रूप में जानी जाने वाली मन की चौथी अवस्था की प्रकृति को
निम्नानुसार परिभाषित किया गया है-

Nature of the 4th state of mind known as Nidrā vṛtti
(sleep) is defined as under:

अभावप्रत्ययालम्बना वृत्तिर्निद्रा ॥ 10 ॥
abhāvapratyayālambanā vṛttirnidrā

10. मन में जागरूकता या ज्ञान की अनुपस्थिति को निद्रा वृत्ति (मन की
नींद की स्थिति) के रूप में जाना जाता है।

नोट: नींद के दौरान मन तमोगुण से संचालित होता है, इसलिए अंधकार की
स्थिति में रहता है । जागरूकता या ज्ञान अनुपस्थित है, जैसे कि मन को कोई
ज्ञान नहीं है या नींद के दौरान कुछ भी पता नहीं है । हालांकि इसका अनैच्छिक
हिस्सा काम कर रहा है, यह नींद के अनुभव सहित जो भी प्रभाव प्राप्त करता है,
उसे दर्ज करता है, इसलिए जागने पर याद आता है कि वह अच्छी तरह सोया था
या अच्छी नींद नहीं ली थी या नींद के दौरान बेचैन रहा था, आदि ।

10. Absence of awareness or knowledge in the mind is
known as *nidrā vṛtti* (sleeping state of mind).

Note: During sleep, the mind is governed by *tamas*,
so remains in the state of darkness. The awareness or

knowledge is absent, as such the mind has no knowledge or is not aware of anything during sleep. Although the involuntary part of it is in operation, it records whatever impressions it receives including the experience of sleep itself, hence one recalls on waking up that he or she slept well or did not sleep well or remained restless during sleep, etc.

व्यासभाष्य -सा च संप्रबोधे प्रत्यवमर्शात्प्रत्ययविशेषः। कथं सुखमहमस्वाप्सम्। प्रसन्नं मे मनः प्रज्ञां मे विशारदी करोति। दुःखमहमस्वाप्सं स्यानं मे मनो भ्रमत्यनवस्थितम्। गाढं मूढोऽहमस्वाप्सम्। गुरूणि मे गात्राणि। क्लान्तं मे चित्तम्। अलसं मुषितमिव तिष्ठतीति। स खल्वयं प्रबुद्धस्य प्रत्यवमर्शो न स्यादसति प्रत्ययानुभवे तदाश्रिताः स्मृतयश्च तद्विषया न स्युः। तस्मात्प्रत्ययविशेषो निद्रा। सा च समाधावितरप्रत्ययवन्निरोद्धव्येति।

भोजवृत्ति-अभावप्रत्यय आलम्बनं यस्या वृत्तेः सा तथोक्ता। तदुक्तं भवति या सन्ततमुद्रिक्तत्वात्तमसः समस्तविषयपरित्यागेन प्रवर्त्तते वृत्तिः सा निद्रा। तस्याश्च सुखमहमस्वाप्समिति स्मृतिदर्शनात् स्मृतेश्चानुभवव्यतिरेकेणानुपपत्तेर्वृत्तित्वम्। स्मृतिं व्याख्यातुमाह

5. Memory

Nature of the 5th state of mind known as Smṛti vṛtti (memory) is defined as under:

अनुभूतविषयासंप्रमोषः स्मृतिः ॥ 11 ॥

anubhūta viṣayāsampramoṣaḥ smṛtiḥ

9. Non-forgetfulness of the perceived, experienced, or realized fact or thing is called as Smṛti vṛtti (memory state of mind).

Memory is non-forgetting the perceived/experienced/or realized objects.

Here the word non-forgetting is important. It points to the desirability of a selective memory.

Yoga philosopher Patañjali's definition of memory, i.e. non-forgetting an experienced knowledge or fact clearly shows that memory consists of recalling a past experience which has been retained in the mind encoded as sanskāra. It involves retention and recall.

Process of Memory

The Memory according to Patañjali may be divided into the following parts :

Anubhava: First part of the process of memory is Anubhava. Anubhava is gained through perceiving a fact. In fact, anubhava is a sort of learning that consists in perceiving facts.

Sanskāra: Sanskāra is the second part of memory. Perceived or experienced knowledge or facts are impressed upon the mind in the form of sanskāras or karmas and retained therewith forever.

Recall or non-forgetting is the third part. It is reproduction. It consists in the revival of the impressed sanskaras or past experiences.

Here regarding the second part of memory one can raise a question as to whether sanskāras impressed upon the mind are retained temporarily for a short period or forever. The answer of Patañjali in this regard is very simple. According to him, sanskāras are an inseparable part of memory. In fact, memory is formed of sanskāras. So sanskāras are factors in memory. Once they are impressed upon the mind, they are never written off. Mind is part of eternal consciousness. It is continuous and carries the record of its memory and sanskāras through successive births.

jātideśakālavyavahitānāmapyānantarya'smṛtisa'skārayorekrū patvāt (Y.D. 4.9)

So memory is an eternal process of the mind. It can be recalled regardless of interruption of place, time, or birth. This is why we meet with people who are able to recall the memories of their past lives.

Contents of Memory

Śabda (word) artha (object or reality) and knowledge (jñāna) of association of object and word is the contents of memory. It may exist either in terms of words, or objects, or in terms of the knoweldg of association of both words and objects.

So long as memory has all the three contents, a yoga practitioner is able to meditate on either of them or these three taken together, i.e. an object, the word, and the knowledge of their association.

So his meditation is related to or conditioned by and directed to an object, word or knowledge of integration of both. Suppose he concentrates on Iśvara. There is a name Aum or some other word for him. There is the reality called Iśvara, with his attributes or non-attributes and there is knowledge or awareness of association of word Aum with the entity called Īśvara. Thus his concentration is either on word or object or knowledge of word and object association which is called savitarka samādhi.

tatra śabdārthavikalpaiḥsaṅkīrṇā savitrkā samāpatti (Y.D. 1.42)

'Samādhi practised with words, object, and the knowledge (awareness) of association of both is known as savitrkā samāpatti.'

Purging of Memory

The actual aim of Patañjali is to engineer one's mind for self-realization, and the aim of self-realization cannot be attained through savitarka smāpatti. A practitioner has to move from savitarka samāpatti to nirvitarka samāpatti. Movement from savitarka samāpatti to nirvitarka samāpatti is not possible until and unless the memory is cleared of the above-discussed contents. This process is known as the purging of memory. Memory can thus be purged with the help of the mind meditating upon the object only i.e. Iśvara, leaving its word and knowledge of association of word and object. After perfection in savitarka samādhi, this type of practice for nīrvītārkā samādhi slowly purges the mind of all contents.

According to Patañjali, on the purging of memory, one attains a state of mind as if void of itself and the light of the object alone shines. This state of meditation is called nivitarkā samādhi.

smṛtipariśuddhau svarūpa-śunyevārtha mātra nirbhāsā nirvitarkā (Y.D. 1.43)

The perfection of this nirvitarkā samādhi is said to be essential in the achievement of spiritual light and bliss.

nirvicāravaiśāradye' dhyātma prāsādaḥ (Y.D. 1.47)

When the mind is exposed to the external world objects, these vṛttis develop which are a hurdle for a seeker on the path of yoga. As these vṛttis keep the picture of a visible world alive in the mind in the form of sanskāras. So long as the visible world is alive in mind, a seeker cannot attain mokṣa. Thus, a seeker endowed with these vṛttis cannot become a yogi. To get rid of these vṛttis or disallow the rise of these vṛttis, it is essential to withdraw the mind from the external world.

Now one may ask a question as to how to withdraw the mind from external objects. The answer is given by

Patañjali.

व्यासभाष्य - किं प्रत्ययस्य चित्तं स्मरति आहोस्विद्विषयस्येति । ग्राह्योपरक्तः प्रत्ययो ग्राह्यग्रहणोभयाकारनिर्भासस्तज्जातीयकं संस्कारमारभते । स संस्कारः स्वव्यञ्जनकाञ्जनस्तदाकारामेव ग्राह्यग्रहणोभयात्मिकां स्मृतिं जनयति । तत्र ग्रहणाकारपूर्वा बुद्धिः । ग्राह्याकारपूर्वा स्मृतिः । सा च द्वयी भावितस्मर्तव्या चाभावितस्मर्तव्या च । स्वप्ने भावितस्मर्तव्या । जाग्रत्समये त्वभावितस्मर्तव्येति । सर्वाश्चैताः स्मृतयः प्रमाणविपर्ययविकल्पनिद्रास्मृतीनामनुभवात्प्रभवन्ति । सर्वाश्चैता वृत्तयः सुखदुःखमोहात्मिकाः । सुखदुःखमोहाश्च क्लेशेषु व्याख्येयाः । सुखानुशयी रागः । दुःखानुशयी द्वेषः । मोहः पुनरविद्येति । एताः सर्वा वृत्तयो निरोद्धव्याः । आसां निरोधे संप्रज्ञातो वा समाधिर्भवत्यसंप्रज्ञातो वेति । अथाऽऽसां निरोधे क उपाय इति

भोजवृत्ति-प्रमाणेनानुभूतस्य विषयस्य योऽयमसंप्रमोषः संस्कारद्वारेण बुद्धावारोहः सा स्मृतिः । तत्र प्रमाणविपर्ययविकल्पा जाग्रदवस्था । त एव तदनुभवबलात् प्रत्यक्षायमाणाः स्वप्नाः । निद्रा तु असंवेद्यमानविषया । स्मृतिश्च प्रमाणविपर्ययविकल्पनिद्रानिमित्ता । एवं वृत्तीर्व्याख्याय सोपायं निरोधं व्याख्यातुमाह

अभ्यासवैराग्याभ्यां तन्निरोधः ॥12॥

abhyāsavairāgyābhyāṃ tannirodhaḥ

12. Through Abhyāsa (constant efforts) and vairāgya (detachment to the objects of the mundane world (external world), the mind can be withdrawn from the visible world.

व्यासभाष्य - चित्तनदी नामोभयतोवाहिनी वहति कल्याणाय वहति पापाय च । या तु कैवल्यप्राग्भारा विवेकविषयनिम्ना सा कल्याणवहा । संसारप्राग्भाराऽविवेकविषयनिम्ना पापवहा । तत्र वैराग्येण विषयस्रोतः खिली क्रियते । विवेकदर्शनाभ्यासेन विवेकस्रोत उद्घाट्यत इत्युभयाधीनश्चित्तवृत्तिनिरोधः ।

भोजवृत्ति-अभ्यासवैराग्ये वक्ष्यमाणलक्षणे ताभ्यां प्रकाशवृत्तिनियमरूपा या वृत्तयस्तासां निरोधो भवतीत्युक्तं भवति । तासां विनिवृत्तबाह्याभिनिवेशानां अन्तर्मुखतया स्वकारण एव चित्ते शक्तिरूपतयाऽवस्थानम् । तत्र विषयदोषदर्शनजेन वैराग्येण तद्वैमुख्यमुत्पाद्यते । अभ्यासेन च सुखजनकशान्तप्रवाहप्रदर्शनद्वारेण दृढं स्थैर्य्यमुत्पाद्यते । इत्थं ताभ्यां भवति चित्तवृत्तिनिरोधः । अभ्यासं व्याख्यातुमाह

Hereunder the nature of *abhyāsa* is defined.

तत्र स्थितौ यत्नोऽभ्यासः ॥13॥

tatra sthitau yatno'bhyāsaḥ

13. Efforts to stabilize the mind are called *abhyāsa.*

व्यासभाष्य -चित्तस्यावृत्तिकस्य प्रशान्तवाहिता स्थितिः। तदर्थः प्रयत्नो वीर्यमुत्साहः।
तत्संपिपादयिषया तत्साधनानुष्ठानमभ्यासः।

.भोजवृत्ति.-वृत्तिरहितस्य चित्तस्य स्वरूपनिष्ठः परिणामः स्थितिस्तस्यां यत्र उत्साहः पुनः
पुनस्तत्त्वेन चेतसि निवेशनमभ्यास इत्युच्यते। तस्यैव विशेषमाह

स तु दीर्घकालनैरन्तर्यसत्कारासेवितो दृढभूमिः ॥14॥

sa tu dīrghakālanairantaryasatkārāsevito dṛḍhabhūmiḥ

14. If *abhyāsa* (efforts to stabilize the mind) is done
constantly for a long time with positive thinking, it
becomes firmly grounded.

व्यासभाष्य - दीर्घकालासेवितो निरन्तरासेवितः सत्कारासेवितः। तपसा ब्रह्मचर्येण विद्यया
श्रद्धया च संपादितः सत्कारवान्दृढभूमिर्भवति। व्युत्थानसंस्कारेण द्रागित्येवानभिभूतविषयः इत्यर्थः।

व.भोजवृत्ति.-बहुकालं नैरन्तर्येण आदरातिशयेन च सेव्यमानो दृढभूमिः स्थिरो भवति।
दार्ढ्याय प्रभवतीत्यर्थः। वैराग्यस्य लक्षणमाह

What is Vairāgya? Vācaspati Miśra in his commentary
on the Sāṅkhya-kārikā of Iśvara Kṛṣṇa defines vairāgya as
follows:

Vairāgya = abhāva of rāga, i.e. the absence of rāga
(sanskāra of the worldly things in the chitta).

Here, the word rāga refers to sanskāras of worldly
things also called as kaśāyas. The word kaśāya means
sanskāra in the chitta. In essence, these sanskāras are
caused by the two emotions of rāga (attachment to
worldly things) and dveśa (hatred to worldly things), and
they impel the senses to seek out their corresponding
sense objects. तैरिन्द्रियाणि यथास्वं विषयेषु प्रवर्त्यन्ते   (*tairindriyāṇi
yathāsvaṁ viṣayeṣu pravartyante*).

Note: Rāga (attachment/love/affection/sympathy) for
worldly things and Dveṣa (hatred/apathy) towards
worldly things both cause sanskāras of affection or
hatred, so the best way to get rid of sanskāras is to

develop a sense of (Audāsinya) indifference to the worldly things.

Vairāgya is of two types. Lower and Higher

Lower level of vairāgya are of four types: yatamāna, vyatireka, ekendriya and vaśīkāra.

These four types of vairāgyas are defined by Vācaspati Miśra further divides vairāgya into four types or stages.

तस्य- यतमानसंज्ञा व्यतिरेकसंज्ञा एकेन्द्रियसंज्ञा वशीकारसंज्ञा इति चतस्रः संज्ञाः ।

(*tasya- yatamānasaṁjñā vyatirekasaṁjñā ēkendriyasaṁjñā vaśīkārasaṁjñā iti chatasraḥ saṁjñāḥ*)

Meaning: There are four stages of vairāgya: yatamāna, vyatireka, ekendriya and vaśikāra.

These four stages correspond to the extent to which the sanskāras (kaśāyas) are 'cooked' (paripācana) i.e. removed from the chitta. His commentary is summarized below:

1. Yatamāna is an endeavor or practicing stage, where none of the sanskāras (kaśāyas) have been deactivated, but where an effort has started to deactivate or cook them.

Here, the effort involves restraining the senses from their stimuli/ sense objects. At this stage, the Sādhaka has recognized that there are sanskāras of the outside world in the chitta and wishes to get rid of them.

2. Vyatireka: This is the stage where some sanskāras (kaśāyas) have been deactivated/cooked, while others have not. Vyatireka refers to discrimination between those kaśāyas that are cooked or deactivated, and those

that are not. For example, one's sense of hearing may no longer be attracted to non-devotional music. But one's tongue may still not be under control. When a seeker knows this, he/she may place him/her at the stage of vyatireka.

3. Ekendriya: the stage where all sanskaras (kasāyas) are cooked, but a curiosity for the sense objects remains. Here none of the senses are allowed to run towards sense objects. However, there is still a curiosity or taste/longing in the chitta.

4. Vaśikāra is complete loss of any lingering taste.

Nature of Vaśikāra *vairāgya* (non-attachment) is defined by Patañjali as:

दृष्टानुश्रविकविषयवितृष्णस्य वशीकारसंज्ञा वैराग्यम् ॥15॥

dṛṣṭānuśravikaviṣayavitṛṣṇasya vaśīkārasaṃjñā vairāgyam

15. Vaśikāra named vairāgya (absence of sanskaras of the outside world) is that where a seeker has no desire for all that has been experienced in the past, and all that has been heard [but not experienced]. Vaśīkāra type of vairāgya is lower level vairāgya.

This is the stage of complete control over the senses.

व्यासभाष्य -स्त्रियोऽन्नपानमैश्वर्यमिति दृष्टविषये वितृष्णस्य स्वर्गवैदेह्यप्रकृतिलयत्व-प्राप्त्यावानुश्रविकविषये वितृष्णस्य दिव्यादिव्यविषयसंयोगेऽपि चित्तस्य विषयदोषदर्शिनः प्रसंख्यानबलादनाभोगात्मिका हेयोपादेयशून्या वशीकारसंज्ञा वैराग्यम्

भोजवृत्ति—द्विविधो हि विषयो दृष्ट आनुश्रविकश्च । दृष्ट इहैवोपलभ्यमानः शब्दादिः । देवलोकादावानुश्रविकः । अनुश्रूयते गुरुमुखादित्यनुश्रवो वेदस्तत्समधिगत आनुश्रविकः तयोर्द्वयोरपि विषययोः परिणामविरसत्वदर्शनाद्विगतगर्द्धस्य या वशीकारसंज्ञा ममैते वश्या नाहमेतेषां वश्य इति योऽयं विमर्षस्तद्वैराग्यमुच्यते । तस्यैव विशेषमाह

After defining the nature of vaśīkāra type of lower

level of vairāgya, nature of highest vairāgya is defined.

तत्परं पुरुषख्यातेर्गुणवैतृष्ण्यम् ॥16॥

tatparaṃ puruṣakhyāterguṇavaitṛṣṇyam

16. The highest/main vairāgya (permanent absence of sanskāras of the worldly things) is attained by the self-realization or realization of the true nature of the self. It is called Guṇa vaitṛṣṇya vairāgya.

Note: Guṇa vaitṛṣṇya means vitṛṣṇā (detachment or indifference) to triguṇātmaka Jagat (outside world made of three guṇas). When the true nature of self is known, a person automatically becomes immune to the worldly sanskāras. Otherwise, so long as guṇa vaitṛṣṇya vairāgya is not achieved, a person had to be cautious about having not imprinted the sanskāras of the outside world on his mind.

व्यासभाष्य—दृष्टानुश्रविकविषयदोषदर्शी विरक्तः पुरुषदर्शनाभ्यासात्तच्छुद्धि प्रविवेकाप्यायितबुद्धिर्गुणेभ्यो व्यक्ताव्यक्तधर्मकेभ्यो विरक्त इति । तद्द्वयं वैराग्यम् । तत्र यदुत्तरं तज्ज्ञानप्रसादमात्रम् । यस्योदये योगी प्रत्युदितख्यातिरेवं मन्यते प्राप्तं प्रापणीयं क्षीणाः क्षेतव्याः क्लेशाः छिन्नः श्लिष्टपर्वा भवसंक्रमः । यस्याविच्छेदाज्जनित्वाम्रियते मृत्वा च जायत इति । ज्ञानस्यैव परा काष्ठा वैराग्यम् । एतस्यैव हि नान्तरीयकं कैवल्यमिति । अथोपायद्वयेन निरुद्धचित्तवृत्तेः कथमुच्यते संप्रज्ञातः समाधिरिति ।

भोजवृत्ति—तद्वैराग्यं परं प्रकृष्टं प्रथमं वैराग्यं विषयविषयम् । द्वितीयं गुणविषयमुत्पन्नगुणपुरुषविवेकख्यातेरेव भवति निरोधसमाधेरत्यन्तानुकूलत्वात् । एवं योगस्य स्वरूपमुक्त्वा संप्रज्ञातस्वरूपं भेदमाह ।

Now nature of samprajñāta and asamprajñāta yoga which is attainable through highest vairāgya is defined.

वितर्कविचारानन्दास्मितारूपानुगमात् संप्रज्ञातः ॥17॥

vitarkavicārānandāsmitārūpānugamāt samprajñātaḥ

According to the four stages of yoga, samprajñāta yoga is of four types: vitarka, vichāra, ānanda and asmita type (fig.11).

Figure 11: Four types of Yoga

Note: Just as the practice of aim is started with a bigger size of the target. Afterwards the size of the target is continued to be reduced in order until the aim is achieved. Similarly, to attain perfection in samprajñāta yoga, a seeker has to pass through four stages of practicing the yoga starting from material targets and ending with soul.

The first stage is called vitarka yoga. In vitarka yoga, a material target is given, as the seeker cannot focus his mind on an abstract target. So, at vitarka level, the target of realization of a seeker is the shape or size of material elements or the shape and size of objects made of material elements (earth, water, fire, air, and ākāśa).

The second stage of yoga is called vichāra yoga. In vichāra yoga, the meditation goes a step higher. The seeker is given an abstract target that is subtler than the material elements. The material elements are qualified by their tanmātrās (sensations) of smell, taste, sight, touch, and sound which are subtler than them. So the target of meditation for the seeker at this stage is tanmātrās (sensations). At this, he meditates upon the sensations qualifying the material elements instead of their shapes. For example, in vichāra yoga, a seeker meditates not upon the size or shape of the sun, but the sight of the sun or we can say that a seeker meditates upon the fragrance of a flower and not upon the shape of a flower.

The third stage of yoga is called ānanda yoga. In ānanda yoga, the target of meditation is the mind devoid of sanskāras of material world. At this stage, the seeker attains comfort or bliss through the mind which is devoid of the guṇas, the material world.

When bliss is attained, and connection from outside world is broken, the seeker gets settled in his/her own self. This fourth stage is called asmitā yoga. In asmitā yoga, the target of meditation is own soul or self. At this stage, the seeker realizes his/her true nature.

व्यासभाष्य—वितर्कश्चित्तस्याऽऽलम्बने स्थूल आभोगः । सूक्ष्मो विचारः । आनन्दो ह्लादः । एकात्मिका संविदस्मिता । तत्र प्रथमश्चतुष्टयानुगतः समाधिः सवितर्कः । द्वितीयो वितर्कविकलः सविचारः । तृतीयो विचारविकलः सानन्दः । चतुर्थस्तद्द्विकलोऽस्मितामात्र इति । सर्व एते सालम्बनाः समाधयः । अथासंप्रज्ञातः समाधिः किमुपायः किंस्वभाव इति ।

भोजवृत्ति—समाधिरिति शेषः । सम्यक्संशयविपर्ययरहितत्वेन प्रज्ञायते प्रकर्षेण ज्ञायते भाव्यस्य स्वरूपं येन स संप्रज्ञातः समाधिर्भावनाविशेषः । स वितर्कादिभेदाच्चतुर्विधः सवितर्कः सविचारः सानन्दः सास्मितश्च । भावना भाव्यस्य विषयान्तरपरिहारेण चेतसि पुनः पुनर्निवेशनम् । भाव्यं च द्विविधम् ईश्वरस्तत्त्वानि च । तान्यपि द्विविधानि जडाजडभेदात् । जडानि चतुर्विंशतिः । अजडः पुरुषः । तत्र यदा महाभूतेन्द्रियाणि स्थूलानि विषयत्वेनाऽऽदाय पूर्वापरानुसंधानेन शब्दार्थोल्लेखसंभेदेन च भावना क्रियते तदा सवितर्कः समाधिः । अस्मिन्नेवाऽऽलम्बने पूर्वापरानुसन्धानशब्दोल्लेखशून्यत्वेन यदा भावना प्रवर्त्तते तदा निर्वितर्कः । तन्मात्रान्तःकरणलक्षणं सूक्ष्मविषयमालम्ब्य तस्य देशकालधर्मावच्छेदेन यदा भावना प्रवर्त्तते तदा सविचारः । तस्मिन्नेवावलम्बने देशकालधर्मावच्छेदं विना धर्मिमात्रावभासित्वेन भावना क्रियमाणा निर्विचार इत्युच्यते । एवं पर्यन्तः समाधिर्ग्राह्यसमापत्तिरिति व्यपदिश्यते । यदा तु रजस्तमोलेशानुविद्धमन्तःकरणसत्त्वं भाव्यते तदा गुणाभावाच्चितिशक्तेः सुखप्रकाशमयस्य सत्त्वस्य भाव्यमानस्योद्रेकात् सानन्दः समाधिर्भवति । अस्मिन्नेव समाधौ ये बद्धधृतयस्तत्त्वान्तरं प्रधानपुरुषरूपं न पश्यन्ति ते विगतदेहाहङ्कारत्वाद्विदेहशब्दवाच्याः । इयं ग्रहणसमापत्तिः । ततः परं रजस्तमोलेशानभिभूतं शुद्धसत्त्वमालम्बनीकृत्य या प्रवर्त्तते भावना तस्यां ग्राह्यस्य सत्त्वस्य न्यग्भवात्

चितिशक्तेरुद्रेकात् सत्तामात्रावशेषत्वेन समाधिः सास्मित इत्युच्यते । न चाहङ्कारास्मितयोरभेदः
शङ्कनीयः । यतो यत्रान्तः करणमहमिति उल्लेखेन विषयान् वेदयते सोऽहङ्कारः । यत्रान्तर्मुखतया
प्रतिलोमपरिणामे प्रकृतिलीने चेतसि सत्तामात्रं अवभाति साऽस्मिता । अस्मिन्नेव समाधौ ये
कृतपरितोषा परं परमात्मानं पुरुषं न पश्यन्ति तेषां चेतसि स्वकारणे लयमुपागते प्रकृतिलया
इत्युच्यन्ते । ये परं पुरुषं ज्ञात्वा भावनायां प्रवर्त्तन्ते तेषामियं विवेकख्यातिर्ग्रहीतृसमापत्तिरित्युच्यते ।
तत्र संप्रज्ञाते समाधौ चतस्रोऽवस्थाः शक्तिरूपतयाऽवतिष्ठन्ते । तत्रैकैकस्यास्त्याग उत्तरोत्तरा इति
चतुरवस्थोऽस्यं संप्रज्ञातः समाधिः । असंप्रज्ञातमाह

Now the nature of asamprajñāta yoga is defined.

विरामप्रत्ययाभ्यासपूर्वः संस्कारशेषोऽन्यः ॥18॥

virāmapratyayābhyāsapūrvaḥ saṃskāraśeṣo'nyaḥ

(Anya) There is another yoga called asamprajñāta yoga which is attained (*abhyāsa pūrvaḥ*) by the practice of main vairāgya (guṇa vaitṛṣṇya vairāgya (*Samadhi Pāda, Sūtra* 15), which is (pratyaya) the cause of (virāma) the absence of vṛttis. At this stage, the mind accumulates no new sanskāra but (*sanskāra śeṣa*) retains only the past sanskāras.

व्यासभाष्य—सर्ववृत्तिप्रत्यस्तमये संस्कारशेषो निरोधश्चित्तस्य समाधिरसंप्रज्ञातः । तस्य परं
वैराग्यमुपायः । सालम्बनो ह्यभ्यासस्तत्साधनाय न कल्पत इति विरामप्रत्ययो निर्वस्तुक आलम्बनी
क्रियते । स चार्थशून्यः । तदभ्यासपूर्वकं हि चित्तं निरालम्बनमभावप्राप्तमिव भवतीत्येष निर्बीजः
समाधिरसंप्रज्ञातः । स खल्वयं द्विविधः उपायप्रत्ययो भवप्रत्ययश्च । तत्रोपायप्रत्ययो योगिनां भवति

भोजवृत्ति—विरम्यतेऽनेनेति विरामो वितर्कादिचिन्तात्यागः विरामश्चासौ प्रत्ययश्चेति
विरामप्रत्ययस्तस्याभ्यासः पौनःपुन्येन चेतसि निवेशनम् । तत्र या काचित् वृत्तिरुल्लसति तस्या नेति
नेतीतिनैरन्तर्येण पर्युदसनं तत्पूर्वः संप्रज्ञातसमाधेः संस्कारशेषोऽन्यस्तद्विलक्षणोऽसंप्रज्ञात इत्यर्थः । न
तत्र किञ्चिद्वेद्यम् संप्रज्ञायते इति असंप्रज्ञातो निर्बीजः समाधिः । इह चतुर्विधश्चित्तस्य परिणामः ।
व्युत्थानं समाधिप्रारम्भो एकाग्रता निरोधश्च । तत्र क्षिप्तमूढे चित्तभूमी व्युत्थानं । विक्षिप्ताभूमिः
सत्त्वोद्रेकात् समाधिप्रारम्भः । निरुद्धैकाग्रते च पर्यन्तभूमी । प्रतिपरिणामञ्च संस्काराः । तत्र
व्युत्थानजनिताः संस्काराः समाधिप्रारम्भजैः संस्कारैः प्रत्याहन्यन्ते । तज्जाश्चैकाग्रताजैः
निरोधजनितैरैकाग्रताजाः संस्काराः स्वरूपञ्च हन्यन्ते । यथा सुवर्णसम्वलितं ध्मायमानं
सीसकमात्मानं सुवर्णमलञ्च निर्दहति । एवमेकाग्रता जनितान् संस्कारान् निरोधजः स्वात्मानञ्च
निर्दहन्ति । तदेवं योगस्य स्वरूपं भेदं संक्षेपेणोपायञ्च अभिधाय विस्तररूपेणोपायं
योगाभ्यासप्रदर्शनपूर्वकं वक्तुमुपक्रमते

Asamprajñāta yoga is further divided into two

categories: Bhava pratyaya and Upāya pratyaya.

भवप्रत्ययो विदेहप्रकृतिलयानाम् ॥19॥
bhavapratyayo videhaprakṛtilayānām

Samādhi of Videha-layas (those that don't identify themselves with their bodies) and Prakṛti-layas (those that are merged in their own true self/nature) is called bhava pratyaya (cause of reincarnation/rebirth in this visible world) and does not lead them to emancipation.

Note: Videha-laya and Prakṛti-laya yogis are called devas. Their sanskāras of the visible world have not yet been completely exhausted, so their samādhi does not lead them to Mokṣa. They reincarnate or take rebirth at certain intervals of time.

व्यासभाष्य—विदेहानां देवानां भवप्रत्ययः। ते हि स्वसंस्कारमात्रोपयोगेन चित्तेन कैवल्यपदमिवानुभवन्तः स्वसंस्कारविपाकं तथाजातीयकमतिवाहयन्ति। तथा प्रकृतिलयाः साधिकारे चेतसि प्रकृतिलीने कैवल्यपदमिवानुभवन्ति यावन्न पुनरावर्त्ततेऽधिकारवशाच्चित्तमिति।

व्यासभाष्य—विदेहा प्रकृतिलयाश्च वितर्कादिभूमिकासूत्रे व्याख्याताः तेषां समाधिर्भवप्रत्ययः भवः संसारः स एव प्रत्ययः कारणं यस्य स भवप्रत्ययः। अयमर्थः अधिमात्रान्तर्भूता एव ते संसारे तथाविधसमाधिभाजो भवन्ति। तेषां परतत्त्वादर्शनाद्योगाभासोऽयम्। अतः परतत्त्वज्ञाने तद्भावनायाञ्च मुक्तिकामेन महान्यत्नो विधेय इत्येतदर्थमुपदिष्टम्। तदन्येषान्तु

श्रद्धावीर्यस्मृतिसमाधिप्रज्ञापूर्वक इतरेषाम् ॥20॥
śraddhāvīryasmṛtisamādhiprajñāpūrvaka itareṣām

Others (Upāya pratyayas), whose sanskāras of the visible world have completely effaced from their mind by (upāyas) means of (śraddhā) positive thought, (vīrya) energy, (smṛti) memory, (samādhi) contemplation and (prajñā) ṛtambharā prajñā, attain asamprajñāta samādhi.

Here it may be pointed out that Ṛtambharā prajñā helps a yogī to have true knowledge of the laws of creation.

Note: Positive thought gives energy, energy reminds the seeker about emancipation, which ultimately inspires him/her to observe samādhi and samādhi helps the seeker to be endowed with ṛtambharā prajñā.

व्यासभाष्य—उपायप्रत्ययो योगिनां भवति। श्रद्धा चेतसः संप्रसादः। सा हि जननीव कल्याणी योगिनं पाति। तस्य हि श्रद्दधानस्य विवेकार्थिनो वीर्यमुपजायते। समुपजातवीर्यस्य स्मृतिरुपतिष्ठते। स्मृत्युपस्थाने च चित्तमनाकुलं समाधीयते। समाहितचित्तस्य प्रज्ञाविवेक उपावर्तते। येन यथार्थं वस्तु जानाति। तदभ्यासत्तद्विषयाच्च वैराग्यादसंप्रज्ञातः समाधिर्भवति। ते खलु नव योगिनो मृदुमध्याधिमात्रोपाया भवन्ति। तद्यथामृदूपायो मध्योपायोऽधिमात्रोपाय इति। तत्र मृदूपायस्त्रिविधिः मृदुसंवेगो मध्यसंवेगस्तीव्रसंवेग इति। तथा मध्योपायस्तथाधिमात्रोपाय इति। तत्राधिमात्रोपायानां

भोजवृत्ति—विदेहप्रकृतिलयव्यतिरिक्तानां योगिनां श्रद्धादिपूर्वकः श्रद्धादयः पूर्वे उपाया यस्य स श्रद्धादिपूर्वकः। ते च श्रद्धादयः क्रमादुपायोपेयभावेन प्रवर्त्तमानाः संप्रज्ञातसमाधेरुपायतां प्रतिपद्यन्ते। तत्र श्रद्धा योगविषये चेतसः प्रसादः। वीर्यमुत्साहः। स्मृतिरनुभूतासंप्रमोधः। समाधिरेकाग्रता। प्रज्ञा प्रज्ञातव्यविवेकः। तत्रश्रद्धावतो वीर्यं जायते योगविषये उत्साहवान् भवति। सोत्साहस्य च पाश्चात्यानुभूतिषु भूमिषु स्मृतिरुत्पद्यते तत्स्मरणाच्च चेतः समाधीयते। समाहितचित्तश्च भाव्यं सम्यग्विवेकेन जानाति। त एते संप्रज्ञातस्य समाधेरुपायाः। तस्याभ्यासात् पराच्च वैराग्यात् भवत्यसंप्रज्ञातः। उक्तोपायवतां योगिनां उपायभेदाद्भेदानाह

तीव्रसंवेगानामासन्नः ॥21॥

tīvrasaṃvegānāmāsannaḥ

The one who has a (tivra) strong (saṃvega) sanskāra of samādhi from past life, attains samādhi (āsannaḥ) immediately.

व्यासभाष्य—समाधिलाभः समाधिफलं च भवतीति।

भोजवृत्ति—समाधिलाभः इति शेषः। संवेगः क्रियाहेतुर्दृढतरः संस्कारः। स तीव्रो येषामधिमात्रोपायानां तेषामासन्नः समाधिलाभः समाधिफलाऽऽसन्नं भवति शीघ्रमेव सम्पद्यत इत्यर्थः। के ते तीव्रसंवेगा इत्यत आह

मृदुमध्याधिमात्रत्वात् ततोऽपि विशेषः ॥22॥

mṛdumadhyādhimātratvāt tato'pi viśeṣaḥ

The success in samādhi is relative to the sanskāra like mild, medium, and intense. For instance, mild sanskāra will lead to slow samādhi, medium to medium and intense to fast.

व्यासभाष्य—मृदुतीव्रो मध्यतीव्रोऽधिमात्रतीव्र इति । ततोऽपि विशेषः । तद्विशेषादपि मृदुतीव्रसंवेगस्याऽऽसन्नः ततो मध्यतीव्रसंवेगस्याऽऽसन्नतरः तस्मादधिमात्रतीव्र-संवेगस्याधिमात्रोपायस्याप्यासन्नतमः समाधिलाभः समाधिफलं चेति । किमेतस्मादेवाऽऽसन्नतमः समाधिर्भवति । अथास्य लाभे भवत्यन्योऽपि कश्चिदुपायो न वेति

भोजवृत्ति—तेभ्य उपायेभ्यो मृद्वादिभेदभिन्नेभ्य उपायवतां विशेषो भवति । मृदुर्मध्योऽधिमात्र इत्युपायभेदः । ते प्रत्येकं मृदुसंवेदमध्यसंवेगतीव्रसंवेगभेदात् त्रिधा । तद्भेदेन च नवयोगिनो भवन्ति । मृदूपायोमृदुसंवेगो मध्यसंवेगस्तीव्रसंवेगश्च । मध्योपायोमृत्युसंवेगो मध्यसंवेगस्तीव्रसंवेगश्च । अधिमात्रोपायोमृदुसंवेगो मध्यसंवेगस्तीव्रसंवेगश्च । अधिमात्रोपाये तीव्रसंवेगे च महान् यत्नः कर्त्तव्य इति भेदोपदेशः । इदानीमेतदुपायविलक्षणं सुगममुपायान्तरं दर्शयितुमाह

ईश्वरप्रणिधानाद्वा ॥23॥

īśvarapraṇidhānādvā

Samādhi is fast achieved by meditating upon Īśvara. According to Vyāsa, when we meditate upon Īśvara, he blesses us with his grace soon. Īśvara is defined in the following sūtra.

व्यासभाष्य—प्रणिधानाद्भक्तिविशेषादावर्जित ईश्वरस्तमनुगृह्णात्यभिध्यानमात्रेण । तदभिध्यानमात्रादपि योगिन आसन्नतरः समाधिलाभः समाधिफलं च भवतीति । अथ प्रधानपुरुषव्यतिरिक्तः कोऽयमीश्वरो नामेति

भोजवृत्ति—ईश्वरो वक्ष्यमाणलक्षणः तत्र प्रणिधानं भक्तिविशेषो विशिष्टमुपासनं सर्वक्रियाणां तत्रार्पणं विषयसुखादिकं फलमनिच्छन् सर्वाः क्रियास्तस्मिन्परमगुरावर्पयति तत् प्रणिधानं समाधेस्तत्फललाभस्य च प्रकृष्ट उपायः । ईश्वरस्य प्रणिधानात् समाधिलाभ इत्युक्तं तत्रेश्वरस्य स्वरूपं प्रमाणं प्रभावं वाचकं उपासनाक्रमं तत्फलञ्च क्रमेण वक्तुमाह

क्लेशकर्मविपाकाशयैरपरामृष्टः पुरुषविशेष ईश्वरः ॥24॥

kleśakarmavipākāśayairaparāmṛṣṭaḥ puruṣaviśeṣa īśvaraḥ

Īśvara is the specific Puruṣa that do not subject to (kleśas) afflictions, (karmas) actions, (karma-phala) their fruits, and the (āśayas) sanskāras of the visible world.

Note: In the present sūtra, two types of Puruṣas have been described. One type is Puruṣa in general. Souls of living beings are Puruṣa is general, but Prama-Puruṣa, Paramātmā, Para-Brahma is specific Puruṣa or Puruṣa Viśeṣa (as there is no other Puruṣa equal to him).

व्यासभाष्य—अविद्यादयः क्लेशाः। कुशलाकुशलानि कर्माणि। तत्फलं विपाकः। तदनुगुणा वासना आशयाः। ते च मनसिवर्तमानाः पुरुषे व्यपदिश्यन्ते स हि तत्फलस्य भोक्तेति। यथा जयः पराजयो वा योद्धृषु वर्तमानः स्वामिनि व्यपदिश्यते। यो ह्यनेन भोगेनापरामृष्टः स पुरुषविशेष ईश्वरः। कैवल्यं प्राप्तस्तर्हि सन्ति च बहवः केवलिनः। ते हि त्रीणि बन्धनानि च्छित्त्वा कैवल्यं प्राप्ता ईश्वरस्य च तत्संबन्धो न भूतो न भावी। यथा मुक्तस्य पूर्वा बन्धकोटिः प्रज्ञायते नैवमीश्वरस्य। यथा वा प्रकृतिलीनस्योत्तरा बन्धकोटिः संभाव्यते नैवमीश्वरस्य। स तु सदैव मुक्तः सदैवेश्वर इति। योऽसौ प्रकृष्टसत्त्वोपादानादीश्वरस्य शाश्वतिक उत्कर्षः स किं सनिमित्त आहोस्विन्निर्निमित्त इति। तस्य शास्त्रं निमित्तम्। शास्त्रं पुनः किंनिमित्तं प्रकृष्टसत्त्वनिमित्तम्। एतयो शास्त्रोत्कर्षयोरीश्वरसत्त्वे वर्तमानयोरनादिः संबन्धः। एतस्मादेतद्भवति सदैवेश्वर सदैव मुक्त इति। तच्च तस्यैश्वर्यं साम्यातिशयविनिर्मुक्तम्। न तावदैश्वर्यान्तरेण तदतिशय्यते। यदेवातिशयिस्यात्तदेव तत्स्यात्। तस्माद्यत्र काष्ठाप्राप्तिरैश्वर्यस्य स ईश्वर इति। न च तत्समानमैश्वर्यमस्ति। कस्मात् द्वयोस्तुल्ययोरेकस्मिन्युगपत्कामितेऽर्थे नवमिदमस्तु पुराणमिदमस्त्वित्येकस्य सिद्धावितरस्य प्राकाम्यविघातादूनलं प्रसक्तम्। द्वयोश्च तुल्ययोर्युगपत्कामितार्थप्राप्तिर्नास्ति। अर्थस्य विरुद्धत्वात्। तस्माद्यस्य साम्यातिशयैर्विनिर्मुक्तैश्वर्य स एवेश्वरः। स च पुरुषविशेष इति। किं च

भोजवृत्ति—क्लिश्नन्तीति क्लेशा अविद्यादयो वक्ष्यमाणाः। विहितप्रतिषिद्धव्यामिश्ररूपाणि कर्माणि। विपच्यन्त इति विपाकाः कर्मफलानि जात्यायुर्भोगाः। आ फलविपाकाच्चित्तभूमौ शेरत इत्याशया वासनाख्याः संस्कारास्तैरपरामृष्टश्चिष्वपि कालेषु च संसृष्टः। पुरुषविशेषः अन्येभ्यः पुरुषेभ्यो विशिष्यत इति विशेषः। ईश्वर ईशनशील इच्छामात्रेण सकलजगदुद्धरणक्षमः। यद्यपि सर्वेषामात्मनां क्लेशादिस्पर्शो नास्ति तथापि चित्तगतास्तेषामपदिश्यते। यथा योद्धृगतौ जयपराजयौ स्वामिनः। अस्य तु त्रिष्वपि कालेषु तथाविधोऽपि क्लेशादिपरामर्शो नास्ति। अतः स विलक्षण एव भगवानीश्वरः। तस्य च तथाविधमैश्वर्यमनादेः सत्त्वोत्कर्षात्। तस्य सत्त्वोत्कर्षश्च प्रकृष्टाज्ञानादेव। न च अनयोर्ज्ञानैश्वर्य्ययोरितरेतराश्रयत्वं परस्परानपेक्षत्वात्। ते द्वे ज्ञानैश्वर्ये ईश्वरसत्त्वे वर्तमाने अनादिभूते तेन च तथाविधेन सत्त्वेन तस्यानादिरेव सम्बन्धः प्रकृतिपुरुषसंयोगवियोग-योरीश्वरेच्छाव्यतिरेकेणानुपपत्तेः यथेतरेषां प्राणिनां सुखदुःखमोहात्मकतया परिणतं चित्तं निर्मले सात्त्विके धर्मात्मप्रख्ये प्रतिसंक्रान्तं चिच्छायासंक्रान्ते संवेद्यं भवति नैवमीश्वरस्य तस्य केवल एव सात्त्विकः परिणाम उत्कर्षवाननादिसंबन्धेन भोग्यतया व्यवस्थितः अतः पुरुषान्तरविलक्षणतया स एवेश्वरः। मुक्तात्मानां तु पुनः क्लेशादियोगस्तैस्तैः शास्त्रोक्तैरुपायैर्निवर्तितः। अस्य पुनः सर्वदैव तथाविधत्वान्न मुक्तात्मतुल्यत्वम्। न चेश्वराणामनेकत्वं तेषां तुल्यत्वे भिन्नाभिप्रायत्वात्कार्यस्यैवानुपपत्तेः। उत्कर्षापकर्षयुक्त्वे च एवोत्कृष्टः स एवेश्वरस्तत्रैव काष्ठाप्राप्तत्वादैश्वर्यस्य। एवमीश्वरस्य स्वरूपमभिधाय प्रमाणमाह

तत्र निरतिशयं सर्वज्ञबीजम् ॥25॥

tatra niratiśayaṃ sārvajñabījam

(Tatra) There in Him is (niratiśaya) the climax of knowledge, so he is called (bīja) source of (sarvajña) all knowledge.

व्यासभाष्य—यदिदमतीतानागतप्रत्युत्पन्नप्रत्येकसमुच्चयातीन्द्रियग्रहणमल्पं बह्विति सर्वज्ञबीजमेतद्विवर्धमानं यत्र निरतिशयं स सर्वज्ञः । अस्ति काष्ठाप्राप्तिः सर्वज्ञबीजस्य सातिशयत्वात्परिमाणवदिति । यत्र काष्ठाप्राप्तिर्ज्ञानस्य स सर्वज्ञः । स च पुरुषविशेष इति । सामान्यमात्रोपसंहारे च कृतोपक्षयमनुमानं न विशेषप्रतिपत्तौ समर्थमिति । तस्य संज्ञादिविशेषप्रतिपत्तिरागमतः पर्यन्वेष्या । तस्याऽत्मानुग्रहाभावेऽपि भूतानुग्रहः प्रयोजनम् । ज्ञानधर्मोपदेशेन कल्पप्रलयमहाप्रलयेषु संसारिणः पुरुषानुद्धरिष्यामीति । तथा चोक्तम् आदिविद्वान्निर्माणचित्तमधिष्ठाय कारुण्याद्भगवान्परमर्षिरासुरये जिज्ञासमानाय तन्त्रं प्रोवाचेति ।

भोजवृत्ति—तस्मिन्भगवति सर्वज्ञत्वस्य यद्बीजमतीतानागतादिग्रहणस्याल्पत्वं महत्त्वं च मूलत्वाद्बीजमिव बीजं तत्त्र निरतिशयं काष्ठां प्राप्तम् । दृष्टा ह्यल्पत्वमहत्त्वादीनां धर्माणां सातिशयानां काष्ठाप्राप्तिः । यथा परमाणावल्पत्वस्याऽकाशे परममहत्त्वस्य । एवं ज्ञानादयोऽपि चित्तधर्मास्तारतम्येन परिदृश्यमानाः क्वचिन्निरतिशयतामासादयन्ति । यत्र चैते निरतिशयाः स ईश्वरः । यद्यपि सामान्यमात्रेऽनुमानमात्रस्य पर्यवसितत्वान्न विशेषावगतिः संभवति तथाऽपि शास्त्रादस्य सर्वज्ञत्वादयो विशेषा अवगन्तव्याः । तस्य स्वप्रयोजनाभावे कथं प्रकृतिपुरुषयोः संयोगवियोगावापादयतीति नाऽशङ्कनीयं तस्य कारुणिकत्वाद्भूतानुग्रह एव प्रयोजनम् । कल्पप्रलयमहाप्रलयेषु निःशेषान्संसारिण उद्धरिष्यामीति तस्याध्यवसायः । यद्यस्येष्टं तत्तस्य प्रयोजनम् । एवमीश्वरस्य प्रमाणमभिधाय प्रभावमाह

स पूर्वेषामपि गुरुः कालेनानवच्छेदात् ॥26॥

sa pūrveṣāmapi guruḥ kālenānavacchedāt

He is older than those who were born first in the beginning of creation, because he is not subject to time.

व्यासभाष्य—पूर्वे हि गुरवः कालेनावच्छिद्यन्ते । यत्रावच्छेदार्थेन कालो नोपावर्तते स एष पूर्वेषामपि गुरुः । यथाऽस्य सर्गस्याऽऽदौ प्रकर्षगत्या सिद्धस्तथातिक्रान्तसर्गादिष्वपि प्रत्येतव्यः ।

भोजवृत्ति—आद्यानां स्रष्टृणां ब्रह्मादीनामपि स गुरुरुपदेष्टा । यतः स कालेन नावच्छिद्यते अनादित्वात् । तेषां पुनरादिमत्त्वादस्ति कालेनावच्छेदः । एवं प्रभावमुक्त्वोपासनोपयोगाय वाचकमाह

तस्य वाचकः प्रणवः ॥27॥

tasya vācakaḥ praṇavaḥ

His nomenclature is AUM.

व्यासभाष्य—वाच्य ईश्वरः प्रणवस्य। किमस्य संकेतकृतं वाच्यवाचकत्वमथ प्रदीपप्रकाशवदवस्थितमिति। स्थितोऽस्य वाच्यस्य वाचकेन सह संबन्धः। संकेतस्त्वीश्वरस्य स्थितमेवार्थमभिनयति। यथाऽवस्थितः पितापुत्रयो संबन्धः संकेतेनावद्योत्यते अयमस्य पिता अयमस्य पुत्र इति। सर्गान्तरेष्वपिवाच्यवाचकशक्त्यपेक्षस्तथैव संकेतः क्रियते। संप्रतिपत्तिनित्यतया नित्यः शब्दार्थसंबन्ध इत्यागमिनः प्रतिजानते। विज्ञात वाच्यवाचकत्वस्य योगिनः

भोजवृत्ति.—इत्थमुक्तस्वरूपस्येश्वरस्य वाचकोऽभिधायकः प्रकर्षेण नूयते स्तूयतेऽनेनेति नौति स्तौतीति वा प्रणव ओंकारः तयोश्च वाच्यवाचकभावलक्षणः सम्बन्धो नित्यः संकेतेन प्रकाश्यते न तु केनचिच्क्रियते यथा   पितापुत्रयो विद्यमान एव संबन्धोऽस्यायं पिताऽस्यायं पुत्र इति केनचित्प्रकाश्यते। उपासनमाह

तज्जपस्तदर्थभावनम् ॥28॥

tajjapastadarthabhāvanam

The (*japa*) repetition of Aum means contemplation of its object, i.e., Iśvara.

व्यासभाष्य—प्रणवस्य जपः प्रणवाभिधेयस्य चेश्वरस्य भावनम्। तदस्य योगिनः प्रणवं जपतः प्रणवार्थ च भावयतश्चित्तमेकाग्रं संपद्यते। तथा चोक्तम्
स्वाध्यायाद्योगमासीत योगात्स्वाध्यायमासते।
स्वाध्याययोगसंपत्त्या परमात्मा प्रकाशते इति।।   28।। किं चास्य भवति

भोजवृत्ति.—तस्य सार्धत्रिमात्रस्य प्रणवस्य जपो यथावदुच्चारणं तद्वाच्यस्य चेश्वरस्य भावनं पुनः पुनश्चेतसि विनिवेशनमेकाग्रताया उपायः। अतः समाधिसिद्धये योगिना प्रणवो जप्यस्तदर्थ ईश्वरश्च भावनीय इत्युक्तं भवति।
उपासनायाः फलमाह

ततः प्रत्यक्चेतनाधिगमोऽप्यन्तरायाभावश्च ॥29॥

tataḥ pratyakcetanādhigamo'pyantarāyābhāvaśca

Because of the japa of AUM, (*pratyak chetana adhigamaḥ*) self-realization (api) and realization of Iśvara takes place (*antarāyābhāvaśca*) and all obstacles are removed.

What are those obstacles? is explained in the next sutra.

व्यासभाष्य—ये तावदन्तराया व्याधिप्रभृतयस्ते तावदीश्वरप्रणिधानान्न भवन्ति। स्वरूपदर्शनमप्यस्य भवति। यथैवेश्वरः पुरुषः शुद्धः प्रसन्नः केवलोऽनुपसर्गस्तथाऽयमपि बुद्धे प्रतिसंवेदी पुरुष इत्येवमधिगच्छति। अथ केऽन्तरायाः। ये चित्तस्य विक्षेपाः। के पुनस्ते कियन्तो

वेति

.भोजवृत्ति—तसमाज्जपात्तदर्थभावनाच्च योगिनः प्रत्यक्चेतनाधिगमो भवति विषय प्रातिकूल्येन स्वान्तःकरणाभिमुखमञ्चति या चेतना दृक्शक्तिः सा प्रत्यक्चेतना तस्या अधिगमो ज्ञानं भवति । अन्तराया वक्ष्यमाणास्तेषामभावः शक्तिप्रतिबन्धोऽपि भवति । अथ केऽन्तराया इत्याशङ्क्रायामाह

व्याधिस्त्यानसंशयप्रमादालस्याविरति-

भ्रान्तिदर्शनालब्धभूमिकत्वानवस्थितत्वानि

चित्तविक्षेपास्तेऽन्तरायाः ॥30॥

vyādhi-styāna-saṃśaya-pramādālasyāvirati-
bhrāntidarśanālabdhabhūmikatvānavasthitatvāni
cittavikṣepāste'ntarāyāḥ

(Vyādhi) imbalance of dhātus[2] rasas[3] and karaṇas sense organs) in the body, (styāna) dullness of mind, (sañśaya) doubt regarding an issue, like it may be or may not be, (pramāda) unwillingness for samādhi, (ālasya) feeling of heaviness in the body and mind debarring one from samādhi, (avirati) mind's indulgence into sensory

---

[2] Rasa (juice of food), rakta (blood), mānsa (flesh/muscle), meda (fat), asthi (bone), majjā (marrow), śukra (semen)

[3] Madhura (Sweet), (amla) sour, (lavaṇa) salty, (kaṭu) bitter, (tikta) pungent, and (kaṣāya) astringent

1. Kapha- Madhura, Amla, Lavaṇa will aggaravate kapha. Kaṭu Tikta, Kaṣāya will pacify kapha. Śodhana treatment- Vamana (vomiting) with madhura

2. Pitta- Amala, Lavaṇa and Kaṭu aggravate pitta. Kaṣāya, Tikta and Madhura will pacify it. Śodhana treatment: Virechana with ghee.

3. Vāta- Kaṭu Tikta and Kaṣāya will aggravate vāta. Madhura, Amla and Lavaṇa will pacify vāta. Śodhana Treatment: Basti with oil

objects, (bhrānti darśana) false knowledge, (alabdha-bhūmikatva) deprivation of conducive atmosphere for samādhi, (anavasthiti) instability of mind even if conducive atmosphere is available, these are distractors of the mind and obstacles to Samādhi.

व्यासभाष्य—नवान्तरायाश्चित्तस्य विक्षेपाः । सहैते चित्तवृत्तिभिर्भवन्ति । एतेषामभावे न भवन्ति पूर्वोक्ताश्चित्तवृत्तयः । तत्र 1 व्याधिर्धातुरसकरणवैषम्यम् । 2 स्त्यानमकर्मण्यता चित्तस्य । 3 संशय उभयकोटिस्पृग्विज्ञानं स्यादिदमेवं नैवं स्यादिति । 4 प्रमादः समाधिसाधनानामभावनम् । 5 आलस्यं कायस्य चित्तस्य च गुरुत्वादप्रवृत्तिः । 6 अविरतिश्चित्तस्य विषयसंप्रयोगात्मा गर्धः । 7 भ्रान्तिदर्शनं विपर्ययज्ञानम् । 8 अलब्धभूमिकत्वं समाधिभूमेरलाभः । 9 अनवस्थितत्वं लब्धायां भूमौ चित्तस्याप्रतिष्ठा । समाधिप्रतिलम्भे हि सति तदवस्थितं स्यादिति । एते चित्तविक्षेपा नव योगमला योगप्रतिपक्षा योगान्तराया इत्यभिधीयन्ते ।

भोजवृत्ति—नवैते रजस्तमोबलात्प्रवर्तमानाश्चित्तस्य विक्षेपा भवन्ति । तैरैकाग्रताविरोधिभिश्चित्तं विक्षिप्यत इत्यर्थः । तत्र 1 व्याधिर्धातुवैषम्यनिमित्तो ज्वरादिः । 2 स्त्यानमकर्मण्यता चित्तस्य । 3 उभयकोट्यालम्बनं ज्ञानं संशयः योगः साध्यो न वेति । 4 प्रमादोऽननुष्ठानशीलता समाधिसाधनेष्वौदासीन्यम् । 5 आलस्यं कायचित्तयोर्गुरुत्वं योगविषये प्रवृत्यभावहेतुः । 6 अविरतिश्चित्तस्य विषयसंप्रयोगात्मा गर्धः । 7 भ्रान्तिदर्शनं शुक्तिकायां रजतवद्विपर्ययज्ञानम् । 8 अलब्धभूमिकत्वं कुतश्चिन्निमित्तात्समाधिभूमेरलाभोऽसंप्राप्तिः । 9 अनवस्थितत्वं लब्धायामपि समाधिभूमाव चित्तस्य तत्राप्रतिष्ठा । त एते समाधेरेकाग्रताया यथायोगं प्रतिपक्षत्वादन्तराया इत्युच्यन्ते । चित्तविक्षेपकारकानन्यानप्यन्तरायान्प्रतिपादयितुमाह

दुःखदौर्मनस्याङ्गमेजयत्वश्वासप्रश्वासा विक्षेपसहभुवः ॥31॥

duḥkhadaurmanasyāṅgamejayatvaśvāsapraśvāsā vikṣepasahabhuvaḥ

(Duḥkha) Ādhyātmika, ādhidaivika and ādhibhautika pains, (daurmanasya) frustration when desires are not fullfilled, (aṅgameyajatva) shakiness dis-equilibrium of body parts, (śvāsa) breathlessness in inhalation and (praśvāsa) exhalation, these are companions of the distractions.

व्यासभाष्य—दुःखमाध्यात्मिकमाधिभौतिकमाधिदैविकं च । येनाभिहताः प्राणिनस्तदुपघाताय प्रयत्ने तद्दुःखम् । दौर्मनस्यमिच्छाविघाताच्चेतसः क्षोभः । यदङ्गान्येजयति कम्पयति तदङ्गमेजयत्वम् । प्राणो यद्बाह्यं वायुमाचामति स श्वासः । यत्कौष्ठ्यं वायु निःसारयति स प्रश्वासः । एते विक्षेपसहभुवो विक्षिप्तचित्तस्यैते भवन्ति । समाहितचित्तस्यैते न भवन्ति । अथैते विक्षेपाः समाधिप्रतिपक्षास्ताभ्यामेवाभ्यासवैराग्याभ्यां निरोद्धव्याः । तत्राभ्यासस्य विषयमुपसंहरन्निदमाह

भोजवृत्ति—कुतश्चित्रिभिक्तादुत्पन्नेषु विक्षेपेषु एते दुःखादयः प्रवर्तन्ते । तत्र दुःखं चित्तस्य राजसः परिणामो बाधनालक्षणः । यद्बाधात्प्राणिनस्तदपघाताय प्रवर्तन्ते । दौर्मनस्यं बाह्याभ्यन्तरैः कारणैर्मनसोदौस्थ्यम् । अङ्गमेजयत्वो सर्वाङ्गीणो वेपथुरासनमनः स्थैर्यस्य बाधकः । प्राणो यद्बाह्यं वायुमाचामति स श्वासः । यत्कौष्ठ्यं वायुं निःश्वसिति सः प्रश्वासः । त एते विक्षेपैः सह प्रवर्तमाना यथोदिताभ्यासवैराग्याताभ्यां निरोद्धव्या इत्येषामुपदेशः । सोपद्रवविक्षेपप्रतिषेधार्थमुपायान्तरमाह

तत्प्रतिषेधार्थमेकतत्त्वाभ्यासः ॥32॥

tatpratiṣedhārthamekatattvābhyāsaḥ

To counteract (these distractions), practice meditation on the one Principle or Reality, i.e. Īśvara.

व्यासभाष्य—विक्षेपप्रतिषेधार्थमेकतत्त्वालम्बनं चित्तमभ्यसेत् । यस्य तु प्रत्यर्थनियतं प्रत्ययमात्रं क्षणिकं च चित्तं तस्य सर्वमेव चित्तमेकाग्रं नास्त्येव विक्षिप्तम् । यदि पुनरिदं सर्वतः प्रत्याहृत्यैकस्मिन्नर्थे समाधीयते सदा भवत्येकाग्रमित्यतो न प्रत्यर्थनियतम् । योऽपि सदृशप्रत्ययप्रवाहेण चित्तमेकाग्रं मन्यते तस्यैकाग्रता यदि प्रवाहचित्तस्य धर्मस्तदैकं नास्ति प्रवाहचित्तं क्षणिकत्वात् । अथ प्रवाहांशस्यैव प्रत्ययस्य धर्मः स सर्वः सदृशप्रत्ययप्रवाही वा विसदृशप्रत्ययप्रवाही वा प्रत्यर्थनियतत्वादेकाग्र एवेति विक्षिप्तचित्तानुपपत्तिः तस्मादेकमनेकार्थमवस्थितं चित्तमिति । यदि च चित्तेनैकेनान्विताः स्वभावभिन्नाः प्रत्यया जायेरन्नथ कथमन्यप्रत्ययदृष्टस्यान्यः स्मर्ता भवेत् । अन्यप्रत्ययोपचितस्य च कर्माशयस्यान्यः प्रत्यय उपभोक्ता भवेत् । कथंचित्समाधीयमानमप्येतद्गोमयपायसीयन्यायमाक्षिपति । किं च स्वात्मानुभवापह्नवश्चित्तस्यान्यत्वे प्राप्नोति । कथं यदहमद्राक्षं तत्स्पृशामि यच्चास्प्राक्षं तत्पश्यामीत्यहमिति प्रत्ययः सर्वस्य प्रत्ययस्य भेदे सति प्रत्ययिन्यभेदेनोपस्थितः । एकप्रत्ययविषयोऽयमभेदात्माऽहमिति प्रत्ययः । कथमत्यन्तभिन्नेषु चित्तेषु वर्तमानः सामान्यमेकं प्रत्ययिनमाश्रयेत् स्वानुभवग्राह्यश्चायमभेदात्माऽहमिति प्रत्ययः । न च प्रत्यक्षस्य माहात्म्यं प्रमाणान्तरेणाभिभूयते । प्रमाणान्तरं च प्रत्यक्षबलेनैव व्यवहारं लभते । तस्मादेकमनेकार्थमवस्थितं च चित्तम् । यच्चित्तस्यावस्थितस्येदं शास्त्रेण परिकर्म निर्दिश्यते तत्कथम्

भोजवृत्ति—तेषां विक्षेपाणां प्रतिषेधार्थमेकस्मिन्कस्मिंश्चिदभिमते तत्त्वेऽभ्यासश्चेतसः पुनः पुनर्निवेशनं कार्यः । मद्दलात् प्रत्युदितायामेकाग्रतायां विक्षेपाः प्रशममुपायान्ति । इदानीं चित्तसंस्कारापादकपरिकर्मकथनमुपायान्तरमाह

मैत्रीकरुणामुदितोपेक्षाणां सुखदुःखपुण्यापुण्यविषयाणां भावनातश्चित्तप्रसादनम् ॥33॥

maitrī-karuṇā-muditopekṣāṇāṃ sukha-duḥkha-puṇyāpuṇya-viṣayāṇāṃ bhāvanātaś-chittaprasādanam

(chitta-prasādanam) Mind is pacified with the (bhāvanā) attitude of (maitrī) friendliness toward the (sukha) happy; (karuṇā) compassion toward the (duḥkha) unhappy; (muditā) gladness toward the (puṇya) virtuous; and (upekṣā) indifference toward the (apuṇya) wicked.

व्यासभाष्य—तत्र सर्वप्राणिषु सुखसंभोगापन्नेषु मैत्रीं भावयेत्। दुःखितेषु करुणाम्। पुण्यात्मकेषु मुदिताम्। अपुण्यशीलेषूपेक्षाम्। एवमस्य भावयतः शुक्लो धर्म उपजायते। ततश्च चित्तं प्रसीदति। प्रसन्नमेकाग्रं स्थितिपदं लभते।

भोजवृत्ति—मैत्री सौहार्दम्। करुणा कृपा। मुदिता हर्षः। उपेक्षौदासीन्यम्। एता यथाक्रमं सुखितेषु दुःखितेषु पुण्यवत्सु अपुण्यवत्सु च विभावयेत्। तथा हि सुखितेषु साधु एषां सुखित्वमिति मैत्रीं कुर्यान्न तु ईर्ष्याम्। दुःखितेषु कथं नु नामैषां दुःखनिवृत्तिः स्यादिति कृपामेव कुर्यान्न ताटस्थ्यम्। पुण्यवत्सु पुण्यानुमोदनेन हर्षमेव कुर्यान्न तु किमेते पुण्यवन्त इति विद्वेषम्। अपुण्यवत्सु चौदासीन्यमेव भावयेन्नानुमोदनं न वा द्वेषम्। सूत्रे सुखदुःखादिशब्दैस्तद्वन्तः प्रतिपादिताः। तदेव मैत्र्यादिपरिकर्मणा चित्ते प्रसीदति सुखेन समाधेराविर्भावो भवति। परिकर्म चैतद्वाह्यं कर्म। यथा गणिते मिश्रकादिव्यवहारो गणितनिष्पत्तये संकलितादिकर्मोपकारकत्वेन प्रधानकर्मनिष्पत्तये भवति एवं द्वेषरागादिप्रतिपक्षभूतमैत्र्यादिभावनया समुत्पादितप्रसादं चित्तं संप्रज्ञातादिसमाधियोग्यं संपद्यते। रागद्वेषावेव मुख्यतया विक्षेपमुत्पादयतः। तौ चेत्समूलमुन्मूलितौ स्यातां तदा प्रसन्नत्वान्मनसो भवत्येकाग्रता। उपायान्तरमाह

प्रच्छर्दनविधारणाभ्यां वा प्राणस्य ॥34॥
pracchardanavidhāraṇābhyāṃ vā prāṇasya

Or, by the rechaka (release) and puraka (retention) prāṇāyāma is the steadiness of mind attained.

व्यासभाष्य—कौष्ठ्यस्य वायोर्नासिकापुटाभ्यां प्रयत्नविशेषाद्वमनं प्रच्छर्दन विधारणं प्राणायामस्ताभ्यां वा मनसः स्थितिं संपादयेत्।

भोजवृत्ति—प्रच्छर्दनं कौष्ठ्यस्य वायोः प्रयत्नविशेषान्मात्राप्रमाणेन बहिर्निःसारणम्। विधारणं मात्राप्रमाणेनैव प्राणस्य वायोर्बहिर्गतिविच्छेदः। स च द्वाभ्यां प्रकाराभ्यां बाह्यस्याभ्यन्तरापूरणेन पूरितस्य वा तत्रैव निरोधेन। तदेवं रेचकपूरककुम्भकभेदेन त्रिविधः प्राणायामश्चित्तस्य स्थितिमेकाग्रतया निबध्नाति सर्वासामिन्द्रियवृत्तिनां प्राणवृत्तिपूर्वकत्त्वात्। मनः प्राणयोश्च स्वव्यापारे परस्परमेकयोगक्षेमत्वाल्लक्षीयमाणः प्राणः समस्तेन्द्रियवृत्तिनिरोधद्वारेण चित्तस्यैकाग्रतायां प्रभवति। समस्तदोषक्षयकारित्वं चास्याऽऽगमे श्रूयते। दोषकृताश्च सर्वा विक्षेपवृत्तयः। अतो दोषनिर्हरणद्वारेणाप्यस्यैकाग्रतायां सामर्थ्यम्। इदानीमुपायान्तरप्रदर्शनोपक्षेपेण संप्रज्ञातस्य समाधेः पूर्वाङ्गं कथयति

विषयवती वा प्रवृत्तिरुत्पन्ना मनसःस्थितिनिबन्धिनी ॥35॥
viṣayavatī vā pravṛttirutpannā manasaḥ sthitinibandhinī

The tendency of the mind toward an object of sense,

brings about a steady state of mind.

Note: The commentator Vyāsa says that if the mind becomes concentrated on the tip of nose, one begins to smell the desired perfume. If it becomes concentrated at the root of tongue, one begins to hear distant sounds; if on tip of tongue, one begins to taste wonderful flavours; if on the middle of tongue, one feels as if one were coming in contact with something.

व्यासभाष्य—नासिकाग्रे धारयतोऽस्य या दिव्यगन्धसंवित्सा गन्धप्रवृत्तिः। जिह्वाग्रे रससंवित्। तालुनि रूपसंवित्। जिह्वामध्ये स्पर्शसंवित्। जिह्वामूले शब्दसंविदित्येता वृत्तय उत्पन्नाश्चित्तं स्थितौ निबध्नन्ति संशयं विधमन्ति समाधिप्रज्ञायां च द्वारी भवन्तीति। एतेन चन्द्रादित्यग्रहमणिप्रदीपपरश्म्यादिषु प्रवृत्तिरुत्पन्ना विषयत्येव वेदितव्या। यद्यपि हि तत्तच्छास्त्रानुमानाचार्योपदेशैखगतमर्थतत्त्वं सद्भूतमेव भवति एतेषां यथाभूतार्थप्रतिपादनसामर्थ्यात् तथापि यावदेकदेशोऽपि कश्चिन्न स्वकरणसंवेद्यो भवति तावत्सर्वं परोक्षमिवापवर्गादिषु सूक्ष्मेष्वर्थेषु न दृढां बुद्धिमुत्पादयति। तस्माच्छास्त्रानुमानाचार्योपदेशोपोद्बलनार्थमेवावश्यं कश्चिदर्थविशेषः प्रत्यक्षीकर्तव्यः। तत्र तदुपदिष्टार्थैकदेशप्रत्यक्षत्वे सति सर्वं सूक्ष्मविषयमपि आऽपवर्गाच्छ्रद्धीयते। एतदर्थमेवेदं चित्तपरिकर्म निर्दिश्यते। अनियतासु वृत्तिषु तद्विषयायां वशीकारसंज्ञायामुपजातायां समर्थ स्यात्तस्य तस्यार्थस्य प्रत्यक्षीकरणायेति। तथा च सति श्रद्धावीर्यस्मृतिसमाधयोऽस्याप्रतिबन्धेन भविष्यन्तीति।

भोजवृत्ति—विषया गन्धरसरूपस्पर्शशब्दास्ते विद्यन्ते फलत्वेन यस्याः सा विषयवती प्रवृत्तिर्मनसः स्थैर्यं करोति। तथा हि नासाग्रे चित्तं धारयतो दिव्यगन्धसंविदुपजायते। तादृश्येव जिह्वाग्रे रससंवित्। ताल्वग्रे रूपसंवित्। जिह्वामध्ये स्पर्शसंवित्। जिह्वामूले शब्दसंवित्। तदेव तत्तदिन्द्रियद्वारेण तस्मिंस्तस्मिन्दिव्यविषये जायमाना संविच्चित्तस्यैकाग्रताया हेतुर्भवति। अस्ति योगस्य फलमिति योगिनः समाश्वासोत्पादनात्। एवंविधमेवोपायान्तरमाह

विशोका वा ज्योतिष्मती ॥36॥
viśokā vā jyotiṣmatī

Or (viśokā) an undisturbed mind when tends towards (jyotiṣmatī) self-realization attains a steady state.

Note: Self-realization and realization of Brahman are associated with the light. So Jyotiṣmati here means self-realisation or realisation of Brahman.

व्यासभाष्य—प्रवृत्तिरुत्पन्ना मनसः स्थितिनिबन्धनीत्यनुवर्तते। हृदयपुण्डरीके धारयतो या बुद्धिसंवित् बुद्धिसत्त्वं हि भास्वरमाकाशकल्पं तत्र स्थितिवैशारद्यात्प्रवृत्तिः

सूर्येन्दुग्रहमणिप्रभारूपाकारेण विकल्पते । तथाऽस्मितायां समापन्नं चित्तं निस्तरङ्गमहोदधिकल्पं शान्तमनन्तमस्मितामात्रं भवति । यत्रेदमुक्तम् तमणुणमात्रमात्मानमनुविद्यास्मीत्येवं तावत्संप्रजानीते इति । एषा द्वयी विशोका विषयवती अस्मितामात्रा च प्रवृत्तिज्योतिष्मतीत्युच्यते । यया योगिनश्चित्तं स्थितिपदं लभत इति ।

भोजवृत्ति.—प्रवृत्तिरुत्पन्ना चित्तस्य स्थितिनिबन्धिनीति वाक्य शेषः । ज्योतिः शब्देन सात्विकः प्रकाश उच्यते । स प्रशस्तो भूयानतिशयवांश्च विद्यते यस्यां सा ज्योतिष्मति प्रवृत्तिः । विशोका विगतः सुखमयत्वाभ्यासवशाच्छोको रजः परिणामो यस्याः सा विशोका चेतसः स्थितिनिबन्धिनी । अयमर्थः हृत्पद्मसंपुटमध्ये प्रशान्तकल्लोलक्षीरोदधिप्रख्यं चित्तसत्त्वं भावयतः प्रज्ञालोकात्सर्ववृत्तिपरिक्षये चेतसः स्थैर्यमुत्पद्यते । उपायान्तरप्रदर्शनद्वारेण संप्रज्ञातसमाधिर्विषयं दर्शयति

वीतरागविषयं वा चित्तम् ॥37॥
vītarāgaviṣayaṃ vā cittam

Or a mind detached from sensory objects of the visible world becomes steady.

व्यासभाष्य—वीतरागचित्तालम्बनोपरक्तं वा योगिनश्चित्तं स्थितिपदं लभत इति ।

भोजवृत्ति.—मनसः स्थितिनिबन्धनं भवतीति शेषः । वीतरागः परित्यक्तविषयाभिलाषस्तस्य यच्चित्तं परिहृतक्लेशं तदालम्बनीकृतं चेतसः स्थितिहेतुर्भवति ।

स्वप्ननिद्राज्ञानालम्बनं वा ॥38॥
svapnanidrājñānālambanaṃ vā

Or, the concentration of mind on the subject of the dream or the sleep state also makes it steady.

व्यासभाष्य—स्वप्रज्ञानालम्बनं वा निद्राज्ञानालम्बनं वा तदाकारं योगिनश्चित्तं स्थितिपदं लभत इति ।

भोजवृत्ति.—प्रत्यस्तमितबाह्येन्द्रियवृत्तेर्मनोमात्रेणैव यत्र भोक्तृत्वमात्मनः स स्वप्नः । निद्रा पूर्वोक्तलक्षणा । तदालम्बनं स्वप्रालम्बनं निद्रालम्बनं वा ज्ञानमालम्ब्यमानं चेतसः स्थितिं करोति । नानारुचित्वात्प्राणिनां यस्मिन्कस्मिंश्चिद्वस्तुनि योगिनः श्रद्धा भवति तस्य ध्यानेनापीष्टसिद्धिरिति प्रतिपादयितुमाह

यथाभिमतध्यानाद्वा ॥39॥
yathābhimatadhyānādvā

Or concentration on the objects of one's choice makes the mind steady.

व्यासभाष्य—यदेवाभिमतं तदेव ध्यायेत्। तत्र लब्धस्थितिकमन्यत्रापि स्थितिपदं लभत इति।

भोजवृत्ति—यथाभिमतवस्तुनि बाह्ये चन्द्रादावाभ्यन्तरे नाडीचक्रादौ वा भाव्यमाने चेतः स्थिरीभवति। एवमुपायान्तरदर्श्य फलदर्शनायाऽऽह

परमाणु परममहत्त्वान्तोऽस्य वशीकारः ॥40॥

paramāṇu paramamahattvānto'sya vaśīkāraḥ

The power of concentration of the mind extends from the smallest particle, i.e. atom to the vast sky.

व्यासभाष्य—सूक्ष्मे निविशमानस्य परमाण्वन्तं स्थितिपदं लभत इति। स्थूले निविशमानस्य परममहत्त्वान्तं स्थितिपदं चित्तस्य। एवं तामुभयीं कोटिमनुधावतो योऽस्याप्रतीघातः स परो वशीकारः। तद्वशीकारात्परिपूर्णं योगिनश्चित्तं न पुनरभ्यासकृतं परिकर्मापेक्षत इति। अथ लब्धस्थितिकस्य चेतसः किंस्वरूपा किंविषया वा समापत्तिरिति तदुच्यते

भोजवृत्ति—एभिरुपायैश्चित्तस्य स्थैर्य भावयतो योगिनः सूक्ष्मविषयभावनाद्वारेण परमाण्वन्तो वशीकारोऽप्रतिघातरूपो जायते न क्वचित्तपरमाणुपर्यन्ते सूक्ष्मे विषयेऽस्य मनः प्रतिहन्यत इत्यर्थः। एवं स्थूलमाकाशादिपरममहत्पर्यन्तं भावयतो न क्वचिच्चेतसः प्रतिघात उत्पद्यते सर्वत्र स्वातन्त्र्यं भवतीत्यर्थः। एवमेभिरुपायैः संस्कृतस्य चेतसः कीदृग्रूपं भवतीत्याह

क्षीणवृत्तेरभिजातस्येव मणेर्ग्रहीतृग्रहणग्राह्येषु तत्स्थतदञ्जनता समापत्तिः ॥41॥

kṣīṇavṛtterabhijātasyeva maṇergrahītṛgrahaṇagrāhyeṣu
tatsthatadañjanatā samāpattiḥ

(Kṣīṇavṛtteh) On the elimination of vṛttis, the mind becomes (iva) like that of (abhijātasya maṇeḥ) a pure jewel/crystal; (tatstha samāpatti) in this state of saṃprajñāta samādhi, (tadañjanatā) the difference of (grahitā) knower (soul), (grāhya) the known (Brahman or any other object), and (garhaṇa) the knowledge is eliminated to a yogī, or, we can say that knower, known and knowledge becomes one and the same thing to a yogī.

व्यासभाष्य—क्षीणवृत्तेरिति प्रत्यस्तमितप्रत्ययस्येत्यर्थः। अभिजातस्येव मणेरिति दृष्टान्तोपादानम्। यथा स्फटिक उपाश्रयभेदात्तत्तद्रूपोपरक्त उपाश्रयरूपाकारेण निर्भासते तथा

ग्राह्यालम्बनोपरक्तं चित्तं ग्राह्यसमापन्नं ग्राह्यस्वरूपाकारेण निर्भासते । तथा भूतसूक्ष्मोपरक्तं भूतसूक्ष्मसमापन्नं भूतसूक्ष्मस्वरूपाभासं भवति । तथा स्थूलालम्बनोपरक्तं स्थूलरूपसमापन्नं स्थूलरूपाभासं भवति । तथा विश्वभेदोपरक्तं विश्वभेदसमापन्नं विश्वरूपाभासं भवति । तथा ग्रहणेष्वपीन्द्रियेषु द्रष्टव्यम् । ग्रहणालम्बनोपरक्तं ग्रहणसमापन्नं ग्रहणस्वरूपाकारेण निर्भासते । तथा ग्रहीतृपुरुषालम्बनोपरक्तं ग्रहीतृपुरुषसमापन्नं ग्रहीतृपुरुषस्वरूपाकारेण निर्भासते । तथा मुक्तपुरुषालम्बनोपरक्तं मुक्तपुरुषसमापन्नं मुक्तपुरुषस्वरूपाकारेण निर्भासते । तदेवमभिजातमणिकल्पस्य चेतसो ग्रहीतृग्रहणग्राह्येषु पुरुषेन्द्रियभूतेषु या तत्स्थतदञ्जनता तेषु स्थितस्य तदाकारापत्तिः सा समापत्तिरित्युच्यते ।

भोजवृत्ति—क्षीणा वृत्तयो यस्य तत्क्षीणवृत्ति तस्य ग्रहीतृग्रहणग्राह्येषु आत्मेन्द्रियविषयेषु तत्स्थतदञ्जनता समापत्तिर्भवति । तत्स्थत्वं तत्रैकाग्रता तदञ्जनता तन्मयत्वं क्षीणभूते चित्ते विषयस्य भाव्यमानस्यैवोत्कर्षः तथाविधा समापत्तिः तद्रूपः परिणामो भवतीत्यर्थः । दृष्टान्तमाह अभिजातस्येव मणेर्यथाभिजातस्य निर्मलस्य स्फटिकमणेस्तत्तदुपाधिवशात्तद्रूपापत्तिरेवं निर्मलस्य चित्तस्य तत्तद्भावनीयवस्तूपरागात्तत्तद्रूपापत्ति । यद्यपि ग्रहीतृग्रहणग्राह्येषु इत्युक्तं तथाऽपि भूमिकाक्रमवशाद्ग्राह्यग्रहणग्रहीतृषु इति बोध्यम् । यतः प्रथमं ग्राह्यनिष्ठ एव समाधिस्ततो ग्रहणनिष्ठस्ततोऽस्मितामात्ररूपो ग्रहीतृनिष्ठ केवलस्य पुरुषस्य ग्रहीतुर्भाव्यत्वासंभवात् । ततश्च स्थूलसूक्ष्मग्राह्योपरक्तं चित्तं तत्र समापन्नं भवति । एवं ग्रहणे ग्रहीतरि च समापन्नं तद्रूपपरिणामत्वं बोध्यम् । इदानीमुक्ताया एव समापत्तेश्चातुर्विध्यमाह

In the next sūtras, different categories of samprajñāta samādhi are defined. First of all, samādhi dealing with the gross objects is described.

तत्र शब्दार्थज्ञानविकल्पैः संकीर्णा सवितर्का समापत्तिः ॥42॥

tatra śabdārthajñānavikalpaiḥ saṃkīrṇā savitarkā samāpattiḥ

There, the samādhi in which the word, its object (like the 'animal gau or cow'), and the knowledge of the association of a particular word with a particular object is (saṅkīrṇa) fused or mixed up, is known as Savitarkā Samāpatti (achievement).

Note: To sum up, the savitarkā samāpatti is the first stage of Sabija Samādhi.

Thus in the beginning, when a seeker starts the practice of samādhi, his awareness of all three things: word, its object, and the knowledge of the association of a particular word with a particular object. When he advances in his practice of samadhi, the distinction between object, the word denoting it, and the knowledge of the association of the word with object fizzles out or say dissipates. This first stage is called Savitarka Samāpatti towards the perfection of Sabīja Samādhi.

व्यासभाष्य—तद्यथा गौरितिशब्दो गौरित्यर्थो गौरिति ज्ञानमित्यविभागेन विभक्तानामपि ग्रहणं दृष्टम् । विभज्यमानाश्चान्ये शब्दधर्मा अन्येऽर्थधर्मा अन्ये ज्ञानधर्मा इत्येतेषां विभक्तः पन्थाः । तत्र समापन्नस्य योगिनो यो गवाद्यर्थे समाधिप्रज्ञायां समारूढः स चेच्छब्दार्थज्ञानविकल्पानुविद्ध उपावर्तते सा संकीर्णा समापत्तिः सवितर्केत्युच्यते । यदा पुनः शब्दसंकेतस्मृतिपरिशुद्धौ श्रुतानुमानज्ञान विकल्पशून्यायां समाधिप्रज्ञायां स्वरूपमात्रेणावस्थितोऽर्थस्तत्स्वरूपाकारमात्रतयैवावच्छिद्यते । सा च निर्वितर्का समापत्ति । तत्परं प्रत्यक्षम् । तच्च श्रुतानुमानयोर्बीजम् । ततः श्रुतानुमाने प्रभवतः । न च श्रुतानुमानज्ञानसहभूतं तद्दर्शनम् । तस्मादसंकीर्णं प्रमाणान्तरेण योगिनो निर्वितर्कसमाधिजं दर्शनमिति । निर्वितर्कायाः समापत्तेरस्याः सूत्रेण लक्षणं द्योत्यते

व्यासभाष्य .भोजवृत्ति—श्रोत्रेन्द्रियग्राह्यः स्फोटरूपो वा शब्दः । अर्थो जात्यादिः । ज्ञानं सत्त्वप्रधाना बुद्धिवृत्तिः । विकल्प उक्तलक्षणः । तैः संकीर्णा यस्यामेते शब्दादयः परस्पराध्यासेन प्रतिभासन्ते गौरिति शब्दो गौरित्यर्थो गौरिति ज्ञानमित्यनेनाऽऽकारेण सा सवितर्का समापत्तिरुच्यते । उक्तलक्षणविपरीतां निर्वितर्कामाह

स्मृतिपरिशुद्धौ स्वरूपशून्येवार्थमात्रनिर्भासा निर्वितर्का ॥43॥

smṛtipariśuddhau svarūpaśūnyevārthamātranirbhāsā nirvitarkā

The second stage is that of Nirvitarka Samāpatti.

When the mind is purged of memory, it becomes void of itself, free from the words and their association with the objects; in this state the object of concentration sensations qualifying the material elements instead of their shapes, that is Nirvitarkā Samāpatti (achievement).

Note: Subject matter of Savitarka and Nirvitarka Samādhi is material objects and their sensations (tanmatras).

The scope of Savichāra and Nirvichāra samāpattis is dealt with in the next sūtra.

व्यासभाष्य—या शब्दसंकेतश्रुतानुमानज्ञानविकल्पस्मृतिपरिशुद्धौ ग्राह्यस्वरूपोपरक्ता प्रज्ञा स्वमिव प्रज्ञास्वरूपं ग्रहणात्मकं त्यक्त्वा पदार्थमात्रस्वरूपा ग्राह्यस्वरूपापन्नेव भवति सा निर्वितर्का समापत्तिः। तथा च व्याख्यातम् तस्या एकबुद्ध्युपक्रमो ह्यर्थात्माणुप्रचयविशेषात्मा गवादिर्घटादिर्वा लोकः।

स च संस्थानविशेषो भूतसूक्ष्माणां साधारणो धर्म आत्मभूतः फलेन व्यक्तेनानुमितः स्वव्यञ्जकाञ्जनः प्रादुर्भवति। धर्मान्तरस्य कपालादेरुदये च तिरो भवति। स एष धर्मोऽवयवीत्युच्यते। योऽसावेकश्च महांश्चारणीयांश्च स्पर्शवांश्च क्रियाधर्मकश्चानित्यश्च तेनावयविना व्यवहाराः क्रियन्ते।

यस्य पुनरवस्तुकः स प्रचयविशेषः सूक्ष्मं च कारणमनुपलभ्यमविकल्पस्य तस्यावयव्यभावादतद्रूपप्रतिष्ठं मिथ्याज्ञानमिति प्रायेण सर्वमेव प्राप्तं मिथ्याज्ञानमिति।

तदा च सम्यग्ज्ञानमपि किं स्याद्विषयाभावात्। यद्युपलभ्यते तत्तदवयविलेनाऽऽम्नातम्। तस्मादस्त्यवयवी यो महत्त्वादिव्यवहारापन्नः समापत्तेर्निर्वितर्काया विषयी भवति।

भोजवृत्ति—शब्दार्थस्मृतिप्रविलये सति प्रत्युदितस्पष्टग्राह्याकारप्रतिभासितया न्यग्भूतज्ञानांशत्वेन स्वरूपशून्येव निर्वितर्का समापत्तिः। भेदान्तरं प्रतिपादयितुमाह

एतयैव सविचारा निर्विचारा च सूक्ष्मविषया

व्याख्याता ॥44॥

etayaiva savicārā nirvicārā ca sūkṣmaviṣayā vyākhyātā

On the pattern of Nirvitarka and Savitarka samāpattis, one can define Savichārā and Nirvichārā samāpattis which have the minutest objects as the subject matter of concentration.

व्यासभाष्य—तत्र भूतसूक्ष्मेष्वभिव्यक्तधर्मकेषु देशकालनिमित्तानुभवावच्छिन्नेषु या समापत्तिः सा सविचारेत्युच्यते। तत्राप्येकबुद्धिनिग्राह्यमेवोदितधर्मविशिष्टं भूतसूक्ष्ममालम्बनीभूतं समाधिप्रज्ञायामुपतिष्ठते।

या पुनः सर्वथा सर्वतः शान्तोदिताव्यपदेश्यधर्मावच्छिन्नेषु सर्वधर्मानुपातिषु सर्वधर्मात्मकेषु समापत्तिः सा निर्विचारेत्युच्यते। एवं स्वरूपं हि तद्भूतसूक्ष्ममेतेनैव स्वरूपेणाऽऽलम्बनीभूतमेव समाधिप्रज्ञास्वरूपमुपरञ्जयति।

प्रज्ञा च स्वरूपशून्येवार्थमात्रा यदा भवति तदा निर्विचारेत्युच्यते। तत्र महद्वस्तुविषया सवितर्का निर्वितर्का च सूक्ष्मवस्तुविषया सविचारा निर्विचारा च। एवमुभयोरेतयैव निवितर्कया विकल्पहानिर्व्याख्यातेति।

भोजवृत्ति—एतयैव सवितर्कया निर्वितर्कया च समापत्या सविचारा निर्विचारा च व्याख्याता । कीदृशी सूक्ष्मविषया सूक्ष्मस्तन्मात्रेन्द्रियादिर्विषयो यस्याः सा तथोक्ता । एतेन पूर्वस्याः स्थूलविषयत्वं प्रतिपादितं भवति । सा हि महाभूतेन्द्रियालम्बना । शब्दार्थविषयत्वेन शब्दार्थविकल्पसहितत्वेन देशकालधर्माद्यवच्छिन्नः सूक्ष्मोऽर्थः प्रतिभाति यस्यां सा सविचारा । देशकालधर्मादिरहितो धर्मिमात्रतया सूक्ष्मोऽर्थस्तन्मात्रेन्द्रियरूपः प्रतिभाति यस्यां सा निर्विचारा । अस्या एव सूक्ष्मविषयायाः किंपर्यन्तः सूक्ष्मविषय इत्याह

सूक्ष्मविषयत्वं चालिङ्गपर्यवसानम् ॥45॥

sūkṣmaviṣayatvaṃ cāliṅgaparyavasānam

The limit of atomicity (micro-ness) of abstract things starting from tanmātras extends up to aliṅga (Prakṛti).

For instance, the particles are the minutest from of the matter; tanmātras (smell, touch, taste, sound, sight) are minuter than particles; ahaṅkāra (principle of individuality of atom) is minuter than tanmātras; liṅga (maha tattva or intelligence) is minuter than aham tattva; and aliṅga (prakṛti or homogeneous state of sattva, rajas and tamas) is the most-minute.

Note: As pointed out above, the subject matter of Savichāra and Nirvichāra samāpattis is not material objects, but abstract things which are beyond matter particles (which are the minutest object of matter). So the samāpattis are called Savichāra and Nirvichāra. Their subject matter starts with tanmātrās (smell, touch, taste, sound, sight) and goes through ahaṅkāra, mahat-tattva till pradhāna (prakṛti-the state of equilibrium of sattva, rajas and tamas).

व्यासभाष्य—पार्थिवस्याणोर्गन्धतन्मात्रं सूक्ष्मो विषयः । आप्यस्य रसतन्मात्रम् । तैजसस्य रूपतन्मात्रम् । वायवीयस्य स्पर्शतन्मात्रम् । आकाशस्य शब्दतन्मात्रमिति । तेषामहंकारः । अस्यापि लिङ्गमात्रं सूक्ष्मो विषयः ।   लिङ्गमात्रस्याप्यलिङ्गं सूक्ष्मो विषयः । न चालिङ्गात्परं सूक्ष्ममस्ति । नन्वस्ति पुरुषः सूक्ष्म इति । सत्यम् । यथा लिङ्गात्परमलिङ्गस्य सौक्ष्म्यं न चैवं पुरुषस्य । किन्तु लिङ्गस्यान्वयिकारणं पुरुषो न भवति । हेतुस्तु भवतीति । अतः प्रधाने सौक्ष्म्यं निरतिशयं व्याख्यातम् ।

भोजवृत्ति—सविचारनिर्विचारयोः समापत्त्योर्यत्सूक्ष्मविषयत्वमुक्तं तदलिङ्गपर्यवसानं न क्वचिल्लीयते न वा किंचिल्लिङ्गति गमयतीत्यलिङ्गं प्रधानं तत्पर्यन्तं सूक्ष्मविषयत्वम्। तथा हि गुणानां परिणामे चत्वारि पर्वाणि विशिष्टलिङ्गमविशिष्टलिङ्गं लिङ्गमात्रमलिङ्गं चेति। विशिष्टलिङ्गं भूतेन्द्रियाणि। अविशिष्टलिङ्गं तन्मात्रेन्द्रियाणि। लिङ्गमात्रं बुद्धिः। अलिङ्गं प्रधानमिति। नातः परं सूक्ष्ममस्तीत्युक्तं भवति। एतासां समापत्तिनां प्रकृते प्रयोजनमाह

ता एव सबीजः समाधिः ॥46॥

tā eva sabījaḥ samādhiḥ

These four Samāpattis are known as Sabīja samādhi or say, Samprajñāta Samādhi.

Note: These four Samāpattis (Savitarka and Nirvitarka, Samādhi Savichāra and Nirvichāra) are called Sabīja or Samprajñāta Samādhi, because during those states of samādhi the prakṛti in material or abstract form continues to be the subject matter. In other words, since prakṛti in seed form is present as subject matter during these four stages of samādhi, the samādhi is called Sabīja.

व्यासभाष्य—ताश्चतस्रः समापत्तयो बहिर्वस्तुबीजा इति समाधिरपि सबीजः। तत्र स्थूलेऽर्थे सवितर्को निर्वितर्कः। सूक्ष्मेऽर्थे सविचारो निर्विचार इति चतुर्धोपसंख्यातः समाधिरिति।

भोजवृत्ति—ता एवोक्तलक्षणाः समापत्तयः सह बीजेनाऽऽलम्बनेन वर्तत इति सबीजः संप्रज्ञातः समाधिरित्युच्यते सर्वासां सालम्बनत्वात्। अथेतरासां समापत्तीनां निर्विचारफलत्वान्निर्विचारायाः फलमाह

निर्विचारवैशारद्येऽध्यात्मप्रसादः ॥47॥

nirvicāravaiśāradye'dhyātmaprasādaḥ

On the perfection of pure Nirvichāra (Samādhi) the dawn of spiritual light and bliss takes place.

When a high profile yogī attains perfection in nirvichāra Samādhi his intellect becomes free from rajas and tamas guṇas, clears off all thoughts and settles down permanently in sattva guṇa. At this stage, his intellect transforms into 'ṛtambhara-prajñā' which is the highest form of intellect.

व्यासभाष्य—अशुद्ध्यावरणमलापेतस्य प्रकाशात्मनो बुद्धिसत्त्वस्य रजस्तमोभ्यामनभिभूतः स्वच्छः स्थितिप्रवाहो वैशारद्यम् । यदा निर्विचारस्य समाधेर्वैशारद्यमिदं जायते तदा योगिनो भवत्यध्यात्मप्रसादो भूतार्थविषयः क्रमाननुरोधी स्फुटः प्रज्ञालोकः । तथा चोक्तम्

प्रज्ञाप्रसादमारुह्य अशोच्यः शोचतो जनान् ।
भूमिष्ठानिव शैलस्थः सर्वान्प्राज्ञोऽनुपश्यति ।।47।।

भोजवृत्ति—निर्विचारत्वं व्याख्यातम् । वैशारद्यं नैर्मल्यम् । सवितर्कात् स्थूलविषयामपेक्ष्य निर्वितर्कायाः प्राधान्यम् । ततोऽपि सूक्ष्मविषयायाः सविचारायाः ततोऽपि निर्विकल्परूपाया निर्विचारायाः तस्यास्तु निर्विचारायाः प्रकृष्टाभ्यासवशाद्वैशारद्ये नैर्मल्ये सत्यध्यात्मप्रसादः समुपजायते । चित्तं क्लेशवासनारहितं स्थितिप्रवाह योग्यं भवति । एतदेव चित्तस्य वैशारद्यं यत्स्थितौ दार्ढ्यम् । तस्मिन्सति किं भवतीत्याह

ऋतम्भरा तत्र प्रज्ञा ।।48।।

ṛtambharā tatra prajñā

Thereafter rises the ṛtambharā prajñā. Ṛta means eternal laws of creation. So, ṛtambharā means intellect that bears the eternal laws of creation.

Here 'prajñā' bears the 'ṛta' (cosmic laws) directly. When a person rises to the state of ṛtambharā-prajñā, he knows the truth directly without the intermediary of language or thought. He achieves a state of direct enlightenment. His knowledge then is perfect. What he sees is the truth, because it is directly realized and free of subjective and situational conditions and the limitations of thought and language. His knowledge is not relative now. It is absolute which is nothing else but the Vedas. This is how Agni, Vāyu, Āditya and Aṅgirā had direct access to the knowledge of creation through their prajñā at the beginning of human creation. In fact, this creation is the embodiment of the Vedas. It is the vāk (speech) of Brahman.

व्यासभाष्य—तस्मिन्समाहितचित्तस्य या प्रज्ञा जायते तस्या ऋतंभरेति संज्ञा भवति । अन्वर्था च सा सत्यमेव बिभर्ति न च तत्र विपर्यासज्ञानगन्धोऽप्यस्तीति । तथा चोक्तम्

आगमेनानुमानेन ध्यानाभ्यासरसेन च ।

त्रिधा प्रकल्पयन्प्रज्ञां लभते योगमुत्तमम् ।।इति ।।   48 ।। सा पुनः

भोजवृत्ति—ऋतं सत्यं बिभर्ति कदाचिदपि न विपर्ययेणाऽच्छाद्यते सा ऋतंभरा प्रज्ञा तस्मिन्सति भवतीत्यर्थः । तस्माच्च प्रज्ञालोकात्सर्वं यघावत्पश्यन्योगी प्रकृष्टं योगं प्राप्नोति । अस्याः प्रज्ञान्तराद्वैलक्षण्यमाह

श्रुतानुमानप्रज्ञाभ्यामन्यविषया विशेषार्थत्वात् ।।49।।
śrutānumānaprajñābhyāmanyaviṣayā viśeṣārthatvāt

(Viśeṣārthtvāt) The knowledge of things that are beyond the power of sense organs or any material instruments (like prakṛti, soul, and Brahman) gained by ṛtambharā prajñā is unique and (anyaviṣayā) different from what is gained through (śruta) words (written in texts or spoken by experts) or (anumāna) inference because it is direct and primary knowledge.

Note: Here words mean both written in Śāstras and spoken by seers. If you see life and infer the existence of the soul, that is called inference. But the knowledge of things that are beyond the power of sense organs or any material instruments gained through ṛtambhara prajñā is direct and primary like the one had by sensory organs.

व्यासभाष्य—श्रुतमागमविज्ञानं तत्सामान्यविषयम् । न ह्यागमेन शक्यो विशेषोऽभिधातुं । कस्मात् । न हि विशेषेण कृतसंकेतः शब्द इति । तथाऽनुमानं सामान्यविषयमेव । यत्र प्राप्तिस्तत्र गतिर्यत्राप्राप्तिस्तत्र न गतिरित्युक्तम् । अनुमानेन च सामान्येनोपसंहारः । तस्माच्छ्रुतानुमानविषयो न विशेषः कश्चिदस्तीति । न चास्य सूक्ष्मव्यवहितविप्रकृष्टस्य वस्तुनो लोकप्रत्यक्षेण ग्रहणमस्ति । न चास्य विशेषस्याप्रमाणकस्याभावोऽस्तीति समाधिप्रज्ञानिर्ग्राह्य एव स विशेषो भवति भूतसूक्ष्मगतो वा पुरुषगतो वा । तस्माच्छ्रुतानुमानप्रज्ञाभ्यामन्यविषया सा प्रज्ञा विशेषार्थत्वादिति । समाधिप्रज्ञाप्रतिलम्भे योगिनः प्रज्ञाकृतः संस्कारो नवो नवो जायते

भोजवृत्ति—श्रुतमागमज्ञानम् अनुमानमुक्तलक्षणम् ताभ्यां या जायते प्रज्ञा सा सामान्यविषया । न हि शब्दलिङ्गयोरिन्द्रियवद्विशेषप्रतिपत्तौ सामर्थ्यम् । इयं पुनर्निर्विचारवैशारद्यसमुद्भवा प्रज्ञा ताभ्यां विलक्षणा विशेषविषयत्वात् । अस्यां हि प्रज्ञायां सूक्ष्मव्यवहितविप्रकृष्टानामपि विशेषः स्फुटेनैव रूपेण भासते । अतस्तस्यामेव योगिना परः प्रयत्नः कर्तव्य इत्युपदिष्टं भवति । अस्याः प्रज्ञायाः फलमाह

तज्जः संस्कारोऽन्यसंस्कारप्रतिबन्धी ।।50।।

tajjaḥ saṃskāro'nyasaṃskārapratibandhī

The sanskāra of knowledge gained through ṛtambharā prajñā supersedes all other sanskāras of knowledge gained through other secondary means.

Note: After the development of ṛtambharā prajñā, the knowledge of the creation and decreation of this material world is revealed to the yogī. So, now his sanskāras of this true knowledge developed due to ṛtambharā superseding all the previous sanskāras pertaining to the material world. Thus during this state, a yogī imbibes the complete knowledge of the material world. Here it should be known that now a yogī has refined sanskāras of the material world, but sanskāras are still there. If he stops here, he will not attain mokṣa. Mokṣa is attained when sanskāras developed through ṛtambharā prajñā are also eliminated. So, how can it happen? The same has been discussed in the following sūtra.

व्यासभाष्य—समाधिप्रज्ञाप्रभवः संस्कारो व्युत्थानसंस्काराशयं बाधते । व्युत्थानसंस्काराभिभवात्तत्प्रभवाः प्रत्यया न भवन्ति । प्रत्ययनिरोधे समाधिरुपतिष्ठते । ततः समाधिजा प्रज्ञा ततःप्रज्ञाकृताः संस्कारा इति नवो नवः संस्काराशयो जायते । ततश्च प्रज्ञा ततश्च संस्कारा इति । कथमसौ संस्काराशयश्चित्तं साधिकारं न करिष्यतीति । न ते प्रज्ञाकृताः संस्काराः क्लेशक्षयहेतुत्वाच्चित्तमधिकारविशिष्टं कुर्वन्ति । चित्तं हि ते स्वकायादवसादयन्ति । ख्यातिपर्यवसानं हि चित्तचेष्टितमिति । किं चास्य भवति

भोजवृत्ति—तया प्रज्ञया जनितो यः संस्कारः सोऽन्यान्व्युत्थानजान्समाधिजांश्च संस्कारान्प्रतिबध्नाति स्वकार्यकरणाक्षमान्करोतीत्यर्थः । यतस्तत्त्वरूपतयाऽनया जनिताः संस्कारा बलबत्त्वादतत्त्वरूपप्रज्ञाजनितान्संस्कारान्बाधितुं शक्नुवन्ति । अतस्तामेव प्रज्ञामभ्यसेदित्युक्तं भवति । एवं संप्रज्ञातं समाधिमभिधायासंप्रज्ञातं वक्तुमाह

तस्यापि निरोधे सर्वनिरोधान्निर्बीजः समाधिः ॥51॥

tasyāpi nirodhe sarvanirodhānnirbījaḥ samādhiḥ

While doing practice of Samādhi constantly, a yogī switches from Sabīja Samādhi over to Nirbīja Samādhi. At this stage, his Sabīja Samādhi ceases to occur. At the cessation of Sabīja Samādhi, the sanskāras gained through ṛtambharā prajñā during Nirvichāra Samādhi are also eliminated, then all the sanskāras having been eliminated, Nirbīja samādhi is attained.

व्यासभाष्य—स न केवलं समाधिप्रज्ञाविरोधी प्रज्ञाकृतानामपि संस्काराणां प्रतिबन्धी भवति । कस्मात् । निरोधजः संस्कारः समाधिजान्संस्कारान्बाधत इति ।

निरोधस्थितिकालक्रमानुभवेन निरोधचित्तकृतसंस्कारास्तित्वमनुमेयम् । व्युत्थाननिरोधसमाधिप्रभवैः सह कैवल्यभागीयैः संस्कारैश्चित्तं स्वस्यां प्रकृताववस्थितायां प्रविलीयते । तस्मात्ते संस्काराश्चित्तस्याधिकारविरोधिनो न स्थितिहेतवो भवन्तीति । यस्मादवसिताधिकारं सह कैवल्यभागीयैः संस्कारैश्चित्तं निवर्तते तस्मिन्निवृत्ते पुरुषः स्वरूपमात्रप्रतिष्ठोऽतः शुद्धः केवलो मुक्त इत्युच्यत इति ।

इति श्रीपातञ्जले सांख्यप्रवचने योगशास्त्रे श्रीमद्व्यासभाष्ये प्रथमः समाधिपादः ।।1।।

भोजवृत्ति—तस्यापि संप्रज्ञातस्य निरोधे प्रविलये सति सर्वासां चित्तवृत्तीनां स्वकारणे प्रविलयाद्या या संस्कारमात्राद्वृत्तिरुदेति तस्यास्तस्या नेति नेतीति केवलं पर्युदसनान्निर्बीजः समाधिराविर्भवति । यस्मिन्सति पुरुषः स्वरूपनिष्ठः शुद्धो भवति । तदत्राधिकृतस्य योगस्य लक्षणं चित्तवृत्तिनिरोधपदानां च व्याख्यानमभ्यासवैराग्यलक्षणं तस्योपायद्वयस्य स्वरूपं भेदं चाभिधाय संप्रज्ञातासंप्रज्ञातभेदेन योगस्य मुख्यामुख्यभेदमुक्त्वा योगाभ्यासप्रदर्शनपूर्वकं विस्तरेणोपायान्प्रदर्श्य सुगमोपायप्रदर्शनपरतयेश्वरस्य स्वरूपप्रमाणप्रभाववाचकोपासनाक्रमं तत्फलानि च निर्णीय चित्तविक्षेपांस्तत्सहभुवश्च दुःखादीन्विस्तरेण च तत्प्रतिषेधोपायानेकत्त्वाभ्यास-मैत्र्यादीन्प्राणायामादीन्संप्रज्ञातासंप्रज्ञातपूर्वाङ्गभूतविषयवती प्रवृत्तिरित्यादीन् च आख्यायोपसंहारद्वारेण च समापत्तीः सलक्षणाः सफलाः स्वस्वविषयसहिताश्चोक्त्वा संप्रज्ञातासंप्रज्ञातयोरुपसंहारमभिधाय सबीजपूर्वको निर्बीजः समाधिरभिहित इति व्याकृतो योगपादः ।

इति श्री भोजदेवविरचितायां पातञ्जलयोगशास्त्रसूत्रवृत्तौ प्रथमः समाधिपादः ।।1।।

इति पतञ्जलि-विरचिते योग-सूत्रे प्रथमः समाधि-पादः ॥

iti patañjali-viracite yoga-sūtre prathamaḥ samādhi-pādaḥ

Here ends the Samādhi-pāda composed by Patañjali

द्वितीयोऽध्यायः
Dvitīyo'dhyāyaḥ

साधन-पादः
Sādhana-pāda

(Means to practice Yoga)

तपःस्वाध्यायेश्वरप्रणिधानानि क्रियायोगः ॥1॥
tapaḥsvādhyāyeśvarapraṇidhānāni kriyāyogaḥ

Observance of yamas and niyamas, āsana and prāṇāyāma, etc. study of Vedas and other Śāstras, and meditation on God is called Kriyāyoga (practice of yoga).

i). Tapaḥ

According to the Gita, tapas is of three types:-

1- शारीरिकतप (Austerity of the body) 2- वाक्तप (Austerity of speech) 3- मानसतप (Austerity of Mind)

1. शारीरिकतप (Austerity of the body): According to Bhagvadgitā, this type of Tapas consists in giving respect to and care of the scholars, learned people, Gurus (Āchārya, Mother and Father), maintenance of cleanliness, simplicity, celibacy, and non-violence. It is said-

देवद्विजगुरुप्राज्ञपूजनं शौचमार्जवम् ।

ब्रह्मचर्यम अहिंसा च शरीरं तप उच्यते ॥

2. वाक्तप (Austerity of speech): The tapas consists in speaking words that are truthful, pleasing, beneficial and not agitating to others and also in regularly reciting Vedic hymns. The same is said:

अनुद्वेगकरं वाक्यं सत्यं प्रियं हितं च यत् ।

स्वाध्यायाभ्यसनं चैव वाङ्मयं तप उच्यते ॥

3. मानसतप (Austerity of Mind): This kind of Tapas consists in the serenity of mind, gentleness, silence, self-restraint, and the purity of thought.

मनः प्रसाद सौम्यत्वं मौनमात्मविनिग्रहः ।

भावसंशुद्धिरित्येतत् तपो मानसमुच्यते ॥

Tapas is to tolerate the pairs of opposites - 'तपो द्वन्द्वसहनम्' The pairs of opposites are hunger and thirst, heat and cold, etc. Maharṣi Patañjali said all the impurities can be removed by penance so that perfection of the body and the senses can be achieved. 'कायेन्द्रियसिद्धिरशुद्धिक्षयात्तपसः' Kena Upaniṣad describes the three pillars of the entire structure of Brahmavidyā or Spiritual Science as Tapas (austerity), Dama (self-restraint) and Karma (Action). The trio of Tapas, Brahmacharya, and Satya has been repeatedly emphasized in Praśnopaniṣad (5.3) and other Upaniṣads. So Tapas is one of the necessary elements to attain perfection

ii) Svādhyāya

The study and practice of Vedas, Śāstras, and spirituality is Svādhyāya. The self-contemplation is also known as Japa. Japa consists in reciting the Sacred syllable 'AUM' the name of Lord.

'स्वाध्यायः मोक्षशास्त्राणामध्ययनं प्राणवजपोवा'

The study of the Śāstras, the Vedas, and the Upaniṣads including the other literature associated with these influences thoughts, takes away the fickleness of mind, ennobles the soul and removes malice and evils.

A Kriyāyogī is neither worried about his past nor

cares about the future. He is a creature of the present. He doesn't permit others to assess him. He is ever progressive. He knows his weakness and he is also conscious of the hurdles that he is likely to face on his path.

iii) Iśvara Praṇidhāna

Iśvara-Praṇidhāna means to dedicate all actions to the Supreme soul. 'ईश्वरप्रणिधानं तस्मिन्परमगुरौ सर्वकर्मार्पणम् ।'.

Iśvara-Praṇidhāna is one of the alternate means of attaining Samādhi. It is said in Yogadarśana- 'ईश्वरप्रणिधानाद्वा ।'

Iśvara is distinguishable from us - so he is called as Puruṣa Viśeṣa (Special Puruṣa) who remains unbound and unclung to pains and sufferings, to actions, to the fruits of actions, and to the tendencies left there after. Iśvara is Omniscient; the depth of his knowledge is unfathomable. He is the teacher of the ṛṣis. AUM (praṇava) is the designation of Iśvara. Iśvara, is the surest way of obtaining concentration and thereby liberation. Iśvarapranidana is the means to Samādhi. The same is said: समाधिसिद्धिरीश्वप्रणिधानात् ।

व्यासभाष्य—नातपस्विनो योगः सिध्यति । अनादिकर्मक्लेशवासनाचित्रा प्रत्युपस्थितविषयजाला चाशुद्धिर्नान्तरेण तपः संभेदमापद्यत इति तपस उपादानम् । तच्च चित्तप्रसादनमबाधमानमनेनाऽऽसेव्यमिति मन्यते । स्वाध्यायः प्रणवादिपवित्राणां जपो मोक्षशास्त्राध्ययनं वा । ईश्वरप्रणिधानं सर्वक्रियाणां परमगुरावर्पणं तत्फलसंन्यासो वा । स हि क्रियायोगः

भोजवृत्ति—तदेवं प्रथमे पादे समाहितचित्तस्य सोपायं योगमभिधाय व्युत्थितचित्तस्यापि कथमुपायाभ्यासपूर्वको योगः स्वास्थ्यम् उपयातीति तत्साधनानुष्ठानप्रतिपादनाय क्रियायोगमाह ।

तपः शास्त्रान्तरोपदिष्टं कृच्छ्रचान्द्रायणादि । स्वाध्यायः प्रणवपूर्वाणां मन्त्राणां जपः । ईश्वरप्रणिधानं सर्वक्रियाणां तस्मिन्परमगुरौ फलनिरपेक्षतया समर्पणम् । एतानि क्रियायोग इत्युच्यते । स किमर्थ इत्यत आह

समाधिभावनार्थः क्लेशतनूकरणार्थश्च ॥2॥

samādhibhāvanārthaḥ kleśatanūkaraṇārthaśca

Kriya-yoga (practice) is for bringing about perfection in samadhi and minimising the afflictions (kleśas).

व्यासभाष्य—स ह्यासेव्यमानः समाधि भावयति क्लेशांश्च प्रतनू करोति । प्रतनूकृतान्क्लेशान्प्रसंख्यानाग्निना दग्धबीजकल्पानप्रसवधर्मिणः करिष्यतीति । तेषां तनूकरणात्पुनः क्लेशैरपरामृष्टा सत्त्वपुरुषान्यतामात्रख्यातिः सूक्ष्मा प्रज्ञा समाप्ताधिकारा प्रतिप्रसवाय कल्पिष्यत इति । अथ के क्लेशाः कियन्तो वेति

भोजवृत्ति—क्लेशा वक्ष्यमाणस्तेषां तनूकरणं स्वकार्यकारणप्रतिबन्धः । समाधिरुक्तलक्षणस्तस्य भावना चेतसि पुनः पुनर्निवेशनं सोऽर्थः प्रयोजन यस्य स तथोक्तः । एतदुक्तं भवति एते तपः प्रभृतयोऽभ्यस्यमानाश्चित्तगतानविच्चादीन्क्लेशाञ्छिथिली कुर्वन्तः समाधेरुपकारकतां भजन्ते । तस्मात्प्रथमतः क्रियायोगवधानपरेण योगिना भवितव्यमित्युपदिष्टम् । क्लेशतनूकरणार्थ इत्युक्तं तत्र के क्लेशा इत्यत आह

अविद्यास्मितारागद्वेषाभिनिवेशाः क्लेशाः ॥3॥

avidyāsmitārāgadveṣābhiniveśāḥ kleśāḥ

The afflictions are: avidyā, asmitā, rāga, dveṣa, and abhiniveśa. They will be explained by Patañjali in the following sūtras.

व्यासभाष्य—क्लेशा इति पञ्च विपर्यया इत्यर्थः । ते स्यन्दमाना गुणाधिकारदृढयन्ति परिणाममवस्थापयन्ति कार्यकारणस्रोत उन्नमयन्ति परस्परानुग्रहतन्त्री भूत्वा कर्मविपाकं चाभिनिर्हरन्तीति ।

भोजवृत्ति—अविद्यादयो वक्ष्यमाणलक्षणाः पञ्च । ते च बाधनालक्षणं परितापमुपजनयन्तः क्लेशशब्दवाच्या भवन्ति । ते हि चेतसि प्रवर्तमानाः संस्कारलक्षणं गुणपरिणामं दृढयन्ति । सत्यपि सर्वेषां तुल्ये क्लेशत्वे मूलभूतत्वादविद्यायाः प्राधान्यं प्रतिपादयितुमाह

अविद्या क्षेत्रमुत्तरेषां प्रसुप्ततनुविच्छिन्नोदाराणाम् ॥4॥

avidyā kṣetramuttareṣāṃ prasuptatanuvicchinnodārāṇām

Avidyā is the breeding ground of the succeeding ones, i.e, asmitā, rāga, dveṣa, and abhiniveśa, whether they are dormant (sleeping), attenuated (weak), fitful or active and strong.

Dormant (प्रसुप्तावस्था):- This is the stage in which they

(Kleśas) are hidden like the tree in the seed. They are manifested when they find a conducive atmosphere.

Weak (तनु):- In this stage, they are (kleśas) are in an attenuated condition. They can be weakened. For example, one evil vāsanā (sanskāra) can be weakened by developing a good vāsanā to counter it. Anger can be weakened by developing mercy, love, and forgiveness, etc.

Active or fitful (विच्छिन्न): In this stage, kleśas are active or occurring spasmodically or intermittently; but not regular or steady. For example, anger or hatred doesn't occur when a person is in love.

Strong (उदार):- In this stage, the kleśas are very powerful. Their operation will be in force.

व्यासभाष्य—अत्राविद्या क्षेत्रं प्रसवभूमिरुत्तरेषामस्मितादीनां चतुर्विधविकल्पानां प्रसुप्ततनुविच्छिन्नोदाराणाम्। तत्र का प्रसुप्तिः। चेतसि शक्तिमात्रप्रतिष्ठानां बीजभावोपगमः। तस्य प्रबोध आलम्बने संमुखीभावः। प्रसंख्यानवतो दग्धक्लेशबीजस्य संमुखीभूतेऽप्यालम्बने नासौ पुनरस्ति। दग्धबीजस्य कुतः प्ररोह इति। अतः क्षीणक्लेशः कुशलश्चरमदेह इत्युच्यते। तत्रैव सा दग्धबीजभावा पञ्चमी क्लेशावस्था नान्यत्रेति। सतां क्लेशानां तदा बीजसामर्थ्यं दग्धमिति विषयस्य संमुखीभावेऽपि सति न भवत्येषां प्रबोध इत्युक्ता प्रसुप्तिर्दग्धबीजानामप्ररोहश्च।

तनुत्वमुच्यते प्रतिपक्षभावनोपहताः क्लेशास्तनवो भवन्ति। तथा विच्छिद्य विच्छिद्य तेन तेनाऽऽत्मना पुनः पुनः समुदाचरन्तीति विच्छिन्न। कथं रागकाले क्रोधस्यादर्शनात्। न हि रागकाले क्रोधः समुदाचरति। रागश्च क्वचिद्दृश्यमानो न विषयान्तरे नास्ति। नैकस्यां स्त्रियां चैत्रो रक्त इत्यन्यासु स्त्रीषु विरक्तः किं तु तत्र रागो लब्धवृत्तिरन्यत्र तु भविष्यद्वृत्तिरिति। स हि तदा प्रसुप्ततनुविच्छिन्नो भवति।

विषये यो लब्धवृत्तिः स उदारः। सर्व एवैते क्लेशविषयलंघनातिक्रामन्ति। कस्तर्हि विच्छिन्नः प्रसुप्ततनुरुदारो वा क्लेश इति। उच्यते सत्यमेवैतत् किंतु विशिष्टानामेवैतेषां विच्छिन्नादित्वम्। यथैव प्रतिपक्षभावनातो निवृत्तस्तथैव स्वव्यञ्जकाञ्जनेनाभिव्यक्त इति। सर्व एवामी क्लेशा अविद्याभेदाः। कस्मात् सर्वेष्वविद्यैवाभिप्लवते। यदविद्यया वस्त्वाकार्यत तदेवानुशेरते क्लेशा विपर्यासप्रत्ययकाल उपलभ्यन्ते क्षीयमाणां चाविद्यामनु क्षीयन्त इति। तत्राविद्यास्वरूपमुच्यते

भोजवृत्ति—अविद्या मोहः अनात्मन्यात्माभिमान इति यावत्। सो क्षेत्रं प्रसवभूमिरुत्तरेषामस्मितादीनां प्रत्येकं प्रसुप्ततन्वादिभेदेन चतुर्विधानाम्। अतो यत्राविद्या विपर्ययज्ञानरूपा शिथिली भवति तत्र क्लेशानामस्मितादीनां नोद्भवो दृश्यते। विपर्ययज्ञानसद्भावे च

तेषामुद्बवदर्शनात्स्थितमेव मूलत्वमविद्यायाः । प्रसुप्ततनुविच्छित्रोदाराणामिति । तत्र ये क्लेशाश्चित्तभूमौ स्थितः प्रबोधकाभावे स्वकार्यं नाऽऽरभन्ते ते प्रसुप्ता इत्युच्यन्ते । यथा बालावस्थायां बालस्य हि वासनारूपेण स्थिता अपि क्लेशाः प्रबोधकसहकार्यभावे नाभिव्यज्यन्ते । ते तनवो ये स्वस्वप्रतिपक्षभावनया शिथिलीकृतकार्यसंपादनशक्तयो वासनावशेषतया चेतस्यवस्थिताः प्रभूतां सामग्रीमन्तरेण स्वकार्यमारब्धुमक्षमाः । यथाऽभ्यासवतो योगिनः । ते विच्छिन्ना ये केनचिद्वलवता क्लेशेनाभिभूतशक्तयस्तिष्ठन्ति यथा द्वेषावस्थायां रागः रागावस्थायां वा द्वेषः न ह्यनयोः परस्परविरुद्धयोर्युम्मत्संभवोऽस्ति । त उदारा ये प्राप्तसहकारिसंनिधयः स्वं स्वं कार्यमभिनिर्वर्तयन्ति यथा सदैव योगपरिपन्थिनो व्युत्थानदशायाम् । एषां प्रत्येकं चतुर्विधानामपि मूलभूतत्वेन स्थिताऽप्यविद्याऽन्वयित्वेन प्रतीयते । न हि क्वचिदपि क्लेशानां विपर्ययान्वयनिरपेक्षाणां स्वरूपमुपलभ्यते । तस्यां च मिथ्यारूपायामविद्यायां सम्यग्ज्ञानेन निवर्तितायां दग्धबीजकल्पानामेषां न क्वचित्प्ररोहोऽस्ति अतोऽविद्यानिमित्तत्वमविद्यान्वयश्चैतेषां निश्चियते । अतः सर्वेऽपि अविद्याव्यपदेशभाजः । सर्वेषां च क्लेशानां चित्तविक्षेपकारित्वायोगिना प्रथममेव तदुच्छेदे यत्नः कार्य इति । अविद्याया लक्षणमाह

अनित्याशुचिदुःखानात्मसु नित्यशुचिसुखात्मख्यातिरविद्या ॥5॥

anityāśuciduḥkhānātmasu nityaśucisukhātmakhyātiravidyā

Avidyā is the sense of permanence in transient, of purity in the impure, of pleasure in the painful, of soul in the matter.

For example, if you think temporary things as permanent and permanent as temporary, it is avidyā. If you think rope as a serpent, it is avidyā. If you think you body as soul, it is avidyā.

व्यासभाष्य—अनित्ये कार्ये नित्यख्यातिः । तद्यथा ध्रुवा पृथिवी ध्रुवा सचन्द्रतारका द्यौः । अमृता दिवौकस इति । तथाऽशुचौ परमबीभत्से काये

स्थानाद्बीजादुपष्टम्भान्निः स्यन्दान्निधनादपि ।
कायमाधेयशौचत्वात्पण्डिता ह्यशुचिं विदुः ॥

इति अशुचौ शरीरे शुचिख्यातिर्दृश्यते । नवेव शशाङ्कलेखा कमनीयेयं कन्या मध्वमृतावयवनिर्मितेव चन्द्रं भित्त्वा निःसृतेव ज्ञायते नीलोत्पलपत्रायताक्षी हावगर्भाभ्यां लोचनाभ्यां जीवलोकमाश्वासयन्तीवेति कस्य केनाभिसंबन्धः । भवति चैवमशुचौ शुचिविपर्यासप्रत्यय इति । एतेनापुण्ये पुण्यप्रत्ययस्तथैवानर्थे चार्थ प्रत्ययो व्याख्यातः ।

तथा दुःखे सुखख्यातिं वक्ष्यति परिणामतापसंस्कारदुःखैर्गुणवृत्तिविरोधाच्च दुःखमेव सर्व विवेकिनः यो ० सू० 2.15 इति । तत्र सुखख्यातिरविद्या । तथाऽनात्मन्यात्मख्यातिर्बाह्योपकरणेषु चेतनाचेतनेषु भोगाधिष्ठाने वा शरीरे पुरुषोपकरणे वा मनस्यनात्मन्यात्मख्यातिरिति । तथैतदत्रोक्तम्

व्यक्तमव्यक्तं वा सत्त्वमात्मत्वेनाभिप्रतीत्य तस्य संपदमनु नन्दत्यात्मसंपदं मन्वानस्तस्य व्यापदमनु शोचत्यात्मव्यापदं मन्वानः स सर्वोऽप्रतिबुद्धः इति । एषा चतुष्पदा भवत्यविद्या मूलमस्य क्लेशसंतानस्य कर्माशयस्य च सविपाकस्येति ।

तस्याश्चामित्रागोष्पदवद्वस्तुसतत्त्वं विज्ञेयम् । यथा नामित्रो मित्राभावो न मित्रभावं किं तु तद्विरुद्धः सपत्नः । यथा वाऽगोष्पदं न गोष्पदाभावो न गोष्पदमात्रं किंतु देश एव ताभ्यामन्यद्वस्त्वन्तरम् एवमविद्या न प्रमाणं न प्रमाणाभावः किन्तु विद्याविपरीतं ज्ञानान्तरमविद्येति ।

भोजवृत्ति—अतस्मिंस्तदिति प्रतिभासोऽविद्येत्यविद्यायाः सामान्यलक्षणम् । तस्या एव भेदप्रतिपादनम् अनित्येषु घटादिषु नित्यत्वाभिमानोऽविद्येत्युच्यते । एवमशुचिषु कायादिषु शुचित्वाभिमानः दुःखेषु च विषयेषु सुखत्वाभिमानः अनात्मनि शरीर आत्मत्वाभिमानः । एतेनापुण्ये पुण्यभ्रमोऽनर्थे चार्थभ्रमो व्याख्यातः । अस्मितां लक्षयितुमाह

दृग्दर्शनशक्त्योरेकात्मतेवास्मिता ॥6॥
dṛgdarśanaśaktyorekātmatevāsmitā

Asmitā is the identification of the seer with the power of the seeing.

The soul is the seer and eyes are the power of Seeing, so considering eyes as a seer is asmitā.

व्यासभाष्य —पुरुषो दृक्शक्तिर्बुद्धिर्दर्शनशक्तिरित्येतयोरेकस्वरूपापत्तिरिवास्मिता क्लेश उच्यते । भोक्तृभोग्यशक्त्योरत्यन्तविभक्तयोरत्यन्तसंकीर्णयोरविभागप्राप्ताविव सत्यां भोगः कल्पते । स्वरूपप्रतिलम्भे तु तयोः कैवल्यमेव भवति कुतो भोग इति । तथा चोक्तम् बुद्धितः परं पुरुषमाकारशीलविद्यादिभिर्विभक्तपश्यन्कुर्यात्तत्राऽऽत्मबुद्धिं मोहेन इति ।

भोजवृत्ति—दृक्शक्तिः पुरुषः दर्शनशक्ति रजस्तमोभ्यामनभिभूतः सात्त्विकः परिणामोऽन्तः करणरूपः अनयोर्भोग्यभोक्तृत्वेन जडाजडत्वेनात्यन्तभिन्नरूपयोरेकताभिमानोऽस्मितेति उच्यते । यथा प्रकृतिवता कर्तृत्वभोक्तृत्वरहितेनापि कर्त्यहं भोक्र्यहमित्यभिमन्यते । सोऽयमस्मिताख्यो विपर्यासः क्लेशः । रागस्य लक्षणमाह

सुखानुशयी रागः ॥7॥
sukhānuśayī rāgaḥ

Once having gone through a pleasurable experience, the desire to seek the pleasure again is called Rāga or attachment.

व्यासभाष्य—सुखाभिज्ञस्य सुखानुस्मृतिपूर्वः सुखे तत्साधने वा यो गर्धस्तृष्णा लोभः स राग इति ।

व्यासभाष्य—सुखमनुशेत इति सुखानुशयी सुखज्ञस्य सुखानुस्मृतिपूर्वकः सुखसाधनेषु तृष्णारूपो गर्धो रागसंज्ञकः क्लेशः । द्वेषस्य लक्षणमाह

दुःखानुशयी द्वेषः ॥8॥
duḥkhānuśayī dveṣaḥ

Once having gone through a painful experience, the arousal of aversion from pain is known as dveṣa.

व्यासभाष्य—दुःखाभिज्ञस्य दुःखानुस्मृतिपूर्वो दुःखे तत्साधने वा यः प्रतिघोमन्युर्जिघांसा क्रोधः स द्वेषः ।

भोजवृत्ति—दुःखमुक्तलक्षणं तदभिज्ञस्य तदनुस्मृतिपूर्वकं तत्साधनेषु अनभिलषतो योऽयं निन्दात्मकः क्रोधः स द्वेषलक्षण क्लेशः । अभिनिवेशस्य लक्षणमाह

स्वरसवाही विदुषोऽपि तथारूढोऽभिनिवेशः ॥9॥
svarasavāhī viduṣo'pi tathārūḍho'bhiniveśaḥ

The natural fear of death which prevails upon learned and laity alike is called abhiniveśa.

Note: Fear of death is natural to all, because everybody has experienced it in past lives.

व्यासभाष्य—सर्वस्य प्राणिन इयमात्माशीर्नित्या भवति मा न भूवं भूयासमिति । न चाननुभूतमरणधर्मकस्यैषा भवत्यात्माशीः । एतया च पूर्वजन्मानुभवः प्रतीयते । स चायमभिनिवेशः क्लेशः स्वरसवाही कृमेरपि जातमात्रस्य प्रत्यक्षानुमानागमैरसंभावितो मरणत्रास उच्छेदटृष्ट्यात्मकः पूर्वजन्मानुभूतं मरणदुःखमनुमापयति ।

यथा चायमत्यन्तमूढेषु दृश्यते क्लेशस्तथा विदुषोऽपि विज्ञातपूर्वापरान्तस्य रूढः । कस्मात् । समाना हि तयोः कुशलाकुशलयोर्मरणदुःखानुभवादियं वासनेति ।

भोजवृत्ति—पूर्वजन्मानुभूतमरणदुःखानुभववासनाबलाद्द्वयरूपः समुपजायमानः शरीरविषयादिभिः मम वियोगो मा भूदिति अन्वहमनुबन्धरूपः सर्वस्यैवाऽऽकृमेर्ब्रह्मपर्यन्तं निमित्तमन्तरेण प्रवर्तमानोऽभिनिवेशाख्यः क्लेशः ।

तदेवं व्युत्थानस्य क्लेशात्मकत्वादेकाग्रताभ्यासकामेन प्रथमं क्लेशाः परिहर्तव्याः । न चाज्ञातानां तेषां परिहार कर्तुं शक्य इति तज्ज्ञानाय तेषामुपदेशं क्षेत्रं विभागं लणणं चाभिधाय स्थूलसूक्ष्मभेदभिन्नानां तेषां प्रहाणोपायविभागमाह

ते प्रतिप्रसवहेयाः सूक्ष्माः ॥10॥

te pratiprasavaheyāḥ sūkṣmāḥ

These afflictions (kleśas) are reduced, through the practice of kriyāyoga, in the form of sanskāras in their source of origin, i.e. mind. However, they find their final resolution when the mind itself is resolved on self-realization.

व्यासभाष्य—ते पञ्च क्लेशा दग्धबीजकल्पा योगिनश्चरिताधिकारे चेतसि प्रलीने सह तेनैवास्तं गच्छन्ति । स्थितानां तु बीजभावोपगतानाम्

भोजवृत्ति—ते सूक्ष्माः क्लेशा ये वासनारूपेणैव स्थिता न वृत्तिरूपं परिणाममारभन्ते ते प्रतिप्रसवेन प्रतिलोमपरिणामेन हेयास्त्यक्तव्याः । स्वकारणास्मितायां कृतार्थं सवासनं चित्तं यदा प्रविष्टं भवति तदा कुतस्तेषां निर्मूलानां संभवः । स्थूलानां हानोपायमाह

ध्यानहेयास्तद्वृत्तयः ॥11॥

dhyānaheyāstadvṛttayaḥ

The tendencies of kleśas are to be eliminated by meditation.

Through Meditation, we can eliminate the tendencies of the five kleśas. By following Kriya-yoga, tapas (austerity), svādhyāya (study of Śāstras), īśvarapraṇidhāna (dedicating all acts to God) one can minimize these kleśas but by meditation, all the kleśas can be eliminated.

व्यासभाष्य—क्लेशानां या वृत्तयः स्थूलास्ताः क्रियायोगेन तनूकृताः सत्य प्रसंख्यानेन ध्यानेन हातव्या यावत्सूक्ष्मीकृता यावद्दग्धबीजकल्पा इति । यथा वस्त्राणां स्थूलो मलः पूर्वं निर्धूयते पश्चात्सूक्ष्मो यत्नेनोपायेन वाऽपनीयते तथा स्वल्पप्रतिपक्षाः स्थूला वृत्तयः क्लेशानां सूक्ष्मास्तु महाप्रतिपक्षा इति ।

भोजवृत्ति—तेषां क्लेशानामारब्धकार्याणां याः सुखदुःखमोहात्मिका वृत्तयस्ता ध्यानेनैव चित्तैकाग्रतालक्षणेन हेया हातव्या इत्यर्थः । चित्तपरिकर्माभ्यासमात्रेणैव स्थूलत्त्वात्तासां निवृत्तिर्भवति । यथा वस्त्रादौ स्थूलो मलः प्रक्षालनमात्रेणैव निवर्तते यस्तु तत्र सूक्ष्मः स तैस्तैरुपायैरुत्तापनप्रभृतिभिरेव निवर्तयितुं शक्यते । एवं क्लेशानां तत्त्वमभिधाय कर्माशयस्याभिधातुमाह

क्लेशमूलः कर्माशयो दृष्टादृष्टजन्मवेदनीयः ॥12॥

kleśamūlaḥ karmāśayo dṛṣṭādṛṣṭajanmavedanīyaḥ

Sanskāras of these afflictions fructify in the present life and in future lives.

व्यासभाष्य—तत्र पुण्यापुण्यकर्माशयः कामलोभमोहक्रोधप्रभवः स दृष्टजन्मवेदनी-यश्चादृष्टजन्मवेदनीयश्च । तत्र तीव्रसंवेगेन मन्त्रतपः समाधिभिर्निर्वर्तितः ईश्वरदेवतामहर्षिमहानुभावानामाराधनाद्वा यः परिनिष्पन्नः स सद्यः परिपच्यते पुण्यकर्माशय इति । तथा तीव्रक्लेशेन भीतव्याधितकृपणेषु विश्वासोपगतेषु वा महानुभावेषु वा तपस्विषु कृतः पुनः पुनरपकारः स चापि पापकर्माशयः सद्य एव परिपच्यते । यथा नन्दीश्वरः कुमारो मनुष्यपरिणामं हित्वा देवत्वेन परिणतः । तथा नहुषोऽपि देवानामिन्द्रः स्वकं परिणामं हित्वा तिर्यक्त्वेन परिणत इति । तत्र नारकाणां नास्ति दृष्टजन्मवेदनीयः कर्माशयः । क्षीणक्लेशानामपि नास्त्यदृष्टजन्मवेदनीयः कर्माशय इति ।

भोजवृत्ति—कर्माशय इत्यनेन तस्य स्वरूपमभिहितम् । यतो वासनारूपाण्येव कर्माणि क्लेशमूल इत्यनेन कारणमभिहितम् । यतः कर्मणां शुभाशुभानां क्लेशा एव निमित्तम् । दृष्टादृष्टजन्मवेदनीय इत्यनेन फलमुक्तम् । अस्मिन्नेव जन्मनि अनुभवनीयो दृष्टजन्मवेदनीयः । जन्मान्तरानुभवनीयोऽदृष्टजन्मवेदनीयः । तथा हि कानिचित्पुण्यानि कर्माणि देवताराधनादीनि तीव्रसंवेगेन कृतानीहैव जन्मनि जात्यायुर्भोगलक्षणं फलं प्रयच्छन्ति यथा नन्दीश्वरस्य भगवन्महेश्वराराधनबलादिहैव जन्मनि जात्यादयो विशिष्टाः प्रादुर्भूताः । एवमन्येषां विश्वामित्रादीनां तपः प्रभावाज्जात्यायुषी । केषांचिज्जातिरेव यथा तीव्रसंवेगेन दुष्कर्मकृतां नहुषादीनां जात्यन्तरादिपरिणामः । उर्वश्याश्च कार्तिकेयवने लतारूपतया । एवं व्यस्तसमस्तरूपत्वेन यथायोगं योज्यम् । इदानीं कर्माशयस्य स्वभेदभिन्नस्य फलमाह

सति मूले तद्विपाको जात्यायुर्भोगाः ॥13॥

sati mūle tadvipāko jātyāyurbhogāḥ

As long as the kleśas are there in the mind in the form of sanskāras, they are bound to result in Jāti (yoni or species), Āyu (life span), and Bhoga (rewards of karmas).

The Kleśas if not completely uprooted would lead to three consequences- Jati (yoni or species), Āyu (life span), and Bhoga (rewards of karmas). Āyu is the whole life span in a particular Jāti (the species or yoni in which a person is to be born according to his/her kārmika sanskāras) and not the span of a life in a yoni. For man, the normal expectancy of one life is a hundred years or so. For dog, the expectancy of one life would be eight to ten years and a cow may live for 20 years, etc. Here, it may be known that sanskāras determine the total life span of an individual in a particular yoni (species), whether he/she lives it in one life or many lives in that particular yoni. For example, if a person is to live human life for 1000 years as per his/her sanskāras, he/she may live it in as many lives as allowed by his health conditions in those lives. So Āyu is fixed for the Jāti (yoni) and not for a one life in that yoni. So also Bhoga - rewards of karmas is also fixed based on Jāti. Bhoga depends on the limitations placed on organs of perception and enjoyment. Bhoga or the carnal satisfaction depends on the type of sense organs that have been given to you in a particular species. The organs of perception and carnal satisfaction in a bat or a cat are different from those given to a man, cow, or horse. A Sheep does not enjoy the music in the same sense as the man does. Bats are capable of hearing and transmitting those wavelengths of sound which normally are beyond the reach of human ears. Cats and owls have very sensitive eyes which enable them to see quite a lot in the range that we call darkness. Dogs have a remarkable sense of smell, which makes them fine police dogs. In that senses, the range of satisfaction is fixed up when happens to be born in a particular living species. Jāti, Āyu, and Bhoga are possessed as the fruits of pleasure and pain on account of their origination in virtue and vice.

व्यासभाष्य—सत्सु क्लेशेषु कर्माशयो विपाकारम्भी भवति । नोच्छिन्नक्लेशमूलः । यथा तुषावनद्धाः शालितण्डुला अदग्धबीजभावाः प्रोहसमर्था भवन्ति नापनीततुषा दग्धबीजभावा वा तथा क्लेशावनद्धः कर्माशयो विपाकप्रोही भवति नापनीतक्लेशो न प्रसंख्यानदग्धक्लेशबीजभावो वेति । स च विपाकस्त्रिविधो जातिरायुर्भोग इति ।

तत्रेदं विचार्यते किमेकं कर्मैकस्य जन्मनः कारणमथैकं कर्मानेकं जन्माऽऽक्षिपतीति । द्वितीया विचारणा किमनेकं कर्मानेकं जन्म निर्वर्तयति अथानेकं कर्मैकं जन्म निर्वर्तयतीति । न तावदेकं कर्मैकस्य जन्मनः कारणम् । कस्मात् अनादिकालप्रचितस्यासंख्येयस्यावशिष्टस्य कर्मणः सांप्रतिकस्य च फलक्रमानियमादनाश्वासो लोकस्य प्रसक्तः स चानिष्ट इति । न चैकं कमानेकस्य जन्मनः कारणम् । कस्मात् अनेकेषु कर्मसु एकैकमेव कर्मानेकस्यजन्मनः कारणमित्यवशिष्टस्य विपाककालाभावः प्रसक्तः स चाप्यनिष्ट इति । न चानेकं कर्मानेकस्य जन्मनः कारणम् । कस्मात् तदनेकं जन्म युगपन्न संभवतीति क्रमेणैव वाच्यम् । तथा च पूर्वदोषानुषङ्गः ।

तस्माज्जन्मप्रायणान्तरे कृतः पुण्यापुण्यकर्माशयप्रचयो विचित्रः प्रधानोपसर्जनभावेनावस्थितः प्रायणाभिव्यक्त एकप्रघट्टकेन मरणं प्रसाध्य संमूर्च्छित एकमेव जन्म करोति । तच्च जन्म तेनैव कर्मणा लब्धायुष्कं भवति । तस्मिन्नायुषि तेनैव कर्मणा भोगः संपद्यत इति । असौ कर्माशयो जन्मायुर्भोगहेतुत्वात् त्रिविपाकोऽभिधीयत इति । अत एकभविकः कर्माशय उक्त इति ।

दृष्टजन्मवेदनीयस्त्वेकविपाकारम्भी भोगहेतुत्वाद्द्विविपाकारम्भी वाऽऽयुर्भोगहेतुत्वा-न्नन्दीश्वरवन्नहुषवद्वेति । क्लेशकर्मविपाकानुभवनिर्वर्तिताभिस्तु वासनाभिर-नादिकालसंमूर्च्छितमिदं चित्तं विचित्रीकृतमिव सर्वतो मत्स्यजालं ग्रन्थिभिरिवाऽऽततमित्येता अनेकभवपूर्विका वासनाः । यस्स्वयं कर्माशय एष एवैकभविक उक्त इति । ये संस्काराः स्मृतिहेतवस्ता वासनास्ताश्चानादिकालीना इति ।

यस्त्वसावेकभविकः कर्माशयः स नियतविपाकश्चानियतविपाकश्च । तत्र दृष्टजन्मवेदनीयस्य नियतविपाकस्यैवायं नियमो न त्वदृष्टजन्मवेदनीयस्यानियतविपाकस्य । कस्मात् । यो ह्यदृष्टजन्मवेदनीयोऽनियतविपाकस्तस्य त्रयो गतिः कृतस्याविपक्वस्य विनाशः प्रधानकर्मण्यावापगमनं वा नियतविपाकप्रधानकर्मणाऽभिभूतस्य वा चिरमवस्थानमिति ।

तत्र कृतस्याविपक्वस्य नाशो यथा शुक्लकर्मोदयादिहैव नाशः कृष्णस्य । यत्रेदमुक्तम् द्वे द्वे ह वै कर्मणी वेदितव्ये पापकस्यैको राशिः पुण्यकृतोऽपहन्ति तदिच्छस्व कर्माणि सुकृतानि कर्तुमिहैव ते कर्म कवयो वेदयन्ते प्रधानकर्मण्यावापगमनम् । यत्रेदमुक्तं स्यात्स्वल्पः संकरः सपरिहारः सप्रत्ययवमर्षः कुशलस्य नापकर्षयालम् । कस्मात् कुशलं हि मे बह्वन्यदस्ति यत्रायमावापं गतः स्वर्गेऽप्यपकर्षमल्पं करिष्यति इति ।

नियतविपाकप्रधानकर्मणाऽभिभूतस्य वा चिरमवस्थानम् । कथमिति अदृष्टजन्मवेदनीयस्यैव नियतविपाकस्य कर्मणः समानं मरणमभिव्यक्तिकारणमुक्तम् न त्वदृष्टजन्मवेदनीयस्यानियतविपाकस्य । यत्त्वदृष्टजन्मवेदनीयं कर्मानियतविपाकं तन्नश्येदावापं वा गच्छेदभिभूतं वा चिरमप्युपासीत यावत्समानं कर्माभिव्यञ्जकं निमित्तमस्य न विपाकाभिमुखं करोतीति । तद्विपाकस्यैव देशकालनिमित्तानवधारणादियं कर्मगतिश्चित्रा दुर्विज्ञाना चेति न चोत्सर्गस्यापवादनिवृत्तिरित्येकभविकः कर्माशयोऽनुज्ञायत इति ।

भोजवृत्ति—मूलमुक्तलक्षणाः क्लेशाः । तेष्वनभिभूतेषु सत्सु कर्मणां कुशलाकुशलरूपाणां विपाकः फलं जात्यायुर्भोगा भवन्ति । जातिर्मनुष्यत्वादि । आयुश्चिरकालमेकशरीरसम्बन्धः । भोगा विषया इन्द्रियाणि सुखसंविदुःखसंविच्च कर्मकरणभावसाधनव्युत्पत्त्या भोगशब्दस्य । इदमत्र तात्पर्यम् चित्तभूमावनादिकालसंचिताः कर्मवासना यथा यथा पाकमुपयान्ति तथा तथा गुणप्रधानभावेन स्थिता जात्यायुर्भोगलक्षणं स्वकार्यमारभन्ते । उक्तानां कर्मफलत्वेन जात्यादीनां

स्वकारणकर्मानुसारिणां कार्यकर्तृत्वमाह

ते ह्लादपरितापफलाः पुण्यापुण्यहेतुत्वात् ॥14॥

te hlādaparitāpaphalāḥ puṇyāpuṇyahetutvāt

Jāti, Āyu, and Bhoga can be pleasurable or painful according to as they proceed from pāpa karmas and puṇya karmas.

Pāpa karmas result in painful Jāti, Āyu, and Bhoga and puṇya karmas result in pleasurable Jāti, Āyu and Bhoga.

व्यासभाष्य—ते जन्मायुर्भोगाः पुण्यहेतुकाः सुखफला अपुण्यहेतुका दुःखफला इति । यथा चेदं दुःखं प्रतिकूलात्मकमेवं विषयसुखकालेऽपि दुखःमस्त्येव प्रतिकूलात्मकं योगिनः । कथं तदुपपद्यते

भोजवृत्ति—ह्लादः सुखं परितापो दुःखं ह्लादपरितापौ फलं येषां ते तथोक्ताः । पुण्यं कुशलं कर्म । तद्विपरीतमपुण्यं ते पुण्यापुण्ये कारणं येषां ते तेषां भावस्तस्मात् । एतदुक्तं भवति पुण्यकर्मारब्धा जात्यायुर्भोगा ह्लादफला अपुण्यकर्मारब्धास्तु परितापफलाः । एतच्च प्राणिमात्रापेक्षया द्वैविध्यम् । योगिनस्तु सर्वं दुःखमित्याह

परिणामतापसंस्कारदुःखैर्गुणवृत्तिविरोधाच्च दुःखमेव सर्वं विवेकिनः
॥15॥

pariṇāmatāpasaṁskāraduḥkhairguṇavṛttivirodhācca
duḥkhameva sarvaṁ vivekinaḥ

The enlightened (yogī) can foresee the pariṇām duḥkha (pleasures earned through puṇya karmas also end in pains), tāpa duḥkha (sufferings earned through pāpa karmas), sanskāra duḥkha (sufferings caused by the sanskāras of pāpa karmas and kleśas), and suffering caused by the conflicts of the vṛttis of guṇas (sattva, rajas and tamas respectively), so he finds pain in everything.

Note: Sattva guṇa vṛtti gives us sukha, rajoguṇa vṛtti gives us duḥkha and tamoguṇi vṛtti gives us moha (error, delusion, hallucination, distraction, infatuation, etc.)

व्यासभाष्य—सर्वस्यायं रागानुविद्धश्चेतनाचेतनसाधनाधीनः सुखानुभव इति तत्रास्ति रागजः

कर्माशयः । तथा च द्वेष्टी दुःखसाधनानि मुह्यति चेति द्वेषमोहकृतोऽप्यस्ति कर्माशयः । तथा चोक्तम् नानुपहत्य भूतान्युपभोगः संभवतीति हिंसाकृतोऽप्यस्ति शरीरः कर्माशयः इति । विषयसुखं चाविद्येत्युक्तम् ।

या भोगेष्विन्द्रियाणां तृप्तेरुपशान्तिस्तत्सुखम् । या लौल्यादनुपशान्तिस्तद्दुःखम् । न चेन्द्रियाणां भोगाभ्यासेन वैतृष्ण्यं कर्तुं शक्यम् । कस्मात् यतो भोगाभ्यासमनु विवर्धन्ते रागाः कौशलानि चेन्द्रियाणामिति । तस्मादनुपायः सुखस्य भोगाभ्यास इति । स खल्वयं वृश्चिकविषभीत इवाऽऽशीविषेण दष्टो यःसुखार्थी विषयानुवासितो महति दुःखपङ्के निमग्न इति । एषा परिणामदुःखता नाम प्रतिकूला सुखावस्थायामपि योगिनमेव क्लिश्नाति ।

अथ का तापदुःखता सर्वस्य द्वेषानुविद्धश्चेतनाचेतनसाधनाधीनस्तापानुभव इति तत्रास्ति द्वेषजः कर्माशयः । सुखसाधनानि च प्रार्थयमानः कायेन वाचा मनसा च परिस्यन्दते ततः परमनुगृह्णात्युपहन्ति चेति परानुग्रहपीडाभ्याम् धर्माधर्मावुपचिनोति । स कर्माशयो लोभान्मोहाच्च भवतीत्येषा तापदुःखतोच्यते । का पुनःसंस्कारदुःखता सुखानुभवात्सुखसंस्काराशयो दुःखानुभवादपि दुःखसंस्काराशय इति । एवं कर्मभ्यो विपाकेऽनुभूयमाने सुखे दुःखे वा पुनः कर्माशयप्रचय इति ।

एवमिदमनादि दुःखस्रोतो विप्रसृतं योगिनमेव प्रतिकूलात्मकत्वादुद्वेजयति । कस्मात् अक्षिपात्रकल्पो हि विद्वानिति । यथोर्णातन्तुरक्षिपात्रे न्यस्तः स्पर्शेन दुःखयति न चान्येषु गात्रावयवेषु एवमेतानि दुःखान्यक्षिपात्रकल्पं योगिनमेव क्लिश्नन्ति नेतरं प्रतिपत्तारम् । इतरं तु स्वकर्मोपहतं दुःखमुपात्तमुपात्तं त्यजन्तं त्यक्तं त्यक्तमुपाददानमनादिवासनाविचित्रतया चित्तवृत्त्या समन्ततोऽनुविद्धमिवाविद्यया हातव्य एवाहंकारममकारानुपातिनं जातं जातं वाह्याध्यात्मिकोभयनिमित्तास्त्रिपर्वाणस्तापा अनुप्लवन्ते । तदेवमना दिना दुःखस्रोतसा व्यूह्यमानमात्मानं भूतग्रामं च दृष्ट्वा योगी सर्वदुःखक्षयकारणं सम्यग्दर्शनं शरणं प्रपद्यत इति ।

गुणवृत्तिविरोधाच्च दुःखमेव सर्वं विवेकिनः । प्रख्याप्रवृत्तिस्थितिरूपा बुद्धिगुणाः परस्परानुग्रहतन्त्री भूत्वा शान्तं घोरं मूढं वा प्रत्ययं त्रिगुणमेवाऽऽरभन्ते । चलं च गुणवृत्तिमिति क्षिप्रपरिणामि चित्तमुक्तम् । रूपातिशया । वृत्त्यतिशयाश्च परस्परेण विरुध्यन्ते सामान्यानि त्वतिशयैः सह प्रवर्तन्ते । एवमेते गुणा इतरेतराश्रयेणोपार्जितसुखदुःखमोहप्रत्ययाः सर्वे सर्वरूपा भवन्तीति गुणप्रधानभावकृतस्त्वेषां विशेष इति । तस्मादुःखमेव सर्वं विवेकिन इति ।

तदस्य महतो दुःखसमुदायस्य प्रभवबीजमविद्या । तस्याश्च सम्यग्दर्शनमभावहेतुः । यथा चिकित्साशास्त्रं चतुर्व्यूहम् रोगो रोगहेतुरारोग्यं भैषज्यमिति एवमिदमपि शास्त्रं चतुर्व्यूहमेव । तद्यथा संसारः संसारहेतुर्मोक्षो मोक्षोपाय इति । तत्र दुःखबहुलः संसारो हेयः प्रधानपुरुषयोः संयोगो हेयहेतुः । संयोगस्याऽऽत्यन्तिकी निवृत्तिर्हानम् । हानोपायः सम्यग्दर्शनम् । तत्र हातुः स्वरूपमुपादेयं वा हेयं वान भवितुमर्हतीति हाने तस्योच्छेदवादप्रसङ्ग उपादाने च हेतुवादः । उभयप्रत्याख्याने शाश्वतवाद इत्येतत्सम्यग्दर्शनम् तदेतच्छास्त्रं चतुर्व्यूहमित्यभिधीयते ।

भोजवृत्ति—विवेकिनः परिज्ञातक्लेशादिविवेकस्य दृश्यमात्रं सकलमेव भोगसाधनं सविषं स्वाद्वन्नमिव दुःखमेव प्रतिकूलवेदनीयमेवेत्यर्थः । यस्मादत्यन्ताभिजातो योगी दुःखलेशेनाप्युद्विजते । यथाऽक्षिपात्रमूर्णातन्तुस्पर्शमात्रेणैव महतीं पीडामनुभवति नेतरदङ्गं तथा विवेकी स्वल्पदुःखानुबन्धेनापि उद्विजते । कथमित्याह परिणामतापसंस्कारदुःखै । विषयाणामुपभुज्यमानानां यथायथं गर्धाभिवृद्धेस्तदप्राप्तिकृतस्य दुःखस्यापरिहार्यतया दुःखान्तरसाधनात्वाच्चास्त्येव

दुःखरूपतेति परिणामदुःखत्वम्। उपभुज्यमानेषु सुखसाधनेषु तत्प्रतिपन्थिनं प्रति द्वेषस्य सर्वदैवावस्थितत्वात्सुखानुभवकालेऽपि तापदुःखं दुष्परिहरमिति तापदुःखता। संस्कारदुःखत्वं च स्वाभिमतानभिमतविषयसंनिधाने सुखसंविदुःखसंविच्चोपजायमाना तथाविधमेव स्वक्षेत्रे संस्कारमारभते। संस्काराच्च पुनस्तथाविधसंविदनुभव इत्यपरिमितसंस्कारोत्पत्तिद्वारेण संसारानुच्छेदात्सर्वस्यैव दुःखत्वम्। गुणवृत्तिविरोधाच्चेति। गुणानां सत्त्वरजस्तमसां या वृत्तयः सुखदुःखमोहरूपाः परस्परमभिभाव्याभिभावकत्वेन विरुद्धा जायन्ते तासां सर्वत्रैव दुःखान्वेधाद्दुःखत्वम्। एतदुक्तं भवति ऐकान्तिकीमात्यन्तिकीं च दुःखनिवृत्तिमिच्छतो विवेकिन उक्तरूपकारणचतुष्टयं यावत्सर्वे विषया दुखःरूपतया प्रतिभान्ति तस्मात्सर्वकर्मविपाको दुःखरूप एवेत्युक्तं भवति। तदेवमुक्तस्य क्लेशकर्माशयविपाकराशेरविद्याप्रभवत्वादविद्यायाश्च मिथ्याज्ञानरूपतया सम्यग्ज्ञानोच्छेद्यत्वात्सम्यग्ज्ञानस्य च साधनहेयोपादे-
यावधारणरूपत्वात्तदभिधानायाऽऽह

हेयं दुःखमनागतम् ॥16॥

heyaṃ duḥkhamanāgatam

The pain or misery which has not yet come ought to be eliminated.

व्यासभाष्य—दुःखमतीतमुपभोगेनातिवाहितं न हेयपक्षे वर्तते। वर्तमानं च स्वक्षणे भोगरूढमिति न तत्क्षणान्तरे हेयतामापद्यते। तस्माद्यदेवानागतं दुःखं तदेवाक्षिपात्रकल्पं योगिनं क्लिश्नाति नेतरं प्रतिपत्तारम्। तदेवहेयतामापद्यते। तस्माद्देव हेयमित्युच्यते तस्यैव कारणं प्रतिनिर्दिश्यते

भोजवृत्ति—भूतस्यातिक्रान्तत्वादनुभूयमानस्य च त्यक्तुमशक्यत्वादनागतमेव संसारदुःखं हातव्यमित्युक्तं भवति। हेयहेतुमाह

द्रष्टृदृश्ययोः संयोगो हेयहेतुः ॥17॥

draṣṭṛdṛśyayoḥ saṃyogo heyahetuḥ

The union of the seer (soul) with the (seen) prakṛti/matter or the visible world is the (hetu) cause of (heya duḥkha) misery that needs to be eliminated.

व्यासभाष्य—द्रष्टा बुद्धेः प्रतिसंवेदी पुरुषः। दृश्या बुद्धिसत्त्वोपारूढा सर्वे धर्माः। तदेतद्दृश्यमयस्कान्तमणिकल्पं संनिधिमात्रोपकारिदृश्यत्वेन स्वं भवति पुरुषस्य दृशिरूपस्य स्वामिनः अनुभवकर्मविषयतामापन्नं यतः। अन्यस्वरूपेण प्रतिपन्नमन्यस्वरूपेण प्रतिलब्धात्मकं स्वतन्त्रमपि परार्थत्वात्परतन्त्रम्।
तयोर्दृग्दर्शनशक्त्योरनादिरर्थकृतः संयोगो हेयहेतुर्दुःखस्य कारणमित्यर्थः।

तथा चोक्तम् तत्संयोगहेतुविवर्जनात्स्यादयमात्यन्तिको दुःखप्रतीकारः। कस्मात्

दुःखहेतोः परिहार्यस्य प्रतीकारदर्शनात्। तद्यथा पादतलस्य भेद्यता कण्टकस्य भेत्तत्वं परिहारः कण्टकस्य पादाऽनधिष्ठानं पादत्राणव्यवहितेन वाऽधिष्ठानम् एतत्त्रयं यो वेद लोके स तत्र प्रतीकारमारभमाणो भेदजं दुःखं नाऽऽप्नोति। कस्मात् त्रित्वोपलब्धिसामर्थ्यादिति। अत्रापि तापकस्य रजसः सत्त्वमेव तप्यम्। कस्मात् तपिक्रियायाः कर्मस्थत्वात् सत्त्वे कर्मणि तपिक्रिया नापरिणामिनि निष्क्रिये क्षेत्रज्ञे दर्शितविषयत्वात्। सत्त्वे तु तप्यमाने तदाकारानुरोधी पुरुषेऽप्यनुतप्यत इति। दृश्यस्वरूपमुच्यते

प्रकाशक्रियास्थितिशीलं भूतेन्द्रियात्मकं भोगापवर्गार्थं दृश्यम् ॥18॥

prakāśakriyāsthitiśīlaṁ bhūtendriyātmakaṁ
bhogāpavargārthaṁ dṛśyam

This dṛśya (visible world) (bhūtātmaka) consisting of matter and (indriyātmaka) living beings is made of sattvaguṇa (intelligence), rajoguṇa (motion) and tamoguṇa (inertia/inaction). This dṛśya (visible world) is meant for enjoyment and liberation of the soul.

Prakāśa is the property of sattva guṇa

Motion is the property of rajoguṇa

Inaction or inertia is the property of tamoguṇa

व्यासभाष्य—प्रकाशशीलं सत्त्वम्। क्रिया शीलं रजः। स्थितिशीलं तम इति। एते गुणाः परस्परोपरक्तविभागाः परिणामिन संयोगवियोगधर्मिण इतरेतरोपाश्रयेणोपार्जितमूर्तयः परस्पराङ्गाङ्गित्वेऽप्यसंभिन्नशक्तिप्रविभागास्तुल्यजातीयातुल्यजातीयशक्तिभेदानुपातिनः प्रधानवेलायामुपदर्शितसंनिधाना गुणत्वेऽपि च व्यापारमात्रेण प्रधानान्तर्णीतानुमितास्तिता पुरुषार्थकर्तव्यतया प्रयुक्तसामर्थ्याः संनिधिमात्रोपकारिणोऽयस्कान्तमणिकल्पाः प्रत्ययमन्तरेणैकतमस्य वृत्तिमनु वर्तमाना प्रधानशब्दवाच्या भवन्ति। एतद्दृश्यमित्युच्यते।

तदेतद्भूतेन्द्रियात्मकं भूतभावेन पृथिव्यादिना सूक्ष्मस्थूलेन परिणमते। तथेन्द्रियभावेन श्रोत्रादिना सूक्ष्मस्थूलेन परिणमत इति। तत्तु नाप्रयोजनमपि तु प्रयोजनमुररीकृत्य प्रवर्तत इति भोगापवर्गार्थं हि तद्दृश्यंपुरुषस्येति। तत्रेष्टानिष्टगुणस्वरूपावधारणमविभागापन्नं भोगो भोक्तुः स्वरूपावधारणमपवर्ग इति। द्वयोरतिरिक्तमन्यद्दर्शनं नास्ति। तथा चोक्तम् अयं तु खलु त्रिषु गुणेषु कर्तृष्वकर्तरि च पुरुषे तुल्यातुल्यजातीये चतुर्थे तक्रियासाक्षिण्युपनीय-मानान्सर्वभावानुपपन्नाननुपश्यन्नदर्शनमन्यच्छङ्कत इति।

तावेतौ भोगापवर्गौ बुद्धिकृतौ बुद्धावेव वर्तमानौ कथं पुरुषे व्यपदिश्येते इति। यथा विजयः पराजयो वा योद्धृषु वर्तमानः स्वामिनि व्यपदिश्यते स हि तत्फलस्य भोक्तेति एवं बन्धमोक्षौ

बुद्धावेव वर्तमानौ पुरुषे व्यपदिश्यते स हि तत्फलस्य भोक्तेति। बुद्धेरेव
पुरुषार्थपरिसमाप्तिर्बन्धस्तदर्थावसायो मोक्ष इति। एतेन ग्रहणधारणोहापोहतत्त्वज्ञानाभिनिवेशो बुद्धौ
वर्तमानाः पुरुषेऽध्यारोपितसद्भावा। स हि तत्फलस्य भोक्तेति।

द्रश्यानां गुणानां स्वरूपभेदावधारणार्थमिदमारभ्यते

भोजवृत्ति.—प्रकाशः सत्त्वस्य धर्मः क्रिया प्रवृत्तिरूपा रजसः स्थितिर्नियमरूपा तमसः ताः
प्रकाशक्रियास्थितयः शीलं स्वाभाविकं रूपं यस्य तत्तथाविधमिति स्वरूपमस्य निर्दिष्टम्।
भूतेन्द्रियात्मकमिति। भूतानि स्थूलसूक्ष्मभेदेन द्विविधानि पृथिव्यादीनि गन्धतन्मात्रादीनि च।
इन्द्रियाणि बुद्धीन्द्रियकर्मेन्द्रियान्तःकरणभेदेन त्रिविधानि। उभयमेतद्ग्राह्यग्रहणरूपात्मा स्वरूपाभिन्नाः
परिणामो यस्य तत्तथाविधमित्यनेनास्य कार्यमुक्तम्। भोगः कथितलक्षणः अपवर्गो
विवेकख्यातिपूर्विका संसारनिवृत्तिः तौ भोगापवर्गावर्थः प्रयोजनं यस्य तत्तथाविधं द्रश्यमित्यर्थः।
तस्य च द्रश्यस्य नानावस्थारूपपरिणामात्मकस्य हेयत्वेन ज्ञातव्यत्वात्तदवस्थाः कथयितुमाह

Now the nature of dṛśya jagat (visible world) is explained.

विशेषाविशेषलिङ्गमात्रालिङ्गानि गुणपूर्वाणि ॥19॥
viśeṣāviśeṣaliṅgamātrāliṅgāni guṇaparvāṇi

The three guṇas undergo four stages (from invisible to the visible) of transformation (fig.12): aliṅga (Prakṛti alone), liṅga (mahat-tattva or intelligence), aviśeṣa (ahaṅkāra and five tanmātras like smell, taste, sight, touch and sound) and viśeṣa [a set of five gross bhūtas, like pṛthivī, jala, agni, vāyu and ākāśa and a set of 11 senses like mind (inner sense), five external sense organs and five external motor organs].

Here it may be known that the last three stages, viz. liṅga, aviśeṣa, and viśeṣa are caused by the union of puruṣa (soul) with prakṛti occurred due to sanskāras of soul.

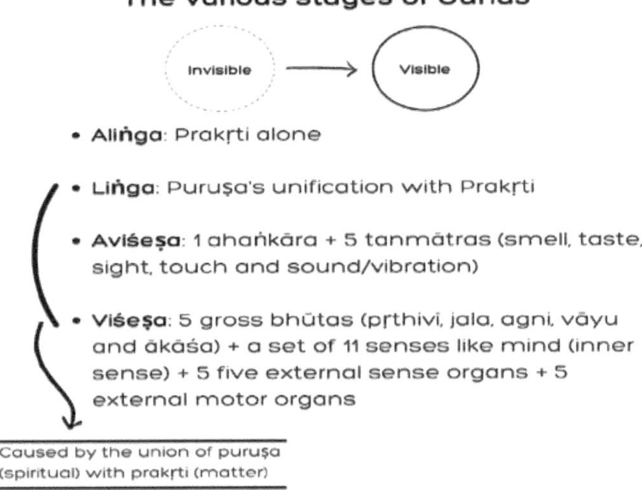

Figure 12: The various stages of Gunas

Before this union, the constituents of prakṛti, i.e. intelligence, motion, and inertia were in a dormant state or balanced state, or critically balanced state. When the Puruṣa united with Prakṛti, motion activated inactive energy or say rajoguṇa (motion) reacted with tamoguṇa (inertia) causing the prakāśa (of creation). Thus all three guṇas are imbalanced. This state is called as vikṛti or entropy. Due to vikṛti, the mahat-tattva (element of intelligence in human beings) came into being. This is called the liṅga (identifiable) stage of sattva, rajas, and tamas which may be termed as the beginning of the dṛśya jagat or visible world.

व्यासभाष्य—तत्राऽऽकाशवाय्वग्न्युदकभूमयो भूतानि शब्दस्पर्शरूपरसगन्धतन्मात्राणामविशेषाणां विशेषाः । तथा श्रोत्रत्वक्चक्षुर्जिह्वाघ्राणानि बुद्धीन्द्रियाणि वाक्पाणिपादपायूपस्थानि कर्मेन्द्रियाणि एकादशं मनः सर्वार्थम् इत्येतान्यस्मितालक्षणस्याविशेषस्य विशेषाः । गुणानामेष षोड़शको विशेषपरिणामः ।

षडविशेषाः । तद्यथा शब्दतन्मात्रं स्पर्शतन्मात्रं रूपतन्मात्रं रसतन्मात्रं गन्धतन्मात्रं चेति एकद्वित्रिचतुष्पञ्चलक्षणाः शब्दादयः पञ्चाविशेषाः षष्ठश्चाविशेषोऽस्मितामात्र इति । एते सत्तामात्रस्याऽऽत्मनो महतः षडविशेषपरिणामाः । यत्तत्परमविशेषेभ्यो लिङ्गमात्रं महत्तत्त्वं तस्मिन्नेते

सत्तामात्रे महत्यात्मन्यवस्थाय
विवृद्धिकाष्ठामनुभवन्ति।

प्रतिसंसृज्यमानाश्च तस्मिन्नेव सत्तामात्रे महत्यात्मन्यवस्थाय यत्तन्त्रिः सत्तासत्तं
निःसदसन्निरसदव्यक्तमलिङ्गं प्रधानं तत्प्रतियन्ति। एष तेषां लिङ्गमात्रः परिणामो निःसत्तासत्तं
चालिङ्गपरिणाम इति।

आलिङ्गावस्थायां न पुरुषार्थो हेतुर्नलिङ्गावस्थायामादौ पुरुषार्थता कारणं भवतीति। न तस्याः
पुरुषार्थता कारणं भवतीति। नासौ पुरुषार्थकृतेति नित्याऽऽख्यायते। त्रयाणां त्ववस्थाविशेषणमादौ
पुरुषार्थता कारणं भवति। स चार्थो हेतुर्निमित्तं कारणं भवतीत्यनित्याऽऽख्यायते गुणास्तु
सर्वधर्मानुपातिनो न प्रत्यस्तमयन्ते नोपजायन्ते। व्यक्तिभिरेवातीतानागत-
व्ययागमवतीभिगुणान्वयिनीभिरुपजननापायधर्मका इव प्रत्यवभासन्ते। यथा देवदत्तो दरिद्राति।
कस्मात्। यतोऽस्य म्रियन्ते गाव इति गवामेव मरणात्तस्य दरिद्रता न स्वरूपहानादिति समः
समाधिः।

लिङ्गमात्रमलिङ्गस्य प्रत्यासत्रं तत्र तत्संसृष्टं विविच्यते क्रमानतिवृत्ते:। तथा षडविशेषा
लिङ्गमात्रे संसृष्टा विविच्यन्ते परिणामक्रमनियमात्। तथा तेष्वविशेषेषु भूतेन्द्रियाणि संसृष्टानि
विविच्यन्ते। तथा चोक्तं पुरस्तात्। न विशेषेभ्यः परं तत्त्वान्तरमस्तीति विशेषाणां नास्ति
तत्त्वान्तरपरिणामः। तेषां तु धर्मलक्षणावस्थापरिणामा व्याख्यायिष्यन्ते।

व्याख्यातं दृश्यमथ द्रष्टुः स्वरूपावधारणार्थमिदमारभ्यते
भोजवृत्ति—गुणानां पर्वाण्यवस्थाविशेषाश्चत्वारो ज्ञातव्या इत्युपदिष्टं भवति। तत्र विशेषा
महाभूतेन्द्रियाणि अविशेषास्तन्मात्रान्तःकरणानि लिङ्गमात्रं बुद्धिः अलिङ्गमव्यक्तमित्युक्तम्। सर्वत्र
त्रिगुणरूपस्याव्यक्तस्यान्वयित्वेन प्रत्यभिज्ञानादवश्यं ज्ञातव्येन योगकाले चत्वारि पर्वाणि
निर्दिष्टानि। एवं हेयत्वेन दृश्यस्य प्रथमं ज्ञातव्यात्वात्तदवस्थासहितं व्याख्यायोपादेयं द्रष्टारं
व्याकर्तुमाह

Now the nature of drasṭā (seer) or Ātmā (soul) is
explained.

द्रष्टा दृशिमात्रः शुद्धोऽपि प्रत्ययानुपश्यः ॥20॥
drasṭā dṛśimātraḥ śuddho'pi pratyayānupaśyaḥ

The drasṭā (soul) is the seer only or has the power to
see things as they are. Though it is pure, i.e not
adulterated by the properties of prakṛti, yet it sees things
according to the mind modified by the vision of outside
world or say sanskāras of mind (due to identifying itself
with the material mind).

व्यासभाष्य—दृशिमात्र इति दृक्शक्तिरेव विशेषणापरामृष्टेत्यर्थः। स पुरुषो बुद्धेः प्रतिसंवेदी।

स बुद्धेर्न सरूपो नात्यन्तं विरूप इति। न तावत्सरूपः। कस्मात्। ज्ञाताज्ञातविषयत्वात्परिणामिनि हि बुद्धिः। तस्याश्च विषयो गवादिर्घटादिर्वा ज्ञातश्चाज्ञातश्चेति परिणमित्वं दर्शयति।

सदाज्ञातविषयत्वं तु पुरुषस्यापरिणामित्वं परिदीपयति। कस्मात्। नहि बुद्धिश्च नाम पुरुषविषयश्च स्यादगृहीता चेति सिद्धं पुरुषस्य सदाज्ञातविषयत्वं ततश्चापरिणामित्वमिति। किं च परार्था बुद्धिः संहत्यकारित्वात् स्वार्थः पुरुष इति। तथा सर्वार्थाध्यवसायकत्वात्त्रिगुणा बुद्धिस्त्रिगुणत्वादचेतनेति। गुणानां तूपद्रष्टा पुरुष इत्यतो न सरूपः।

अस्तु तर्हि विरूप इति। नात्यन्तं विरूपः। कस्मात् शुद्धोऽप्यसौ प्रत्ययानुपश्यो यतः। प्रत्ययं बौद्धमनुपश्यति तमनुपश्यन्नतदात्माऽपि तदात्मक इव प्रत्यवभासते। तथा चोक्तम् अपरिणामिनीहि भोक्तृशक्तिरप्रतिसंक्रमा च परिणामिन्यर्थे प्रतिसंक्रान्तेव तद्वृत्तिमनु पतति तस्याश्च प्राप्तचैतन्योपग्रहरूपाया बुद्धिवृत्तेरनुकारमात्रतया बुद्धिवृत्त्यविशिष्टा हि ज्ञानवृत्तिरित्याख्यायते।

भोजवृत्ति—द्रष्टा पुरुषो दृशिमात्रश्चेतनामात्रः। मात्रग्रहणं धर्मधर्मिनिरासार्थम्। केचिद्धि चेतनामात्मनो धर्ममिच्छन्ति। स शुद्धोऽपि परिणामित्वाद्यभावेन स्वप्रतिष्ठोऽपि प्रत्ययानुपश्यः प्रत्यया विषयोपरक्तानि ज्ञानानि तानि अनु अव्यवधानेन प्रतिसंक्रमाद्यभावेन पश्यति। एतदुक्तं भवति जातविषयोपरागायामेव बुद्धौ संनिधिमात्रेणैव पुरुषस्य द्रष्टृत्वमिति। स एव भोक्तेत्याह

<h2 style="text-align:center">तदर्थ एव दृश्यस्यात्मा ॥21॥</h2>

tadartha eva dṛśyasyātmā

(dṛśyasya) This visible body (of ātmā) came into being due its kārmika sanskāras, (tadartham) so that soul may bear fruits of its past karmas and do new karmas to make its future.

व्यासभाष्य—दृशिरूपस्य पुरुषस्य कर्मविषयतामापन्नं दृश्यमिति तदर्थ एव दृश्यस्याऽऽत्मा भवति। स्वरूपं भवतीत्यर्थः। तत्स्वरूपं तु पररूपेण अतिलब्धात्मकं भोगापवर्गार्थतायां कृतायां पुरुषेण न दृश्यत इति। स्वरूपहानादस्य नाशः प्राप्तो न तु विनश्यति। कस्मात्

भोजवृत्ति—दृश्यस्य प्रागुक्तलक्षणस्याऽऽत्मा यत्स्वरूपं स तदर्थस्तस्य पुरुषस्य भोक्तृत्वसंपादनं नाम स्वार्थपरिहारेण प्रयोजम्। न हि प्रधानं प्रवर्तमानमात्मनः किंचित्प्रयोजनमपेक्ष्य प्रवर्तते किंतु पुरुषस्य भोक्तृत्वं संपादयितुमिति।

यद्येवं पुरुषस्य भोगसंपादनमेव प्रयोजनं तदा संपादिते तस्मिंस्तन्निष्प्रयोजनं विरतव्यापारं स्यात् तस्मिंश्च परिणामशून्ये शुद्धत्वात्सर्वे द्रष्टारो बन्धरहिताः स्युः ततश्च संसारोच्छेद इत्याशङ्क्याऽऽह

<h2 style="text-align:center">कृतार्थं प्रति नष्टमप्यनष्टं तदन्यसाधारणत्वात् ॥22॥</h2>

kṛtārthaṃ prati naṣṭam apyanaṣṭaṃ tadanyasādhāraṇatvāt

The dṛśya or visible body (naṣṭam) is eliminated (kṛtārthaṃ prati) for the drastās (souls) who have complete their bhogas (reaped the fruits of their karmas), i.e. who are liberated; (api) but (anaṣṭam) it is not eliminated for those draṣṭās (souls) who have not completed their bhogas (not yet reaped the fruits of their karmas, i.e. attained liberation.

This sūtra shows that draṣṭās (souls) are many like Sāṅkhya says: *puruṣa bahutvaṁ siddham.* The multiplicity of Puruṣas (souls) is a proven principle.

व्यासभाष्य—कृतार्थमेकं पुरुषं प्रति दृश्यं नष्टमपि नाशं प्राप्तमप्यनष्टं तदन्यपुरुषसाधारणत्वात् । कुशलं पुरुषं प्रति नाशं प्राप्तमप्यकुशलान्पुरुषान्प्रति न कृतार्थमिति तेषां दृशेः कर्मविषयतामापन्नं लभत एव पुरुषेणाऽऽत्मरूपमिति । अतश्च दृग्दर्शनशक्त्योर्नित्यत्वादनादिः संयोगो व्याख्यात इति । तथा चोक्तम् धर्मिणामनादिसंयोगाद्धर्ममात्राणामप्यनादिः संयोग इति । संयोगस्वरूपाभिधित्सयेदं सूत्रं प्रवर्तते

भोजवृत्ति—यद्यपि विवेकख्यातिपर्यन्ताद्भोगसंपादनात्मकपि कृतार्थं पुरुषं प्रति तन्नष्टं विरतव्यापारं तथापि सर्वपुरुषसाधारणत्वादन्यान्प्रत्यनष्टव्यापारमवतिष्ठते । अतःप्रधानस्य सकलभोक्तृसाधारणत्वान्न कृतार्थता न कदाचिदपि विनाशः । एकस्य मुक्तौ वा न सर्वमुक्तिप्रसङ्ग इत्युक्तं भवति । दृश्यद्रष्टारौ व्याख्याय संयोगं व्याख्यातुमाह

स्वस्वामिशक्त्योः स्वरूपोपलब्धिहेतुः संयोगः ॥23॥

svasvāmiśaktyoḥ svarūpopalabdhihetuḥ saṁyogaḥ

The (hetu) purpose of (sañyoga) the union of Puruṣa (soul) and Prakṛti (body) is to make both (sva) the dṛśya body and (svāmī) its lord, the draṣṭā (seer or embodied soul) (svarūpopalabdhi) realise their true nature.

Note: The true nature of the body is its being the means of bhoga or say means of reaping the fruits of karmas and the true nature of the embodied soul is its mokṣa. Until and unless the union of Puruṣa and Prakṛti takes place, neither body can play its real role of acting as a means of bhoga, nor soul can attain emancipation after completing the bhoga of karmas (reaping the fruits of karmas).

व्यासभाष्य—पुरुषः स्वामी दृश्येन स्वेन दर्शनार्थं संयुक्तः। तस्मात्संयोगाद् दृश्यस्योपलब्धिर्या स भोगः। या तु द्रष्टुः स्वरूपोपलब्धिः सोऽपवर्गः। दर्शनकार्यावसानः संयोग इति दर्शनं वियोगस्य कारणमुक्तम्। दर्शनमदर्शनस्य प्रतिद्वंद्वीत्यदर्शनं संयोगनिमित्तमुक्तम्। नात्र दर्शनं मोक्षकारणमदर्शनाभावादेव बन्धाभावः स मोक्ष इति। दर्शनस्य भावे बन्धकारणस्यादर्शनस्य नाश इत्यतो दर्शनं ज्ञानं कैवल्यकारणमुक्तम्।

किंचेदमदर्शनं नाम किं गुणानामधिकार आहोस्विद्दृशिरूपस्य स्वामिनो दर्शितविषयस्य प्रधानचित्तस्यानुत्पादः। स्वस्मिन्दृश्ये विद्यमाने यो दर्शनाभावः।

किमर्थवत्तागुणानाम्। अथाविद्या स्वचित्तेन सह निरुद्धा स्वचित्तस्योत्पत्तिबीजम्। किं स्थितिसंस्कारक्षये गतिसंस्काराभिव्यक्तिः। यत्रेदमुक्तं प्रधानं स्थित्यैव वर्तमानं विकाराकरणादप्रधानं स्यात्।

तथा गत्यैव वर्तमानं विकारनित्यत्वादप्रधानं स्यात्। उभयथा चास्य वृत्तिः प्रधानव्यवहारं लभते नान्यथा। करणान्तरेष्वपि कल्पितेष्वेव समानश्चर्चः। दर्शनशक्तिरेवादर्शनमित्येके प्रधानस्याऽऽत्मख्यापनार्था प्रवृत्तिः इतिश्रुतेः।

सर्वबोध्यबोधसमर्थः प्राक्प्रवृत्तेः पुरुषो न पश्यति सर्वकार्यकारणसमर्थं दृश्यं तदा न दृश्यत इति। उभयस्याप्यदर्शनं धर्म इत्येके।

तत्रेदं दृश्यस्य स्वात्मभूतमपि पुरुषप्रत्ययापेक्षं दर्शनं दृश्यधर्मत्वेन भवति। तथा पुरुषस्यानात्मभूतमपि दृश्यप्रत्ययापेक्षं पुरुषधर्मत्वेनेवादर्शनमवभासते। दर्शनं ज्ञानमेवादर्शनमिति केचिदभिदधति। इत्येते शास्त्रगता विकल्पाः। तत्र विकल्पबहुत्वमेतत्सर्वपुरुषाणां गुणानां संयोगे साधारणविषयम्। यस्तु प्रत्यक्चेतनस्य स्वबुद्धिसंयोगः

भोजवृत्ति—कार्यद्वारेणास्य लक्षणं करोति स्वशक्तिर्दृश्यस्य स्वभावः स्वामिशक्तिर्दृष्टुः स्वरूपं तयोर्द्वयोरपि संवेद्यसंवेदकत्वेन व्यवस्थितयोर्या स्वरूपोपलब्धिस्तस्याः कारणं यः स संयोगः। स च सहजभोग्यभोक्तृभावस्वरूपान्नान्यः। न हि तयोर्नित्ययोर्व्यापकयोश्च स्वरूपादतिरिक्तः कश्चित् संयोगः। यदेव भोग्यस्य भोग्यत्वं भोक्तृश्च भोक्तृत्वमनादिसिद्धं स एव संयोगः। तसयापि कारणमाह

तस्य हेतुरविद्या ॥24॥
tasya heturavidyā

This union of Puruṣa (soul) and Prakṛti (body) is caused by Avidyā (soul's identification with prakṛti).

Avidyā is real souls' identifying with unreal body.

Here unreal means, non-eternal, changeable.

व्यासभाष्य—विपर्ययज्ञानवासनेत्यर्थः। विपर्ययज्ञानवासनावासिता च न कार्यनिष्ठां पुरुषख्यातिं बुद्धिः प्राप्नोति साधिकारा पुनरावर्तते। सा तु पुरुषख्यातिपर्यवसानां कार्यनिष्ठां प्राप्नोति चरिताधिकारा निवृत्तादर्शना बन्धकारणाभावान्न पुनरावर्तते।

अत्र कश्चित्षण्डकोपाख्यानेनोद्घाटयति मुग्धया भार्यायाऽभिधीयते षण्डकाऽऽर्यपुत्र अपत्यवती मे भगिनी किमर्थं नाहमिति स तामाह मृतस्तेऽहमपत्यमुत्पादयिष्यामीति । तथेदं विद्यमानं ज्ञानं चित्तनिवृत्तिं न करोति विनष्टं करिष्यतीति का प्रत्याशा । तत्राऽऽचार्यदेशीयो वक्ति ननु बुद्धिनिवृत्तिरेव मोक्षोऽदर्शनकरणाभावाद्बुद्धिनिवृत्तिः । तच्चादर्शनं बन्धकारणं दर्शनान्निवर्तते । तत्र चित्तनिवृत्तिरेव मोक्षः किमर्थमस्थान एवास्य मतिविभ्रमः ।

हेयं दुःखमुक्तम् हेय कारणं च संयोगाख्यं सनिमित्तमुक्तमतः परं हानं वक्तव्यम्

.भोजवृत्ति.—या पूर्वं विपर्यासात्मिका मोहरूपाऽविद्या व्याख्याता सा तस्याविवेकख्यातिरूपस्य संयोगस्य कारणम् । हेयं हानक्रियाकर्मोच्यते किं पुनस्तद्धानमित्यत आह

तदभावात् संयोगाभावो हानं तद्दृशेः कैवल्यम् ॥25॥

tadabhāvāt samyogābhāvo hānam taddṛśeh kaivalyam

The absence of avidyā leads to the absence of union of Puruṣa (soul) with Prakṛti (body) which is called as (hāna) abandonment of union of Prakṛti with Puruṣa. (tad) That is called as the (kaivalyam) emancipation of (dṛśeh) draṣṭā (soul).

व्यासभाष्य—तस्यादर्शनस्याभावादबुद्धिपुरुषसंयोगाभाव आत्यन्तिको बन्धनोपरम इत्यर्थः । एतद्धानम् । तद्दृशेः कैवल्यं पुरुषस्यामिश्रीभावः पुनरसंयोगो गुणैरित्यर्थः । दुःखकारणनिवृत्तौ दुःखोपरमो हानम् । तदा स्वरूपप्रतिष्ठः पुरुष इत्युक्तम् । अथ हानस्य कः प्राप्त्युपाय इति

.भोजवृत्ति.—तस्या अविद्यायाः स्वरूपविरुद्धेन सम्यग्ज्ञानेनोन्मूलिताया योऽयमभावस्तस्मिन्सति तत्कार्यस्य संयोगस्याप्यभावस्तद्धानमित्युच्यते । अयमर्थः नैतस्य मूर्तद्रव्यवत्परित्यागो युज्यते किंतु जातायां विवेकख्यातावविवेकनिमित्तः संयोगः स्वयमेव निवर्तत इति तस्य हानम् । यदेव च संयोगस्य हानं तदेव नित्यं केवलस्यापि पुरुषस्य कैवल्यं व्यपदिश्यते ।

तदेवं संयोगस्य स्वरूपं कारणं कार्यं चाभिहितम् । अथ हानोपायकथनद्वारेणोपादेयकारणमाह

विवेकख्यातिरविप्लवा हानोपायः ॥26॥

vivekakhyātiraviplavā hānopāyah

The realization of its true nature by the soul is called vivekakhyāti. When the soul is able to realize its true nature, it withdraws its prakṛti buddhi[4], that is, it stops

---

4 My German friend, Mr. Alois Heinrich on this prakṛti buddhi of
   soul referred to the English word buddy, which is referred to a

identifying itself with prakṛti/mind. This Vivekakhyāti (aviplavā) when reaches the stage of uniterruption or maturity, (upāyaḥ) becomes the means of (hāna) the end of the union of puruṣa (souls) and prakṛti (body), i.e. the means of emancipation.

व्यासभाष्य—सत्त्वपुरुषान्यताप्रत्ययो विवेकख्यातिः । सा त्वनिवृत्तमिथ्याज्ञाना प्लवते । यदा मिथ्याज्ञानं दग्धबीजभावं वन्ध्यप्रसवं संपद्यते तदा विधूतक्लेशरजसः सत्त्वस्य परे वैशारद्ये परस्यां वशीकारसंज्ञायां

वर्तमानस्य विवेकप्रत्ययप्रवाहो निर्मलो भवति । सा विवेकख्यातिरविप्लवा हानोपायः । ततो मिथ्याज्ञानस्य दग्धबीजभावोपगमः पुनश्चाप्रसव इत्येष मोक्षस्य मार्गो हानस्योपाय इति ।

भोजवृत्ति—अन्ये गुणा अन्यः पुरुष इत्येवंविधस्य विवेकस्य या ख्यातिः प्रख्या साऽस्य हानस्य दृश्यदुःख परित्यागस्योपायः कारणम् । कीदृशी अविप्लवा न विद्यते विप्लवो विच्छेदोऽन्तराऽन्तरा व्युत्थानरूपो यस्याः साऽविप्लवा । इदमत्र तात्पर्यम् प्रतिपक्षभावनाबलादविद्याप्रविलये विनिवृत्तज्ञातृत्वकर्तृत्वाभिमानायाः रजस्तमोमलानभिभृताया बुद्धेरन्तर्मुखा या चिच्छायासंक्रान्तिः सा विवेकख्यातिरुच्यते । तस्यां च संततत्वेन प्रवृत्तायां सत्यां दृश्यस्याधिकारनिवृत्तिर्भवत्येव कैवल्यम् । उत्पन्नविवेकख्यातेः पुरुथस्य यादृशी प्रज्ञा भवति तां कथयन्विवेकख्यातेरेव स्वरूपमाह

तस्य सप्तधा प्रान्तभूमिः प्रज्ञा ॥27॥
tasya saptadhā prāntabhūmiḥ prajñā

(tasya) A Yogī who has attained vivekakhyāti undergoes (saptadhā) sevenfold (prajñā) experiences. These sevenfold experiences have been given by the Vyāsa as under:

1. I have known the sufferings to be eliminated along with their causes, now there is nothing more to be known. This is his first experience.

2. The cause of pain, i.e. avidyā have been eliminated, now nothing is left to be eliminated. This is his second experience.

---

good friend. Buddhi is your buddy which helps you in emancipation.

3. Through Asamprajñāta samādhi, I have realized the state of Mokṣa, now nothing is left to be realized. This is his third experience.

4. I have attained perfection in Viveka-khyāti which is the means of Mokṣa, now nothing is left to be perfected. This is his fourth experience.

The above-cited four experiences cover freedom from action. The next three will cover the freedom of mind (chitta).

5. The objective of prakṛti buddhi (soul identifying itself with the prakṛti) is bhoga (enjoyment) and mokṣa. A yogī feels that the objectives of prakṛti buddhi has been achieved. This is his fifth experience.

6. The guṇas have resolved into their cause along with mind. Now they will not rise again. This is the sixth experience.

7. Lastly the yogī feels that he/she has risen above the guṇas born of prakṛti and realizes his/her true nature and Brahman. This is the state of self-realization and realization of Brahman which is also called emancipation.

Having experienced these seven types of stages, a yogī is called living liberated.

व्यासभाष्य—तस्येति प्रत्युदितख्यातेः प्रत्याम्नायः । सप्तधेति अशुद्ध्यावरणमलापगमाच्चित्तस्य प्रत्ययान्तरानुत्पादे सति सप्तप्रकारैव प्रज्ञा विवेकिनो भवति ।

तद्यथा 1 परिज्ञातं हेयं नास्य पुनः परिज्ञेयमस्ति ।   2 क्षीणा हेय हेतवो न पुनरेतेषां क्षेतव्यमस्ति । 3 साक्षात्कृतं निरोधसमाधिना हानम् । 4 भावितो विवेकख्यातिरूपो हानोपाय इति । एषा चतुष्टयी कार्या विमुक्तिः प्रज्ञायाः । चित्तविमुक्तिस्तु त्रयी ।   5 चरिताधिकारा बुद्धिः । 6 गुणा गिरिशिखरतटच्युता इव ग्रावाणो निरवस्थानाः स्वकारणे प्रलयाभिमुखाः सह तेनास्तं गच्छन्ति । न चैषां प्रविलीनानां पुनरस्त्युत्पादः प्रयोजनाभावादिति ।   7 एतस्यामवस्थायां गुणसम्बन्धातीतः स्वरूपमात्रज्योतिरमलः केवली पुरुष इति । एतां सप्तविधां प्रान्तभूमिप्रज्ञानमनुपश्यन्पुरुषः कुशल इत्याख्यायते । प्रतिप्रसवेऽपि चित्तस्य मुक्तः कुशल इत्येव भवति गुणातीतत्वादिति ।

सिद्धा भवति विवेकख्यातिर्हानोपाय इति । न च सिद्धिरन्तरेण साधनमित्येतदारभ्यते

भोजवृत्ति—तस्योत्पन्नविवेकज्ञानस्य ज्ञातव्यविवेकरूपा प्रज्ञा प्रान्तभूमौ सकलसालम्बनसमाधिभूमिपर्यन्ते सप्तप्रकारा भवति । तत्र कार्यविमुक्तिरूपा चतुष्प्रकारा   1 ज्ञातं मया ज्ञेयं न ज्ञातव्यं किंचिदस्ति । 2 क्षीणा मे क्लेशा न किंचित्क्षेतव्यमस्ति । 3 अधिगतं मया ज्ञानं 4 प्राप्तं मया विवेकख्यातिरिति । प्रत्ययान्तरपरिहारेण तस्यामवस्थायामीदृश्येव प्रज्ञा जायते । ईदृशी प्रज्ञा कार्यविषयं निर्मलं ज्ञानं कार्यविमुक्तिरित्युच्यते । चित्तविमुक्तिस्त्रिधा   5 चरितार्था मे बुद्धिर्गुणा हताधिकारा गिरिशिखरनिपतिता इव ग्रावाणो न पुनः स्थितिं यास्यन्ति   6 स्वकारणे प्रविलयाभिमुखानां गुणानां मोहभिधानमूलकारणाभावान्निष्प्रयोजनत्वाच्चामीषां कुतः प्ररोहो भवेत् 7 सात्मीभूतश्च मे समाधिस्तस्मिन्सति स्वरूपप्रतिष्ठोऽहमिति । ईदृशी त्रिप्रकारा चित्तविमुक्तिः । तदेवमीदृश्यां सप्तविधप्रान्तभूमिप्रज्ञायामुपजातायां पुरुषः कुशलः इत्युच्यते । विवेकख्यातिः संयोगाभावहेतुरित्युक्तं तस्यास्तूत्पत्तौ किं निमित्तमित्यत आह

योगाङ्गानुष्ठानादशुद्धिक्षये ज्ञानदीप्तिरा विवेकख्यातेः ॥28॥

yogāṅgānuṣṭhānādaśuddhikṣaye jñānadīptirā vivekakhyāteḥ

(anuṣṭhānāt) By the practice of (yogāṅga) 8 parts of yoga, (aśuddhi) impurities of afflictions (kleśas) are (kṣaya) eliminated and so the (jñāna-diptiḥ) light of right knowledge starts shining and it culminates (vivekakhyāteḥ) at Vivekakhyāti.

व्यासभाष्य—योगाङ्गान्यष्टावभिधायिष्यमाणानि । तेषामनुष्ठानात्पञ्चपर्वणो विपर्ययस्याशुद्धिरूपस्य क्षयो नाशः । तत्क्षये सम्यग्ज्ञानस्याभिव्यक्तिः । यथा यथा च साधनान्यनुष्ठीयन्ते तथा तथा तनुत्वमशुद्धिरापद्यते । यथा यथा च क्षीयते तथा तथा क्षयक्रमानुरोधिनी ज्ञानस्यापि दीप्तिर्विवर्धते । सा खल्वेषा विवृद्धिः प्रकर्षमनुभवत्या विवेकख्यातेः आ गुणपुरुषस्वरूपविज्ञानादित्यर्थः । योगाङ्गानुष्ठानमशुद्धेर्वियोगकारणम् ।

यथा परशुश्छेद्यस्य । विवेकख्यातेस्तु प्राप्तिकारणं यथा धर्मः सुखस्य नान्यथा कारणम् । कति चैतानि कारणानि शास्त्रे भवन्ति । नवैवेत्याह । तद्यथा

उत्पत्तिस्थित्यभिव्यक्तिविकारप्रत्ययाप्तयः ।

वियोगान्यत्वधृतयः कारणं नवधा स्मृतम् ।।इति ।।

तत्रोत्पत्तिकारणं मनो भवति विज्ञानस्य स्थितिकारणं मनसः पुरुषार्थता शरीरस्येवाऽऽहार इति । अभिव्यक्तिकारणं यथा रूपस्याऽऽलोकस्तथा रूपज्ञानं विकारकारणं मनसो विषयान्तरम् । यथाऽग्निः पाक्यस्य । प्रत्ययकारणं धूमज्ञानमग्निज्ञानस्य । प्राप्तिकारणं योगाङ्गानुष्ठानं विवेकख्यातेः ।

वियोगकारणं तदेवाशुद्धेः । अन्यत्वकारणं यथा सुवर्णस्य सुवर्णकारः । एवमेकस्य स्त्रीप्रत्ययस्याविद्या मूढत्वे द्वेषो दुःखत्वे रागः सुखत्वे तत्त्वज्ञानं माध्यस्थ्ये । धृतिकारणं

शरीरमिन्द्रियाणाम्। तानि च तस्य। महाभूतानि शरीराणां तानि च परस्परं सर्वेषां तैर्यग्यौनमानुषदैवतानि च परस्परार्थत्वादित्येवं नव कारणानि। तानि च यथासंभवं पदार्थान्तरेष्वपि योज्यानि। योगाङ्गानुष्ठानं तु द्विधैव कारणत्वं लभत इति। तत्र योगाङ्गान्यवधार्यन्ते

भोजवृत्ति—योगाङ्गानि वक्ष्यमाणानि तेषामनुष्ठानाज्ज्ञानपूर्वकादभ्यासादा विवेकख्यातेरशुद्धिक्षये चित्तसत्त्वस्य प्रकाशावरणलक्षणक्लेशरूपाशुद्धिक्षये या ज्ञानदीप्तिस्तारतम्येन सात्त्विकः परिणामो विवेकख्यातिपर्यन्तः स तस्याः ख्यातेर्हेतुरित्यर्थः। योगाङ्गानुष्ठानादशुद्धिक्षय इत्युक्तं कानि पुनस्तानि योगाङ्गानीति तेषामुपदेशमाह

यमनियमासनप्राणायामप्रत्याहारधारणाध्यानसमाधयोऽष्टावङ्गानि ॥29॥

*yamaniyamāsanaprāṇāyāmapratyāhāradhāraṇādhyānasamā
dhayo'ṣṭāvaṅgāni*

Yama (social discipline), niyama (personal discipline), Āsana (posture), prāṇyāma (control of breath), pratyāhāra (withdrawal of the senses), dhāraṇā (concentration of mind), dhyāna (meditation) and samādhi, these eight parts of yoga.

व्यासभाष्य—यथाक्रममेषामनुष्ठानं स्वरूपं च वक्ष्यामः। तत्र

भोजवृत्ति—इह कानिचित्समाधेः साक्षादुपकारकत्वेनान्तरङ्गाणि यथा धारणादीनि। कानिचित्प्रतिपक्षभूतहिंसादिवितर्कोन्मूलनद्वारेण समाधिमुपकुर्वन्ति। यथा यमनियमादीनि। तत्रासनादिनामुत्तरोत्तरमुपकारकत्वम्। तद्यथा सत्यासनजये प्राणायामस्थैर्यम्। एवमुत्तरत्रापि योज्यम्। क्रमेणैषां स्वरूपमाह

अहिंसासत्यास्तेयब्रह्मचर्यापरिग्रहा यमाः ॥30॥

ahiṃsāsatyāsteyabrahmacaryāparigrahā yamāḥ

1. Ahinsā - Non-violence,

2. Satya - Truthfulness

3. Asteya - Non-Stealing

4. Brahmcharya - Celibacy

5. Aparigraha - (Non-hoarding), these are yamas or social discipline.

Hereunder we give a detailed description of the yamas.

Ahinsā (Non-violence) - Ahinsā does not mean just killing or wounding some creature, but Sāstra says that Ahinsā means not to kill or even hurt any living being in any way by speech, thought, or action. Ahinsā is the most important of all other yamas and niyamas. Vyāsa says: 'तत्राहिंसा सर्वदा सर्वभूतानामनभिद्रोहः । ' ('*tatrāhimsā sarvadā sarvabhūtānāmanabhidrohah*'). Ahimsā means having not enmity with anybody. Patañjali says that one who is firmly (strongly) established in Ahinsā even rivals become friends. 'अहिंसाप्रतिष्ठायां तत्सन्निधौ वैरत्यागः ' (*ahimsāpratiṣṭhāyām tatsannidhau vairatyāgaḥ*).

Satya (Truthfulness) - Vyāsa said 'सत्यं यथार्थे वाङ्मनसे यथा दृष्टं यथा श्रुतं तथा वाङ्मनश्चेति (*satyam yathārthe vānmanase yathā dṛṣṭam yathā śrutam tathā vānmanaścheti*). Whatever seen or heard must be followed in mind and speech. The words one speaks should not harm any creature and has to produce happiness and joy to all. The words should be pleasing, beneficial and not agitating. One who is established in truthfulness, his/her actions will yield desired fruits. 'सत्यप्रतिष्ठायां क्रियाफलाश्रयत्वम्' (*satyapratiṣṭhāyām kriyāphalāśrayatvam*) ।

Asteya (non-stealing) अस्तेयमशास्त्रपूर्वकं द्रव्याणां परतः स्वीकरणम् तत्प्रतिषेधः - पुनरस्पृहारूपम् अस्तेयमिति (*asteyamaśāstrapūrvakam dravyāṇām parataḥ svīkaraṇam tatpratiṣedhaḥ - punarasprhārūpam asteyamiti*)- Due to attraction or desires the idea of stealing arises. So, one who is firmly established in non-stealing all the gems and wealth comes to him. 'अस्तेयप्रतिष्ठायां सर्वरत्नोपस्थानम् (*asteyapratiṣṭhāyām sarvaratnopasthānam*)

Brahmacharya (celibacy)-'ब्रह्मचर्यं गुप्तेन्द्रियाणां संयमः ' (*brahmamacharyam guptendriyāṇām samyamaḥ*) Brahmacharya means control of sexual desire. If a man saves his vital energy or seminal fluid his body becomes brilliant and fragrant and takes him near to Brahman. One who is firmly established in Brahmacharya, vigour can be gained. The same is said 'ब्रह्मचर्य प्रतिष्ठायां वीर्यलाभः (*brahmacharya pratiṣṭhāyāṁ vīryalābhaḥ*) ।

Aparigraha-Vyasa says: 'विषयाणामार्जनरक्षणक्षयसंगहिंसादोष-दर्शनादिस्वीकरणमपरिग्रहः (*viṣayānāmārjanarakṣaṇakṣayasaṁgahiṁs ādoṣa-darśanādisvīkaraṇamaparigrahaḥ*) So, parigraha is a process of hoarding, preserving, and attachment to the objects more than wha is required. Aparigraha can be attained easily by developing detachment to all material objects. By doing so the Sādhaka acquires the knowledge of his past, present, and future. 'अपरिग्रहस्थैर्ये जन्मकथन्तासम्बोधः ' (*aparigrahasthairye janmakathantāsambodhaḥ*).

व्यासभाष्य—तत्राहिंसा सर्वथा सर्वदा सर्वभूतानामनभिद्रोहः । उत्तरे च यमनियमास्तन्मूलास्तत्सिद्धिपरतयैव तत्प्रतिपादनाय प्रतिपाद्यन्ते । तदवदातरूपकरणायैवोपादीयन्ते । तथा चोक्तम् स खल्वयं ब्राह्मणो यथा यथा व्रतानि बहूनि समादित्सते तथा तथा प्रमादकृतेभ्यो हिंसानिदानेभ्यो निवर्तमानस्तामेवावदातरूपामहिंसां करोति ।

सत्यं यथार्थे वाङ्मनसे । यथा दृष्टं यथाऽनुमितं यथा श्रुतं तथा वाङ्मनश्चेति । परत्र स्वबोधसंक्रान्तये वागुक्ता सा यदि न वञ्चिता भ्रान्ता वा प्रतिपत्तिवन्ध्या वा भवेदिति । एषा सर्वभूतोपकारार्थं प्रवृत्ता न भूतोपघाताय । यदि चैवमप्यभिधीयमाना भूतोपघातपरैव स्यान्न सत्यं भवेत्पापमेव भवेत्तेन पुण्याभासेन पुण्यप्रतिरूपकेण कष्टं तमः प्राप्नुयात् । तस्मात्परीक्ष्य सर्वभूतहितं सत्यं ब्रूयात् ।

स्तेयमशास्त्रपूर्वकं द्रव्याणां परतः स्वीकरणं तत्प्रतिषेधः पुनरस्पृहारूपमस्तेयमिति । ब्रह्मचर्य गुप्तेन्द्रियस्योपस्थस्य संयमः । विषयाणामर्जनरक्षणाक्षयसङ्घहिंसादोषदर्शनादस्वीकरणमपरिग्रह इत्येते यमाः । ते तु

.**भोजवृत्ति.**—तत्र प्राणवियोगप्रयोजनव्यापारो हिंसा । सा च सर्वानर्थहेतुः । तदभावोऽहिंसा । हिंसायाः सर्वकालं परिहार्यत्वात्प्रथमं तदभावरूपाया अहिंसाया निर्देशः । सत्यं वाङ्मनसयोर्यथार्थत्वम् । स्तेयं परस्वापहरणं तदभावोऽस्तेयम् । ब्रह्मचर्यमुपस्थसंयमः । अपरिग्रहो भोगसाधनानामनङ्गीकारः । त एतेऽहिंसादयः पञ्च यमशब्दवाच्या योगाङ्गत्वेन निर्दिष्टाः । एषां विशेषमाह

जातिदेशकालसमयानवच्छिन्नाः सार्वभौमा महाव्रतम् ॥31॥

*jātideśakālasamayānavacchinnāḥ sārvabhaumā
mahāvratam*

Yamas (social disciplines) are great universal observances. They are to be observed beyond the limits of yonis (species), time, and place.

For instance, violence is violence if it is done intentionally to a small creature like an ant or to a human being, if it is done at the battlefield or on any date and time.

व्यासभाष्य—तत्राहिंसा जात्यवच्छिन्ना मत्स्यवधकस्य मत्स्येष्वेव नान्यत्र हिंसा। सैव देशावच्छिन्ना न तीर्थे हनिष्यामीति। सैव कालावच्छिन्ना न चतुर्दश्यां न पुण्येऽहनि हनिष्यामीति। सैव त्रिभिरुपरतस्य समयावच्छिन्ना देवब्राह्मणार्थे नान्यथा हनिष्यामीति। यथा च क्षत्रियाणां युद्धा एव हिंसा नान्यत्रेति। एभिर्जातिदेशकालसमयैरनवच्छिन्ना अहिंसादयः सर्वथैव परिपालनीयाः। सर्वभूमिषु सर्वविषयेषु सर्वथैवाविदितव्यभिचाराः सार्वभौमामहाव्रतमित्युच्यन्ते।

भोजवृत्ति—जातिर्ब्राह्मणत्वादिः। देशस्तीर्थादिः। कालश्चतुर्दश्यादिः। समयो ब्राह्मणप्रयोजनादिः। एतैश्चतुर्भिरनवच्छिन्नाः पूर्वोक्ता अहिंसादयो यमाः सर्वासु क्षित्यादिषु चित्तभूमिषु भवा महाव्रतमित्युच्यन्ते। तद्यथा ब्राह्मणं न हनिष्यामि तीर्थे न कंचन हनिष्यामि चतुर्दश्यां न हनिष्यामि देवब्राह्मणप्रयोजनव्यतिरेकेण कमपि न हनिष्यामीति। एवं चतुर्विधावच्छेदव्यतिरेकेण किंचित्क्वचित्कदाचित्कस्मिंश्चिदर्थे न हनिष्यामीत्यनवच्छिन्नाः। एवं सत्यादिषु यथायोगं योज्यम्। इत्थमनियतीकृताः सामान्येनैव प्रवृत्ता महाव्रतमित्युच्यते न पुनः परिच्छिन्नावधारणम्। नियमानाह

शौचसंतोषतपःस्वाध्यायेश्वरप्रणिधानानि नियमाः ॥32॥

śaucasaṃtoṣatapaḥsvādhyāyeśvarapraṇidhānāni niyamāḥ

Niyamas (self-discipline) are also of five kinds.

1. Śaucha - Cleanliness

2. Santoṣa - Contentment

3. Tapas - Austerity

4. Svādhyāya- Study

5. Iśvarapraṇidhāna- Surrendering everything to God.

Śauca - (Cleanliness) - This śauca is of two types :

1. External, 2. Internal

External purity will be achieved by taking bath etc, internal purity by purifying the mind with satya and jñāna, etc., by doing this external Śaucha, the Sādhaka shows detachment to his own body without comparing with others. The same is said, 'शौचात्स्वाङ्गजुगुप्सा परैरसंसर्गः ' (śauchātsvāngajugupsā parairasaṁsargaḥ) । By internal purity, purification of mind, concentration, control of organs and self-realization can be attained. 'सत्वशुद्धिसौमनस्यैकाग्रयेन्द्रियजयात्मदर्शनयोग्यत्वानि च   ' (satvaśuddhisaumanasyaikāgrayendriyajayātmadarśanayogy atvāni cha)

Santoṣa - (Contentment)-'सन्तोषः सन्निहितसाधनाद्धिकस्यानु - पादिता' (santoṣaḥ sannihitasādhanāddhikasyānu-pāditā) contentment means not earning more than what is needed. It is a state in which the aspirant is satisfied with what he is having by developing detachment to material objects   'सन्तोषादनुत्तमसुखलाभः' (santoṣādanuttamasukhalābhaḥ) ।'

Tapas (Austerity) - 'तपो द्वन्द्वसहनम् द्वन्द्वश्च जिघत्सापिपासे   , शीतोष्णे, स्थानासने' (tapo dvandvasahanam dvandvaścha jighatsāpipāse, śītoṣṇe, sthānāsane). Means austerity is the power to tolerate opposite feelings like hunger-thirst, cold-hot, happiness-unhappiness, etc., equally. By practicing austerity all the impurities will be removed and a perfection of body and senses can be attained. 'कायेन्द्रियसिद्धिरशुद्धिक्षयात्तपसः (kāyendriyasiddhiraśuddhikṣayāttapasaḥ) ।'

Svādhyāya (Study) - 'स्वाध्यायः मोक्षशास्त्राणामध्ययनं प्रणवजपो वा (svādhyāyaḥ mokṣaśāstrāṇāmadhyayanaṁ praṇavajapo vā)'

Svādhyāya means, study of the Vedas and the Śāstras or chanting of 'AUM' (Praṇava) which shows us the path of liberation. By perfectly following the Svādhyāya the sādhaka realizes the intended sense of the Śāstra or Veda. 'स्वाध्यायादिष्टदेवतासम्प्रयोगः' *svadhyāyādiṣṭadevatāsamprayogaḥ.*

Iśvara praṇidhāna (surrender to God) - It is said, 'ईश्वरपप्रणिधानं तस्मिन्परमगुरो सर्वकर्मार्पणम् ।' (*iśvarapapraṇidhānaṁ tasminparamaguro sarvakarmārpaṇam*) That is Iśvara praṇidhāna means to surrender himself/herself and his/her actions to God. By doing so सम्प्रज्ञातसमाधि can be attained. Patañjali said- 'समाधिसिद्धिरीश्वरप्रणिधानात् ।' (*samādhisiddhirīśvarapraṇidhānāt*).

व्यासभाष्य—तत्र शौचं मृज्जलादिजनितं मेध्याभ्यवहरणादि च बाह्यम् । आभ्यन्तरं चित्तमलानामाक्षालनम् । संतोषः संनिहितसाधनादधिकस्यानुपादित्सा । तपो द्वंद्वसहनम् । द्वंद्वं च जिघत्सापिपासे शीतोष्णे स्थानासने काष्ठमौनाकारमौने च । व्रतानि चैषां यथायोगं कृच्छ्रचान्द्रायणसांतपनादीनि । स्वाध्यायो मोक्षशास्त्राणामध्ययनं प्रणवजपो वा । ईश्वरप्रणिधानं तस्मिन्परमगुरौ सर्वकर्मार्पणम् ।

शय्यासनस्थोऽथ पथि व्रजन्वा स्वस्थः परिक्षीणवितर्कजालः ।
संसारबीजक्षयमीक्षमाणः स्यान्नित्ययुक्तोऽमृतभोगभागी ।।
यत्रेदमुक्तं ततः प्रत्यक्चेतनाधिगमोऽप्यन्तरायाभावश्चेति । ।32 ।।

एतेषां यमनियमानाम्

भोजवृत्ति—शौचं द्विविधं बाह्यमाभ्यन्तरं च । बाह्यं मृज्जलादिभिः कायादिप्रक्षालनम् । आभ्यन्तरं मैत्र्यादिभिश्चित्तमलानां प्रक्षालनम् । संतोषस्तुष्टिः । शेषाः प्रागेव कृतव्याख्यानाः । एते शौचादयो नियमशब्दवाच्याः । कथमेषां योगाङ्गत्वमित्यत आह

वितर्कबाधने प्रतिपक्षभावनम् ॥33॥
vitarkabādhane pratipakṣabhāvanam

When wicked ideas become the hurdle in observing yamas and niyamas, control them with the thought of their dreadful consequences.

The process of thinking of the dreadful consequences of wicked acts is cited in the following sūtra.

व्यासभाष्य—यदास्य ब्राह्मणस्य हिंसादयो वितर्का जायेरन्हनिष्याम्यहमपकारिणमनृतमपि वक्ष्यामि द्रव्यमप्यस्य स्वी करिष्यामि दारेषु चास्य व्यवायी भविष्यामि परिग्रहेषु चास्य स्वामी भविष्यामीति । एवमुन्मार्गप्रवणवितर्कज्वरेणातिदीप्तेन बाध्यमानस्तत्प्रतिपक्षान्भावयेत् । घोरेषु संसाराङ्गारेषु पच्यमानेन मया शरणमुपागतः सर्वभूताभयप्रदानेन योगधर्मः । स खल्वहं त्यक्त्वा वितर्कान्पुनस्तानाददानस्तुल्यः श्ववृत्तेनेति भावयेत् । यथा श्वा वान्तावलेही तथा त्यक्तस्य पुनराददान इति । एवमादि सूत्रान्तरेष्वपि योज्यम् ।

व्यासभाष्य—वितर्क्यन्त इति वितर्का योगपरिपन्थिनो हिंसादयस्तेषां प्रतिपक्षभावने सति यदा बाधा भवति तदा योगः सुकरो भवतीति भवत्येव यमनियमानां योगाङ्गत्वम् । इदानीं वितर्काणां स्वरूपं भेदप्रकारं कारणं फलं न क्रमेणाऽऽह

वितर्का हिंसादयः कृतकारितानुमोदिता लोभक्रोधमोहपूर्वका मृदुमध्याधिमात्रा दुःखाज्ञानानन्तफला इति प्रतिपक्षभावनम् ॥34॥

*vitarkā himsādayah kṛtakāritānumoditā
lobhakrodhamohapūrvakā mṛdumadhyādhimātrā
duhkhājñānānantaphalā iti pratipakṣabhāvanam*

Violence, etc. are the wicked acts. These wicked acts whether (*kṛt*) committed, (*kārita*) abetted, or (*anumodita*) supported are born of (lobha) greed, (krodha) anger, and (moha) attachment. Whether their intensity is (mṛdu) mild, (madhya) moderate, or (adhimātra) high, they will result in (ananta) endless (duḥkha) pain and (ajñāna) ignorance. This is how we can (bhāvanam) think of their (pratipakṣa) dreadful consequences.

व्यासभाष्य—तत्र हिंसा तावत् कृता कारिताऽनुमोदितेति त्रिधा । एकैका पुनस्त्रिधा लोभेन मांसचर्मार्थेन क्रोधेनापकृतमनेनेति मोहेन धर्मो मे भविष्यतीति । लोभक्रोधमोहाः पुनस्त्रिविधा मृदुमध्याधिमात्रा इति । एवं सप्तविंशतिभेदा भवन्ति हिंसायाः । मृदुमध्याधिमात्राः पुनस्त्रिविधाः मृदुमृदुर्मध्यमृदुस्तीव्रमृदुरिति । तथा मृदुमध्यो मध्यमध्यस्तीव्रमध्य इति । तथा मृदुतीव्रो मध्यतीव्रोऽधिमात्रतीव्र इति एवमेकाशीतिभेदा हिंसा भवति । सा पुनर्नियमविकल्पसमुच्चयभेदादसंख्येया प्राणभृद्भेदस्यापरिसंख्येयत्वादिति । एवमनृतादिष्वपि योज्यम् ।

ते खल्वमी वितर्का दुःखाज्ञानानन्तफला इति प्रतिपक्षभावनम् । दुःखमज्ञानं चानन्तं फलं येषामिति प्रतिपक्षभावनम् । तथा च हिंसकस्तावत्प्रथमं वध्यस्य वीर्यमाक्षिपति । ततश्च शस्त्रादिनिपातेन दुःखयति । ततो जीवितादपि मोचयति । ततो वीर्याक्षेपादस्य चेतनाचेतनमुपकरण

क्षीणावीर्यं भवति ।

दुःखोत्पादान्नरकतिर्यक्मनुष्यादिषु दुःखमनुभवति । जीवितव्यपरोपणात्प्रतिक्षणं च जीवितात्यये वर्तमानो मरणमिच्छन्नपि दुःखविपाकस्य नियतविपाकवेदनीयत्वात्कथंचिदेवोच्छ्वसिति । यदि च कथंचित्पुण्यावापगता हिंसा भवेत्तत्र सुखप्राप्तौ भवेदल्पायुरिति । एवमनृतादिष्वपि योज्यं यथासंभवम् । एवं वितर्काणां चामुमेवानुगतं विपाकमनिष्टं भावयन्न वितर्केषु मनः प्रणिदधीत ।

भोजवृत्ति.—एते पूर्वोक्ताः वितर्काः हिंसादयः प्रथमं त्रिधा भिद्यन्ते कृतकारितानुमोदिता भेदेन । तत्र स्वयं निष्पादिताः कृताः । कुरु कुर्विति प्रयोजकव्यापारेण समुत्पादिताः कारिताः । अन्येन क्रियमाणाः साध्वित्यङ्गीकृता अनुमोदिताः । एतच्च त्रैविध्यं परस्परव्यामोहनिवारणायोच्यते । अन्यथा मन्दमतिरेवं मन्येत न मया स्वयं हिंसा कृतेति नास्ति मे दोष इति । एतेषां कारणप्रतिपादनाय लोभक्रोधमोहपूर्वका इति । यद्यपि लोभक्रोधौ प्रथमं निर्दिष्टौ तथाऽपि सर्वक्लेशानां मोहस्यानात्मनि आत्माभिमानलक्षणस्य निदानत्वात्तस्मिन्सति स्वपरविभागपूर्वकत्वेन लोभक्रोधादीनामुद्भवान्मूलत्वमवसेयम् । मोहपूर्विका सर्वा दोषजातिरित्यर्थः । लोभस्तृष्णा । क्रोधः कृत्याकृत्यविवेकोन्मूलकः प्रज्वलनात्मकश्चित्तधर्मः । प्रत्येकं कृतादिभेदेन त्रिप्रकारा अपि हिंसादयो मोहादिकारणत्वेन त्रिधा भिद्यन्ते । एषामेव पुनरवस्थाभेदेन त्रैविध्यमाह मृदुमध्याधिमात्राः । मृदवो मन्दा न तीव्रा नापि मध्याः । मध्या नापि मन्दा नापि तीव्राः । अधिमात्रास्तीव्राः । पाश्चात्या नव भेदाः । इत्थं त्रैविध्ये सति सप्तविंशतिर्भवति । मृद्वादीनामपि प्रत्येकं मृदुमध्याधिमात्रभेदात्त्रैविध्यं संभवति । तद्यथायोगं योज्यम् । तद्यथा मृदुमृदुर्मृदुमध्यो मृदुतीव्र इति । एषां फलमाह दुःखाज्ञानानन्तफलाः । दुःखं प्रतिकूलतयाऽवभासमानो राजसश्चित्तधर्मः । अज्ञानं मिथ्याज्ञानं संशयविपर्ययरूपं ते दुःखाज्ञाने अनन्तमपरिच्छिन्नं फलं येषां ते तथोक्ताः । इत्थं तेषां स्वरूपकारणादिभेदेन ज्ञातानां प्रतिपक्षभावनया योगिना परिहारः कर्तव्य इत्युपदिष्टं भवति । एषामभ्यासवशात्प्रकर्षमागच्छतामनुनिष्पादिन्यः सिद्धयो यथा भवन्ति तथा क्रमेण प्रतिपादयितुमाह

Hereunder the result of perfection attained in yamas is delineated.

अहिंसाप्रतिष्ठायां तत्सन्निधौ वैरत्यागः ॥35॥

ahiṃsāpratiṣṭhāyāṃ tatsannidhau vairatyāgaḥ

Should a yogī attains perfection in Ahinsā (Non-violence), all living beings around him/her leave enmity.

व्यासभाष्य—सर्वप्राणिनां भवति ।

भोजवृत्ति.—तस्याहिंसां भावयतः संनिधौ सहज विरोधिनामप्यहिनकुलादीनां वैरत्यागो निर्मत्सरतयाऽवस्थानं भवति । हिंसा अपि हिंस्रत्वं परित्यजन्तीत्यर्थः । सत्याभ्यासवतः किं भवतीत्याह

सत्यप्रतिष्ठायां क्रियाफलाश्रयत्वम् ॥36॥
satyapratiṣṭhāyāṃ kriyāphalāśrayatvam

When perfection in truth is attained, whatever a yogī thinks or speaks is instantly materialized on the ground.

व्यासभाष्य—धार्मिको भूया इति भवति धार्मिकः। स्वर्गंप्राप्नुहीति स्वर्गं प्राप्नोति। अमोघाऽस्य वाग्भवति।

भोजवृत्ति—क्रियमाणा हि क्रिया यागादिकाः फलं स्वर्गादिकं प्रयच्छन्ति तस्य तु सत्याभ्यासवतो योगिनस्तथा सत्यं प्रकृष्यते यथा क्रियायामकृतायामपि योगी फलमाप्नोति। तद्वचनाद्यस्य कस्यचित्क्रियामकुर्वतोऽपि क्रियाफलं भवतीत्यर्थः। अस्तेयाभ्यासवतः फलमाह

अस्तेयप्रतिष्ठायां सर्वरत्नोपस्थानम् ॥37॥
asteyapratiṣṭhāyāṃ sarvaratnopasthānam

On achieving perfection in non-stealing, a yogī never has the shortage of things desired by him at any place or time.

व्यासभाष्य—सर्वदिक्स्थान्यस्योपतिष्ठन्ते रत्नानि।

भोजवृत्ति—अस्तेयं यदाऽभ्यस्यति तदाऽस्य तत्प्रकर्षान्निरभिलाषस्यापि सर्वतो दिव्यानि रत्नानि उपतिष्ठन्ते। ब्रह्मचर्याभ्यासस्य फलमाह

ब्रह्मचर्यप्रतिष्ठायां वीर्यलाभः ॥38॥
brahmacaryapratiṣṭhāyāṃ vīryalābhaḥ

On perfection in Brahmacharya, a yogī attains unrestricted energy and is able to transmit energy and knowledge to a humble seeker of it.

व्यासभाष्य—यस्य लाभादप्रतिघानगुणानुत्कर्षयति। सिद्धश्च विनेयेषु ज्ञानमाधातुं समर्थो भवतीति।

भोजवृत्ति—यः किल ब्रह्मचर्यमभ्यस्यति तस्य तत्प्रकर्षान्निरतिशयं वीर्यं सामर्थ्यमाविर्भवति। वीर्यनिरोधो हि ब्रह्मचर्यं तस्य प्रकर्षाच्छरीरेन्द्रियमनः सु वीर्यं प्रकर्षमागच्छति। अपरिग्रहाभ्यासस्य फलमाह

अपरिग्रहस्थैर्ये जन्मकथंतासम्बोधः ॥39॥
aparigrahasthairye janmakathaṃtāsambodhaḥ

On attaining perfection in non-hoarding, the secrets of past, present, and future lives reveal to a yogī. For instance, who is he? How did he attain this body? What is this life? How is this life coming into existence? What will be his future life? etc. etc.

व्यासभाष्य—अस्य भवति । कोहमासं कथमहमासं किंस्विदिदं कथं स्विदिदं के वा भविष्याम: कथं वा भविष्याम इत्येवमस्य पूर्वान्तपरान्तमध्येष्वात्मभावजिज्ञासा स्वरूपेणोपावर्तते । एता यमस्थैर्ये सिद्धय: । नियमेषु वक्ष्याम:

भोजवृत्ति—कथमित्यस्यभाव: कथंता जन्मन: कथंता जन्मकथंता तस्या: संबोध: सम्यग्ज्ञानं जन्मान्तरे कोऽहमासं कीदृश: किंकार्यकारीति जिज्ञासायां सर्वमेव सम्यग्ज्ञानातीत्यर्थ: । न केवलं भोगसाधनपरिग्रह एव परिग्रहो यावदात्मन: शरीरपरिग्रहोऽपि परिग्रह भोगसाधनत्वाच्छरीरस्य । तस्मिन्सति रागानुबन्धाद्बहिर्मुखायामेव प्रवृत्तौ न तात्त्विकज्ञानप्रादुर्भव: । यदा पुन: शरीरादिपरिग्रहनैरपेक्ष्येण माध्यस्थ्यमवलम्बते तदा मध्यस्थस्य रागादित्यागात्सम्यग्ज्ञानहेतुर्भवत्येव पूर्वापरजन्मसंबोध: ।

Now the results of attaining perfection in Niyamas are described.

शौचात् स्वाङ्गजुगुप्सा परैरसंसर्गः ॥40॥

śaucāt svāṅgajugupsā parairasaṃsargaḥ

On attaining perfection in Śaucha (cleanliness), a yogī develops aversion from his own body and avoids contact with others.

व्यासभाष्य—स्वाङ्गे जुगुप्सायां शौचमारभमाण: कायावद्दर्शी कायानभिष्वङ्गी यतिर्भवति । किं च परैरसंसर्ग: कायस्वभावावलोकी स्वमपि कायं जिहासुर्मृज्जलादिभिराक्षालयन्नपि कायशुद्धिमपश्यन्कथं परकायैरत्यन्तमेवाप्रयतै: संसृज्येत । किं च

भोजवृत्ति—य: शौचं भावयति तस्य स्वाङ्गेष्वपि कारणस्वरूपपर्यालोचनद्वारेण जुगुप्सा घृणा समुपजायतेऽशुचिरयं कायो नात्राऽऽग्रह: कार्य इति अमुनैव हेतुना परैरन्यैश्च कायवद्भिरसंसर्ग: संसर्गाभाव: संसर्गपरिवर्जनमित्यर्थ: । य: किल स्वमेव कायं जुगुप्सते तत्तदवद्यदर्शनात्स कथं परकीयैस्तथाभूतै: कायै: संसर्गमनुभवति । शौचस्यैव फलान्तरमाह

सत्त्वशुद्धिसौमनस्यैकाग्र्येन्द्रियजयात्मदर्शन-
योग्यत्वानि च ॥41॥

sattvaśuddhisaumanasyaikāgryendriyajayātmadarśana-

yogyatvāni ca

One also becomes (yogyatvāni) quaified for (sattva-śuddhi) purity of the mind, (saumanasya) cheerfulness of the heart, (ekāgrayya) concentration, (indriya-jaya) control of the senses, and (ātmadarśana) fitness for self-realization.

व्यासभाष्य—भवन्तीति वाक्यशेषः । शुचेः सत्त्वशुद्धिस्ततः सौमनस्यं तत एकाग्र्यं तत इन्द्रियजयस्ततश्चाऽऽत्मदर्शनयोग्यत्वं बुद्धिसत्त्वस्य भवतीत्येच्छौचस्थैर्यादधिगम्यत इति ।

भोजवृत्ति—भवन्तीति वाक्यशेषः । सत्त्वं प्रकाशसुखाद्यात्मकं तस्य शुद्धी रजस्तमोभ्यामनभिवः सौमनस्यं खेदाननुभवेन मानसी प्रीतिः । एकाग्रता नियतेन्द्रियविषये चेतसः स्थैर्यम् । इन्द्रियजयो विषयपराङ्मुखाणामिन्द्रियाणामात्मनि अवस्थानम् । आत्मदर्शने विवेकख्यातिरूपे चित्तस्य योग्यत्वंसमर्थत्वम् । शौचाभ्यसवत एते सत्त्वशुद्ध्यादयः क्रमेण प्रादुर्भवन्ति । तथा हि सत्त्वशुद्धेः सौमनस्यं सौमनस्यादैकाग्र्यमैकाग्र्यादिन्द्रियजय इन्द्रियजयादात्मदर्शनयोग्यतेति । संतोषाभ्यासवतः फलमाह

संतोषादनुत्तमसुखलाभः ॥42॥

saṃtoṣādanuttamasukhalābhaḥ

From perfection in contentment, superior type of happiness is achieved which cannot be achieved through through sensory enjoyment.

व्यासभाष्य—तथा चोक्तम्

यच्च कामसुखं लोके यच्च दिव्यं महत्सुखम् ।
तृष्णाक्षयसुखस्यैते नार्हतः षोडशीं कलाम् ।।इति । ।42 । ।

भोजवृत्ति—संतोषप्रकर्षेण योगिनस्तथाविधमान्तरं सुखमाविर्भवति । यस्य बाह्यं सुखं लेशेनापि न समम् । तपसः फलमाह

कायेन्द्रियसिद्धिरशुद्धिक्षयात् तपसः ॥43॥

kāyendriyasiddhiraśuddhikṣayāt tapasaḥ

From perfection in tapas (austerity), (aśuddhi) all impurities of the body, mind and sensory organs (kṣaya) are eliminated and a yogī attains (siddhi) divine powers of (kāya) the body like reducing the body to the size of an atom and inflating it to gigantic size; as well as the divine power of (indriyaa) senses like microscopic and telescopic vision, smelling of distant objecrs, hearing sounds of inaudible frequency and distance sounds, etc.

व्यासभाष्य—निर्वर्त्यमानमेव तपो हिनस्त्यशुद्ध्यावरणमलं तदावरणमलापग-मात्कायसिद्धिरणिमाद्या ।तथेन्द्रियसिद्धिर्दूराच्छ्रवणदर्शनाद्येति ।

भोजवृत्ति—तपः समभ्यस्यमानं चेतसः क्लेशादिलक्षणाशुद्धिक्षयद्वारेण कायेन्द्रियाणां सिद्धिमुत्कर्षमादधाति । अयमर्थः चान्द्रायणादिना चित्तक्लेशक्षयस्तत्क्षयादिन्द्रियाणां सूक्ष्मव्यवहितविप्रकृष्टदर्शनादिसामर्थ्यमाविर्भवति । कायस्य यथेच्छमणुत्वमहत्त्वादीनि । स्वाध्यायस्य फलमाह

स्वाध्यायाद् इष्टदेवतासंप्रयोगः ॥44॥
svādhyāyād iṣṭadevatāsaṃprayogaḥ

On attaining perfection in the (svādhyāya) study of Śāstras and Vedas, a yogī is able to know the (iṣṭa devatā) intended meaning of the Śāstra and Vedas.

On attaining siddhi in chanting a particular mantra, a yogī is able to achieve intended purpose of chanting the mantra.

व्यासभाष्य—देवा ऋषयः सिद्धाश्च स्वाध्यायशीलस्य दर्शनं गच्छन्ति कार्ये चास्य वर्तन्त इति ।

भोजवृत्ति—अभिप्रेतमन्त्रजपादिलक्षणे स्वाध्याये प्रकृष्यमाणे योगिन इष्ट्याऽभिप्रेतया देवतया संप्रयोगो भवति । सा देवता प्रत्यक्षीभवतीत्यर्थः । ईश्वरप्रणिधानस्य फलमाह

समाधिसिद्धिरीश्वरप्रणिधानात् ॥45॥
samādhisiddhirīśvarapraṇidhānāt

When a yogī completely surrenders himself/herself to God, he attains perfection in Samādhi.

व्यासभाष्य—ईश्वरार्पितसर्वभावस्य समाधिसिद्धिर्यया सर्वमीप्सितमवितथं जानाति देशान्तरे देहान्तरे कालान्तरे च । ततोऽस्य प्रज्ञा यथाभूतं प्रजानातीति ।
उक्ताः सह सिद्धिभिर्यमनियमाः । आसनादीनि वक्ष्यामः । तत्र

भोजवृत्ति—ईश्वरे यत्प्रणिधानं भक्तिविशेषस्तस्मात्समाधेरुक्तलक्षणस्याऽविर्भावो भवति । यस्मात्स भगवानीश्वरः प्रसन्नः सन्नान्तरायरूपान्क्लेशान्परिहृत्य समाधिं संबोधयति ।

यमनियमानुक्त्वाऽऽसनमाह

स्थिरसुखम् आसनम् ॥46॥
sthirasukham āsanam

Steady and comfortable posture is Āsana.

व्यासभाष्य—तद्यथा पद्मासनं वीरासनं भद्रासनं स्वस्तिकं दण्डासनं सोपाश्रयं पर्यङ्कं क्रौञ्चनिषदनं हस्तिनिषदनमुष्ट्रनिषदनं समसंस्थानं स्थिरसुखं यथासुखं चेत्येवमादीनि ।

भोजवृत्ति—आस्यतेऽनेनेत्यासनं पद्मासनदण्डासनस्वस्तिकासनादि । तद्यदा स्थिरं निष्कम्पं सुखमनुद्वेजनीयं च भवति तदा योगाङ्गतां भजते । तस्यैव स्थिरसुखत्वप्राप्त्यर्थमुपायमाह

प्रयत्नशैथिल्यानन्तसमापत्तिभ्याम् ॥47॥
prayatnaśaithilyānantasamāpattibhyām

(prayatna) Leaving all physical and mental activities and (śaithilya) with a relaxed body and mind; (samāpatti) and meditating (ananta) on the Infinite, the perfection in Āsana is attained.

व्यासभाष्य—भवतीति वाक्यशेषः । प्रयत्नोपरमात्सिध्यत्यासनं येन नाङ्गमेजयो भवति । अनन्ते वा समापन्नं चित्तमासनं निर्वर्तयतीति ।

भोजवृत्ति—तदासनं प्रयत्नशैथिल्येनाऽऽनन्त्यसमापत्त्या च स्थिरं सुखं भवतीति संबन्धः । यदा यदाऽऽसनं बध्नामीतीच्छां करोति प्रयत्नशैथिल्येऽपि अक्लेशेनैव तदा तदाऽऽसनं संपद्यते । यदा चाऽऽकाशादिगत आनन्त्ये चेतसः समापत्तिः क्रियतेऽव्यवधानेन तादात्म्यमापद्यते तदा देहाहंकाराभावान्नाऽऽसनं दुःखजनकं भवति । अस्मिंश्चाऽऽसनजये सति समाध्यन्तरायभूता न प्रभवन्ति अङ्गमेजयत्वादयः । तस्यैवानुनिष्पादितं फलमाह

ततो द्वन्द्वानभिघातः ॥48॥
tato dvandvānabhighātaḥ

On the perfection of Āsana, immunity against (dvandvas) dualities is attained, i.e. a yogī is not disturbed by heat and cold, etc.

व्यासभाष्य—शीतोष्णादिभिर्द्वंद्वैरासनजयान्नाभिभूयते ।

भोजवृत्ति—तस्मिन्नासनजये सति द्वंद्वैः शीतोष्णक्षुत्तृष्णादिभिर्योगी नाभिहन्यत इत्यर्थः । आसनजयानन्तरं प्राणायाममाह

तस्मिन्सति श्वासप्रश्वासयोर्गतिविच्छेदः प्राणायामः ॥49॥

tasminsati śvāsapraśvāsayorgativicchedaḥ prāṇāyāmaḥ

Having attained the perfection of Āsana, the reduction or absence in the speed of inhalation and exhalation, is Prāṇāyāma.

व्यासभाष्य—सत्यासने बाह्यस्य वायोराचमनं श्वासः कौष्ठ्यस्य वायोर्निःसारणं प्रश्वासः तयोर्गतिविच्छेद उभयाभावः प्राणायामः । स तु

भोजवृत्ति—आसनस्थैर्ये सति तन्निमित्तकः प्राणायामलक्षणो योगाङ्गविशेषोऽनुष्ठेयो भवति । कीदृशः श्वासप्रश्वासयोर्गतिविच्छेदलक्षणः । श्वासप्रश्वासौ निरुक्तौ । तयोस्त्रिधा रेचनस्तम्भनपूरणद्वारेण बाह्याभ्यन्तरेषु स्थानेषु गतेः प्रवाहस्य विच्छेदो धारणं प्राणायाम उच्यते । तस्यैव सुखावगमाय विभज्य स्वरूपं कथयति

बाह्याभ्यन्तरस्तम्भवृत्तिर्देशकालसंख्याभिः परिदृष्टो दीर्घसूक्ष्मः ॥50॥

bāhyābhyantarastambhavṛttirdeśakālasaṃkhyābhiḥ paridṛṣṭo dīrghasūkṣmaḥ

Prāṇyāma is of three types external (rechaka), internal (puraka), and (stambhavṛtti) stilled. They may be classified as (dirgha) long and (sukṣma) short when measuring on the scale of (deśa) distance, (kāla) timespan, and (saṅkhyā) number. For example, long distance breathing will be called long and short-distance breathing will be called short. Similarly, breathing involving a longer timespan is called long, if involving a short timespan, it will be called short breathing. If breathing involves long counting, it will be called long and if it involves short counting, it will be called as short breathing.

व्यासभाष्य—यत्र प्रश्वासपूर्वको गत्यभावः स बाह्यः । यत्र श्वासपूर्वको गत्यभावः स आभ्यन्तरः । तृतीयः स्तम्भवृत्तिर्यत्रयोभयाभावः । सकृत्प्रयत्नाद्भवति । यथा तप्ते न्यस्तमुपले जलं सर्वतः संकोचमापद्यते तथा द्वयोर्युगपद्वत्यभाव । इति त्रयोऽप्येते देशेन परिदृष्टा इयानस्य विषयो देश इति । कालेन परिदृष्टा क्षणानामियत्तावधारणेनावच्छिन्ना इत्यर्थः । संख्याभिः परिदृष्टा एतावद्भिः श्वासप्रश्वासैः प्रथम उद्घातस्तद्व्रिगृहीतस्यैतावद्भिर्द्वितीय उद्घात एवं तृतीयः । एवं मृदुरेवं मध्य एवं तीव्र इति संख्यापरिदृष्टः । स खल्वयमेवमभ्यस्तो दीर्घसूक्ष्मः ।

भोजवृत्ति—बाह्यवृत्तिः श्वासो रेचकः । अन्तर्वृत्तिः प्रश्वासः पूरकः । अन्तस्तम्भवृत्तिः कुम्भकः । तस्मिञ्जलमिव कुम्भे निश्चलतया प्राणा अवस्थाप्यन्त इति कुम्भकः । त्रिविधोऽयं प्राणायामो देशेन कालेन संख्यया चोपलक्षितो दीर्घसूक्ष्मसंज्ञो भवति । देशेनोपलक्षितो यथा नासाप्रदेशान्तादौ । कालेनोपलक्षितो यथा षट्त्रिंशन्मात्रादिप्रमाणः । संख्ययोपलक्षितो यथा इयतो वारान्कृत एतावद्भिः श्वासप्रश्वासैः प्रथम उद्घातोभवतीति । एतज्ज्ञानाय संख्याग्रहणमुपात्तम् । उद्घातो नाम नाभिमूलात्प्रेरितस्य वायोः शिरसि अभिहननम् । त्रीन्प्राणायामानभिधाय चतुर्थमभिधातुमाह

बाह्याभ्यन्तरविषयाक्षेपी चतुर्थः ॥51॥
bāhyābhyantaraviṣayākṣepī caturthaḥ

The fourth one named Kumbhaka transcends the external/exhalation (Rechaka) and internal/inhalation (Pūraka). Suspension of breathing after inhalation and exhalation is called kumbhaka.

व्यासभाष्य—देशकालसंख्याभिर्बाह्यविषयपरिदृष्ट आक्षिप्तः । तथाऽभ्यन्तरविषयपरिदृष्ट आक्षिप्तः । उभयथा दीर्घसूक्ष्मः । तत्पूर्वको भूमिजयात्क्रमेणोभयोर्गत्यभावश्चतुर्थः प्राणायामः । तृतीयस्तु विषयानालोचितो गत्यभावः सकृदारब्ध एव देशकालसंख्याभिः परिदृष्टो दीर्घसूक्ष्मः । चतुर्थस्तु श्वासप्रश्वासयोर्विषयावधारणात्क्रमेण भूमिजयादुभयाक्षेपपूर्वको गत्यभावश्चतुर्थः प्राणायाम इत्ययं विशेष इति ।

भोजवृत्ति—प्राणस्य बाह्यो विषयो नासाद्वादशान्तादिः । आभ्यन्तरो विषयो हृदयनाभिचक्रादिः । तौ द्वौ विषयावाक्षिप्य पर्यालोच्य सः स्तम्भरूपो गतिविच्छेदः स चतुर्थः प्राणायामः । तृतीयस्मात्कुम्भकाख्यादयमस्य विशेषः स बाह्याभ्यन्तरविषयावपर्यालोच्यैव सहसा तप्तोपलनिपतितजलन्यायेन युगपत्स्तम्भवृत्त्या निष्पद्यते । अस्य तु विषय द्वयाक्षेपक निरोधः । अयमपि पूर्ववद्देशकालसंख्याभिरूपलक्षितो द्रष्टव्यः । चतुर्विधस्यास्य फलमाह

ततः क्षीयते प्रकाशावरणम् ॥52॥
tataḥ kṣīyate prakāśāvaraṇam

From these four Prāṇāyāmas, the veil of rajoguṇā and tamoguṇa over the sattva guṇa is removed. Sattva guṇa becomes dominant. Sattvaguṇa is of the nature of Prakāśa. It means that by these four prāṇāyāmas, the dominance of tamas and rajas guṇas cames to an end and sattva guṇā becomes dominant.

व्यासभाष्य—प्राणायामानभ्यस्यतोऽस्य योगिनः क्षीयते विवेकज्ञानावरणीयं कर्म । यत्तदाचक्षते महामोहमयेनेन्द्रजालेन प्रकाशशीलं सत्त्वमावृत्य तदेवाकार्ये नियुङ्क्त इति । तदस्य प्रकाशावरणं कर्म संसारनिबन्धनं प्राणायामाभ्यासादुर्बल भवति प्रतिक्षणं च क्षीयते । तथा चोक्तम्

तपो न परं प्राणायामात्ततो विशुद्धिर्मलानां दीप्तिश्च ज्ञानस्य इति । किं च

भोजवृत्ति—ततस्तस्मात्प्राणायामात्प्रकाशस्य चित्तसत्त्वगतस्य यदावरणं क्लेशरूपं तत्क्षीयते विनश्यतीत्यर्थः । फलान्तरमाह

धारणासु च योग्यता मनसः ॥53॥
dhāraṇāsu ca yogyatā manasaḥ

And the mind becomes fit or qualified for (Dhāraṇā) concentration.

व्यासभाष्य—प्राणायामाभ्यासादेव । 'प्रच्छर्दनविधारणाभ्यां वा प्राणस्य ' 1.34 इति वचनात् । अथ कः प्रत्याहारः

भोजवृत्ति—धारणा वक्ष्यमाणलक्षणस्तासु प्राणायामैः क्षीणदोष मनो यत्र यत्र धार्यते तत्र स्थिरी भवति न विक्षेपं भजते । प्रत्याहारस्य लक्षणमाह

स्वविषयासंप्रयोगे चित्तस्वरूपानुकार इवेन्द्रियाणां प्रत्याहारः ॥54॥
svaviṣayāsaṃprayoge cittasvarūpānukāra ivendriyāṇāṃ
pratyāhāraḥ

When (indriyāṇām) sense organs (asaṃprayoge) gets disconnected with (sva-viṣaya) their objects, they appear (anukāra iva) as if merged with (chitta-svarūpa) the mind, that is called Pratyāhāra.

व्यासभाष्य—स्वविषयसंप्रयोगाभावे चित्तस्वरूपानुकार इवेति चित्तनिरोधे चित्तवन्निरुद्धानीन्द्रियाणि नेतरेन्द्रियजयवदुपायान्तरमपेक्षन्ते । यथा मधुकरराजं मक्षिका उत्पतन्तमनूत्पतन्ति निविशमानमनुनिविशन्ते तथेन्द्रियाणि चित्तनिरोधे निरुद्धानीत्येष प्रत्याहारः ।

भोजवृत्ति—इन्द्रियाणि विषयेभ्यः प्रतीपमाह्रियन्तेऽस्मिन्निति प्रत्याहारः । स च कथं निष्पद्यत इत्याह चक्षुरादीनामिन्द्रियाणां स्वविषयो रूपादिस्तेन संप्रयोगस्तदाभिमुख्येन वर्तनं तदभावस्तदाभिमुख्यं परित्यज्य स्वरूपमात्रेऽवस्थानं तस्मिन्सति चित्तस्वरूपमात्रानुकारीणीन्द्रियाणि भवन्ति । यतश्चित्तमनु वर्तमानानि मधुकरराजमिव मधुमक्षिकाः सर्वाणीन्द्रियाणि प्रतीयन्तेऽतश्चित्तनिरोधे तानि प्रत्याहृतानि भवन्ति । तेषां तत्स्वरूपानुकारः प्रत्याहारः उक्तः । प्रत्याहारफलमाह

ततः परमावश्यतेन्द्रियाणाम् ॥55॥
tataḥ paramā vaśyatendriyāṇām

On perfection of Pratyāhāra, senses come under the complete control of a yogī.

व्यासभाष्य—शब्दादिष्वव्यसनमिन्द्रियजय इति केचित्। सक्तिर्व्यसनं व्यस्यत्येनं श्रेयस इति। अविरुद्धा प्रतिपत्तिर्न्याय्या। शब्दादिसंप्रयोगः स्वेच्छयेत्यन्ये रागद्वेषाभावे सुखदुःखशून्यं शब्दादिज्ञानमिन्द्रियजय इति केचित्। चित्तैकाग्र्यादप्रतिपत्तिरेवेति जैगीषव्यः। ततश्च परमात्वियं वश्यता यच्चित्तनिरोधे निरुद्धानीन्द्रियाणि नेतरेन्द्रियजयवत्प्रयत्नकृतमुपायान्तरमपेक्षन्ते योगिन इति।

इति श्रीपातञ्जले सांख्यप्रवचने योगशास्त्रे श्रीमद्व्यासभाष्ये द्वितीयः साधनपादः।।2।।

भोजवृत्ति—अभ्यस्यमाने हि प्रत्याहारे तथा वश्यानि आयत्तानीन्द्रियाणि संपद्यन्ते यथा बाह्यविषयाभिभमुखतां नीयमानान्यपि न यान्तीत्यर्थः।

तदेवं प्रथमपादोक्त योगस्याङ्गभूतक्लेशतनूकरणफलं क्रियायोगमभिधाय क्लेशानामुद्देशं स्वरूपं कारणं क्षेत्रं फलं चोक्त्वा कर्मणामपि भेदं कारणं स्वरूपं फलं चाभिधाय विपाकस्य स्वरूपं कारणं चाभिहितम्। ततस्त्याज्यत्वात्क्लेशादीनां ज्ञानव्यतिरेकेण त्यागस्याशक्यत्वाज्ज्ञानस्य न शास्त्रायत्तत्वाच्छास्त्रस्य च हेयहानकारणोपादेयोपादानकारणबोधकत्वेन चतुर्व्यूहत्वाद्धेयस्य च हानव्यतिरेकेण स्वरूपानिष्पत्तेर्हानसहितं चतुर्व्यूहं स्वस्वकारणसहितमभिधायोपादेयनकारणभूताया विवेकख्यातेः कारणभूतानामन्तरङ्गबहिरङ्गभावेन स्थितानां योगाङ्गानां यमादीनां स्वरूपं फलसहितं व्याकृत्याऽऽसनादीनां धारणापर्यन्तानां परस्परमुपकार्योपकारकभावेनावस्थितानामुद्देशमभिधाय प्रत्येकं लक्षणकरणपूर्वकं फलमभिहितम्। तदयं योगो यमनियमादिभिः प्राप्तबीजभाव आसनप्राणायामैरङ्कुरितः प्रत्याहारेण पुष्पितो ध्यानधारणासमाधिभिः फलिष्यतीति व्याख्यातः साधनपादः।

इति श्रीभोजदेवविरचितायां पातञ्जलयोगशास्त्रसूत्रवृत्तौ द्वितीयः साधनपादः।।2।।

इति पतञ्जलि-विरचिते योग-सूत्रे द्वितीयः साधन-पादः

तृतीयोऽध्यायः

Tṛtīyo'dhyāyaḥ

विभूति-पादः

Vibhūti-pāda

The Divine powers

While concluding the previous chapter, it was said that from the four Prāṇāyāmas, the veil of rajoguṇā and tamoguṇa over the sattva guṇa is removed and the mind becomes fit for (Dhāraṇā) concentration. This Chapter is started with the definition of Dhāraṇā.

देशबन्धश्चित्तस्य धारणा ॥3.1॥

deśabandhaścittasya dhāraṇā

Focusing the mind at one point is called Dhāraṇā or concentration.

व्यासभाष्य—नाभिचक्रे हृदयपुण्डरीके मूर्ध्नि ज्योतिषि नासिकाग्रे जिह्वाग्र इत्येवमादिषु देशेषु बाह्ये वा विषये चित्तस्य वृत्तिमात्रेण बन्ध इति धारणा ।

भोजवृत्ति—तदेवं पूर्वोद्दिष्टं धारणाद्यङ्गत्रयं निर्णेतुं संयमसंज्ञाविधानपूर्वकं बाह्याभ्यन्तरादि सिद्धिप्रतिपादनाय लक्षयितुमुपक्रमते । तत्र धारणायाः स्वरूपमाह

तत्र प्रत्ययैकतानता ध्यानम् ॥3.2॥

tatra pratyayaikatānatā dhyānam

(Tatra) In the process of focus of mind at one point, (pratyaya) if the subject of focus (ekatānatā) continues to be the same (without any change), it is called Dhyāna or meditation.

There are three factors in Dhyāna. They are Dhyātā (meditator or soul), Dhyeya (object of meditation), and dhyāna (meditation). In Dhyāna, all the three factors are distinguishable.

व्यासभाष्य—तस्मिन्देशे ध्येयालम्बनस्य प्रत्ययस्यैकतानता सदृशः प्रवाहः प्रत्ययान्तरेणापरामृष्टो ध्यानम्।

भोजवृत्ति—तत्र तस्मिन्प्रदेशे यत्र चित्तं धृतं तत्र प्रत्ययस्य ज्ञानस्य यैकतानता विसदृशपरिणामपरिहारद्वारेण यदेव धारणायामालम्बनीकृतं तदालम्बनतयैव निरन्तरमुत्पत्तिः सा ध्यानमुच्यते। चरमं योगाङ्गं समाधिमाह

तदेवार्थमात्रनिर्भासं स्वरूपशून्यमिव समाधिः ॥3.3॥

tadevārthamātranirbhāsaṃ svarūpaśūnyamiva samādhiḥ

(tadeva) In Dhyāna, when (svarūpaśūnyamiva) meditator forgets about his/her own nature and (arthamātra-nirbhāsaṃ) is aware of the object of meditation only, (samādhiḥ) it is called Samādhi.

In Samādhi, Dhyātā (meditator), Dhyeya (object of meditation), and dhyāna (meditation) are not distinguishable. Or Dhyātā (meditator), and dhyāna (meditation) merge into Dhyeya (object of meditation).

व्यासभाष्य—इदमत्रबोध्यम् ध्यातृध्येयध्यानकलनावत् ध्यानं तद्रहितं समाधिरिति ध्यानसमाध्योर्विभागः। अस्य च समाधिरूपस्य ङ्रस्याङ्गिसंप्रज्ञातयोगादयं भेदो यदत्र चिन्तारूपतया निःशेषतो ध्येयस्य स्वरूपं न भासते। अङ्गिनि तु संप्रज्ञाते ज्ञातव्य साक्षात्कारोदये समाध्यविषया अपि विषया भासन्त इति। तथा च साक्षात्कारयुक्तैकाग्र्यकाले संप्रज्ञातयोगः। अन्यदा ते समाधिमात्रमिति विभागः समाधिः ध्यानमेव ध्येयाकारनिर्भासं प्रत्ययात्मकेन स्वरूपेण शून्यमिव यदा भवति ध्येयस्वभावावेशात्तदा समाधिरित्युच्यते।

भोजवृत्ति—तदेवोक्तलक्षणं ध्यानं यत्रार्थमात्रनिर्भासमर्थाकारसमावेशादुद्भूतार्थरूपन्यग्भूत-ज्ञानस्वरूपत्वेन स्वरूपशून्यतामिवाऽऽपद्यते स समाधिरित्युच्यते। सम्यगाधीयत एकाग्री क्रियते विक्षेपान्परिहृत्य मनो यत्र स समाधिः। उक्तलक्षणस्य योगाङ्गत्रयस्य व्यवहाराय स्वशास्त्रे तान्त्रिकीं संज्ञां कर्तुमाह

त्रयमेकत्र संयमः ॥3.4॥

trayamekatra saṃyamaḥ

If Dhāraṇā, Dhyāna, and Samādhi are aligned or focused on one single object, it is called Sañyama.

Dhāraṇā, Dhyāna and Samādhi, the three together

constitute Sañyama or co-conciliation. (त्रयमेकत्र संयमः)

व्यासभाष्य—तदेतद्धारणाध्यानसमाधित्रयमेकत्र संयमः । एकविषयाणि त्रीणि साधनानि संयमः इत्युच्यते । तदस्य त्रयस्य तान्त्रिकी परिभाषा संयम इति ।

भोजवृत्ति—एकस्मिन्विषये धारणाध्यानसमाधित्रयं प्रवर्तमानं संयमसंज्ञया शास्त्रे व्यवह्रियते । तस्य फलमाह

तज्जयात्प्रज्ञालोकः ॥3.5॥
tajjayātprajñālokaḥ

When the perfection of Sañyama is attained, a yogī attains (samādhi prajñā) divine intellect.

व्यासभाष्य—तस्य संयमस्य जयात्समाधिप्रज्ञाया भवत्यालोको यथा यथा संयमः स्थिरपदो भवति तथा तथेश्वरप्रसादात्समाधिप्रज्ञा विशारदी भवति ।

भोजवृत्ति—तस्य संयमस्य जयादभ्यासेन सात्म्योपादनात्प्रज्ञाया विवेकख्यातेरालोकः प्रसवो भवति । प्रज्ञा ज्ञेयं सम्यगवभासयतीत्यर्थः । तस्योपयोगमाह

तस्य भूमिषु विनियोगः ॥3.6॥
tasya bhūmiṣu viniyogaḥ

That Sañyama should be applied starting from macro objects to micro ones.

First of all, a seeker should do the practice of sañyama on macro objects. When he/she is able to realize the macro objects, he/she should do practice on micro, more micro-objects, and so on.

व्यासभाष्य—तस्य संयमस्य जितभूमेर्याऽनन्तरा भूमिस्तत्र विनियोगः । न ह्यजिताधरभूमिरनन्तरभूमिं विलङ्घ्य प्रान्तभूमिषु संयमं लभते । तदभावाच्च कुतस्तस्य प्रज्ञालोकः । ईश्वरप्रसादाज्जितोत्तरभूमिकस्य च नाधरभूमिषु परचित्तज्ञानादिषु संयमो युक्तः । कस्मात् तदर्थस्यान्यथैवावगतत्वात् । भूमेरस्या इयमनन्तरा भूमिरित्यत्र योग एवोपाध्यायः । कथम् । एवं ह्युक्तम्

योगेन योगो ज्ञातव्यो योगो योगात्प्रवर्तते ।
योऽप्रमत्तस्तु योगेन स योगे रमते चिरम् ॥इति॥6॥

भोजवृत्ति—तस्य संयमस्य भूमिषु स्थूलसूक्ष्मालम्बनभेदेन स्थितासु चित्तवृत्तिषु विनियोगः कर्तव्यः अधरामधरां चित्तभूमिं जितां जितां ज्ञात्वोत्तरस्यां भूमौ संयमः कार्यः । न

ह्यनात्मीकृताधरभूमिरुत्तरस्यां भूमौ संयमंकुर्वाणः फलभाग्भवति ।   साधनपादे योगाङ्गान्यष्टावुद्दिश्य पञ्चानां लक्षणं विधाय त्रयाणां कथं न कृतमित्याशङ्क्याऽऽह

त्रयमन्तरङ्गं पूर्वेभ्यः ॥3.7॥
trayamantaraṅgaṃ pūrvebhyaḥ

Dhāraṇā, Dhyāna, and Samādhi form the internal part of Saṃprajñāta (Sabīja) Samādhi, or say they are directly helpful Saṃprajñāta (Sabīja) Samādhi. So, they are said to be antraṅga (internal) part to Saṃprajñāta (Sabīja) Samādhi as compared to preceding five-Yama, Niyama, Āsana, Prāṇāyāma, Pratyāhāra, as they form the external part of samādhi.

व्यासभाष्य—तदेतद्धारणाध्यानसमाधित्रयमन्तरङ्गं संप्रज्ञातस्य समाधेः पूर्वेभ्यो यमादिभ्यः पञ्चभ्यः साधनेभ्य इति ।

भोजवृत्ति—पूर्वेभ्यो यमादिभ्यो योगाङ्गेभ्यः पारम्पर्येण समाधेरुपकारकेभ्यो धारणादियोगाङ्गत्रयं संप्रज्ञातस्य समाधेरन्तरङ्गं समाधिस्वरूपनिष्पादनात् ।। तस्यापि समाध्यन्तरापेक्षया बहिरङ्गत्वमाह

तदपि बहिरङ्गं निर्बीजस्य ॥3.8॥
tadapi bahiraṅgaṃ nirbījasya

But Dhāraṇā, Dhyāna, and Samādhi form the external part of Asaṃprajñāta (Nirbīja) Samādhi or we can say that they indirectly helpful in Asaṃprajñāta (Nirbīja) Samādhi. In the next sūtra, consequence of Samādhi is stated.

व्यासभाष्य—तदप्यन्तरङ्गं साधनत्रयं निर्बीजस्य योगस्य बहिरङ्गं भवति । कस्मात् तदभावे भावादिति । अथ निरोधचित्तक्षणेषु चलं गुणवृत्तिमिति कीदृशस्तदा चित्तपरिणामः

भोजवृत्ति—निर्बीजस्य निरालम्बनस्य शून्यभावनापरपर्यायस्य समाधेरेतदपि योगाङ्गत्रयं बहिरङ्गं पारम्पर्येणोपकारकत्वात् । इदानीं योगसिद्धिराख्यातुकामः संयमस्य विषयपरिशुद्धिं कर्तुं क्रमेण परिणामत्रयमाह

व्युत्थाननिरोधसंस्कारयोरभिभव-प्रादुर्भावौ
निरोधक्षणचित्तान्वयो निरोध-परिणामः ॥3.9॥

vyutthānanirodhasaṃskārayorabhibhava-prādurbhāvau
nirodhakṣaṇacittānvayo nirodha-pariṇāmaḥ

(Nirodha kṣaṇa) The process of elimination of sanskāras (chittānvaya) of mind takes place in two ways. First (vyutthāna sanskāra abhibhava) is the elimination of the existing sanskāras and the other is (nirodha sanskāra prādurbhāva) restraining further accumulations of sanskāras. This process is known as Nirodha-Pariṇāma (result of withdrawal of mind).

Note: When the mind is involved with the object of the external world, it accumulates sanskāras, this process is called Vyutthāna Sanskāras. Abhibhava means elimination. Similarly when the mind is withdrawn from the external world, then it stops accumulating further sanskāras and the previous sanskāras get exhausted. This exhaustion process is known as Nirodha Sanskāra (fig.13)

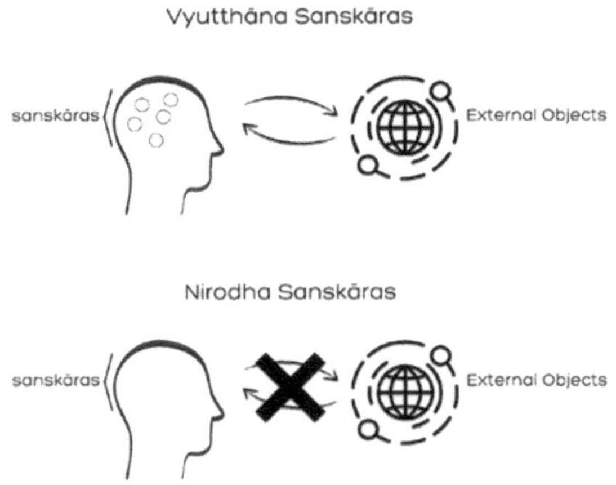

Figure 13: Vyutthāna and Nirodha Sanskāras

व्यासभाष्य—व्युत्थानसंस्काराश्चित्तधर्मा न ते प्रत्ययात्मका इति प्रत्ययनिरोधे न निरुद्धा निरोधसंस्कारा अपि चित्तधर्मास्तयोरभिभवप्रादुर्भावौ व्युत्थानसंस्कारा हीयन्ते निरोधसंस्कारा आधीयन्ते निरोधक्षणं चित्तमन्वेति

तदेकस्य चित्तस्य प्रतिक्षणमिदं संस्कारान्यथात्वं निरोधपरिणामः । तदा संस्कारशेषं चित्तमिति

निरोधसमाधौ व्याख्यातम् ।

भोजवृत्ति—व्युत्थानं क्षिप्तमूढविक्षिप्ताख्यं भूमित्रयम् । निरोधः प्रकृष्टसत्त्वस्याङ्गितया चेतसः परिणामः । ताभ्यां व्युत्थाननिरोधाभ्यां यौ जनितौ संस्कारौ तयोर्यथाक्रममभिभवप्रादुर्भावौ यदा भवतः । अभिभवो न्यग्भूततया कार्यकरणासामर्थ्येनावस्थानम् । प्रादुर्भावो वर्तमानेऽध्वनि अभिव्यक्तरूपतयाऽविर्भावः । तदा निरोधक्षणे चित्तस्योभयवृत्तित्वादन्वयो यः स निरोधपरिणाम उच्यते । अयमर्थः यदा व्युत्थानसंस्काररूपो धर्मस्तिरोभूतो भवति निरोधसंस्काररूपश्चाऽविर्भवति धर्मिरूपतया च चित्तमुभयान्वयिल्वेऽपि निरोधात्मनाऽवस्थितं प्रतीयते तदा स निरोधपरिणामशब्देन व्यवहियते । चलत्वादुणवृत्तस्य यद्यपि चेतसो निश्चलत्वं नास्ति तथाऽपि एवंभूतः परिणामः स्थैर्यमुच्यते । तस्यैव फलमाह

तस्य प्रशान्तवाहिता संस्कारात् ॥3.10॥
tasya praśāntavāhitā saṃskārāt

(Sanskārāt) By virtue of Nirodha Sanskāra (absence of sanskāras) [tasya] the mind (praśānta-vāhitā) becomes steady.

Note: When the mind has sanskāras, then only it becomes active and fickle. Sanskāras are like the products in the shop of mind. If the shop is full of products, there will be hustle, bustle around the shop and its owner will be busy selling of the products. If the shop is empty, then the owner has nothing to do except to sit still. So, a mind devoid of sanskāras becomes steady.

व्यासभाष्य—निरोधसंस्काराभ्यासपाटवापेक्षा प्रशान्तवाहिता चित्तस्य भवति । तत्संस्कारमान्द्ये व्युत्थानधर्मिणा संस्कारेण निरोधधर्मसंस्कारोऽभिभूयत इति ।

भोजवृत्ति—तस्य चेतसो निरुक्तान्निरोधसंस्कारात्प्रशान्तवाहिता भवति । परिहृतविक्षेपतया सदृशप्रवाहपरिणामि चित्तं भवतीत्यर्थः । निरोधपरिणाममभिधाय समाधिपरिणाममाह

सर्वार्थतैकाग्रतयोः क्षयोदयौ चित्तस्य समाधिपरिणामः ॥3.11॥
sarvārthataikāgratayoḥ kṣayodayau cittasya samādhipariṇāmaḥ

(samādhipariṇāmaḥ) The result of Samādhi is (kṣaya) drop of the focus of the mind from (sarvārthatā) all or many objects and (udaya) the rise of (ekāgratā) focus to one object.

The normal tendency of the mind is to focus on many objects at one time. But Samādhi enables the mind to focus one-pointed object.

व्यासभाष्य—सर्वार्थता चित्तधर्मः। एकाग्रताऽपि चित्तधर्मः। सर्वार्थतायाः क्षयस्तिरोभाव इत्यर्थः। एकाग्रताया उदय आविर्भाव इत्यर्थः। तयोर्धर्मित्वेनानुगतं चित्तं तदिदं चित्तमपायोपजनयोः स्वात्मभूतयोर्धर्मयोरनुगतं समाधीयते स चित्तस्य समाधिपरिणामः।

भोजवृत्ति—सर्वार्थता चलत्वान्नानाविधार्थग्रहणं चित्तस्य विक्षेपो धर्मः। एकस्मिन्नेवाऽऽलम्बने सदृशपरिणामितैकाग्रता साऽपि चित्तस्य धर्मः। तयोर्यथाक्रमं क्षयोदयौ सर्वार्थतालक्षणस्य धर्मस्य क्षयोऽत्यन्ताभिभव एकाग्रतालक्षणस्य धर्मस्य प्रादुर्भावोऽभिव्यक्तिश्चित्तस्योद्रिक्त-सत्त्वस्यान्वयितयाऽवस्थानं समाधिपरिणाम इत्युच्यते। पूर्वस्मात्परिणामादस्यायं विशेषः तत्र संस्कारलक्षणयोर्धर्मयोरभिभवप्रादुर्भावौ पूर्वस्य व्युत्थानसंस्काररूपस्य न्यग्भावः। उत्तरस्य निरोधसंस्काररूपस्योद्भवोऽनभिभूतत्वेनावस्थानम्। इह तु क्षयोदयाविति सर्वार्थतारूपस्य विक्षेपस्यात्यन्ततिरस्कारादनुत्पत्तिरतीतेऽध्वनि प्रवेशः क्षय एकाग्रतालक्षणस्य धर्मस्योद्भवो वर्तमानेऽध्वनि प्रकटत्वम्। तृतीयमेकाग्रतापरिणाममाह

ततः पुनः शान्तोदितौ तुल्यप्रत्ययौ चित्तस्यैकाग्रतापरिणामः ॥3.12॥

tataḥ punaḥ śāntoditau tulyapratyayau cittasyaikāgratāpariṇāmaḥ

(tatḥ) When the mind is firmly established in Samādhi, (cittasyaikāgratāpariṇāmaḥ) as a result of the one-pointed concentration of mind, (śānta) the past objects of concentration erasing from mind (udita) and the presently rising new objects of concentration of mind become (tulya-pratyaya) aligned. That is, one forgets the difference between the past and present objects of concentration.

व्यासभाष्य—समाहितचित्तस्य पूर्वप्रत्ययः शान्त उत्तरस्तत्सदृश उदितः समाधिचित्तमुभयोरनुगतं पुनस्तथैवाऽसमाधिभ्रेषादिति। स खल्वयं धर्मिणश्चित्तस्यैकाग्रतापरिणामः।

भोजवृत्ति—समाहितस्यैव चित्तस्यैकप्रत्ययो वृत्तिविशेषः शान्तोऽतीतमध्वानं प्रविष्टः। अपरस्तूदितो वर्तमानेऽध्वनि स्फुरितः। द्वावपि समाहितचित्तत्वेन तुल्यावेकरूपालम्बनत्वेन सदृशौ प्रत्ययावुभयत्रापि समाहितस्यैव चित्तस्यान्वयित्वेनावस्थानं स एकाग्रतापरिणाम इत्युच्यते। चित्तपरिणामोक्तं रूपमन्यत्राप्यतिदिशन्नाह

एतेन भूतेन्द्रियेषु धर्मलक्षणावस्थापरिणामा व्याख्याताः ॥3.13॥

etena bhūtendriyeṣu dharmalakṣaṇāvasthāpariṇāmā
vyākhyātāḥ

(Etena) By way of multi-pointed, one-pointed and aligned concentration of mind, the (pariṇāmāḥ) changes pertaining to dharma (property), lakṣaṇa (symptoms) and avastha (state) of material things and sense organs are explained (by implication).

Change of dharma may be explained as subsidence of past dharma and the rise of new dharma. For example, the transformation of a lump of clay into a pot is called the change of dharma.

When the same change of dharma is described in terms of clay, i.e. change of clay from lump to pot, it is known as change of lakṣaṇa of clay. When clay is in the form of lump, it is one lakṣaṇa of clay and the clay in the form of pot is another lakṣaṇa of clay. Similarly, when a golden bracelet is transformed into an earring, that will be called a change of the lakṣaṇa of gold.

Change of state is discernible when a new pot becomes old with the passage of time.

व्यासभाष्य—एतेन पूर्वोक्तेन चित्तपरिणामेन धर्मलक्षणावस्थारूपेण भूतेन्द्रियेषु धर्मपरिणामो लक्षणपरिणामोऽवस्थापरिणामश्चोक्तो वेदितव्यः । तत्र व्युत्थाननिरोधयोरभिभवप्रादुर्भावौ धर्मिणि धर्मपरिणामः । लक्षणपरिणामश्च । निरोधस्त्रिलक्षणस्त्रिभिरध्वभिर्युक्तः । स खल्वनागतलक्षणमध्वानं प्रथमं हित्वा धर्मत्वमनतिक्रान्तो वर्तमानलक्षणं प्रतिपन्नः । यत्रास्य स्वरूपेणाभिव्यक्तिः । एषोऽस्य द्वितीयोऽध्वा । न चातीतानागताभ्यां लक्षणाभ्यां वियुक्तः ।

तथा व्युत्थानं त्रिलक्षणं त्रिभिरध्वभिर्युक्तं वर्तमानलक्षणं हित्वा धर्मत्वमनतिक्रान्तमतीतलक्षणं प्रतिपन्नम् । एषोऽस्य तृतीयोऽध्वा । न चानागतवर्तमानाभ्यां लक्षणाभ्यां वियुक्तम् । एवं पुनर्व्युत्थानमुपसंपद्यमानमनागतलक्षणं हित्वा धर्मत्वमनतिक्रान्तं वर्तमानलक्षणं प्रतिपन्नम् । यत्रास्य स्वरूपाभिव्यक्तौ सत्यां व्यापारः । एषोऽस्य द्वितीयोऽध्वा । न चातीतानागताभ्यां लक्षणाभ्यां वियुक्तमिति । एवं पुनर्निरोध एवं पुनर्व्युत्थानमिति ।

तथाऽवस्थापरिणामः । तत्र निरोधक्षणेषु निरोधसंस्कारा बलवन्तो भवन्ति दुर्बला

व्युत्थानसंस्कारा इति । एष धर्माणामवस्था परिणामः । तत्र धर्मिणो धर्मैः परिणामो धर्माणां
त्र्यध्वनां लक्षणैः परिणामो लक्षणनामप्यवस्थाभिः परिणाम इति । एवं धर्मलक्षणवस्थापरिणामैः
शून्यं न क्षणमपि गुणवृत्तमवतिष्ठते । चलं च गुणवृत्तम् । गुणस्वाभाव्यं तु प्रवृत्तिकारणमुक्तं
गुणानामिति । एतेन भूतेन्द्रियेषु धर्मधर्मिभेदाच्चिविधः परिणामो वेदितव्यः ।

परमार्थतस्त्वेक एव परिणामः । धर्मिस्वरूपमात्रो हि धर्मो धर्मिविक्रियैवैषा धर्मद्वारा प्रपञ्चयत
इति । तत्र धर्मस्य धर्मिणि वर्तमानस्यैवाध्वस्वतीतानागतवर्तमानेषु भावान्यथात्वं भवति न तु
द्रव्यान्यथात्वम् । यथा सुवर्णभाजनस्य भित्त्वाऽन्यथाक्रियमाणस्य भावान्यथात्वं भवति न
सुवर्णान्यथात्वमिति ।

अपर आह धर्मानभ्यधिको धर्मी पूर्वतत्त्वानतिक्रमात् । पूर्वापरावस्थाभेदमनुपतितः
कौटस्थ्येनैव परिवर्तेत यद्यन्वयी स्यादिति । अयमदोषः । कस्मात् । एकान्ततानभ्युपगमात् ।
तदेतत्त्रैलोक्यं व्यक्तेरपैति नित्यत्वप्रतिषेधात् । अपेतमप्यस्ति विनाशप्रतिषेधात् । संसर्गाच्चास्य
सौक्ष्म्यं सौक्ष्म्याच्चानुपलब्धिरिति ।

लक्षणपरिणामो धर्मोऽध्वसु वर्तमानोऽतीतोऽतीतलक्षणयुक्तोऽनागतवर्तमानाभ्यां
लक्षणाभ्यामवियुक्तः । तथाऽनागतोऽनागतलक्षणयुक्तो वर्तमानातीताभ्यां लक्षणभ्यामवियुक्तः । तथा
वर्तमानो वर्तमानलक्षणयुक्तोऽतीतानागताभ्यां लक्षणाभ्यामवियुक्त इति । यथा पुरुष एकस्यां स्त्रियां
रक्तो न शेषासु विरक्तो भवतीति ।

अत्र लक्षणपरिणामे सर्वस्य सर्वलक्षणयोगादध्वसंकरः प्राप्नोतीति परैर्दोषश्चोद्यत इति । तस्य
परिहारः धर्माणां धर्मत्वमप्रसाध्यम् । सति च धर्मत्वे लक्षणभेदोऽपि वाच्यो न वर्तमानसमय एवास्य
धर्मत्वम् । एवं हि न चित्तं रागधर्मकं स्यात्क्रोधकाले रागस्यासमुदाचारादिति ।

किञ्च त्रयाणां लक्षणानां युगपदेकस्यां व्यक्तौ नास्ति संभवः । क्रमेण तु स्वव्यञ्जकाञ्जनस्य
भावो भवेदिति । उक्तं च रूपातिशया वृत्त्यतिशयाश्च विरुध्यते सामान्यानि त्वतिशयैः सह प्रवर्तन्ते ।
तस्मादसंकरः । यथा रागस्यैव क्वचित्समुदाचार इति न तदानीमन्यत्राभावः किंतु केवलं सामान्येन
समन्वागत इत्यस्ति तदा तत्र तस्य भावः । तथा लक्षणस्येति ।

न धर्मी त्र्यध्वा धर्मास्तु त्र्यध्वानस्ते लक्षिता अलक्षितास्तत्र लक्षितास्तां तामवस्थां
प्राप्नुवन्तोऽन्यत्वेन प्रतिनिर्दिश्यन्तेऽवस्थान्तरतो न द्रव्यान्तरतः । यथैका रेखा शतस्थाने शतं दशस्थाने
दशैका चैकस्याने । यथा चैकत्वेऽपि स्त्री माता चोच्यते दुहिता च स्वसा चेति ।

अवस्थापरिणामे कौटस्थ्यप्रसङ्गदोषः कैश्चिदुक्तः । कथम् । अध्वनो व्यापारेण व्यवहितत्वात् ।
यदा धर्मः स्वव्यापारं न करोति तदाऽनागतो यदा करोति तदा वर्तमानो यदा कृत्वा
निवृत्तस्तदाऽतीत इत्येवं धर्मधर्मिणोर्लक्षणानामवस्थानां च कौटस्थ्यं प्राप्नोतीति परैर्दोष उच्यते ।

नासौ दोषः । कस्मात् । गुणिनित्यत्वेऽपि गुणानां विमर्दवैचित्र्यात् । यथा संस्थानमादिमद्धर्ममात्रं
शब्दादीनां गुणानां विनाश्यविनाशिनामेवं लिङ्गमादिमद्धर्ममात्रं सत्त्वादीनां गुणानां विनाश्यविनाशिनां
तस्मिन्विकारसंज्ञेति ।

तत्रेदमुदाहरणं मृद्धर्मी पिण्डाकाराद्धर्माद्धर्मान्तरमुपसंपद्यमानो धर्मतः परिणमते घटाकार इति ।
घटाकारोऽनागतं लक्षणं हित्वा वर्तमानलक्षणं प्रतिपद्यत इति लक्षणतः परिणमते । घटो

नवपुराणतां प्रतिक्षणमनुभवन्नवस्थापरिणामं प्रतिपद्यत इति । धर्मिणोऽपि धर्मान्तरमवस्था धर्मस्यापि लक्षणान्तरमवस्थेत्येक एव द्रव्यपरिणामो भेदेनोपदर्शित इति । एवं पदार्थान्तरेष्वपि योज्यमिति । त एते धर्मलक्षणावस्थापरिणामा धर्मिस्वरूपमनतिक्रान्ता इत्येक एव परिणामः सर्वानमून्विशेषानभिप्लवते । अथ कोऽयं परिणामः । अवस्थितस्य द्रव्यस्य पूर्वधर्मनिवृत्तौ धर्मान्तरोत्पत्तिः परिणाम इति । तत्र

भोजवृत्ति—एतेन त्रिविधेनोक्तेन चित्तपरिणामेन भूतेषु स्थूलसूक्ष्मेषु इन्द्रियेषु बुद्धिकर्मलक्षणभेदेनावस्थितेषु धर्मलक्षणावस्थाभेदन त्रिविधः परिणामो व्याख्यातोऽवगन्तव्यः । अवस्थितस्य धर्मिणः पूर्वधर्मनिवृत्तौ धर्मान्तरापत्तिर्धर्म परिणामः । यथा मृल्लक्षणस्य धर्मिणः पिण्डरूपधर्मपरित्यागेन घटरूपधर्मान्तरस्वीकारो धर्मपरिणाम इत्युच्यते । लक्षणपरिणामो यथातस्यैव घटस्यानागताध्वपरित्यागेन वर्तमानाध्वस्वीकारः । तत्परित्यागेन चातीताध्वपरिग्रहः । अवस्थापरिणामो यथा तस्यैव घटस्य प्रथमद्वितीययोः सदृशयोः क्षणयोरन्वयित्वेन । यतश्च गुणवृत्तिर्नापरिणममाना क्षणमप्यस्ति । ननु कोऽयं धर्मीत्याशङ्क्य धर्मिणो लक्षणमाह

शान्तोदिताव्यपदेश्यधर्मानुपाती धर्मी ॥3.14॥
śāntoditāvyapadeśyadharmānupātī dharmī

(Dharmī) The object (anupāti) remains common to all states of changes, i.e. (śānta) past, (udita) present and (avyapadeśya) future.

Clay is the common object (dharmī) to a new pot, old pot, and of the pot to be manufactured in the future.

व्यासभाष्य—योग्यतावच्छिन्ना धर्मिणः शक्तिरेव धर्मः । स च फलप्रसवभेदानुमितसद्भाव एकस्यान्योऽन्यश्च परिदृष्टः । तत्र वर्तमानः स्वव्यापारमनुभवन्धर्मी धर्मान्तरेभ्यः शान्तेभ्यश्चाव्यपदेश्येभ्यश्च भिद्यते । यदा तु सामान्येन समन्वागतो भवति तदा धर्मिस्वरूपमात्रत्वाल्कोऽसौ केन भिद्येत ।

तत्र ये खलु धर्मिणो धर्माः शान्ता उदिता अव्यपदेश्याश्चेति तत्र शान्ता ये कृत्वा व्यापारानुपरताः सव्यापार उदितास्ते चानागतस्य लक्षणस्य समनन्तरा । वर्तमानस्यान्तरा अतीताः । किमर्थमतीतस्यान्तरा न भवन्ति वर्तमानाः । पूर्वपश्चिमताया अभावात् । यथाऽनागतवर्तमानयोः पूर्वपश्चिमता नैवमतीतस्य । तस्मात्रातीतस्यास्ति समनन्तरः । तदनागत एव समनन्तरो भवति वर्तमानस्येति ।

अथाव्यपदेश्याः के । सर्वं सर्वात्मकमिति । यत्रोक्तम् जलभूम्योः पारिणामिकं रसादिवैश्वरूप्यं स्थावरेषु दृष्टम् । तथा स्थावराणां जङ्गमेषु जङ्गमानां स्थावरेष्वित्येवं जात्यनुच्छेदेन सर्वं सर्वात्मकमिति ।

देशकालाकारनिमित्तापबन्धात्र खलु समानकालमात्मनामभिव्यक्तिरिति । य एतेष्वभिव्यक्तानभिव्यक्तेषु धर्मेष्वनुषाती सामान्यविशेषात्मा सोऽन्वयी धर्मी । यस्य तु धर्ममात्रमेवेदं

निरन्वयं तस्य भोगाभावः। कस्मात् अन्येन विज्ञानेन कृतस्य कर्मणोऽन्यत्कथं भोक्तृत्वेनाधिक्रियेत।
तत्स्मृत्यभावश्च नान्यदृष्टस्य स्मरणमन्यस्यास्तीति। वस्तुप्रत्यभिज्ञानाच्च स्थितोऽन्वयी धर्मी यो
धर्मान्यथात्वमभ्युपगतः प्रत्यभिज्ञायते। तस्मान्नेदं धर्ममात्रं निरन्वयमिति।

भोजवृत्ति—शान्ता ये कृतस्वस्वव्यापारा अतीतेऽध्वनि अनुप्रविष्टाः उदिता येऽनागतमध्वानं
परित्यज्य वर्तमानेऽध्वनि स्वव्यापारं कुर्वन्ति अव्यपदेश्या ये शक्तिरूपेण स्थिता व्यपदेष्टुं न शक्यन्ते
तेषां नियतकार्यकारणरूपयोग्यतयाऽवच्छिन्ना शक्तिरेवेह धर्मशब्देनाभिधीयते। तं त्रिविधमपि धर्म
योऽनुपतति अनुवर्ततेऽन्वयित्वेन स्वी करोति स शान्तोदिताव्यपदेश्यधर्मानुपाती धर्मीत्युच्यते। यथा
सुवर्णं रुचकरूपधर्मपरित्यागेन स्वस्तिकरूप धर्मान्तरपरिग्रहे सुवर्णरूपतयाऽनुवर्तमानं तेषु धर्मेषु
कथंचिद्भिन्नेषु धर्मिरूपतया सामान्यात्मना धर्मरूपतया विशेषात्मना स्थितमन्वयित्वेनावभासते।
एकस्य धर्मिणः कथमनेके परिणामा इत्याशङ्कामपनेतुमाह

क्रमान्यत्वं परिणामान्यत्वे हेतुः ॥3.15॥

kramānyatvaṃ pariṇāmānyatve hetuḥ

The (krama-anyatvaṁ) succession of a sequence is the (hetuḥ) cause of (parimāṇa-anyatve) manifold evolution.

For example, a succession of sequences like powder of clay, a wet lump of clay, a dry lump of clay, and baked clay is the cause of manifold products of clay.

व्यासभाष्य—एकस्य धर्मिण एक एव परिणाम इति प्रसक्ते क्रमान्यत्वं परिणामान्यत्वे
हेतुर्भवतीति। तद्यथा चूर्णमृत्पिण्डमृद्घटमृत्कपालमृत्कणमृदिति च क्रमः। यो यस्य धर्मस्य
समनन्तरो धर्मः स तस्य क्रमः। पिण्डः प्रच्यवते घट उपजायत इति धर्मपरिणामक्रमः।
लक्षणपरिणामक्रमो घटस्यानागतभावाद्वर्तमानभावः क्रमः। तथा पिण्डस्य वर्तमानभावादतीतभावः
क्रमः। नातीतस्यास्ति क्रमः। कस्मात्। पूर्वपरतायां सत्यां समनन्तरत्वं सा तु नास्त्यतीतस्य।
तस्माद्द्वयोरेव लक्षणयोः क्रमः। तथाऽवस्थापरिणामक्रमोऽपि घटस्याभिनवस्य प्रान्ते पुराणता
दृश्यते। सा च क्षणपरम्परानुपातिना क्रमेणाभिव्यज्यमाना परां व्यक्तिमापद्यत इति। धर्मलक्षणाभ्यां
च विशिष्टोऽयं तृतीयः परिणाम इति।

य एते क्रमा धर्मधर्मिभेदे सति प्रतिलब्धस्वरूपाः। धर्मोऽपि धर्मी
भवत्यन्यधर्मस्वरूपापेक्षयेति। यदा तु परमार्थतो धर्मिण्यभेदोपचारसाद्वारेण स एवाभिधीयते
धर्मस्तदाऽयमेकत्वेनैव क्रमः प्रत्यवभासते।

चित्तस्य द्वये धर्मा परिदृष्टाश्चापरिदृष्टाश्च। तत्र प्रत्ययात्मकाः परिदृष्टा वस्तुमात्रात्मका
अपरिदृष्टाः। ते च सप्तैव भवन्त्यनुमानेन प्रापितवस्तुमात्रसद्भावाः।

निरोधधर्मसंस्काराः परिणामोऽथ जीवनम्।
चेष्टा शक्तिश्च चित्तस्य धर्मा दर्शनवर्जिताः।।इति।।15।।
अतो योगिन उपात्तसर्वसाधनस्य बुभुत्सितार्थप्रतिपत्तये संयमस्य विषय उपक्षिप्यते

भोजवृत्ति—धर्माणामुक्तलक्षणानां यः क्रमस्तस्य यत्प्रतिक्षणमन्यत्वं परिदृश्यमानं तत्
परिणामस्योक्तलक्षणस्यान्यत्वे नानविधत्वे हेतुर्लिङ्गं ज्ञापकं भवति । अयमर्थः योऽयं नियतः क्रमो
मृच्चूर्णान्मृत्पिण्डस्ततः कपालानि तेभ्यश्च घट इत्येवंरूपः परिदृश्यमानः परिणामस्यान्यत्वमावेदयति
तस्मिन्नेव धर्मिणि यो लक्षणपरिणामस्यावस्थापरिणामस्य वा क्रमः सोऽपि अनेनैव न्यायेन
परिणामान्यत्वे गमकोऽवगन्तव्यः । सर्व एव भावा नियतेनैव क्रमेण प्रतिक्षणं परिणममानाः
परिदृश्यन्ते । अतः सिद्धं क्रमान्यत्वात्परिणामान्यत्वम् । सर्वेषां चित्तादीनां परिणममानानां केचिद्धर्माः
प्रत्यक्षेणैवोपलभ्यन्ते । यथा सुखादयः संस्थानादयश्च । केचिच्चैकान्तेनानुमानगम्याः । यथा
धर्मसंस्काराशक्तिप्रभृतयः । धर्मिणश्च भिन्नाभिन्नरूपतया सर्वत्रानुगमः । इदानीमुक्तस्य संयमस्य
विषयप्रदर्शनद्वारेण सिद्धीः प्रतिपादयितुमाह

<h2 style="text-align:center">परिणामत्रयसंयमाद् अतीतानागतज्ञानम् ॥3.16॥</h2>

pariṇāmatrayasaṃyamād atītānāgatajñānam

By Sañyama on the changes of dharma, lakṣaṇa, and
avasthā of an object, a yogī knows the past and future of
that object.

व्यासभाष्य—धर्मलक्षणावस्थापरिणामेषु संयमाद्योगिनां भवत्यतीतानागतज्ञानम् ।
धारणाध्यानसमाधित्रयमेकत्र संयम उक्तः । तेन परिणामत्रयं साक्षात्क्रियमाणमतीतानागतज्ञानं तेषु
संपादयति ।

भोजवृत्ति—धर्मलक्षणावस्थाभेदेन यत्परिणामत्रयमुक्तं तत्र संयमात्तस्मिविषये पूर्वोक्तसंयमस्य
कारणादतीतानागतज्ञानं योगिनः समाधेराविर्भवति । इदमत्र तात्पर्यम् अस्मिन्धर्मिणि अयं धर्म इदं
लक्षणमियमवस्था चानागतादध्वनः समेत्य वर्तमानेऽध्वनि स्वं व्यापारं विधायातीतमध्वानं
प्रविशतीत्येवं परिहृतविक्षेपतया यदा संयमं करोति तदा यत्किंचिदनुत्पन्नमतिक्रान्तं वा तत्सर्वं योगी
जानाति । यतश्चित्तस्य शुद्धसत्त्वप्रकाशरूपत्वात्सर्वार्थग्रहणसामर्थ्यमविद्यादिभिर्विक्षेपैरपक्रियते । यदा
तु तैस्तैरुपायैर्विक्षेपाः परिह्रियन्ते तदा निवृत्तमलस्येवाऽऽदर्शस्य सर्वार्थग्रहण-
सामर्थ्यमेकाग्रताबलादाविर्भवति । सिद्ध्यन्तरमाह

<h2 style="text-align:center">शब्दार्थप्रत्ययानामितरेतराध्यासात्</h2>

<h2 style="text-align:center">सङ्करस्तत्प्रविभागसंयमात्सर्वभूतरुतज्ञानम् ॥3.17॥</h2>

śabdārthapratyayānāmitaretarādhyāsāt
saṅkarastatpravibhāgasaṃyamātsarvabhūtarutajñānam

(Adhyāsāt) By reading/knowing the co-relation of one
with another, there is an (saṅkara) integration of (śabda)
words, (artha) their objects, and (pratyaya) the
knowledge of the objects (though each is otherwise
separate). (Sañyamāt) By Sañyama on the (pravibhāga)

separate natures of the words, objects, and their knowledge, a yogī can (jñāna) understand (ruta) the language of (sarva-bhūta) all living beings (animals, birds, plants, small creatures, etc.)

व्यासभाष्य—तत्र वाग्वर्णेष्वेवार्थवती । श्रोत्रं च ध्वनिपरिणाममात्रविषयम् । पदं पुनर्नादानुसंहारबुद्धिनिग्राह्यमिति ।

वर्णा एकसमयासंभवित्वात्परस्परनिरनुग्रहात्मानस्ते पदमसंस्पृश्यानुपस्थाप्याऽऽविर्भूतास्तिरो-भूताश्चेति प्रत्येकमपदस्वरूपा उच्यन्ते ।

वर्णः पुनरेकैकः पदात्मा सर्वाभिधानशक्तिप्रचितः सहकारिवर्णान्तर-प्रतियोगित्वाद्वैश्वरूप्यमिवाऽऽपन्नः पूर्वश्चोत्तरेणोत्तरश्च पूर्वेण विशेषेऽवस्थापित इत्येवं बहवो वर्णाः क्रमानुरोधिनोऽर्थसंकेतेनावच्छिन्ना इयन्त एते सर्वाभिधानशक्तिपरिवृता गकारौकारविसर्जनीयाः सास्नादिमन्तमर्थं द्योतयन्तीति ।

तदेतेषामर्थसंकेतेनावच्छिन्नानामुपसंहृतध्वनिक्रमाणां य एको बुद्धिनिर्भासस्तत्पदं वाचकं वाच्यस्य संकेत्यते । तदेकं पदमेकबुद्धिविषयमेकप्रयत्नक्षिप्तमभागमक्रमवर्णं बौद्धमन्त्यवर्णप्रत्ययव्यापारोपस्थापितं परत्र प्रतिपिपादयिषया वर्णैरेवाभिधीयमानैः श्रूयमाणैश्च श्रोतृभिरनादिवाग्व्यवहारवासनानुविद्धया लोकबुद्ध्या सिद्धवत्संप्रतिपत्त्या प्रतीयते ।

तस्य संकेतबुद्धितः प्रविभागः एतावतामेवंजातीयकोऽनुसंहार एकस्यार्थस्य वाचक इति । संकेतस्तु पदपदार्थयोरितरेतराध्यासरूपः स्मृत्यात्मको योऽयं शब्दः सोऽयमर्थो योऽयमर्थः सोऽयं शब्द इति । एवमितरेतराध्यासरूपः संकेतो भवतीति । एवमेते शब्दार्थप्रत्यया इतरेतराध्यासात्संकीर्णा गौरिति शब्दो गौरित्यर्थो गौरिति ज्ञानम् । य एषां प्रविभागज्ञः स सर्ववित् ।

सर्वपदेषु चास्ति वाक्यशक्तिर्वृक्ष इत्युक्तेऽस्तीति गम्यते ।

न सत्तां पदार्थो व्यभिचरतीति । तथा न ह्यासाधना क्रियास्तीति ।

तथा च पचतीत्युक्ते सर्वाकारकाणामाक्षेपो नियमार्थोऽनुवादः कर्तृकरणकर्मणां चैत्राग्नितण्डुलानामिति । दृष्टं च वाक्यार्थे पदरचनं श्रोत्रियश्छन्दोऽधीते जीवति प्राणान्धारयति । तत्र वाक्ये पदार्थाभिव्यक्तिस्ततः पदं प्रविभज्य व्याकरणीयं क्रियावाचकं वा कारकवाचकं वा । अन्यथा भवत्यश्वोऽजापय इत्येवमादिषु नामाख्यातसारूप्यादनिर्ज्ञातं कथं क्रियायां कारके वा व्याक्रियेतेति ।

तेषां शब्दार्थप्रत्ययानां प्रविभागः । तद्यथा श्वेतते प्रासाद इति क्रियार्थः श्वेतः प्रासाद इति कारकार्थः शब्दः क्रियाकारकात्मा तदर्थः प्रत्ययश्च । कस्मात् । सोऽयमित्यभिसंबन्धादेकाकार एव प्रत्ययः संकेत इति ।

यस्तु श्वेतोऽर्थः स शब्दप्रत्यययोरालम्बनीभूतः । स हि स्वाभिरवस्थाभिर्विक्रियमाणो न शब्दसहगतो न बुद्धिसहगतः । एवं शब्द एव प्रत्ययो नेतरेतरसहगत इत्यन्यथा शब्दोऽन्यथाऽर्थोऽन्यथा प्रत्यय इति विभागः । एवं तद्विभागसंयमाद्योगिनः सर्वभूतरुतज्ञानं संपद्यत इति ।

भोजवृत्ति—शब्दः श्रोत्रेन्द्रियग्राह्यो नियतक्रमवर्णात्मा नियतैकार्थप्रतिपत्त्यवच्छिन्नः । यदि वा क्रमरहितः स्फोटात्मा शास्त्रसंस्कृतबुद्धिग्राह्यः । उभयथापि पदरूपो वाक्यरूपश्च तयोरेकार्थप्रतिपत्तौ सामर्थ्यात् । अर्थो जातिगुणक्रियादिः । प्रत्ययो ज्ञानं विषयाकारा बुद्धिवृत्तिः । एषां शब्दार्थज्ञानानां व्यवहार इतरेतराध्यासाद्धिन्नानामपि बुद्ध्येकरूपतासंपादनात्संकीर्णत्वम् । तथा हि गामानयेत्युक्ते कश्चिद्रोलक्षणमर्थं गोत्वजात्यवच्छिन्नं सास्नादिमत्पिण्डरूपं शब्दं च तद्वाचकं ज्ञानं च तद्ग्राहकमभेदेनैवाध्यवस्यति न त्वस्य गोशब्दो वाचकोऽयं गोशब्दस्य वाच्यस्तयोरिदं ग्राहकं ज्ञानमिति भेदेन व्यवहरति । तथा हि कोऽयमर्थः कोऽयं शब्दः किमिदं ज्ञानमिति पृष्टः सर्वत्रैकरूपमेवोत्तरं ददाति गौरिति । स यद्येकरूपतां न प्रतिपद्यते कथमेकरूपमुत्तरं प्रयच्छति । एतस्मिन्स्थिते योऽयं प्रविभागं इदं शब्दस्य तत्त्वं यद्वाचकत्वं नाम इदमर्थस्य यद्वाच्यत्वमिदं ज्ञानस्य यत्प्रकाशकत्वमिति प्रविभागं विधाय तस्मिन्प्रविभागे यः संयमं करोति तस्य सर्वेषां भूतानां मृगपशुपक्षिसरीसृपादीनां यद्रुतं यः शब्दस्तत्र ज्ञानमुत्पद्यतेऽनेनैवाभिप्रायेणैतेन प्राणिनाऽयं शब्द समुच्चारित इति सर्वं जानाति । सिद्ध्यन्तरमाह

संस्कारसाक्षात्करणात्पूर्वजातिज्ञानम् ॥3.18॥

saṃskārasākṣātkaraṇātpūrvajātijñānam

[saṃskārasākṣātkaraṇāt] By sañyama on the sanskāras of a particular living being, [pūrvajātijñānam] a yogī can know the previous species of birth of that living being.

व्यासभाष्य—द्वये खल्वमी संस्काराः स्मृतिक्लेशहेतवो वासनारूपा विपाकहेतवो धर्माधर्मरूपाः । ते पूर्वभवाभिसंस्कृताः परिणामचेष्टानिरोधशक्तिजीवनधर्मवदपरिदृष्टाश्चित्तधर्माः । तेषु संयमः संस्कारसाक्षात्क्रियायै समर्थः । न च देशकालनिमित्तानुभवैर्विना तेषामस्ति साक्षात्करणम् । तदित्थं संस्कारसाक्षात्करणात्पूर्वजातिज्ञानमुत्पद्यते योगिनः । परत्राप्येवमेव संस्कारसाक्षात्करणात्परजातिसंवेदनम् ।

अत्रेदमाख्यानं श्रूयते भगवतो जैगीषव्यस्यं संस्कारसाक्षात्करणाद्दशसु महासर्गेषु जन्मपरिणामक्रममनुपश्यतो विवेकजं ज्ञानं प्रादुरभूत । अथ भगवानावट्यस्तनुधरस्तमुवाच दशसु महासर्गेषु भव्यत्वादनभिभूतबुद्धिसत्त्वेन त्वया नरकतिर्यग्गर्भसंभवं दुःखं संपश्यता देवमनुष्येषु पुनःपुनरुत्पद्यमानेन सुखदुःखयोः किमधिकमुपलब्धमिति भगवन्तमावट्यं जैगीषव्य उवाच दशसु महासर्गेषु भव्यत्वादनभिभूतबुद्धिसत्त्वेन मया नरकतिर्यग्भवं दुःखं संपश्यता देवमनुष्येषु पुनः पुनरुत्पद्यमानेन यत्किंचिदनुभूतं तत्सर्वं दुःखमेव प्रत्यवैमि । भगवानावट्य उवाच यदिदमायुष्मतः प्रधानवशित्वमनुत्तमं च संतोषसुखं किमिदमपि दुःखपक्षे निक्षिप्तमिति । भगवाञ्जैगीषव्य उवाच विषयसुखापेक्षयैवेदमनुत्तमं संतोषसुखमुक्तम् कैवल्यसुखापेक्षया दुःखमेव । बुद्धिसत्त्वस्यायं धर्मस्त्रिगुणस्त्रिगुणश्च प्रत्ययो हेयपक्षे न्यस्त इति दुःखरूपस्तृष्णातन्तुः । तृष्णादुःखसंतापापगमात्तु प्रसन्नमबाधं सर्वानुकूलं सुखमिदमुक्तमिदि ।

भोजवृत्ति—द्विविधाश्चित्तस्य वासनारूपाः संस्काराः । केचित्स्मृतिमात्रोत्पादनफलाः केचिज्जात्यायुर्भोगलक्षणविपाकहेतवः यथा धर्माधर्माख्याः । तेषु संस्कारेषु यदा संयमं करोति एवं मया

सोऽर्थोऽनुभूत एवं मया सा क्रिया निष्पादितेति पूर्ववृत्तमनुसंदधानो भावयन्नेव
प्रबोधकमन्तरेणोद्बुद्धसंस्कारः सर्वमतीतं स्मरति । क्रमेण साक्षात्कृतेष्वबुद्धेषु संस्कारेषु
पूर्वजन्मानुभूतानपि जात्यादीन्प्रत्यक्षेण पश्यति । सिद्ध्यन्तरमाह

प्रत्ययस्य परचित्तज्ञानम् ॥3.19॥
pratyayasya paracittajñānam

[pratyayasya] By sañyama on the mind of the other
person, [paracittajñānam] a yogī can read his, her mind.

व्यासभाष्य—प्रत्यये संयमात्प्रत्ययस्य साक्षात्करणात्ततः परचित्तज्ञानम् ।

भोजवृत्ति—प्रत्यस्य परचित्तस्य केनचिन्मुखरागादिना लिङ्गेन गृहीतस्य यदा संयमं करोति
तदा परकीयचित्तस्य ज्ञानमुत्पद्यते सरागमस्य चित्तं विरागं वेति । परचित्तगतानपि
धर्मार्ज्ञानातीत्यर्थः । अस्यैव परचित्तज्ञानस्य विशेषमाह

न च तत्सालम्बनं तस्याविषयीभूतत्वात् ॥3.20॥
na ca tatsālambanaṃ tasyāviṣayībhūtatvāt

A yogī can read the state of mind of another person,
(na cha) but he is not able to read (sālambanam) the
cause of that state of the concerned person, as (tasya) the
same (aviṣayībhūtatvāt) is not the subject matter of
sañyama.

व्यासभाष्य—रक्तं प्रत्ययं जानात्यमुष्मिन्नालम्बने रक्तमिति न जानाति । परप्रत्ययस्य
यदालम्बनं तद्योगिचित्तेन नाऽऽलम्बनीकृतं परप्रत्ययमात्रं तु योगिचित्तस्यालम्बनीभूतमिति ।

भोजवृत्ति—तस्य परस्य यच्चित्तं तत्सालम्बनं स्वकीयेनाऽऽलम्बनेन सहितं न शक्यते
ज्ञातुमालम्बनस्य केनचिल्लिङ्गेनाविषयीकृतत्वात् । लिङ्गाच्चित्तमात्रं परस्यावगतं ननु नीलविषयमस्य
चित्तं पीतविषयमिति वा । यच्च न गृहीतं तत्र संयमस्य कर्तुमशक्यत्वान्न भवति परचित्तस्य यो
विषयस्तत्र ज्ञानम् । तस्मात्परकीयचित्तं नाऽऽलम्बनसहितं गृह्यते तस्वाऽऽलम्बनस्यागृहीतत्वात् ।
चित्तधर्माः पुनर्गृह्यन्त एव । यदा तु किमनेनाऽऽलम्बितमिति प्रणिधानं करोति तदा
तत्संयमात्तद्विषयमपि ज्ञानमुत्पद्यत एव । सिद्ध्यन्तरमाह

How Does a Yogī Become Invisible?

कायरूपसंयमात्तद्ग्राह्यशक्तिस्तम्भे चक्षुःप्रकाशासंप्रयोगेऽन्तर्धानम्

॥3.21॥
kāyarūpasaṃyamāttadgrāhyaśaktistambhe

cakṣuḥprakāśāsamprayoge'ntardhānam

(Sañyamāt) By sañyama on (kāyarūpa) the form of the body, (grāhyaśakti) the light waves emitted by the body are (stambha) obstructed, thence (asañyoge) disconnection of (chakṣu) the eyes with (prakāśa) the light emitted by the body takes place and a yogī (antardhānam) becomes invisible.

व्यासभाष्य—कायस्य रूपे संयमाद्रूपस्य या ग्राह्या शक्तिस्तां प्रतिष्टभ्राति । ग्राह्यशक्तिस्तम्भे सति चक्षुप्रकाशासंप्रयोगेऽन्तर्धनिमुत्पद्यते योगिनः । एतेन शब्दाद्यन्तर्धानमुक्तं वेदितव्यम् ।

भोजवृत्ति—कायः शरीरं तस्य रूपं चक्षुर्ग्राह्यो गुणस्तस्मिन्नस्त्यस्मिन्काये रूपमिति संयमात्तस्य रूपस्य चक्षुर्ग्राह्यत्वरूपा या शक्तिस्तस्याः स्तम्भे भावनावशात्प्रतिबन्धे चक्षुष्प्रकाशासंयोगे चक्षुषः प्रकाशः सत्त्वधर्मस्तस्यासंयोगे तद्ग्रहणव्यपाराभावे योगिनोऽन्तर्धानं भवति न केनचिदसौ दृश्यत इत्यर्थः । एतेनैव रूपाद्यन्तर्धानोपायप्रदर्शनेन शब्दादीनां श्रोत्रादिग्राह्याणामन्तर्धानमुक्तं वेदितव्यम् । सिद्ध्यन्तरमाह

सोपक्रमं निरुपक्रमं च कर्म तत्संयमादपरान्तज्ञानमरिष्टेभ्यो वा

॥3.22॥

sopakramaṃ nirupakramaṃ ca karma
tatsaṃyamādaparāntajñānamariṣṭebhyo vā

(Tat sañyamāt) By sañyama on past life karmic sanskāras (sopakramam) to be fructified sooner or (nirupakramam) later (ariṣṭebhyo vā) and from signs called portents, (aparānta jñāna) a yogī knows the exact time of death.

Portents are of three types: Spiritual: 1.1 By inserting a finger into the ear cavity, if one is not able to hear the sound of blood flowing into veins and arteries. 1.2 By closing eyes, if one is not able to see the inner light of the body.

2. Ādhibhautika: Meet with the dead people or invited by dead persons.

3. Ādhidaivika: Seeing unnatural things in nature.

व्यासभाष्य—आयुर्विपाकं कर्म द्विविधं सोपक्रमं निरुपक्रमं च । तथा यथाऽऽर्द्रं वस्त्रं वितानितं लघीयसा कालेन शुष्येत्तथा सोपक्रमम् । यथा च तदेव संपिण्डितं चिरेण संशुष्येदेवं निरुपक्रमम् । यथा वाऽग्निः शुष्के कक्षे मुक्तो वातेन समन्ततो युक्तः क्षेपीयसा कालेन दहेत्तथा सोपक्रमम् । यथा वा स एवाग्निस्तृणराशौ क्रमशोऽवयवेषु न्यस्तश्चिरेण दहेत्तथा निरुपक्रमम् । तदैकभविकमायुष्करं कर्म द्विविधं सोपक्रमं निरुपक्रमं च । तत्संयमादपरान्तस्य प्रायणस्य ज्ञानम् ।

अरिष्टेभ्यो वेति । त्रिविधमरिष्टमाध्यात्मिकमाधिभौतिकमाधिदैविकं च । तत्राऽऽध्यात्मिकं घोषं स्वदेहे पिहितकर्णो न शृणोति ज्योतिर्वा नेत्रेऽवष्टब्धे न पश्यति । तथाऽधिभौतिकं यमपुरुषान्पश्यति पितृनतीतानकस्मात्पश्यति । तथाऽधिदैविकं स्वर्गमकस्मात्सिद्धान्वा पश्यति । विपरीतं वा सर्वमिति । अनेन वा जानात्यपरान्तमुपस्थितमिति ।

भोजवृत्ति—आयुर्विपाकं यत्पूर्वकृतं कर्म तद्द्विप्रकारं सोपक्रमं निरुपक्रमं च । तत्र सोपक्रमं यत्फलजननायोपक्रमेण कार्यकारणाभिमुख्येन सह वर्तते । यथोष्णप्रदेशे प्रसारितमार्द्रवासः शीघ्रमेव शुष्यति । उक्तरूपविपरीतं निरुपक्रमं यथा तदेवाऽऽर्द्रवासः संवर्तितमनुष्णदेशे चिरेण शुष्यति । तस्मिन्द्विविधे कर्मणि यः संयमं करोति किं मम कर्म शीघ्रविपाकं चिरविपाकं वा एवं ध्यानादाढ्योदपरान्तज्ञानमस्योत्पद्यते । अपरान्तः शरीरवियोगस्तस्मिंज्ज्ञानममुष्मिन्कालेऽमुष्मिन्देशे मम शरीरवियोगो भविष्यतीति निःसंशयं जानाति । अरिष्टेभ्यो वा । अरिष्टानि त्रिविधानि आध्यात्मिकाधिभौतिकाधिदैविकभेदेन । तत्राऽऽध्यात्मिकानि पिहितकर्णः कोष्ठ्यस्य वायोर्घोषं न शृणोतीत्येवमादीनि । आधिभौतिकानि अकस्माद्विकृतपुरुषदर्शनादीनि । आधिदैविकानि अकाण्ड एव द्रष्टुमशक्यस्वर्गादिपदार्थदर्शनादीनि । तेभ्यः शरीरवियोगकालं जानाति । यद्यपि अयोगिनामप्यरिष्टेभ्यः प्रायेण तज्ज्ञानमुत्पद्यते तथापि तेषां सामान्याकारेण तत्संशयरूपं योगिनां पुनर्नियत देशकालतया प्रत्यक्षवदव्यभिचारि । परिकर्मनिष्पादिताः सिद्धिः प्रतिपादयितुमाह

मैत्र्यादिषु बलानि ॥3.23॥
maitryādiṣu balāni

Through sañyama on (maitrī) friendliness with happy persons; (karuṇā) compassion with miserables; and (muditā) gladness with righteous persons; a yogī gains the highest states of happiness, compassion, and gladness.

Here the word, maitrī, etc. suggests the three words in series: maitrī (friendliness), karuṇā (compassion) and muditā (gladness).

व्यासभाष्य—मैत्री करुणा मुदितेति तिस्रो भावनास्तत्र भूतेषु सुखितेषु मैत्रीं भावयित्वा मैत्रीबलं लभते । दुःखितेषु करुणां भावयित्वा करुणाबलं लभते । पुण्यशीलेषु मुदितां भावयित्वा मुदिताबलं लभते । भावनातः समाधिर्यः स संयमस्ततो बलान्यवन्ध्यवीर्याणि जायन्ते । पापशीलेषूपेक्षा न तु भावना । ततश्च तस्यां नास्ति

समाधिरित्यतो न बलमुपेक्षातस्तत्र संयमाभावादिति ।

भोजवृत्ति—मैत्रीकरुणामुदितोपेक्षासु यो विहितसंयमस्तस्य बलानि मैत्र्यादीनां संबन्धीनि प्रादुर्भवन्ति । मैत्रीकरुणामुदितोपेक्षास्तथाऽस्य प्रकर्षं गच्छन्ति यथा सर्वस्य मित्रत्वादिकमयं संपद्यते । सिद्ध्यन्तरमाह

बलेषु हस्तिबलादीनि ॥3.24॥

baleṣu hastibalādīni

By sañyama on (physical) strength, a yogī can attain power like that of an elephant.

व्यासभाष्य—हस्तिबले संयमाद्धस्तिबलो भवति । वैनतेयबले संयमाद्वैनतेय बलो भवति । वायुबले संयमाद्वायुबलो भवतीत्येवमादि ।

भोजवृत्ति—हस्त्यादिसंबन्धिषु बलेषु कृतसंयमस्य तद्बलानि हस्त्यादिबलानि आविर्भवन्ति । यदयमर्थः यस्मिन्हस्तिबले वायुवेगे सिंहवीर्ये वा तन्मयीभावेनायं संयमं करोति तत्तत्सामर्थ्ययुक्त्वात्सर्वमस्य प्रादुर्भव तीत्यर्थः । सिद्ध्यन्तरमाह

प्रवृत्त्यालोकन्यासात्सूक्ष्मव्यवहितविप्रकृष्टज्ञानम् ॥3.25॥

pravṛttyālokanyāsātsūkṣmavyavahitaviprakṛṣṭajñānam

(Nyāsāt) By putting sañyama on (*āloka*) the sāttvika light developed due to (*pravṛtti) jyotiṣmati* state of mind (focus of mind on self-realization) and *viṣayavati* state of mind (focus of mind on objects of sense), a yogī can have the knowledge of the (sūkṣma) atomic, (vyavahita) covered and (viprakṛṣṭa) remote objects.

Note: For jyotiṣmati pravṛtti and Viṣayavatī pravṛtti of mind, see sūtras 1.35 and 1.36.

व्यासभाष्य—ज्योतिष्मती प्रवृत्तिरुक्ता मनसस्तस्यां च आलोकस्तं योगी सूक्ष्मे वा व्यवहिते वा विप्रकृष्टे वाऽर्थे विन्यस्य तमर्थमधिगच्छति ।

भोजवृत्ति—प्रवृत्तिर्विषयवती ज्योतिष्मती च प्रागुक्ता तस्या योऽसावालोकः सात्त्विकप्रकाशप्रसरस्तस्य निखिलेषु विषयेषु न्यासात्तद्वासितानां विषयाणां भावनात्सान्तःकरणेषु इन्द्रियेषु प्रकृष्टशक्तिमापन्नेषु सूक्ष्मस्य परमाण्वादेर्व्यवहितस्य भूम्यन्तर्गतस्य निधानादेर्विप्रकृष्टस्य मेर्वपरपार्श्ववर्तिनो रसायनादेर्ज्ञानमुत्पद्यते । एतत्समानवृत्तान्तं सिद्ध्यन्तरमाह

भुवनज्ञानं सूर्ये संयमात् ॥3.26॥

bhuvanajñānaṃ sūrye saṃyamāt

By sañyama on the sun, the mystery of the universe is unfolded to the yogī.

व्यासभाष्य—तत्प्रस्तारः सप्त लोकाः । तत्रावीचेः प्रभृति मेरुपृष्ठं यावदित्येवं भूर्लोकः मेरुपृष्ठादारभ्य आध्रुवाद्ग्रहनक्षत्रताराविचित्रोऽन्तरिक्षलोकः । ततः परः स्वर्लोकः पञ्चविधो माहेन्द्रस्तृतीयो लोकः । चतुर्थः प्राजापत्यो महर्लोकः त्रिविधो ब्राह्मः । तद्यथा जनलोकस्तपोलोकः सत्यलोक इति ।

ब्राह्मस्त्रिभूमिको लोकः प्राजापत्यस्ततो महान् ।
माहेन्द्रश्च स्वरित्युक्तो दिवि तारा भुवि प्रजाः ।। इति संग्रहश्लोकः ।

तत्रावीचेरुपर्युपरि निविष्टाः षण्महानरकभूमयो घनसलिलानलानिलाकाशतमः प्रतिष्ठा महाकालाम्बरीषरौरवमहारौरवकालसूत्रान्धतामिस्राः । यत्र स्वकर्मोपार्जितदुःखवेदनाः प्राणिनः कष्टमायुर्दीर्घमाक्षिप्य जायन्ते । ततो महातलरसातलातलसुतलवितलतलातलपातालाख्यानि सप्त पातालानि । भूमिरियमष्टमी सप्तद्वीपा वसुमती यस्याः सुमेरुर्मध्ये पर्वतराजः काञ्चनः । तस्य राजतवैदूर्यस्फटिकहेममणिमयानि शृङ्गाणि । तत्र वैदूर्यप्रभानुरागान्नीलोत्पलपत्रश्यामो नभसो दक्षिणो भागः श्वेतः पूर्वः स्वच्छः पश्चिमः कुरण्टकाभ उत्तरः । दक्षिणपार्श्वे चास्य जम्बूर्यतोऽयं जम्बूद्वीपः । तस्य सूर्यप्रचाराद्रात्रिंदिवं लग्नमिव वर्तते । तस्य नीलश्वेतशृङ्खवन्त उदीचीनास्त्रयः पर्वता द्विसाहस्रायामाः । तदन्तरेषु त्रीणि वर्षाणि नव नव योजनसाहस्राणि रमणकं हिरण्मयमुत्तराः कुरव इति । निषधहेमकूटहिमशैला दक्षिणतो द्विसाहस्रायामाः । तदन्तरेषु त्रीणि वर्षाणि नव नव योजनसाहस्राणि हरिवर्षं किंपुरुषं भारतमिति । सुमेरोः प्राचीना भद्राश्वमाल्यवत्सीमानः प्रतीचीनाः केतुमाला गन्धमादनसीमानः । मध्ये वर्षमिलावृतम् । तदेतद्योजनशतसाहस्रं सुमेरोर्दिशिदिशि तदर्धेन व्यूढम् ।

स खल्वयं शतसाहस्रायामो जम्बूद्वीपस्ततो द्विगुणेन लवणोदधिना वलयाकृतिना वेष्टितः । ततश्च द्विगुणा द्विगुणाः शाककुशक्रौञ्चशाल्मगोमेधपुष्करद्वीपाः समुद्राश्च सर्षपराशिकल्पाः सविचित्रशैलावतंसा इक्षुरससुरासर्पिर्दधिमण्डक्षीरस्वादूदकाः । सप्त समुद्रपरिवेष्टिता वलयाकृतयो लोकालोकपर्वतपरिवाराः पञ्चाशद्योजनकोटिपरिसंख्याताः । तदेतत्सर्वं सुप्रतिष्ठितसंस्थानमण्डमध्ये व्यूढम् । अण्डं च प्रधानस्याणुरवयवो यथाऽऽकाशे खद्योत इति ।

तत्र पाताले जलधौ पर्वतेष्वेतेषु देवनिकाया असुरगन्धर्वकिन्नर-किंपुरुषयक्षराक्षसभूतप्रेतपिशाचापस्मारकाप्सरोब्रह्मराक्षसकूष्माण्डविनायकाः प्रतिवसन्ति । सर्वेषु द्वीपेषु पुण्यात्मनो देवमनुष्याः ।

सुमेरुस्त्रिदशानामुद्यानभूमिः तत्र मिश्रवनं नन्दनं चैत्ररथं सुमानसमित्युद्यानानि । सुधर्मा देवसभा । सुदर्शनं पुरम् । वैजयन्तः प्रासादः । ग्रहनक्षत्रताराकास्तु ध्रुवे निबद्धा वायुविक्षेपनियमेनोपलक्षितप्रचाराः सुमेरोरुपर्युपरि सन्निविष्टा दिवि विपरिवर्तन्ते ।

माहेन्द्रनिवासिनः षड्देवनिकायाः त्रिदशा अग्निष्वात्ता याम्यास्तुषिता अपरिनिर्मितवशवर्तिनः

परिनिर्मितवशवर्तिनश्चेति । सर्वे संकल्पसिद्धा अणिमाद्यैश्वर्योपपन्नाः कल्पायुषो वृन्दारकाः कामभोगिन औपपादिकदेहा उत्तमानुकूलाभिरप्सरोभिः कृतपरिचाराः ।

महति लोके प्राजापत्ये पञ्चविधो देवनिकायः कुमुदा ऋभवः प्रतर्दना अज्ञनाभाः प्रचिताभा इति । एते महाभूतवशिनो ध्यानहाराः अल्पसहस्रायुषः । प्रथमे ब्रह्मणो जनलोके चतुर्विधो देवनिकायो ब्रह्मपुरोहिता ब्रह्मकायिका ब्रह्ममहाकायिका अमरा इति ते भूतेन्द्रियवशिनो द्विगुणद्विगुणोत्तरायुषः ।

द्वितीयो तपसि लोके त्रिविधो देवनिकायः आभास्वरा महाभास्वराः सत्यमहाभास्वराः इति । ते भूतेन्द्रियप्रकृतिवशिनो द्विगुणद्विगुणोत्तरायुषः सर्वे ध्यानाहारा ऊर्ध्वरेतस ऊर्ध्वमप्रतिहतज्ञाना अधरभूमिष्वनावृताज्ञानविषयाः । तृतीये ब्रह्मणः सत्यलोके चत्वारो देवनिकाया अकृतभवनन्यासाः स्वप्रतिष्ठा उपर्युपरिस्थिताः प्रधानवशिनो यावत्सर्गीयुषः ।

तत्राच्युताः सवितर्कध्यानसुखाः शुद्धनिवासाः सविचारध्यानसुखाः सत्याभा आनन्दमात्रध्यानसुखा संज्ञासंज्ञिनश्चास्मितामात्रध्यानसुखाः । तेऽपि त्रैलोक्यमध्ये प्रतितिष्ठन्ति । त एते सप्त लोकाः सर्व एव ब्रह्मलोकाः । विदेहप्रकृतिलयास्तु मोक्षपदे वर्तन्त इति न लोकमध्ये न्यस्ता इति । एतद्योगिना साक्षात्करणीयं सूर्य द्वारे संयम कृत्वा ततोऽन्यत्रापि एवं तावदभ्यसेद्यावदिदं सर्वं दृष्टमिति ।

.**भोजवृत्ति**.—सूर्ये प्रकाशमये यः संयमं करोति तस्य सप्तसु भूर्भुवः स्वः प्रभृतिषु लोकेषु यानि भुवनानि तत्तत्संनिवेशभाञ्जि स्थानानि तेषु यथावदस्य ज्ञानमुत्पद्यते । पूर्वस्मिन्सूत्रे सात्त्विकप्रकाश आलम्बनतयोक्त इह तु भौतिक इति विशेषः । भौतिकप्रकाशालम्बनद्वारेणैव सिद्ध्यन्तरमाह

चन्द्रे ताराव्यूहज्ञानम् ॥3.27॥
candre tārāvyūhajñānam

By sañyama on the moon, knowledge of the constellations takes place.

व्यासभाष्य—चन्द्रे संयमं कृत्वा ताराणां व्यूहं विजानीयात् ।

.**भोजवृत्ति**.—ताराणां ज्योतिषां यो व्यूहो विशिष्टः संनिवेशस्तस्मिंश्चन्द्रे कृतसंयमस्य ज्ञानमुत्पद्यते । सूर्यप्रकाशेन हततेजस्कत्वात्ताराणां सूर्यसंयमात्तज्ज्ञानं न शक्नोति भवितुमिति पृथुगुपायोऽभिहितः । सिद्ध्यन्तरमाह

ध्रुवे तद्गतिज्ञानम् ॥3.28॥
dhruve tadgatijñānam

By sañyama on the pole star, a yogī can know the motion of the pole star and other stars.

व्यासभाष्य—ततो ध्रुवे संयमं कृत्वा ताराणां गतिं विजानीयात् । ऊर्ध्वविमानेषु कृतसंयमस्तानि विजानीयात् ।

भोजवृत्ति.—ध्रुवे निश्चले ज्योतिषां प्रधाने कृतसंयमस्य तासां ताराणां या गतिः प्रत्येकं नियतकाला नियतदेशा च तस्या ज्ञानमुत्पद्यते । इयं ताराऽयं ग्रह इयता कालेनामुं राशिमिदं नक्षत्रं यास्यतीति सर्वं जानाति । इदं कालज्ञानस्य फलमित्युक्तं भवति । बाह्याः सिद्धीः प्रतिपाद्याऽऽन्तराः सिद्धीः प्रतिपादयितुमुपक्रमते

नाभिचक्रे कायव्यूहज्ञानम् ॥3.29॥
nābhicakre kāyavyūhajñānam

By sañyama on the navel centre, knowledge of the constitution of the body takes place.

व्यासभाष्य—नाभिचक्रे संयमं कृत्वा कायव्यूहं विजानीयात् । वातपित्तश्लेष्माणस्त्रयो दोषाः । धातवः सप्त त्वग्लोहितमांसस्नाय्वस्थिमज्जाशुक्राणि । पूर्वं पूर्वमेषां बाह्यमित्येष विन्यासः ।

भोजवृत्ति.—शरीरमध्यवर्ति नाभिसंज्ञकं यत्षोडशारं चक्रं तस्मिन् कृतसंयमस्य योगिनः कायगतो योऽसौ व्यूहो विशिष्टरसमलधातुनाड्यादीनामवस्थानं तत्र ज्ञानमुत्पद्यते । इदमुक्तं भवति नाभिचक्रे शरीरमध्यवर्ति सर्वतः प्रसृतानां नाड्यादीनां मूलभूतमतस्तत्र कृतावधानस्य समग्रसंनिवेशो यथावदाभाति । सिद्ध्यन्तरमाह

कण्ठकूपे क्षुत्पिपासानिवृत्तिः ॥3.30॥
kaṇṭhakūpe kṣutpipāsānivṛttiḥ

By sañyama on the cavity of throat, the yogī gets rid of the urge of hunger and thirst.

व्यासभाष्य—जिह्वाया अधस्तात्तन्तुस्तन्तोरधस्तात्कण्ठस्ततोऽधस्तात्कूपस्तत्र संयमात्क्षुत्पिपासे न बाधेते ।

भोजवृत्ति.—कण्ठे गले कूपः कण्ठकूपः जिह्वामूले जिह्वातन्तोरधस्तात्कूप इव कूपो गर्ताकारः प्रदेशः प्राणोदेर्यत्संस्पर्शात्क्षुत्पिपासादयः प्रादुर्भवन्ति तस्मिन्कृतसंयमस्य योगिनः क्षुत्पिपासादयो निवर्तन्ते । घण्टिकाधस्तात्स्रोतसा धार्यमाणे तस्मिन्भाविते भवत्येवंविधा सिद्धिः । सिद्ध्यन्तरमाह

कूर्मनाड्यां स्थैर्यम् ॥3.31॥
kūrmanāḍyāṁ sthairyam

By sañyama on the Kūrma-nādi located below the cavity of throat, the yogī attains steadiness of body and mind.

व्यासभाष्य—कूपादध उरसिकूर्माकारानाडी तस्यां कृतसंयमः स्थिरपदं लभते । यथा सर्पो गोधा चेति ।

भोजवृत्ति—कण्ठकूपस्याधस्ताद्या कूर्माख्या नाड़ी तस्यां कृतसंयमस्य चेतसः स्थैर्यमुत्पद्यते । तत्स्थानमनुप्रविष्टस्य चञ्चलता न भवतीत्यर्थः । यदि वा कायस्य स्थैर्यमुत्पद्यते न केनचित्स्पन्दयितुं शक्यत इत्यर्थः । सिद्ध्यन्तरमाह

मूर्धज्योतिषि सिद्धदर्शनम् ॥3.32॥
mūrdhajyotiṣi siddhadarśanam

By sañyama on the light emanating from the (Brahmarandhra) crown of the head, one can establish contact with Siddhas (extraterrestrial life or a siddha yogīs) takes place.

व्यासभाष्य—शिरः कपालेऽन्तश्छिद्रं प्रभास्वरं ज्योतिस्तत्र संयमं कृत्वा सिद्धानां द्यावापृथिव्योरन्तरालचारिणां दर्शनम् ।

भोजवृत्ति—शिरः कपाले ब्रह्मरंध्राख्यं छिद्रं प्रकाशाधारत्वाज्ज्योतिः । यथा गृहाभ्यन्तरस्थस्य मणेः प्रसरन्ती प्रभा कुञ्चिताकारेव सर्वप्रदेशे संघटते तथा हृदयस्थः सात्त्विकः प्रकाशः प्रसृतस्तत्र संपिण्डितत्वं भजते । तत्र कृतसंयमस्य ये द्यावापृथिव्योरन्तरालवर्तिनः सिद्धा दिव्याः पुरुषास्तेषामितरप्राणिभिरदृश्यानां तस्य दर्शनं भवति । तान्पश्यति तैश्च स संभाषत इत्यर्थः । सर्वज्ञत्व उपायमाह

प्रातिभाद्वा सर्वम् ॥3.33॥
prātibhādvā sarvam

By the power of (Prātibha Jñāna or Tāraka Jñāna) spontaneous enlightenment, the yogī is able to have the knowledge of all things.

Prātibha Jñāna is also called Tāraka Jñāna in the 54th sūtra of this chapter. This is known as spontaneous enlightenment occurring during the process of self-realization.

व्यासभाष्य—प्रातिभं नाम तारकं तद्विवेकजस्य ज्ञानस्य पूर्वरूपम् । यथोदये प्रभा भास्करस्य । तेन वा सर्वमेव जानाति योगी प्रातिभस्य ज्ञानस्योत्पत्ताविति ।

भोजवृत्ति—निमित्तानपेक्षं मनोमात्रजन्यमविसंवादकं द्रागुत्पद्यमानं ज्ञानं प्रतिभा । तस्यां संयमे क्रियमाणे प्रातिभं विवेकख्यातेः पूर्वभाति तारकं ज्ञानमुदेति । यथा उदेष्यति सवितरि पूर्वं प्रभा प्रादुर्भवति तद्द्विवेकख्यातेः पूर्वं तारकं सर्वविषयं ज्ञानमुत्पद्यते । तस्मिन्सति संयमान्तरानपेक्षः सर्वं जानातीत्यर्थः । सिद्ध्यन्तरमाह-

हृदये चित्तसंवित् ॥3.34॥

hṛdaye cittasaṃvit

By sañyama on the heart-lotus, a yogī is able to know the sanskāras of his mind and the sanskāras of the mind of other persons.

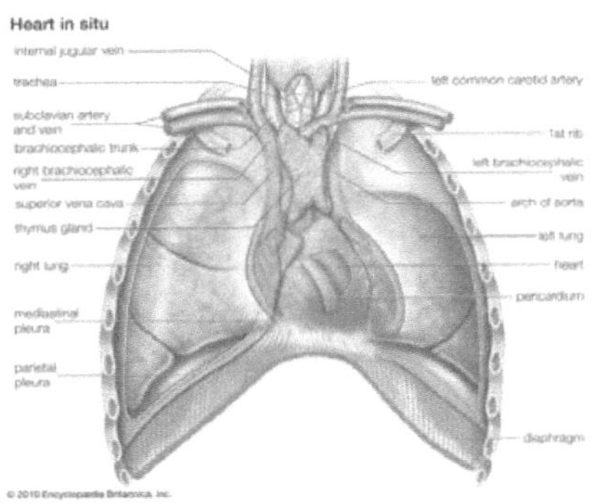

व्यासभाष्य— हृदयं शरीरस्य प्रदेशविशेषस्तस्मिन्नधोमुखस्वल्पपुण्डरीकाऽभ्यन्तरेऽन्तःकरणसत्त्वस्य स्थानं तत्र कृतसंयमस्य स्वपरचित्त............ । .... सर्वा वासनाः परचित्तगतांश्च रागादीज्ञानातीत्यर्थः । सिद्ध्यन्तरमाह- याददमास्मन्ब्रह्मपुर दहरं पुण्डरीकं वेश्म तत्र विज्ञानं तस्मिसंयमाच्चित्तसंवित् ।

सत्त्वपुरुषयोरत्यन्तासंकीर्णयोः प्रत्ययाविशेषो भोगः
परार्थत्वात्स्वार्थसंयमात्पुरुषज्ञानम् ॥3.35॥

sattvapuruṣayoratyantāsaṃkīrṇayoḥ pratyayāviśeṣo
bhogaḥ parārthatvātsvārthasaṃyamātpuruṣajñānam

Though the (sattva) mind and the (puruṣa) soul are two (atyanta) extremely (asaṅkīrṇa) different entities, yet (pratyaya-aviśeṣaḥ) non-discrimination of both (unification of both) results in (bhogaḥ) enjoyment, (prārthatvāt) because mind's actions are for the soul. (Sañyamāt) By sañyama on (svārtha) his/her own self, a yogī (puruṣa-jñānam) realizes his/her true nature of his/her own self.

व्यासभाष्य—बुद्धिसत्त्वं प्रख्याशीलं समानसत्त्वोपनिबन्धने रजस्तमसी वशीकृत्य सत्त्वपुरुषान्यताप्रत्ययेन परिणतम् । तस्माच्च सत्त्वात्परिणामिनोऽत्यन्तविधर्मा विशुद्धोऽन्यश्चितिमात्ररूपः पुरुषः । तयोरत्यन्तासंकीर्णयोः प्रत्ययाविशेषो भोगः पुरुषस्य दर्शितविषयत्वात् । स भोगप्रत्ययः सत्त्वस्य परार्थत्वाद्दृश्यः ।

यस्तु तस्माद्विशिष्टश्चितिमात्ररूपोऽन्यः पौरुषेयः प्रत्ययस्तत्र संयमात्पुरुषविषया प्रज्ञा जायते । न च पुरुषप्रत्ययेन बुद्धिसत्त्वात्मना पुरुषो दृश्यते पुरुष एव तं प्रत्ययं स्वात्मावलम्बनं पश्यति । तथा ह्युक्तम् विज्ञातारमरे केन विजानीयात् बृ० 2.4.14 इति ।

भोजवृत्ति—सत्त्वं प्रकाशसुखात्मकः प्राधानिकः परिणामविशेषः पुरुषो भोक्ताऽधिष्ठातृरूपः । तयोरत्यन्तासंकीर्णयोर्भोग्यभोक्तृरूपत्वाच्चेतनाचेतनत्वाच्च भिन्नयोर्यः प्रत्ययस्याविशेषो भेदेनाप्रतिभासनं तस्मात्सत्त्वस्यैव कर्तृताप्रत्ययेन वा सुखदुःखसंवित्स भोगः । सत्त्वस्य स्वार्थनैरपेक्ष्येण परार्थः पुरुषार्थनिमित्तस्तस्मादन्यो यः स्वार्थः पुरुषस्वरूपमात्रालम्बनः परित्यक्ताहंकारसत्त्वे या चिच्छायासंक्रान्तिस्तत्र कृतसंयमस्य पुरुषविषयं ज्ञानमुत्पद्यते । तत्र तदेवं रूपं स्वालम्बनं ज्ञानं सत्त्वनिष्ठः पुरुषो जानाति न पुनः पुरुषो ज्ञाता ज्ञानस्य विषयभावमापद्यते ज्ञेयत्वापत्तेर्ज्ञातृज्ञेययोश्चात्यन्तविरोधात् । अस्यैव संयमस्य फलमाह

ततः प्रातिभश्रावणवेदनादर्शास्वादवार्ता जायन्ते ॥3.36॥

tataḥ prātibhaśrāvaṇavedanādarśāsvādavārtā jāyante

By sañyama on Puruṣa (soul) there develops (prātibha) spontaneous enlightenment, (śrāvaṇa) divine audition (audition of inaudible sounds), (vedana) divine skin-sensation, (ādarśa) divine vision, (āsvād) divine taste and (vārtā) divine olfacation.

व्यासभाष्य —प्रातिभात्सूक्ष्मव्यवहितविप्रकृष्टातीतानागतज्ञानम् । श्रावणाद्दिव्यशब्दश्रवणम् । वेदनाद्दिव्यस्पर्शाधिगमः ।
आदर्शाद्दिव्यरूपसंवित् । आस्वादाद्दिव्यरससंवित् । वार्तातो दिव्यगन्धविज्ञानमित्येतानि नित्यं जायन्ते ।

भोजवृत्ति—ततः पुरुषसंयमादभ्यस्यमानाद्व्युत्थितस्यापि ज्ञानानि जायन्ते । तत्र प्रातिभं पूर्वोक्तं ज्ञानं तस्याऽविर्भावात्सूक्ष्मादिकमर्थं पश्यति । श्रावणं श्रोत्रेन्द्रियजं ज्ञानं तस्माच्च प्रकृष्टाद्दिव्यंदिवि भवंशब्दं जानाति । वेदना स्पर्शेन्द्रियजं ज्ञानं वेद्यतेऽनेयेति कृत्वा तान्त्रिक्या संज्ञया व्यवह्रियते । तस्माद्दिव्यस्यपर्शिविषयं ज्ञानं समुपजायते । आदर्शश्चक्षुरिन्द्रियजं ज्ञानम् । आ समन्तादृश्यतेऽनुभूयते रूपमनेनेति कृत्वा तस्य प्रकर्षाद्दिव्यं रूपज्ञानमुत्पद्यते । आस्वादो रसनेन्द्रियजं ज्ञानम् । आस्वाद्यतेऽनेनेति कृत्वा तस्मिन्प्रकृष्टे दिव्ये रसे संविदुपजायते । वार्ता गन्धसंवित् । वृत्तिशब्देन तान्त्रिक्या परिभाषया घ्राणेन्द्रियमुच्यते । वर्तते गन्धविषय इहि कृत्वा वृत्तेर्घ्राणेन्द्रिययाजाता वार्ता गन्धसंवित् । तस्यां प्रकृष्यमाणायां दिव्यगन्धोऽनुभूयते । एतेषां फलविशेषाणां विशेषविभागमाह

ते समाधावुपसर्गा व्युत्थाने सिद्धयः ॥3.37॥

te samādhāvupasargā vyutthāne siddhayaḥ

These divine powers are obstacles on the way of Samādhi, however, they are regarded as powers in practical sense or worldly affairs.

व्यासभाष्य—ते प्रातिभादयः समाहितचित्तस्योत्पद्यमाना उपसर्गास्तद्दर्शनप्रत्यनीकत्वात्। व्युत्थितचित्तस्योत्पद्यमानाः सिद्धयः।

भोजवृत्ति—ते प्राक्प्रतिपादिताः फलविशेषाः समाधेः प्रकर्षं गच्छत उपसर्गा उपद्रवा विघ्नकारिणः। तत्र हर्षविस्मयादिकरणेन समाधिः शिथिली भवति। व्युत्थाने तु पुनर्व्यवहारदशायां विशिष्टफलदायकत्वात्सिद्धयो भवन्ति। सिद्धन्तरमाह

बन्धकारणशैथिल्यात्प्रचारसंवेदनाच्च चित्तस्य परशरीरावेशः ॥ 3.38 ॥

bandhakāraṇaśaithilyātpracārasaṃvedanācca cittasya
paraśarīrāveśaḥ

By sañyama on chitta (mind full of sanskāras or information from outside world), (bandha-kāraṇa śaithilyāt) the cause of bondage is weakened and (saṃvedanāt) the knowledge of (prachāra) the movements of mind through sense-organs to stimuli is known; a yogī is able to allow his [chittasya] mind [paraśarīrāveśaḥ] enter into the body of another person.

व्यासभाष्य—लोलीभूतस्य मनसोऽप्रतिष्ठस्य शरीरे कर्माशयवशाद्बन्धः प्रतिष्ठेत्यर्थः। तस्य कर्मणो बन्धकारणस्य शैथिल्यं समाधिबलाद्भवति। प्रचारसंवेदनं च चित्तस्य समादिजमेव। कर्मबन्धक्षयात्स्वचित्तस्य प्रचारसंवेदनाच्च योगी चित्तं स्वशरीरान्निष्कृष्य शरीरान्तरेषु निक्षिपति। निक्षिप्तं चित्तं चेन्द्रियाण्यनु पतन्ति। यथा मधुकरराजानं मक्षिका उत्पतन्तमनूत्पतन्ति निविशमानमनु निविशन्ते तथेन्द्रियाणि परशरीरावेशे चित्तमनु विधियन्त इति।

भोजवृत्ति—व्यापकत्वादात्मचित्तयोर्नियतकर्मवशादेव शरीरान्तर्गतयोभोक्तृभोग्यभावेन यत्संवेदनमुपजायते स एव शरीरे बन्ध इत्युच्यते। तद्यदा समाधिवशाद्बन्धकारणं धर्माधर्माख्यं शिथिलं भवति तानवमापद्यते। चित्तस्य च योऽसौ प्रचारो हृदयप्रदेशादिन्द्रियद्वारेण विषयाभिमुख्येन प्रसरस्तस्य संवेदनं ज्ञानमियं चित्तवहा नाडी अनया चित्तं वहति इयं च रसप्राणादि वहाभ्यो नाडीभ्यो विलक्षणेति स्वपरशरीरयोर्यदा संचारं जानाति तदा परकीयं शरीरं मृतं जीवच्छरीरं वा चित्तसंचारद्वारेण प्रविशति। चित्तं परशरीरे प्रविशदिन्द्रियाण्यपि अनुवर्त्तन्ते मधुकरराजमिव मधुमक्षिकाः। अथ परशरीरप्रविष्टो योगी स्वशरीरवत्तेन व्यवहरति। यतो

व्यापकयोश्चित्तपुरुषयोर्भोगसंकोचे कारणं कर्म तच्चेत्समाधिना क्षिप्तं तदा स्वातन्त्र्यात्सर्वत्रैव भोगनिष्पत्तिः ।

सिद्ध्यन्तरमाह

उदानजयाज्जलपङ्ककण्टकादिष्वसङ्ग उत्क्रान्तिश्च ॥3.39 ॥

udānajayājjalapaṅkakaṇṭakādiṣvasaṅga utkrāntiśca

By mastery over udāna vāyu (located in throat and head), a yogī can walk over water, swamps, and thorns; he never gets drowned in waters; and at the time of death, the soul leaves the body at yogi's will through the upper exit (Brahmandhara).

व्यासभाष्य—समस्तेन्द्रियवृत्तिः प्राणादिलक्षणा जीवनं तस्य क्रिया पञ्चतयी प्राणो मुखनासिकागतिराहृदयवृत्तिः । समं नयनात्समानश्चाऽऽनाभिवृत्तिः । अपनयनादपान आपादतलवृत्तिः । उन्नयनादुदान आशिरोवृत्तिः । व्यापी व्यान इति । एषां प्रधानं प्राणः । उदानजयाज्जलपङ्ककण्टकादिष्वसङ्ग उत्क्रान्तिश्च प्रयाणकाले भवति । तां वशित्वेन प्रतिपद्यते ।

भोजवृत्ति—समस्तानामिन्द्रियाणां तुषज्वालावद्या युगपदुत्थिता वृत्तिः सा जीवन शब्दवाच्या । तस्याः क्रियाभेदात्प्राणापानादिसंज्ञाभिर्व्यपदेशः तत्र । हृदयान्मुखनासिकाद्वारेण वायोः प्रणयनात्प्राण इत्युच्यते । नाभिदेशात्पादाङ्गुष्टपर्यन्तमपनयनादपानः । नाभिदेशं परिवेष्ठ्य समन्तान्नयनात्समानः । कृकाटिकादेशादा शिरोवृत्तेरुन्नयनादुदानः । व्याप्य नयनात्सर्वशरीरेव्यापी व्यानः । तत्रोदानस्य संयमद्वारेण जयादितरेषां वायूनां निरोधादूर्ध्वगतित्वेन जले महानद्यादौ महति वा कर्दमे तीक्ष्णेषु कण्टकेषु वा न सजतेऽतिलघुत्वात् । तूलपिण्डवज्जलादौ मज्जितोऽप्युद्रच्छतीत्यर्थः । सिद्ध्यन्तरमाह-

समानजयाज्ज्वलनम् ॥3.40 ॥

samānajayājjvalanam

By mastery over the Samāna vāyu located in the heart and navel, the yogī develops a radiant aura around his body.

व्यासभाष्य —जितसमानस्तेजस उपध्मानं कृत्वा ज्वलयति ।।

भोजवृत्ति—अग्निमावेष्ठ्य व्यवस्थितस्य समानाख्यस्य वायोर्जयात्संयमेन वशीकारान्निराववरणस्याग्रेरुद्भूतत्वात्तेजसा प्रज्वलन्निव योगी प्रतिभाति । सिद्ध्यन्तरमाह

श्रोत्राकाशयोः सम्बन्धसंयमाद्दिव्यं श्रोत्रम् ॥3.41 ॥

śrotrākāśayoḥ sambandhasamyamāddivyaṃ śrotram

By sañyama on the relation between Akāśa and the

auditory sense, a yogī develops the power of divine audition.

व्यासभाष्य—सर्वश्रोत्राणामाकाशं प्रतिष्ठा सर्वशब्दानां च । यथोक्तम् तुल्यदेशश्रवणानामेकदेशश्रुतित्वं सर्वेषां भवतीति । तच्चैतदाकाशस्य लिङ्गम् ।

अनावरणं चोक्तम् । तथाऽमूर्तस्याप्यन्यत्रानावरणदर्शनाद्विभूत्वमपि प्रख्यातमाकाशस्य । शब्दग्रहणनिमित्तं श्रोत्रम् । बधिराबधिरयोरेकः शब्दं गृह्णात्यपरो न गृह्णातीति । तस्माच्छ्रोत्रमेव शब्द विषयम् । श्रोत्राकाशयोः संबन्धे कृतसंयमस्य योगिनो दिव्यं श्रोत्रं प्रवर्तते ।

भोजवृत्ति—श्रोत्रं शब्दग्राहकमाहंकारिकमिन्द्रियम् । आकाशं व्योम शब्दतन्मात्रकार्यम् । तयोः संबन्धो देशदेशिभावलक्षणस्तस्मिन्कृतसंयमस्य योगिनो दिव्यं श्रोत्रं प्रवर्तते युगपत्सूक्ष्मव्यवहितविप्रकृष्टशब्दग्रहणसमर्थं भवतीत्यर्थः । सिद्ध्यन्तरमाह-

कायाकाशयोः सम्बन्धसंयमाल्लघुतूल समापत्तेश्चाकाशगमनम् ॥42॥

kāyākāśayoḥ sambandhasaṃyamāllaghutūla-
samāpatteścākāśagamanam

By sañyama on the relation between the Body and Ākāśa, a yogī attains the state of the lightness of cotton, etc. and becomes capable to walk in space.

व्यासभाष्य —यत्र कायस्तत्राऽऽकाशं तस्यावकाशदानात्कायस्य तेन सम्बन्धः प्राप्तिस्तत्र कृतसंयमो जित्वा तत्संबन्धं लघुषु वा तूलादिष्वा परमाणुभ्यः समापत्तिं लब्ध्वा जितसंबन्धो लघुर्भवति । लघुत्वाच्च जले पादाभ्यां विहरति । ततस्तूर्णनाभितन्तुमात्रे विहृत्य रश्मिषु विहरति । ततो यथेष्टमाकाशगतिरस्य भवतीति ।

भोजवृत्ति—कायः पाञ्चभौतिकं शरीरं तस्याऽऽकाशेनावकाशदायकेन यः संबन्धस्तत्र संयमं विधाय लघुनि तूलादौ समापत्तिं तन्मयीभावलक्षणां च विधाय प्रासातिलघुभावो योगी प्रथमं यथारुचि जले संचरन्क्रमेणोर्णनाभतन्तुजालेन संचरमाण आदित्यरश्मिभिश्च विहरन्यथेष्टमाकाशेन गच्छति । सिद्ध्यन्तरमाह

बहिरकल्पिता वृत्तिर्महाविदेहा ततः प्रकाशावरणक्षयः ॥3.43॥

bahirakalpitā vṛttirmahāvidehā tataḥ prakāśāvaraṇakṣayaḥ

By sañyama on the (akalpitā) unmodified vṛtti of mind, (bahir) which is not body centric, called Mahāvidehā, the veil of rajoguṇā and tamoguṇa from over the sattvaguṇa is removed.

The vṛtti of mind which is not body centric is called

mahāvidehā vṛtti. That vṛtti is called akalpitā (unmodified). Body centric vṛttis are called kalpitā (modified).

व्यासभाष्य—शरीराद्बहिर्मनसो वृत्तिलाभो विदेहा नाम धारणा । सा यदि शरीरप्रतिष्ठस्य मनसो बहिर्वृत्तिमात्रेण भवति सा कल्पितेत्युच्यते । या तु शरीर निरपेक्षा बहिर्भूतस्यैव मनसो बहिर्वृत्तिः सा खल्वकल्पिता । तत्र कल्पितया साधयन्त्यकल्पितां महाविदेहामिति ।

यया परशरीराण्याविशन्ति योगिनः । ततश्च धारणातः प्रकाशात्मनो बुद्धिसत्त्वस्य यदावरणं क्लेशकर्मविपाकत्रयं रजस्तमोमूलं तस्य च क्षयो भवति ।

भोजवृत्ति—शरीराद्बहिर्या मनसः शरीरनैरपेक्ष्येण वृत्तिः सा महाविदेहा नाम विगतशरीराहंकारदार्ढ्यद्वारेणोच्यते । ततस्तस्यां कृतात्संयमात्प्रकाशावरणक्षयः सात्त्विकस्य चित्तस्य यः प्रकाशस्तस्य यदावरणं क्लेशकर्मादि तस्य क्षयः प्रविलयो भवति । अयमर्थः शरीराहंकारे सति या मनसो बहिर्वृत्तिःसाकल्पितेत्युच्यते । यदा पुनः शरीराहंकारभावं परित्यज्य स्वातन्त्र्येण मनसो वृत्तिः साऽकल्पिता तस्यां संयमाद्योगिनः सर्वे चित्तमलाः क्षीयन्ते ।

तदेवं पूर्वान्तविषयाः परान्तविषया मध्यभवाश्च सिद्धीः प्रतिपाद्यनन्तरं भुवनज्ञानादिरूपा बाह्याः कायव्यूहादिरूपा अभ्यन्तरा परिकर्मनिष्पन्नभूताश्च मैत्र्यादिषु बलानीत्येवमाद्याः समाध्युपयोगिनीश्चान्तःकरणबहिः करणलक्षणेन्द्रियभवाः प्राणादिवायुभवाश्च सिद्धीश्चित्तदार्ढ्यात्समाधौ समाधासोत्पत्तये प्रतिपाद्येदानीं स्वदर्शनोपयोगिसबीजनिर्बीजसमाधिसिद्ध्ये विविधो पायप्रदर्शनायाऽऽह

स्थूलस्वरूपसूक्ष्मान्वयार्थवत्त्वसंयमाद्भूतजयः ॥3.44 ॥

sthūlasvarūpasūkṣmānvayārthavattvasaṃyamādbhūtajayaḥ

By sañyama on [sthūla] gross form, (svarūpa) essential nature, [sukṣma] subtle form, [anvaya] integration or synthesis of different constituents, and [arthavattva] purpose of five bhūtas, a yogī gets control over them.

(Sthūla) Gross form, (svarūpa) essential nature, (sukṣma) subtle form, (anvaya) integration or synthesis of different constituents, and (arthavattva) purpose of five bhūtas are illustrated by the following list:

Pṛthivī, Jala, Agni, Vāyu and Ākāśa

Gross forms: Pṛthivī, Jala, Agni, Vāyu and Ākāśa

Nature: Solid, liquid, heat, blow, all-pervading

Subtle: Smell, taste, luminosity, touch, sound

Anvaya: Sattva (intelligence), Rajas (motion), Tamas (inertia)

Arthavattavam: Bhoga (enjoyment) and Apavarga (Emancipation).

व्यासभाष्य—तत्र पार्थिवाद्याः शब्दादयो विशेषाः सहाऽङ्कारादिभिर्धर्मैः स्थूलशब्देन परिभाषिताः । एतद्भूतानां प्रथमं रूपम् । द्वितीयं रूपं स्वसामान्यं मूर्तिर्भूमिः स्नेहो जलं वह्निरुष्णता वायुः प्रणामी सर्वतोगतिराकाश इत्येतत्स्वरूपशब्देनोच्यते ।

अस्य सामान्यस्य शब्दादयो विशेषाः । तथा चोक्तम् एकजातिसमन्वितानामेषां धर्ममात्रव्यावृत्तिरिति ।

सामान्यविशेषसमुदायोऽत्र द्रव्यम् । दृष्टो हि समूहः प्रत्यस्तमितभेदावयवानुगतः शरीरं वृक्षो यूथं वनमिति । शब्देनोपात्तभेदावयवानुगतः समूह उभये देवमनुष्याः । समूहस्य देवा एको भागो मनुष्या द्वितीयो भागस्ताभ्यामेवाभिधीयते समूहः ।

स च भेदाभेदविवक्षितः । आम्राणां वनं ब्राह्मणानां संघ आम्रवणं ब्राह्मणसंघ इति ।

स पुनर्द्विविधो युतसिद्धावयवोऽयुतसिद्धावयवश्च । युतसिद्धावयवः समूहो वनं संघ इति । अयुतसिद्धावयवः संघातः शरीरं वृक्षः परमाणुरिति । अयुतसिद्धावयवभेदानुगतः समूहो द्रव्यमिति पतञ्जलिः । एतत्स्वरूपमित्युक्तम् ।

अथ किमेषां सूक्ष्मरूपं तन्मात्रं भूतकारणं तस्यैकोऽवयवः परमाणुः सामान्यविशेषात्माऽयुतसिद्धावयवभेदानुगतः समुदाय इत्येवं सर्वतन्मात्राण्येतत्तृतीयम् । अथ भूतानां चतुर्थं रूपं ख्यातिक्रियास्थितिशीला गुणाः कार्यस्वभावानुपातिनोऽन्वयशब्देनोक्ताः । अथैषां पञ्चमं रूपमर्थवत्त्वं भोगापवर्गार्थता गुणेष्वेवान्वयिनी गुणास्तन्मात्रभूतभौतिकेष्विति सर्वमर्थवत् । तेष्विदानीं भूतेषु पञ्चसु पञ्चरूपेषु संयमात्तस्य तस्य रूपस्य स्वरूपदर्शनं जयश्च प्रादुर्भवति । तत्र पञ्च भूतस्वरूपाणि जित्वा भूतजयी भवति । तज्जयाद्धृतानुसारिण्य इव गावोऽस्य संकल्पानुविधायिन्यो भूतप्रकृतयो भवन्ति ।

भोजवृत्ति—पञ्चानां पृथिव्यादीनां भूतानां ये पञ्चावस्थाविशेषरूपा धर्माः स्थूलत्वादयस्तत्र कृतसंयमस्य भूतजयो भवति । भूतानि अस्य वश्यानि भवन्तीत्यर्थः । तथाहि भूतानां परिदृश्यमानं विशिष्टाकारवत्स्थूलरूपं ।

स्वरूपं चैषां यथाक्रमं कार्यं गन्धस्नेहोष्णताप्रेरणावकाशदानलक्षणं ।
सूक्ष्मं च यथाक्रमं भूतानां कारणत्वेन व्यवस्थितानि गन्धादितन्मात्राणि ।

अन्वयिनो गुणाः प्रकाशप्रवृत्तिस्थितिरूपतया सर्वत्रैवान्वयित्वेन समुपलभ्यन्ते । अर्थवत्त्वं तेष्वेव गुणेषु भोगापवर्गसंपादनाख्या शक्तिः । तदेवं भूतेषु पञ्चसूक्तधर्मलक्षणावस्थाभिन्नेषु प्रत्यवस्थं संयमं कुर्वन्योगी भूतजयी भवति । तद्यथा प्रथमं स्थूल रूपे संयमं विधाय तदनु स्वरूपे इत्येवं क्रमेण तस्य कृतसंयमस्य संकल्पानुविधायिन्यो वत्सानुसारिण्य इव गावो भूतप्रकृतयो भवन्ति । तस्यैव भूतजयस्य फलमाह

ततोऽणिमादिप्रादुर्भावः कायसम्पत्तद्धर्मानभिघातश्च ॥3.45॥

tato'nimādiprādurbhāvaḥ
kāyasampattaddharmānabhighātaśca

By control over bhūtas, a yogī [aṇimādi pradurbhāva] attains aṇimā, etc. 9 siddhis (divine powers), [kāyasampat] will be defined in sūtra 46; [tad dharmānabhighātaścha] his functions become free from the obstructions of the bhūtas.

Nine siddhis are as follows:

Through sañyama on gross bhūtas, a yogī attains the following 9 siddhis (divine powers)

1. Aṇimā: Reduction of the body to the level of atom.

2. Laghimā: Becoming light.

3. Mahimā: Becoming very large.

4. Prāpti: Access to all places, even touching the moon sitting on the surface of the earth.

5. Garimā: Becoming very heavy.

6. Through sañyama on nature of bhūtas, a yogī attains the siddhi (divine power) of Prakāmya, i.e. a yogī can enter everything at will, even into the earth like that of waters.

7. Through sañyama on the subtle (atomic) form of bhūtas, a yogī attains the siddhi (divine power) of Vaśitva, i.e. control over all material things and other living beings including gross bhūtas, though a yogī is free from the control of everything.

8. Through sañyama on Anvaya, a yogī attains the siddhi (divine power) of Īśitva, i.e. a yogī attains the power of creation and destruction of all material objects.

9. Through sañyama on Arthavattva (purpose), a yogī attains the siddhi (divine power) of Yatrakāmāvsāyitva (Satyasaṅkalpatā), i.e. instant materialization of desires.

व्यासभाष्य—तत्राणिमा भवत्यणुः । 2 लघिमा लघुर्भवति । 3 महिमा महान्भवति । 4 प्राप्तिरङ्गुल्यग्रेणापि स्पृशति चन्द्रमसम् । 5 प्राकाम्यमिच्छानभिघातः । भूमावुन्मज्जति निमज्जति यथोदके । 6 वशित्वं भूतभौतिकेषु वशी भवत्यवश्यश्चान्येषाम् । 7 ईशितृत्वं तेषां प्रभवाव्ययव्यूहानामीष्टे ।। 8 यत्र कामावसायित्वं सत्यसंकल्पता यथा संकल्पस्तथा भूतप्रकृतीनामवस्थानम् । न च शक्तोऽपि पदार्थविपर्यासं करोति । कस्मात् । अन्यस्य यत्र कामावसायिनः पूर्वसिद्धस्य तथा भूतेषु संकल्पादिति । एतान्यष्टावैश्वर्याणि । यसंपद्धक्ष्यमाणा । तद्धर्मानभिघातश्च पृथ्वी मूर्त्या न निरुणद्धिः योगिनः शरीरादिक्रियां शिलामप्यनुविशतीति । नाऽऽपः स्निग्धाः क्लेदयन्ति । नाग्निरुष्णो दहति । न वायु प्रणामी वहति । अनावरणात्मकेऽप्याकाशे भवत्यावृतकायः सिद्धानामप्यदृश्यो भवति ।

भोजवृत्ति—अणिमा परमाणुरूपतापत्तिः । 2 महिमा महत्त्वम् । 3 लघिमा तूलपिण्डवल्लघुत्वप्राप्तिः । 4 गरिमा गुरुत्वम् । 5 प्राप्तिरङ्गुल्यग्रेण चन्द्रादिस्पर्शनशक्तिः । 6 प्राकाम्यमिच्छानभिघातः । 7 शरीरान्तः करणेश्वरत्वमीशित्वम् । 8 सर्वत्र प्रभविष्णुता वशित्वं सर्वाण्येव भूतानि अनुगामित्वात्तदुक्तं नातिक्रामन्ति । 9 यत्रकामावसायो यस्मिन्विषयेऽस्य काम इच्छा भवति यस्मिन्विषये योगिनो व्यवसायो भवति तं विषयं स्वीकारद्वारेणाभिलाषसमाप्तिपर्यन्तं नयन्तीत्यर्थः । त एतेऽणिमाद्याः समाध्युपयोगिनो भूतजयाद्योगिनः प्रादुर्भवन्ति । यथा परमाणुत्वं प्राप्तो वज्रादीनामप्यन्तः प्रविशति । एवं सर्वत्र योज्यम् । त एतेऽणिमादयोऽष्टौ गुणा महासिद्धयय उच्यन्ते । कायसंपद्धक्ष्यमाणा तां प्राप्नोति तद्धर्मानभिघातश्च तस्य कायस्य ये धर्मा रूपादयस्तेषामनभिघातो नाशो न कुतश्चिद्भवति नास्य रूपमग्निर्दहति न वायुः शोषयतीत्यादि योज्यम् । कायसंपदमाह

रूपलावण्यबलवज्रसंहननत्वानि कायसम्पत् ॥3.46॥

rūpalāvaṇyabalavajrasaṃhananatvāni kāyasampat

Kāyasampat is extreme beauty, grace, strength and a

diamond like unbreakable body.

व्यासभाष्य—दर्शनीयः कान्तिमानतिशयबलो वज्रसंहननश्चेति ।

भोजवृत्ति—रूपलावण्यबलानि प्रसिद्धानि । वज्रसंहननत्वं वज्रवत्कठिना संहतिरस्य शरीरे भवतीत्यर्थः । इति कायस्याऽविर्भूतगुणसंपत् । एवं भूतजयमभिधाय प्राप्तिभूमिकाविशेष इन्द्रियजयमाह

ग्रहणस्वरूपास्मितान्वयार्थवत्त्वसंयमादिन्द्रियजयः ॥3.47॥

grahaṇasvarūpāsmitānvayārthavattvasaṃyamādindriyajayaḥ

By sañyama on grahaṇa (receiving the power of sense organs) svarūpa (knowledge gained by sense organs or sensory perception), asmitā (individuality of sense organs), anvaya (coherence in the knowledge perceived by individual sense organs), arthavattva (purpose of sense organs), a yogī wins over the senses.

व्यासभाष्य—सामान्यविशेषात्मा शब्दादिर्ग्राह्यः । तेष्विन्द्रियाणां वृत्तिर्ग्रहणम् । न च तत्सामान्यमात्रग्रहणाकारं कथमनालोचितः स विषय विशेष इन्द्रियेण मनसाऽनुव्यवसीयेतेति । स्वरूपं पुनः प्रकाशात्मनो बुद्धिसत्त्वस्य सामान्यविशेषयोर्युतसिद्धावयवभेदानुगतः समूहो द्रव्यमिन्द्रियम् । तेषां तृतीयं रूपमस्मितालक्षणोऽहंकारः । तस्य सामान्यस्येन्द्रियाणि विशेषाः । चतुर्थं रूपं व्यवसायात्मकाः प्रकाशक्रियास्थितिशीला गुणा येषामिन्द्रियाणि साहंकाराणि परिणामः । पञ्चमं रूपं गुणेषु यदनुगतं पुरुषार्थवत्त्वमिति । पञ्चस्वेतेष्विन्द्रियरूपेषु यथाक्रमं संयमस्तत्र तत्र जयं कृत्वा पञ्चरूपजयादिन्द्रियजयः प्रादुर्भवति योगिनः ।

भोजवृत्ति—ग्रहणमिन्द्रियाणां विषयाभिमुखी वृत्तिः । स्वरूपं सामान्येनप्रकाशकत्वम् । अस्मिताऽहंकारानुगमः । अन्वयार्थवत्त्वे पूर्ववत् । एतेषामिन्द्रियाणामवस्थापञ्चके पूर्ववत्संयमं कृत्वेन्द्रियजयी भवति । तस्य फलमाह

ततो मनोजवित्वं विकरणभावः प्रधानजयश्च ॥3.48॥

tato manojavitvaṃ vikaraṇabhāvaḥ pradhānajayaśca

Having attained control over senses, a yogi attains the siddhi (power) of Manojavitva (his body becomes as fast as mind), Vikaraṇa-bhāva (to receive information from far off places without being physically present) and Pradhāna-jaya (to have complete control of prakṛti-vikṛti, i.e. from mahat-tattva onward, or say the creation).

व्यासभाष्य—कायस्यानुत्तमो गतिलाभो मनोजवित्वम्। विदेहानामिन्द्रियाणाम-भिप्रेतदेशकालविषयापेक्षो वृत्तिलाभो विकरणभावः। सर्वप्रकृतिविकारवशित्वं प्रधानजय इत्येतास्तिस्रः सिद्धयो मधुप्रतीका उच्यन्ते। एताश्च करणपञ्चरूपजयादधिगम्यन्ते।

भोजवृत्ति—शरीरस्य मनोवदनुत्तगतिलाभो मनोजवित्वम्। कायानिरपेक्षाणामिन्द्रियाणां वृत्तिलाभो विकरभावः। सर्ववशित्वं प्रधानजयः। एताः सिद्धयो जितेन्द्रियस्य प्रादुर्भवन्ति ताश्चास्मिञ्शास्त्रे मधुप्रतीका इत्युच्यन्ते। यथा मधुन एकदेशोऽपि स्वदत एवं प्रत्येकमेताः सिद्धयः स्वदन्त इति मधुप्रतीकाः। इन्द्रियजयमभिधायान्तःकरणजयमाह

सत्त्वपुरुषान्यताख्यातिमात्रस्य सर्वभावाधिष्ठातृत्वं सर्वज्ञातृत्वं च

॥3.49॥

*sattvapuruṣānyatākhyātimātrasya
sarvabhāvādhiṣṭhātṛtvaṃsarvajñātṛtvaṃ ca*

(*sattvapuruṣānyatākhyātimātrasya*) To one who has realized the distinction between Sattva (mind) and Puruṣa (soul) (*sarvabhāvādhiṣṭhātṛtvam*) gains supremacy over all material things and (*sarvajñātṛtvam*) knowledge of everything.

व्यासभाष्य—निर्धूतरजस्तमोमलस्य बुद्धिसत्त्वस्य परे वैशारद्ये परस्यां वशीकारसंज्ञायां वर्तमानस्य सत्त्वपुरुषान्यताख्यातिमात्ररूपप्रतिष्ठस्य सर्वभावाधिष्ठातृत्वम्। सर्वात्मानो गुणा व्यवसायव्यवसेयात्मकाः स्वामिनं क्षेत्रज्ञं प्रत्यशेषदृश्यात्मत्वेनोपस्थिता इत्यर्थः। सर्वज्ञातृत्वं सर्वात्मनां गुणानां शान्तोदिताव्यपदेश्यधर्मत्वेन व्यवस्थितानामक्रमोपारूढं विवेकजं ज्ञानमित्यर्थः। इत्येषा विशोका नाम सिद्धिर्यां प्राप्य योगी सर्वज्ञः क्षीणक्लेशबन्धनो वशी विहरति।

भोजवृत्ति—तस्मिन्शुद्धेः सात्त्विके परिणामे कृतसंयमस्य या सत्त्वपुरुषयोरुत्पद्यते विवेकख्यातिर्गुणानां कर्तृत्वाभिमानशिथिलीभावरूपा तन्माहात्म्यात्तत्रैव स्थितस्य योगिनः सर्वभावाधिष्ठातृत्वं सर्वज्ञातृत्वं च समाधेर्भवति। सर्वेषां गुणपरिणामानां भावानां स्वामिवदाक्रमणं सर्वभावाधिष्ठातृत्वं तेषामेव च शान्तोदिताव्यपदेश्यधर्मित्वेनावस्थितानां यथावद्विवेकज्ञानं सर्वज्ञातृत्वम्। एषां चास्मिञ्शास्त्रे परस्यां वशीकारसंज्ञायो प्राप्तायां विशोका नाम सिद्धिरित्युच्यते। क्रमेण भूमिकान्तरमाह

तद्वैराग्यादपि दोषबीजक्षये कैवल्यम् ॥3.50॥
tadvairāgyādapi doṣabījakṣaye kaivalyam

[*Tadvairāgyādapi*] From aversion of realization of the distinction between Sattva (mind) and Puruṣa (soul), [*doṣabījakṣaye*] sanskāras of afflictions and other karmas having been eliminated, [*kaivalyam*] a yogī attains liberation.

व्यासभाष्य—यदाऽस्यैवं भवति क्लेशकर्मक्षये सत्त्वस्यायं विवेकप्रत्ययो धर्मः सत्त्वं च हेयपक्षे न्यस्तं पुरुषश्चापरिणामी शुद्धोऽन्यः सत्त्वादिति । एवमस्य ततो विरज्यमानस्य यानि क्लेशबीजानि दग्धशालिबीजकल्पान्यप्रसवसमर्थानि तानि सह मनसा प्रत्यस्तं गच्छन्ति । तेषु प्रलीनेषु पुरुषः पुनरिदं तापत्रयं

न भुङ्क्ते । तदेतेषां गुणानां मनसि कर्मक्लेशविपाकस्वरूपेणाभिव्यक्तानां चरितार्थानाम् प्रतिप्रसवे पुरुषस्याऽत्यन्तिको गुणवियोगः कैवल्यम् तदा स्वरूपप्रतिष्ठा चितिशक्तिरेव पुरुष इति ।

भोजवृत्ति—एतस्यामपि विशोकायां सिद्धौ यदा वैराग्यमुत्पद्यते योगिनस्तदा तस्माद्दोषाणां रागादीनां यद्बीजमविद्यादयस्तस्य क्षये निर्मूलने कैवल्यमात्यन्तिकी दुःखनिवृत्तिः पुरुषस्य गुणानामधिकारपरिसमाप्तौ स्वरूपप्रतिष्ठत्वम् । अस्मिन्नेव समाधौ स्थित्युपायमाह

स्थान्युपनिमन्त्रणे सङ्गस्मयाकरणं पुनरनिष्टप्रसङ्गात् ॥3.51॥

sthānyupanimantraṇe saṅgasmayākaraṇam
punaraniṣṭaprasaṅgāt

[*Upanimantraṇe*] On invitation by [*sthāni*] people highly placed in society or state, like kings and emperors, a yogī [*akaraṇama*] should not feel [*saṅga*] temptation or [smaya] pride, [*punar aniṣṭa-prasaṅgāt*] in such a state, he may have the fear of falling from yoga.

व्यासभाष्य—चत्वारः खल्वमी योगिनः प्रथमकल्पिको मधुभूमिकः प्रज्ञाज्योतिरतिक्रान्तभावनीयश्चेति । तत्राभ्यासी प्रवृत्तमात्रज्योतिः प्रथमः । ऋतंभरप्रज्ञो द्वितीयः । भूतेन्द्रियजयी तृतीय सर्वेषु भावितेषु भावनीयेषु कृतरक्षाबन्धः कर्तव्यसाधनादिमान् । चतुर्थो यस्त्वतिक्रान्तभावनीयस्तस्य चित्तप्रतिसर्ग एकोऽर्थः । सप्तविधाऽस्य प्रान्तभूमिप्रज्ञा ।

तत्र मधुमतीं भूमिं साक्षात्कुर्वतो ब्राह्मणस्य स्थानिनो देवाः सत्त्वविशुद्धिमनुपश्यन्तः स्थानैरुपनिमन्त्रयन्ते भो इहाऽऽस्यतामिह रन्यतां ।

कमनीयोऽयं भोगः कमनीयेयं कन्या रसायनमिदं जरामृत्युं बाधते वैहायसमिदं यानममी कल्पद्रुमाः पुण्या मन्दाकिनी सिद्धा महर्षय उत्तमा अनुकूला अप्सरसो दिव्ये श्रोत्रचक्षुषी वज्रोपमः कायः स्वगुणैः सर्वमिदमुपार्जितमायुष्मताप्रतिपद्यतामिदमक्षयमजरममरस्थानं देवानां प्रियमिति एवमभिधीयमानः सङ्गदोषाऩ्भावयेद्घोरेषु संसाराङ्गारेषु पच्यमानेन मया जननमरणान्धकारे विपरिवर्तमानेन कथंचिदासादितः क्लेशतिमिरविनाशी योगप्रदीपस्तस्य चैते तृष्णायोनयो विषयवायवः प्रतिपक्षाः । स खल्वहं लब्धालोकः कथमनया विषयमृगतृष्णया वञ्चितस्तस्यैव पुनः प्रदीप्तस्य संसाराग्रेरात्मानमिन्धनी कुर्यामिति । स्वस्ति वः स्वप्रोपमेभ्यः कृपणजनप्रार्थनीयेभ्यो

विषयेभ्य इत्येवं निश्चितमतिः समाधिं भावयेत् ।

सङ्गमकृत्वा सयमपि न कुर्यादेवमहं देवानामपि प्रार्थनीय इति । सयादयं सुस्थितंमन्यतया मृत्युना केशेषु गृहीतमिवाऽऽत्मानं न भावयिष्यति । तथा चास्य छिन्द्रान्तरप्रेक्षी नित्यं यत्नोपचर्यः प्रमादो लब्धविवरः क्लेशानुत्तम्भाविष्यति ततः पुनरनिष्टप्रसङ्गः । एवमस्य सङ्गस्मयावकुर्वतो भावितोऽर्थो दृढी भविष्यति । भावनीयश्चार्थोऽभिमुखी भविष्यतीति ।

भोजवृत्ति—चत्वारो योगिनो भवन्ति । तत्राभ्यासवान्प्रवृत्तमात्रज्योतिः प्रथमः । ऋतंभरप्रज्ञो द्वितीयः । भूतेन्द्रियजयी तृतीयः । अतिक्रान्तभावनीयश्चतुर्थः । तत्र चतुर्थस्य समाधेः प्राप्तसप्तविधप्रान्तभूमिप्रज्ञो भवति । ऋतंभरप्रज्ञस्य द्वितीयां मधुमतीसंज्ञां भूमिकां साक्षात्कुर्वतः स्थानिनो देवा उपनिमन्त्रयितारो भवन्ति दिव्यस्त्रीरसायनादिकं ढौकयन्ति तस्मिन्नुपनिमन्त्रणे नानेन सङ्गः कर्तव्यः नापि स्मयः सङ्गकरणे पुनर्विषयभोगे पतति स्मयकरणे कृतकृत्यमात्मानं मन्यमानो न समाधावुत्सहते । अतः सङ्गस्मययोस्तेन वर्जनं कर्त्तव्यम् ।

क्षणतत्क्रमयोः संयमाद्विवेकजं ज्ञानम् ॥3.52॥
kṣaṇatatkramayoḥ saṃyamādvivekajaṃ jñānam

By sañyama on the kṣaṇa (smallest unit of time taken by displacement of smallest particle of matter) and sequence thereof, a yogī can have knowledge of things, things are created and decreated in the sequence of kṣaṇas. This type of knowledge is known as born of Viveka.

Vivekajñāna is the knowledge-based upon the sañyama on concerned things.

Kṣaṇa is a time taken by an atom during its displacement (during its movement from one point to another point).

व्यासभाष्य—यथाऽपकर्षपर्यन्तं द्रव्यं परमाणुरेवं परमापकर्षपर्यन्तः कालः क्षणः यावता वा समयेन चलितः परमाणुः पूर्वदेशं जह्यादुत्तरदेशमुपसंपद्येत स कालः क्षणः । तत्प्रवाहाविच्छेदस्तु क्रमः । क्षण तत्क्रमयोर्नास्ति वस्तुसमाहार इति बुद्धिसमाहारो मुहूर्ताहोरात्रादयः । स खल्वयं कालो वस्तुशून्योऽपि बुद्धिनिर्माणः शब्दज्ञानानुपाती लौकिकानां व्युत्थितदर्शनानां वस्तुस्वरूप इवावभासते ।

क्षणस्तु वस्तुपतितः क्रमावलम्बी क्रमश्च क्षणानन्तयात्मा तं कालविदः काल इत्याचक्षते योगिनः । नच द्वौ क्षणौ सह भवतः । क्रमश्च न द्वयोः सहभुवोरसंभवात् । पूर्वस्मादुत्तरभाविनो यदानन्तर्यं क्षणस्य स क्रमः । तस्माद्वर्तमान एवैकः क्षणो न पूर्वोत्तरक्षणाः सन्तीति । तस्मान्नास्ति

तत्समाहारः । ये तु भूतभाविनः क्षणास्ते परिणामान्विता व्याख्येयाः । तेनैकेन क्षणेन कृत्स्नो लोकः परिणाममनुभवति । तत्क्षणोपारूढाः खल्वमी सर्वे धर्माः । तयोः क्षणतत्क्रमयोः संयमात्तयोः साक्षात्करणम् । ततश्च विवेकजं ज्ञानं प्रादुर्भवति । तस्य विषयविशेष उपक्षिप्यन्ते

भोजवृत्ति—क्षणः सर्वान्त्यः कालावयवो यस्य कलाः प्रभवितुं न शक्यन्ते । तथाविधानां कालक्षणानां यः क्रमः पौर्वापर्येण परिणामस्तत्र संयमात्प्रागुक्तं विवेकजं ज्ञानमुत्पद्यते । अयमर्थः अयं कालक्षणोऽमुष्मात्कालक्षणातुत्तरोऽयमस्मांत्पूर्व इत्येवंविधे क्रमे कृतसंयमस्यात्यन्तसूक्ष्मेऽपि क्षणक्रमे यदा भवति । साक्षात्कारस्तदान्यदपि सूक्ष्मं महदादि साक्षात्करोतीति विवेकज्ञानोत्पत्तिः । अस्यैव संयमस्य विषयविवेकोपक्षेपणायाऽऽह

The characteristics of Vivekaja jñāna (knowledge born of Viveka) are described in the next sūtra.

जातिलक्षणदेशैरन्यतानवच्छेदात् तुल्ययोस्ततः प्रतिपत्तिः ॥3.53॥

jātilakṣaṇadeśairanyatānavacchedāt tulyayostataḥ pratipattiḥ

When we are not able to make distinction between two things on the basis of similarity of their species, characteristics, and place, a yogī can make distinction on the basis of vivekajñāna.

Two similarly looking things that are not differentiated by their species, their characteristics, and place, even they can be differentiated by knowledge born of Viveka.

Difference of species: Crow and cuckoo both are of distinct species, but due to similarity, it is difficult to make a distinction of species between them. A yogī can do so.

Difference of characteristics: Suppose there are two cows, there is no distinction of species. One is brown and another is white. This is a difference of characteristics.

Difference of place: Suppose there are two apples from two different regions and they are placed left and right side according to their place of origin. If their position is changed, it will be difficult to make a distinction between them, but a yogī can make a distinction on the basis of his/her knowledge born of Viveka.

व्यासभाष्य—तुल्ययोर्देशलक्षणसारूप्ये जातिभेदोऽन्यताया हेतुः गौरियं वडवेयमिति । तुल्यदेशजातीयत्वे लक्षणमन्यत्वकरं कालाक्षी गौः स्वस्तिमती गौरिति । द्वयोरामलकयोर्जातिलक्षणसारूप्याद्देशभेदोऽन्यत्वकर इदं पूर्वमिदमुत्तरमिति । यदा तु पूर्वमामलकमन्यव्यग्रस्य ज्ञातुरुत्तरदेश उपावर्त्यते तदा तुल्यदेशत्वे पूर्वमेतदुत्तरमे-तदितिप्रविभागानुपपत्तिः । असंदिग्धेन च तत्त्वज्ञानेन भवितव्यमित्यत इदमुक्तं ततः प्रतिपत्तिर्विवेकज्ञानादिति ।

कथं पूर्वामलकसहक्षणो देश उत्तरामलकसहक्षणाद्देशाद्भिन्नः । ते चाऽऽमलके स्वदेशक्षणानुभवभिन्ने । अन्यदेशक्षणानुभवस्तु तयोरन्यत्वे हेतुरिति । एतेन दृष्टान्तेन परमाणोस्तुल्यजातिलक्षणदेशस्य पूर्वपरमाणुदेशसहक्षणसाक्षात्करणादुत्तरस्य परमाणोस्तद्देशा-नुपपत्तावुत्तरस्य तद्देशानुभवो भिन्नः सहक्षणभेदात्तयोरीश्वरस्य योगिनोऽन्यत्वप्रत्ययो भवतीति ।

अपरे तु वर्णयन्ति येऽन्त्या विशेषास्तेऽन्यताप्रत्ययं कुर्वन्तीति । तत्रापि देशलक्षणभेदो मूर्तिव्यवधिजातिभेदश्चान्यत्वे हेतुः । क्षणभेदस्तु योगिबुद्धिगम्य एवेति । अत उक्तं मूर्तिव्यवधिजातिभेदाभावान्नास्ति मूलपृथक्त्वमिति वार्षगण्यः ।

भोजवृत्ति—पदार्थानां भेदहेतवो जातिलक्षणदेशा भवन्ति । कचिद्भेदहेतुर्जातिः यथा गौरियं महिषीऽयमिति । जात्या तुल्ययोर्लक्षणं भेदहेतुः इयं कर्बुरेयमरुणेति । जात्या लक्षणेन चाभिन्नयोर्भेदहेतुर्देशो दृष्टः यथा तुल्यपरिमाणयोरामलकयोर्भिन्न देशस्थितयोः । यत्र पुनर्भेदोऽवधारयितुं न शक्यते यथैकदेशस्थितयोः शुक्लयोः पार्थिवयोः परमाण्वोस्तथाविधे विषये भेदाय कृतसंयमस्य भेदेन ज्ञानमुत्पद्यते तदा तदभ्यासात्सूक्ष्माण्यपि तत्त्वानि भेदेन प्रतिपद्यते । एतदुक्तं भवति यत्र केनचिदुपायेन भेदो नावधारयितुं शक्यस्तत्र संयमाद्भवत्येव भेदप्रतिपत्तिः । सूक्ष्माणां तत्त्वानामुक्तस्य विवेकजन्यज्ञानस्य संज्ञाविषयस्वाभाव्यं व्याख्यातुमाह

Nature of knowledge born of Viveka is described in the following sūtra.

तारकं सर्वविषयं सर्वथाविषयम् अक्रमं चेति विवेकजं ज्ञानम् ॥3.54॥

tārakaṃ sarvaviṣayaṃ sarvathāviṣayam akramaṃ ceti vivekajaṃ jñānam

Knowlledge born of Viveka is called Tāraka Jñāna (spontaneous enlightenment). It is all comprehensive, all-dimensional, and without sequence (simultaneous, instant, and eternal).

व्यासभाष्य   —तारकमिति स्वप्रतिभोत्थमनौपदेशिकमित्यर्थः । सर्वविषयं नास्य किंचिदविषयीभूतमित्यर्थः । सर्वथाविषयमतीतानागतप्रत्युत्पन्नं सर्वं पर्यायैः सर्वथा जानातीत्यर्थः । अक्रममित्येकक्षणोपारूढं सर्वं सर्वथा गृह्णातीत्यर्थः । एतद्विवेकजं ज्ञानं परिपूर्णम् । अस्यैवांशो योगप्रदीपो मधुमतीं भूमिमुपादाय यावदस्य परिसमाप्तिरिति । प्राप्तविवेकजज्ञानस्याप्राप्तविवेकजज्ञानस्य वा

भोजवृत्ति—उक्तसंयमबलादन्त्यायां भूमिकायामुत्पन्नं ज्ञानं तारयत्यगाधात्संसार-सागराद्योगिनमित्यान्वर्थिक्या संज्ञया तारकमित्युच्यते । अस्य विषयमाह सर्वविषयमिति । सर्वाणि तत्त्वानि महदादीनि विषयो यस्येति सर्वविषयम् । स्वभावश्चास्य सर्वथाविषयत्वम् । सर्वाभिरवस्थाभिः स्थूलसूक्ष्मादिभेदेन तेस्तैः परिणामैः सर्वेण प्रकारेणावस्थितानि तत्त्वानि विषयो यस्येति सर्वथाविषयम् । स्वभावान्तरमाह अक्रमं चेति ।
निःशेषनानावस्थापरिणतद्वित्र्यात्मकभावग्रहणे नास्य क्रमो विद्यत इति अक्रमम् । सर्वं करतलामलकवद्युगपत्पश्यतीत्यर्थः । अस्माच्च विवेकजात्तारकाख्याज्ज्ञानात्किं भवतीत्याह

सत्त्वपुरुषयोः शुद्धिसाम्ये कैवल्यमिति ॥3.55॥
sattvapuruṣayoḥ śuddhisāmye kaivalyamiti

When (sattva) mind and (puruṣa) soul are (sāmye) equally (Śuddhi) purified, (kaivalyamiti) liberation is attained.

Purity of mind means freedom of the mind from rajas and tamas; discrimination of mind from the soul; and elimination of the sanskāras of kleśas.

Purity of soul means absence of desire of enjoyment in the soul.

व्यासभाष्य—यदा निर्धूतरजस्तमोमलं बुद्धिसत्त्वं पुरुषस्यान्यताप्रतीतिमात्राधिकारं दग्धक्लेशबीजं भवति तदा पुरुषस्य शुद्धिसारूप्यमिवाऽऽपन्नं भवति तदा पुरुषस्योपचरितभोगाभावः शुद्धिः । एतस्यामवस्थायां कैवल्यं भवतीश्वरस्यानीश्वरस्य वा विवेकजज्ञानभागिन इतरस्य वा । नहि दग्धक्लेशबीजस्य ज्ञाने पुनरपेक्षा काचिदस्ति । सत्त्वशुद्धिद्वारेणैतत्समाधिजमैश्वर्यं ज्ञानं चोपक्रान्तम् । परमार्थतस्तु ज्ञानादर्शनं निवर्तते तस्मिन्निवृत्ते न सन्त्युत्तरे क्लेशाः । क्लेशाभावात्कर्मविपाकाभावः । चरिताधिकाराश्चैतस्यामवस्थायां गुणा न पुरुषस्य पुनर्दृश्यत्वेनोपतिष्ठन्ते । तत्पुरुषस्य कैवल्यं तदा पुरुषः स्वरूपमात्रज्योतिरमलः केवली भवति ।

इति श्री पातञ्जले सांख्यप्रवचने योगशास्त्रे श्रीमद्व्यासभाष्ये तृतीयः विभूतिपादः ॥3॥

भोजवृत्ति— ॥3.55॥ सत्त्वपुरुषावुक्तलक्षणौ तयोः शुद्धिसाम्ये कैवल्यं सत्त्वस्य सर्वकर्तृत्वाभिमाननिवृत्त्या स्वकारणेऽनुप्रवेशः शुद्धिः पुरुषस्य शुद्धिरुपचरितभोगाभाव इति द्वयोः समानायां शुद्धौ पुरुषस्य कैवल्यमुत्पद्यते मोक्षोभवतीत्यर्थः । तदेवमन्तरङ्गं योगाङ्गत्रयमभिधाय तस्य

च संयमसंज्ञां कृत्वा संयमस्य च विषयप्रदर्शनार्थं परिणामत्रयमुपपाद्य संयमबलोत्पद्यमानाः
पूर्वान्तपरान्तमध्यभवाः सिद्धीरुपदर्श्य समाध्याश्वासोत्पत्तये बाह्या भुवनज्ञानादिरूपा आभ्यन्तराश्च
कायव्यूहज्ञानादिरूपाः प्रदर्श्य समाध्युपयोगायेन्द्रियप्राणजयादिपूर्विकाः परमपुरुषार्थसिद्धये
यथाक्रममवस्थासहितभूतजयेन्द्रियजयसत्त्वजयोद्भवाश्च व्याख्याय विवेकज्ञानोत्पत्तये
तांस्तानुपायानुपन्यस्य तारकस्य सर्वसमाध्यवस्थापर्यन्तभवस्य स्वरूपमभिधाय तत्समापत्तेः
कृताधिकारस्य चित्तसत्त्वस्य स्वकारणेऽनुप्रवेशात्कैवल्यमुत्पद्यत इत्यभिहितमिति निर्णीतो
विभूतिपादस्तृतीयः ।

इति श्री भोजदेवविरचितायांपातञ्जलयोगशास्त्रसूत्रवृतौ तृतीयः विभूतिपादः ।।3।।

इति पतञ्जलि-विरचिते योग-सूत्रे तृतीयो विभूति-पादः

iti patañjali-viracite yoga-sūtre tṛtīyo vibhūti-pādaḥ

चतुर्थोऽध्यायः

कैवल्य-पादः
Chaturtho'dhyāyaḥ

Kaivalya-pāda

Liberation

जन्मौषधिमन्त्रतपःसमाधिजाः सिद्धयः ॥1॥

janmauṣadhimantratapaḥsamādhijāḥ siddhayaḥ

(Siddhayaḥ) Divine powers are attained by the (janma) sanskāras of past life, (auṣadhi) administration of rasāyana or particular herbs, mantra, tapa, and samādhi.

व्यासभाष्य—देहान्तरिता जन्मना सिद्धिः। ओषधिभिरसुरभवनेषु रसायनेनेत्येवमादिः। मन्त्रैराकाशगमनाणिमादिलाभः। तपसा संकल्पसिद्धिः कामरूपी यत्र तत्र कामग इत्येवमादि। समाधिजाः सिद्धयो व्याख्याताः। तत्र कायेन्द्रियाणामन्यजातीयपरिणतानाम्

.**भोजवृत्ति**—इदानीं विप्रतिपत्तिसमुत्थभ्रान्तिनिराकरणेन युक्त्या कैवल्यस्वरूपज्ञानाय कैवल्यपादोऽयमारभ्यते। तत्र याः पूर्वमुक्ताः सिद्धयस्तासां नानाविधजन्मादि कारणप्रतिपादनद्वारेणैवं बोधयति। मदि या एताः सिद्धयस्ताः सर्वाः पूर्वजन्माभ्यस्तसमाधि-बलाज्जन्मादिनिमित्तमात्रत्वेनाऽश्रित्य प्रवर्तन्ते। ततश्चानेकभवसाध्यस्य समाधेर्न क्षतिरस्तीत्याश्वासोत्पादनाय समाधिसिद्धेश्च प्राधान्यख्यापनार्थं कैवल्यप्रयोगार्थं चाऽह

जात्यन्तरपरिणामः प्रकृत्यापूरात् ॥2॥

jātyantarapariṇāmaḥ prakṛtyāpūrāt

(prakṛti-āpūrāt) A change in sanskāras (pariṇāmaḥ) causes (jātyantara) the change in yoni (species).

व्यासभाष्य—पूर्वपरिणामापाय उत्तरपरिणामोपजनस्तेषामपूर्वावयवानुप्रवेशाद्भवति। कायेन्द्रियप्रकृतयश्च स्वं स्वं विकारमनुगृह्णन्त्यापूरेण धर्मादिनिमित्तमपेक्षमाणा इति।

.**भोजवृत्ति**—योऽयमिहैव जन्मनि नन्दीश्वरादीनां जात्यादिपरिणामः सप्रकृत्यापूरात् पाश्चात्या एव हि प्रकृतयोऽमुष्मिञ्जन्मनि विकारानापूरयन्ति जात्यन्तराकारेण परिणामयन्ति।

निमित्तमप्रयोजकं प्रकृतीनां वरणभेदस्तु ततः क्षेत्रिकवत् ॥3॥

nimittamaprayojakaṃ prakṛtīnāṃ varaṇabhedastu tataḥ
kṣetrikavat

As described in the previous sūtra, sanskāras are the efficient cause of the change of yoni. In this sūtra, Āchārya says that [*nimittam*] dharma (moral, ethical and spiritual deeds) [*a-prayojakam*] is not the direct cause in the change [*prakṛtinām*] of the prakṛti (sanskāras) of man. [*varaṇa-bhedaḥ*] They are only the breakers of the boundary lines or obstacles prohibitting the accumulation of good sanskas [*kṣetrikvat*] like a farmer who waters his fields, does not create water nor orders water to flow, but breaks the boundary lines to make the water flow from one bed to another bed.

व्यासभाष्य—न हि धर्मादि निमित्तं तत्प्रयोजकं प्रकृतिनां भवति । न कार्येण कारणं प्रवर्त्यत इति । कथं तर्हि वरणभेदस्तु ततः क्षेत्रिकवत् । यथा क्षेत्रिकः केदारादपां पूर्णात्केदारान्तरं पिप्लावयिषुः समं निम्नं निम्नतरं वा नापः पाणिनाऽपकर्षत्यावरणं त्वासां भिनत्ति तस्मिन्भिन्ने स्वयमेवाऽऽपः केदारान्तरमाप्लावयन्ति तथा धर्मः प्रकृतीनामावरणधर्मं भिनत्ति तस्मिन्भिन्ने स्वयमेव प्रकृतयः स्वं स्वं विकारमाप्लावयन्ति । यथा वा स एव क्षेत्रिकस्तस्मिन्नेव केदारे न प्रभवत्यौदकान्भौमान्वा रसान्धान्यमूलान्यनुप्रवेशयितुं किं तर्हि मुद्गगवेधुकश्यामाकादींस्ततोऽपकर्षति । अपकृष्टेषु तेषु स्वयमेव रसा धान्यमूलान्यनुप्रविशन्ति तथा धर्मो निवृत्तिमात्रे कारणधर्मस्य शुद्ध्यशुद्ध्योरत्यन्तविरोधात् न तु प्रकृतिप्रवृत्तौ धर्मो हेतुर्भवतीति । अत्र नन्दीश्वरादय उदाहार्याः । विपर्ययेणाप्यधर्मो धर्मं बाधते । ततश्चाशुद्धिपरिणाम इति । तत्रापि नहुषाजगरादय उदाहार्याः । यदा तु योगी बहुन्कायान्निर्मिमीते तदा किमेकमनस्कास्ते भवन्त्यथानेकमनस्का इति

भोजवृत्ति—निमित्तं धर्मादि तत्प्रकृतीनामर्थान्तरपरिणामे न प्रयोजकम् । नहि कार्येण कारणं प्रवर्तते । कुत्र तर्हि तस्य धर्मादिव्यापार इत्याह वरणभेदस्तु ततः क्षेत्रिकवत् । ततस्तस्मादनुष्ठीयमानाद्धर्माद्वरणमावरकमधर्मादि तस्यैव विरोधिलवाद्भेदः क्षयः क्रियते । तस्मिन्प्रतिबन्धके क्षीणे प्रकृतयः स्वयमभिमतकार्याय प्रभवन्ति दृष्टान्तमाह क्षेत्रिकवत् । यथा क्षेत्रिकः कृषीवलः केदारात्केदारान्तरं जलं निनीषुर्जलप्रतिबन्धकवरणभेदमात्रं करोति तस्मिन्भिन्ने जलं स्वयमेव प्रसरद्रूपं परिणामं गृह्णाति न तु जलप्रसरणे तस्य कश्चित्प्रयत्न एवं धर्मादिर्बोद्धव्यम् । यदा साक्षात्कृततत्त्वस्य योगिनो युगपत्कर्मफलभोगायाऽऽत्मीयनिरतिशयविभूत्यनुभावाद्युगपद्-नेकशरीरनिर्मित्सा जायते तदा कुतस्तानि चित्तानि प्रभवन्तीत्याह

निर्माणचित्तान्यस्मितामात्रात् ॥4॥

nirmāṇacittānyasmitāmātrāt

[*Asmitā-mātrāt*] From ahaṅkāra alone [*nirmāña-chittāni*] minds/chittas are created.

Here the Āchārya wants to propose that ahaṅkāra alone gives birth to the chitta of various souls when they are in the process of attaining their respective bodies in. According to Vyāsa, the commentator of Yogadarśana, when minds are created, all souls become equipped with their concerned chitta. ततः सचित्तानि भवन्ति। After being equipped with their concerned chitta, souls occupies a body with five sense and motor organs. According to Sāṅkyadarśana also, the mind and five sense organs proceed from ahaṅkāra. These minds (chittas) act as the storehouse of sanskāras of concerned living beings which are the impression or psychological genes formed in the mind of living beings according to their actions, thoughts, and tendencies. These sanskāras act as the seeds for their next lives of the concerned living beings. According to the Vedānta Darśana, संस्कार बीजात् सृष्टिः। During the birth of a living being, these psychological genes containing all information of their lives transform into biological genes (DNA/RNA).

व्यासभाष्य—अस्मितामात्रं चित्तकारणमुपादाय निर्माणचित्तानि करोति ततः सचित्तानि भवन्ति।

भोजवृत्ति—योगिनः स्वयं निर्मितेषु कायेषु तानि चित्तानि तानि मूलकारणदस्मितामात्रादेव तदिच्छया प्रसरन्ति अग्रेर्विस्फुलिङ्गा इव युगपत्परिणमन्ति। ननु बहुनां चित्तानां भिन्नाभिप्रायत्वात्रैककार्यकर्तृत्वं स्यादित्यत आह

प्रवृत्तिभेदे प्रयोजकं चित्तमेकमनेकेषाम् ॥5॥

pravṛttibhede prayojakam cittamekamanekeṣām

[*Ekam*] The one single [*chittam*] mind is

[*prayojakam*] the stimulator [*anekeṣām*] of various sense organs in their [*pravṛtti-bhede*] different functions.

व्यासभाष्य—बहूनां चित्तानां कथमेकचित्ताभिप्रायपुरःसरा प्रवृत्तिरिति सर्वचित्तानां प्रयोजकं चित्तमेकं निर्मिमीते ततः प्रवृत्तिभेदः ।

.**भोजवृत्ति**—तेषामनेकेषां चेतसां प्रवृत्तिभेदे व्यापारनानात्व एकं योगिनश्चित्तं प्रयोजकं प्रेरकमधिष्ठातृत्वेन तेन न भिन्नमतत्वम् । अयमर्थः यथाऽऽत्मीय शरीरे मनश्चक्षुः पाण्यादीनि यथेच्छं प्रेरयति अधिष्ठातृत्वेन तथा कायान्तरेष्वपीति । जन्मादिप्रभवत्वात्सिद्धीनां चित्तमपि तत्प्रभवं पञ्चविधमेक अतः जन्मादिप्रभवाच्चित्तात्समाधिप्रभवस्य चित्तस्य वैलक्षण्यमाह

तत्र ध्यानजमनाशयम् ॥6॥
tatra dhyānajamanāśayam

[*Tatra*] Of these, [*dhyānajam*] the mind perfected through samādhi [*anāśayam*] becomes free from the sanskāras.

व्यासभाष्य—पञ्चविधं निर्माणचित्तं जन्मौषधिमन्त्रतपः समाधिजाः सिद्धय इति । तत्र यदेव ध्यानजं चित्तं तदेवानाशयं तस्यैव नास्त्याशयो रागादिप्रवृत्तिर्नतः पुण्यपापाभिसंबन्धः क्षीणक्लेशत्वाद्योगिन इति । इतरेषां तु विद्यते कर्माशयः । यतः

.**भोजवृत्ति**—ध्यानजं समाधिजं यच्चितं तत्पञ्चसु मध्येऽनाशयं कर्मवासनारहितमित्यर्थः । यथेतरचित्तेभ्यो योगिनश्चित्तं विलक्षणं क्लेशादिरहितं तथा कर्मापि विलक्षणमित्याह

कर्माशुक्लाकृष्णं योगिनस्त्रिविधमितरेषाम् ॥7॥
karmāśuklākṛṣṇam yoginastrividhamitareṣām

[*Karma*] The actions [*yoginaḥ*] of yogīs are neither white (good) nor black (bad), [*itareṣām*] but those of others [*trividham*] are of three kinds-good, bad and mixed.

Note: Yogīs do not do kāmya, naimittika and niṣiddha (prohibited) karmas. They do only nitya (daily) karmas, that too they minimise them to the extent possible. So, there is not possibility of either doing good or bad karmas. All karmas good or bad lead to the embidiment of soul.

व्यासभाष्य—चतुष्पदी खल्वियं कर्मजातिः। कृष्णा शुक्लकृष्णा शुक्लाऽशुक्लाकृष्णा चेति। तत्र कृष्णा दुरात्मनाम्। शुक्लकृष्णा बहिःसाधनसाध्या। तत्र परपीड़ानुग्रहद्वारेणैव कर्माशयप्रचयः। शुक्ला तपःस्वाध्यायध्यानवताम्। सा हि केवले मनस्यायत्तत्वादबहिः साधनानधीना न परान्पीड़यित्वा भवति। अशुक्लाकृष्णा संन्यासिनां क्षीणक्लेशानां चरमदेहानामिति। तत्राशुक्लं योगिन एव फलसंयन्सादकृष्णं चानुपादानात्। इतरेषां तु भूतानां पूर्वमेव त्रिविधमिति।

.**भोजवृत्ति**—शुभफलदं कर्म यागादि शुक्लम्। अशुभफलदं ब्रह्महत्यादि कृष्णम्। उभयसंकीर्णं शुक्लकृष्णम्। तत्र शुक्लकर्म विचक्षणानां दानतपः स्वाध्यायादिमतां पुरुषाणाम्। कृष्णं कर्म नारकिणाम्। शुक्लकृष्णं मनुष्याणाम्। योगिनां तु सन्यासवतां त्रिविधकर्मविपरीतं यत्फलत्यागानुसंधानेनैवानुष्ठानात्र किंचित्फलमारभते। अस्यैव कर्मणः फलमाह

ततस्तद्विपाकानुगुणानामेवाभिव्यक्तिर्वासनानाम् ॥8॥

tatastadvipākānuguṇānāmevābhivyaktirvāsanānām

[*Tataḥ*] Then [*tad vipāka-anuguṇānām-eva*] according to the consequences of these three types of actions (good, bad, or mixed) [*vāsanānām*] formation of sanskāras [*abhivyakti*] takes place.

Here the Āchārya wants to inform that according to our good, bad or mixed actions, good, bad or mixed sanskāras are formed in our mind. As stated earlier, sanskāras are the impressions or psychological genes formed in the mind according to our actions, thoughts, and tendencies.

व्यासभाष्य—तत इति त्रिविधात्कर्मणः तद्विपाकानुगुणानामेवेति यज्जातीयस्य कर्मणो यो विपाकस्तस्यानुगुणा या वासनाः कर्मविपाकमनुशेरते तासामेवाभिव्यक्तिः। न हि दैवं कर्म विपच्यमानं नारकतिर्यङ्मनुष्यवासनाभिव्यक्तिनिमित्तं संभवति। किंतु दैवानुगुणा एवास्य वासना व्यज्यन्ते। नारकतिर्यङ्मनुष्येषु चैवं समानश्चर्यः।

.**भोजवृत्ति**—इह हि द्विविधाः कर्मवासनाः स्मृतिमात्रफला जात्यायुर्भोगफलाश्च। तत्र जात्यायुर्भोगफला एकानेकजन्मभवा इत्यनेन पूर्वमेव कृतनिर्णयाः। यास्तु स्मृतिमात्रफलास्तासु ततः कर्मणो येन कर्मणा याद्दक्शरीरमारब्धं देवमनुष्यतिर्यगादिभेदेन तस्य विपाकस्य या अनुगुणा अनुरूपा वासनास्तासामेव तस्मादभिव्यक्तिः वासनानां भवति। अयमर्थः येन कर्मणा पूर्वं देवतादिशरीरमारब्धं जात्यन्तरशतव्यवधानेन पुनस्तथाविधस्यैव शरीरस्यऽऽरम्भे तदनुरूपा एव स्मृतिफला वासनाः प्रकटी भवन्ति। लोकोत्तरेष्वेवार्थेषु तस्य स्मृत्यादयो जायन्ते। इतरास्तु सत्योऽपि अव्यक्तसंज्ञास्तिष्ठन्ति न तस्यां दशायां नारकादिशरीरोद्भवा वासना व्यक्तिमायान्ति। आसामेव वासनानां कार्यकरणभावानुपपत्तिमाशङ्क्य समर्थयितुमाह

जातिदेशकालव्यवहितानामप्यानन्तर्यं स्मृतिसंस्कारयोरेकरूपत्वात् ॥9॥

*jātideśakālavyavahitānāmapyānantaryaṁ
smṛtisaṁskārayorekarūpatvāt*

[*ānantaryaṁ*] Continuity of sanskāras is maintained [*jāti-deśa-kāla-vyavahitānāmapi*] irrespective of yonī (species), place and time, (ekarūpatvāt) there being no difference (*smṛti-sanskārayoḥ*) in the nature of sanskāra and memory.

Here the Āchārya wants to say that nature of sanskāras and memory is the same and their continuity is maintained from one species to another species, one place to another place and one time to another time, whether a soul has accumulated them in a human body or animal body or any other body; whether a soul has accumulated them on the earth or any other planets; whether a soul has accumulated them today or hundred of years ago. As such these sanskāras are aligned in the mind chronologically and accordingly they fructify.

व्यासभाष्य—वृषदंशविपाकोदयः स्वव्यञ्जकाञ्जनाभिव्यक्तः । स यदि जातिशतेन वा दूरदेशतया वा कल्पशतेन वा व्यवहितः पुनश्च स्वव्यञ्जकाञ्जन एवोदियाद्रागित्येवं पूर्वानुभूतवृषदंशविपाकाभिसंस्कृता वासना उपादाय व्यज्येत् । कस्मात् । यतो व्यवहितानामप्यासां सदृशं कर्माभिव्यञ्जकं निमित्तीभूतमित्यानन्तर्यमेव । कुतश्च स्मृतिसंस्कारयोरेकरूपत्वात् । यथाऽनुभवास्तथा संस्काराः । ते च कर्मवासनानुरूपाः । यथा च वासनास्तथा स्मृतिरिति जातिदेशकालव्यवहितेभ्यः संस्कारेभ्यः स्मृतिः । स्मृतेश्च पुनः संस्कारा इत्येवमेते स्मृतिसंस्काराः कर्माशयवृत्तिलाभवशाद्व्यज्यन्ते । अतश्च व्यवहितानामपि निमित्तनैमित्तिभावानुच्छेदादानन्तर्यमेव सिद्धमिति वासनाः संस्कारा आशया इत्यर्थः ।

भोजवृत्ति—इह नानायोनिषु भ्रमतां संसारिणां कांचिद्योनिमनुभूय यदा योन्यन्तरसहस्रव्यवधानेन पुनस्तामेव योनिं प्रतिपद्यते तदा तस्यां पूर्वानुभूतायां योनौ तथाविधशरीरादिव्यञ्जकापेक्षया वासना याः प्रकटीभूता आसंस्तास्तथाविधव्यञ्जकाभावात्तिरोहिताः पुनस्तथाविधव्यञ्जकशरीरादिलाभे प्रकटी भवन्ति । जातिदेशकालव्यवधानेऽपि तासां स्वानुभूतस्मृत्यादिफलसाधने आनन्तर्यं नैरन्तर्यम् कुतः स्मृतिसंस्कारयोरेकरूपत्वात् । तथा ह्यनुष्ठीयमानात्कर्मणश्चित्तसत्त्वे वासनानुरूपः संस्कारः समुत्पद्यते । स च स्वर्गनरकादीनां फलानामङ्कुरीभावः कर्मणां वा यागादीनां शक्तिरूपतयाऽवस्थानम् । कर्तुर्वा

तथाविधभोग्यभोक्तृत्वरूपं सामर्थ्यम्। संस्कारात्स्मृतिः स्मृतेश्च सुखदुःखोपभोगस्तदनुभवाच्च पुनरपि संस्कारस्मृत्यादयः। एवं च यस्य स्मृतिसंस्कारादयो भिन्नास्तयाऽनन्तर्याभिआवे दुर्लभः कार्यकारणभावः। अस्माकं तु यदाऽनुभव एव संस्कारी भवति संस्कारश्च स्मृतिरूपतया परिणमते तदैकस्यैव चित्तस्यानुसंधातृत्वेन स्थितत्वात्कार्यकारणभावो न दुर्घटः। भवत्वानन्तर्यं कार्यकारणभावश्च वासनानां यदा नु प्रथममेवानुभवः प्रवर्तते तदा किं वासनानिमित्त उत निनिमित्त इति शङ्कां व्यपनेतुमाह

तासामनादित्वं चाशिषो नित्यत्वात् ॥10॥

tāsāmanāditvaṃ cāśiṣo nityatvāt

[*Tāsām*] Those sanskāras are [*anāditvam*] beginningless, [*nityatvāt*] there being the eternality [*āṣiśaḥ*] of desires for enjoyment and life.

व्यासभाष्य—तासां वासनानामाशिषो नित्यत्वादनादित्वम्। येयमात्माशीर्मा न भूवं भूयासमिति सर्वस्य दृश्यते सा न स्वाभाविकी। कस्मात्। जातमात्रस्य जन्तोरननुभूतमरणधर्मकस्य द्वेषदुःखानुस्मृतिनिमित्तो मरणत्रासः कथं भवेत्। न च स्वाभाविकं वस्तु निमित्तमुपादत्ते। तस्मादनादिवासनानुविद्धमिदं चित्तं निमित्तवशात्काश्चिदेव वासनाः प्रतिलभ्य पुरुषस्य भोगायोपावर्तत इति।

घटप्रासादप्रदीपकल्पं संकोचविकासि चित्तं शरीरपरिमाणाकारमात्रमित्यपरे प्रतिपन्नाः। तथा चान्तराभावः संसारश्च युक्त इति। वृत्तिरेवास्य विभुनश्चित्तस्य संकोचविकासिनीत्याचार्यः।

तच्च धर्मादिनिमित्तापेक्षम्। निमित्तं च द्विविधम् बाह्यमाध्यात्मिकं च। शरीरादिसाधनापेक्षं बाह्यं स्तुतिदानाभिवादनादि चित्तमात्राधीनं श्रद्धाद्याध्यात्मिकम्। तथा चोक्तम् ये चैते मैत्र्यादयो ध्यायिनां विहारास्ते बाह्यसाधननिरनुग्रहात्मानः प्रकृष्टं धर्ममभिनिर्वर्तयन्ति। तयोर्मानसं बलीयः। कथं ज्ञानवैराग्ये केनातिशय्येते दण्डकारण्यं च चित्तबलव्यतिरेकेण शरीरेण कर्मणा शून्यं कः कर्तुमुत्सहेत समुद्रमगस्त्यवद्वा पिबेत्।

भोजवृत्ति—तासां वासनानामनादित्वं न विद्यत आदिर्यस्य तस्य भावस्तत्त्वं तासा मादिर्नास्तीत्यर्थः। कुत इत्यत आह आशिषो नित्यत्वात्। येयमाशीर्महामोहरूपा सदैव सुखसाधनानि मे भूयासुर्मा कदाचन तैर्मे वियोगो भूदिति यः संकल्पविशेषो वासनानां कारणं तस्य नित्यत्वादनादित्वादित्यर्थः। एतदुक्तं भवति कारणस्य संनिहितत्वादनुभवसंस्कारादीनां कार्याणां प्रवृत्तिः केन वार्यते अनुभवसंस्काराद्यनुविद्धं संकोचविकाशधर्मि चित्तं तत्तदभिव्यञ्जकविपाकलाभात्तत्तत्फलरूपतया परिणमत इत्यर्थः। तासामानन्त्याद्धानां कथं संभवतीत्याशङ्क्य हानोपायमाह

हेतुफलाश्रयालम्बनैः संगृहीतत्वादेषामभावे तदभावः ॥11॥

hetuphalāśrayālambanaiḥ saṃgṛhītatvādeṣāmabhāve tadabhāvaḥ

[*saṅgṛhītatvād*] The sanskaras are accumulated due to [*hetu*] their cause (good, bad or mixed deeds), [*phala*] desire for fruits, [*āśraya*] mind, [*ālambana*] and senses organs. [*tad-abhāva*] Sanskaras disappear [*eṣām*] when these four—good, bad or mixed deeds, desire for fruits, mind, and sense organs —[*abhāve*] disappear.

व्यासभाष्य—हेतुर्धर्मात्सुखमधर्मादुःखं सुखाद्रागो दुःखाद्द्वेषस्ततश्च प्रयत्नस्तेन मनसा वाचा कायेन वा परिस्यन्दमानः परमनुगृह्णात्युपहन्ति वा ततः पुनर्धर्माधर्मौ सुखदुःखे रागद्वेषाविति प्रवृत्तमिदं षडरं संसारचक्रम् । अस्य च प्रतिक्षणमावर्तमानस्याविद्या नेत्री मूलं सर्वक्लेशानामित्येष हेतुः । फलं तु यमाश्रित्य यस्य प्रत्युत्पन्नता धर्मादिः न ह्यपूर्वोपजनः । मनस्तु साधिकारमाश्रयो वासनानाम् । न ह्यवसिताधिकारे मनसि निराश्रया वासनाः स्थातुमुत्सहन्ते । यदभिमुखीभूतं वस्तु यां वासनां व्यनक्ति तस्यास्तदालम्बनम् । एवं हेतुफलाश्रयालम्बनैरेतैः संगृहीताः सर्वा वासनाः । एषामभावे तत्संश्रयाणामपि वासनानामभावः । नास्त्यसतः संभवः न चास्ति सतो विनाश इति द्रव्यत्वेन संभवन्त्यः कथं निवर्तिष्यन्ते वासना इति

.**भोजवृत्ति**.—वासनानामनन्तरानुभवो हेतुस्तस्याप्यनुभवस्य रागादस्तेषामविद्येति साक्षात्पारम्पर्येण हेतुः । फलं शरीरादि स्मृत्यादि च । आश्रयो बुद्धिसत्त्वम् । आलम्बनं यदेवानुभवस्य तदेव वासनानामतस्तैर्हेतुफलाश्रयालम्बनैरनन्तानामपि वासनानां संगृहीतत्वात्तेषां हेत्वादीनामभावे ज्ञानयोगाभ्यां दग्धबीजकल्पत्वे विहिते निर्मलत्वान्न वासनाः प्ररोहन्ति न कार्यमारभन्त इति तासामभावः ।

ननु प्रतिक्षणं चित्तस्य नश्वरत्वाद्भेदोपलब्धेः वासनानां तत्फलानां च कार्यकारणभावेन युगपद्भाविल्वाद्भेदे कथमेकत्वमित्याशङ्क्यै कत्वसमर्थनायाऽऽह

अतीतानागतं स्वरूपतोऽस्त्यध्वभेदाद्धर्माणाम् ॥12॥
atītānāgataṃ svarūpato'styadhvabhedāddharmāṇām

[*Atīta*] The karmas/actions of past [*anāgata*] and the future [*svarūpataḥ asti*] essentially exist in the form of sanskaras. They are rewarded [*adhva-bhedāt*] according to their timings of [*dharmāṇām*] fruition.

व्यासभाष्य—भविष्यद्व्यक्तिकमनागतमनुभूतव्यक्तिकमतीतं व्यापारोपारूढं वर्तमानं त्रयं कैतद्वस्तु ज्ञानस्य ज्ञेयम् । यदि चैतत्स्वरूपतो नाभविष्यन्नेदं निर्विषयं ज्ञानमुदपत्स्यत । तस्मादतीतानागतं स्वरूपतोऽस्तीति । किंच भोगभागीयस्य वाऽपवर्गभागीयस्य वा कर्मणः फलमुत्पित्सु यदि निरुपाख्यमिति तदुद्देशेन तेन निमित्तेन कुशलानुष्ठानं न युज्यते । सतश्च फलस्य निमित्तं वर्तमानीकरणे समर्थं नापूर्वोपजनने । सिद्धं निमित्तं नैमित्तिकस्य विशेषानुग्रहं कुरुते नापूर्वमुत्पादयतीति ।

धर्मी चानेकधर्मस्वभावस्तस्य चाध्वभेदेन धमाः प्रत्यवस्थिताः । न च यथा वर्तमानं
व्यक्तिविशेषापन्नं द्रव्यतोऽस्त्येवमतीतमनागतं च । कथं तर्हि स्वेनैव व्यङ्क्येन स्वरूपेणानागतमस्ति ।
स्वेन चानुभूतव्यक्तिकेन स्वरूपेणातीतमिति । वर्तमानस्यैवाध्वनः स्वरूपव्यक्तिरिति न सा
भवत्यतीतानागतयोरध्वनोः । एकस्य चाध्वनः समये द्वावध्वानौ धर्मिसमन्वागतौ भवत एवेति
नाभूत्वा भावस्त्रयाणामध्वानामिति ।

भोजवृत्ति．—इहात्यन्तमसतां भावानामुत्पत्तिर्न युक्तिमती तेषां सत्त्वसम्बन्धायोगात् । न हि
शशविषाणादीनां क्वचिदपि सत्त्वसंबन्धो दृष्टः । निरुपाख्ये च कार्ये किमुद्दिश्य कारणानि प्रवर्तेरन् ।
न हि विषयमनालोच्य कश्चित्प्रवर्तते । सतामपि विरोधान्नाभावसम्बन्धोऽस्ति । यत्स्वरूपेण
लब्धसत्ताकं तत्कथं निरुपाख्यतामभावरूपतां वा भजते न निरुद्धं रूपं स्वीकारोतीत्यर्थः ।
तस्मात्सतामभावसंभवादसतां चोत्पत्त्यसंभवात्तैस्तैर्धर्मैर्विपरिणममानो धर्मी सदैवैकरूपतयाऽवतिष्ठते ।
धर्मास्तु तत्रैव त्र्यधिकल्वेन त्रैकालिकल्वेन व्यवस्थिताः स्वस्मिन्स्वस्मिन्नध्वनि व्यवस्थिता न स्वरूपं
त्यजन्ति । वर्तमानेऽध्वनि व्यवस्थिताः केवलं भोग्यतां भजन्ते तस्माद्धर्माणा-
मेवातीतानागताद्ध्वभेदस्तेनैव रूपेण कार्यकारणभावोऽस्मिन्दर्शने प्रतिपाद्यते ।
तस्मादपवर्गपर्यन्तमेकमेव चित्तं धर्मितयाऽनुवर्तमानं न निह्नोतुं पार्यते । त एते धर्मधर्मिणः किंरूपा
इत्यत आह

ते व्यक्तसूक्ष्मा गुणात्मानः ॥13॥

te vyaktasūkṣmā guṇātmānaḥ

[*Te*] These kārmic sanskāras, [*vyakta-sūkṣamāḥ*]
whether rewarded or unrewarded, remain [*guṇa-
ātmānaḥ*] transformed in three guṇas—sattva, rajas and
tamas.

Here it is told that sanskāras of karmas whether
rewarded or unrewarded transform into three guṇas—
sattva, rajas, and tamas. In this regard, Vyasa (4.13)
quotes a śloka referring to Śāstrānuśāsana as:

गुणानां परमं रूपं न दृष्टिपथमृच्छति ।

यत्तु दृष्टिपथं प्राप्तं तन्मायेव सुतुच्छककम् ॥

[Meaning] The causal form of the (guṇās) sanskāras is
not subject to perception. Whatever is perceived, that is
the effect (rewarded form) of the sanskāras.

व्यासभाष्य—ते खल्वमी त्र्यध्वानो धर्मा वर्तमाना व्यक्तात्मानोऽतीतानागताः
सूक्ष्मात्मानः षडविशेषरूपाः । सर्वमिदं गुणानां सन्निवेशविशेषमात्रमिति परमार्थतो

गुणात्मानः । तथा च शास्त्रानुशासनम् गुणानां परमं रूपं न दृष्टिपथमृच्छति । यत्तु दृष्टिपथं प्राप्तं तन्मायेव सुतुच्छकम् ।इति । ।।13 ।।

यदा तु सर्वे गुणाः कथमेकः शब्द एकमिन्द्रियमिति

.भोजवृत्ति.—य एते धर्मधर्मिणः प्रोक्तास्ते व्यक्तसूक्ष्मभेदेन व्यवस्थिता गुणाः सत्त्वरजस्तमोरूपास्तदात्मानस्तत्स्वभावास्तत्परिणामरूपा इत्यर्थः । यतः सत्त्वरजस्तमोभिः सुखदुःखमोहरूपैः सर्वासां बाह्याभ्यन्तरभेदभिन्नानां भावव्यक्तीनामन्वयानुगमो दृश्यते । यद्यदन्वयि तत्तत्परिणामरूपं दृष्टं यथा घटादयो मृदन्विता मृत्परिणामरूपाः ।

यद्येते त्रयो गुणाः सर्वत्र मूलकारणं कथमेको धर्मीति व्यपदेश इत्याशङ्क्याऽऽह

परिणामैकत्वाद्वस्तुतत्त्वम् ॥14 ॥
pariṇāmaikatvādvastutattvam

[*Vastutattvam*] Identity of a species [*pariṇām*] is the result of [*ekatvam*] synthesis of the guṇa variables at the end points.

The different species are formed of combinations and permutations of the three guṇas, how is it that different species have their different identities?

The answer is that in each species the combination and permutation of guṇas occupies a unique synthesis, which gives them a unique identity.

व्यासभाष्य—प्रख्याक्रियास्थितिशीलानां गुणानां ग्रहणात्मकानां करणभावेनैकः परिणामः श्रोत्रमिन्द्रियं ग्राह्यात्मकानां शब्दतन्मात्रभावेनैकः परिणामः शब्दो विषय इति शब्दादीनां मूर्तिसमानजातीयानामेकः परिणामः पृथिवीपरमाणुस्तन्मात्रावयवस्तेषां चैकः परिणामः पृथिवी गौर्वृक्षः पर्वत इत्येवमादिभूतान्तरेष्वपि स्नेहौष्ण्यप्रणामित्वावकाशदानान्युपादाय सामान्यमेकविकारारम्भः समाधेयः । नास्त्यर्थो विज्ञानविसहचरः । अस्ति तु ज्ञानमर्थविसहचरं स्वप्नादौ कल्पितमित्यनया दिशा ये वस्तुस्वरूपमपह्नुवते ज्ञानपरिकल्पनामात्रं वस्तु स्वप्नविषयोपमं न परमार्थतोऽस्तीति य आहुस्ते तथेति प्रत्युपस्थितमिदं स्वमाहात्म्येन वस्तु कथमप्रमाणात्मकेन विकल्पज्ञानबलेन वस्तुस्वरूपमुत्सृज्य तदेवापलपन्तः श्रद्धेयवचनाः स्युः । कुतश्चैतदन्याय्यम्

.भोजवृत्ति.—यद्यपि त्रयो गुणस्तथाऽपि तेषामङ्गाङ्गिभावगमनलक्षणयो यः परिणामः क्वचित्सत्त्वमङ्गि क्वचिद्रजः क्वचिच्च तम इत्येवंरूपस्तस्यैकत्वाद्वस्तुनस्तत्त्वमेकत्वमुच्यते । यथेयं पृथिवी अयं वायुरित्यादि । ननु च ज्ञानव्यतिरिक्ते सत्यर्थे वस्त्वेकमनेकं वा वक्तुं युज्यते यदा विज्ञानमेव वासनावशात्कार्यकारणभावेनावस्थितं तथा तथा प्रतिभाति तदा कथमेतच्छक्यते वक्तुमित्याशङ्क्याऽऽह

वस्तुसाम्ये चित्तभेदात्तयोर्विभक्तः पन्थाः ॥15॥

vastusāmye cittabhedāttayorvibhaktaḥ panthāḥ

[*Vastusāmye*] One and the same object is [*cittabhedāt*] identified differently by different minds. This shows that [*tayoḥ*] mind and object [*vibhaktaḥ panthā*] are two different things (fig.14).

Figure 14: Minds and one object

व्यासभाष्य—बहिश्चित्तालम्बनीभूतमेकं वस्तु साधारणम्। तत्खलु नैकचित्तपरिकल्पितं नाप्यनेकचित्तपरिकल्पितं किंतु स्वप्रतिष्ठम्। कथम्। वस्तुसाम्ये चित्तभेदात्। धर्मापेक्षं चित्तस्य वस्तुसाम्येऽपि सुखज्ञानं भवत्यधर्मापेक्षं तत एव दुःखज्ञानमविद्यापेक्षं तत एव मूढज्ञानं सम्यग्दर्शनापेक्षं तत एव माध्यस्थ्यज्ञानमिति। कस्य तच्चित्तेन परिकल्पितम्। न चान्यचित्तपरिकल्पितेनार्थेनान्यस्य चित्तोपरागो युक्तः। तस्माद्वस्तुज्ञानयोर्ग्राह्यग्रहणभेदभिन्नयोर्विभक्तः पन्थाः। नानयोः संकरगन्धोऽप्यस्तीति। सांख्यपक्षे पुनर्वस्तु त्रिगुणं चलं च गुणवृत्तिमिति धर्मादिनिमित्तापेक्षं चित्तैरभिसंबध्यते। निमित्तानुरूपस्य च प्रत्ययस्योत्पद्यमानस्य तेन तेनाऽऽत्मना हेतुर्भवति केचिदाहुः ज्ञानसहभूरेवार्थो भोग्यत्वात्सुखादिवदिति। त एतया द्वारा साधारणत्वं बाधमानाः पूर्वोत्तरक्षणेषु वस्तुरूपमेवापह्नुवते।

भोजवृत्ति.—तयोर्ज्ञानार्थयोः विविक्तः पन्था विविक्तो मार्ग इति यावत्। कथं वस्तुसाम्ये चित्तभेदात्। समाने वस्तुनि ह्यादावुपलभ्यमाने नानाप्रमातृणां चित्तस्य भेदः सुखदुःखमोहरूपतया समुपलभ्यते। तथाहि एकस्यां रूपलावण्यवत्यां योषिति उपलभ्यमानायां सरागस्य सुखमुत्पद्यते सपत्न्यास्तु द्वेष परिव्राजकादेर्घृणेत्येकस्मिन्वस्तुनि नानाविधचित्तोदयात्कथं चित्तकार्यत्वं वस्तुन एकचित्तकार्यत्वे वस्त्वेकरूपतयैवावभासते। किं च चित्तकार्यत्वे वस्तुनो यदीयस्य चित्तस्य तद्वस्तु कार्यं तस्मिन्नर्थान्तरव्यासक्तेऽतद्वस्तु न किञ्चित्स्यात् भवत्विति चेन्न तदेव कथमन्यैर्बहुभिरुपलभ्यते उपलभ्यते च। तस्मान्न चित्तकार्यम्। अथ युगपद्बहुभिः सोऽर्थः क्रियते तदा बहुभिर्निर्मितस्यार्थस्यैकनिर्मिताद्वैलक्षण्यं स्यात्। यदा तु वैलक्षण्यं नेष्यते तदा कारण भेदे सति कार्यभेदस्याभावे निर्हेतुकमेकरूपं या जगत्स्यात् एतदुक्तं भवति सत्यपि भिन्ने कारणे यदि

कार्यस्याभेदस्तदा समग्रं जगन्नानाविधकारणजन्यमेकरूपं स्यात्।

कारणभेदाननुगमात्स्वातन्त्र्येण निर्हेतुकं वा स्यात्। यद्येवं कथं तेन त्रिगुणात्मनार्थेनैकस्यैव प्रमातुः सुखदुःखमोहमयानि ज्ञानानि न जन्यन्ते मैवम् यथार्थस्त्रिगुणस्तथा चित्तमपि त्रिगुणं तस्य चार्थप्रतिभासोत्पत्तौ धर्मादयः सहकारिकारणं तदुद्भवाभिभववशात्कदाविच्चित्तस्य तेन तेन रूपेणाभिव्यक्तिः। तथा च कामुकस्य संनिहितायां योषिति धर्मसहकृतं चित्तं सत्वस्याङ्गितया परिणममानं सुखमंय भवति तदेवाधर्मसहकारि रजसोऽङ्गितया दुःखरूपं सपत्नीमात्रस्य भवति तीव्राधर्मसहकारितया परिणममानं तमसोऽङ्गित्वेन कोपनायाः सपत्न्या मोहमयं भवति। तस्माद्विज्ञानव्यतिरिक्तोऽस्ति बाह्योऽर्थः। तदेवं न विज्ञानार्थयोस्तादात्म्यं विरोधान्न कार्यकारणभावः। कारणाभेदे सत्यपि कार्यभेदप्रसङ्गादिति ज्ञानाद्व्यतिरिक्तत्वमर्थस्य व्यवस्थापितम्।

यद्येवं ज्ञानं चेत्प्रकाशकत्वाद्ग्रहणस्वभावमर्थश्च प्रकाश्यत्वाद्ग्राह्यस्वभावस्तत्कथं गपत्सर्वानर्थान्नि गृह्णाति न स्मरति चेत्याशङ्क्य परिहारं वक्तुमाह

न चैकचित्ततन्त्रं वस्तु तदप्रमाणकं तदा किं स्यात् ॥16॥
na caikacittatantraṃ vastu tadapramāṇakaṃ tadā kiṃ syāt

The existence of an object [*na cha*] does not depend [*eka chitta-tantram*] on its cognition by mind alone. When an object is not cognized by a mind, [*tadapramāṇakaṃ tadā kiṃ syāt*] would it become non-existent?

The answer is no.

व्यासभाष्य—एकचित्ततन्त्रं चेद्वस्तु स्यात्तदा चित्ते व्यग्रे निरुद्धे वाऽस्वरूपमेव तेनापरामृष्टमन्यस्याविषयीभूतमप्रमाणकमगृहीतस्वभावकं केनचित्तदानीं किं तत्स्यात्। संबध्यमानं च पुनश्चित्तेन कुत उत्पद्येत। ये चास्यानुपस्थिता भागास्ते चास्यन स्युरेवं नास्ति पृष्ठमित्युदरमपि न गृह्येत। तस्मात्स्वतन्त्रोऽर्थः सर्वपुरुषसाधारणः स्वतन्त्राणि च चित्तानि प्रति पुरुषं प्रवर्तन्ते। तयोः सम्बन्धादुपलब्धि पुरुषस्य भोग इति।

तदुपरागापेक्षित्वाच्चित्तस्य वस्तु ज्ञाताज्ञातम् ॥17॥
taduparāgāpekṣitvāccittasya vastu jñātājñātam

[*Vastu*] An object [*jñāta*] is called known or [*ajñāta*] unknown depending upon [*chittsya*] the mind [*taduparāgāpekṣitvāt*] being in contact with the object [*cha*] or not.

When the mind is in contact with the object through

sense organs, an object is called known to the mind and when the mind is not in contact with the object, the object remains unknown.

व्यासभाष्य—अयस्कान्तमणिकल्पा विषया अयःसधर्मकं चित्तमभिसंबन्ध्योपरञ्जयन्ति । येन च विषयेणोपरक्तं चित्तं स विषयो ज्ञातस्ततोऽन्यः पुनरज्ञातः । वस्तुनो ज्ञाताज्ञातस्वरूपत्वात्परिणामि चित्तम् । यस्य तु तदेवं चित्तं विषयस्तस्य

.**भोजवृत्ति—**तस्यार्थस्योपरागादाकारसमर्पणाच्चित्ते बाह्यं वस्तु ज्ञातमज्ञातं च भवति । अयमर्थः सर्वः पदार्थ आत्मलाभे चित्तं सामग्रीमपेक्षते । नीलादिज्ञानं चोपजायमानमिन्द्रियणांलिकया समागतमर्थोपरागं सहकारिकारणत्वेनापेक्षते व्यतिरिक्तस्यार्थस्य संबन्धाभावाद्ग्रहीतुमशक्यत्वात् । ततश्च येनैवार्थेनास्य ज्ञानस्य स्वरूपोपरागः कृतस्तमेवार्थ ज्ञानं व्यवहारयोग्यतां नयति ततश्च सोऽर्थो ज्ञात इत्युच्यते येन चाङ्कारो न समर्पितः सोऽज्ञातत्वेन व्यवह्रियते यस्मिंश्चानुभूतेऽर्थे सादृश्यादिः अर्थः संस्कारमुद्बोधयन्सहकारिकारणतां प्रतिपद्यते तस्मिन्नेवार्थे स्मृतिरुपजायते इति न सर्वत्र ज्ञानं नापि सर्वत्र स्मृतिरिति न कश्चिद्विरोधः ।

यद्येवं प्रमाताऽपि पुरुषो यस्मिन्काले नीलं वेदयते न तस्मिन्काले पीतमतस्तस्यापि कदाचित्कत्वं ग्रहीतृरूपत्वादाकारग्रहणे परिणामित्वं प्राप्तमित्याशङ्कां परिहर्तुमाह

सदा ज्ञाताश्चित्तवृत्तयस्तत्प्रभोः पुरुषस्यापरिणामित्वात् ॥18॥
sadā jñātāścittavṛttayastatprabhoḥ puruṣasyāpariṇāmitvāt

[*Chittavṛttayaḥ*] The vṛttis of mind [*sadā*] are always [*jñātā*] known [*tatprabhoḥ*] to its master, [*puruṣasya*] the soul, because the soul is [*apariṇāmī*] not subject to change with the change of vṛttis, i.e. soul never becomes old and dies.

व्यासभाष्य—यदि चित्तवत्प्रभुरपि पुरुषः परिणमेत्ततस्तद्विषयाश्चित्तवृत्तयः शब्दादिविषयवज्ज्ञाताज्ञाताः स्युः । सदाज्ञातत्वं तु मनसस्तत्प्रभोः पुरुषस्यापरिणामित्वमनुमापयति । स्यादाशङ्का चित्तमेव स्वाभासं विषयाभासं च भविष्यतीत्यग्निवत्

.**भोजवृत्ति—**या एताश्चित्तस्य प्रमाणविपर्ययादिरूपा वृत्तयस्तास्तत्प्रभोश्चित्तस्य ग्रहीतुः पुरुषस्य सदा सर्वकालमेव ज्ञेयाः तस्य चिद्रूपतयाऽपरिणामात् परिणामित्वाभावादित्यर्थः । यद्यसौ परिणामी स्यात्तदा परिणामस्य कादाचित्कत्वात्प्रमातुस्तासां चित्तवृत्तीनां सदा ज्ञातत्वं नोपपद्येत । अयमर्थ पुरुषस्य चिद्रूपस्य सदैवाधिष्ठातृत्वेन व्यवस्थितस्य यदन्तरङ्गं निर्मलं सत्त्वं तस्यापि सदैवावस्थितत्वाद्येन येनार्थेनोपरक्तं भवति तथाविधस्यार्थस्य सदैव चिच्छायासंक्रान्तिसद्भावस्तस्यां सत्यां सिद्धं सदा ज्ञातृत्वमिति न कदाचित्परिणामित्वाशङ्का ।

ननु चित्तमेव यदि सत्त्वोत्कर्षात्प्रकाशकं तदा स्वपरप्रकाशकत्वादात्मानमर्थं च प्रकाशयतीति तावतैव व्यवहारसमाप्तेः किं ग्रहीत्रन्तरेणेत्या शङ्कामपनेतुमाह

न तत्स्वाभासं दृश्यत्वात् ॥19॥

na tatsvābhāsaṃ dṛśyatvāt

[*Tat*] The mind [*na*] does not [*svabhāsam*] have its own knowledge, [*dṛśyatvāt*] because it is made of the element of dṛśya jagat (material world). *Ahaṅkāra* is jaḍa (material element).

व्यासभाष्य—यथेतराणीन्द्रियाणि शब्दादयश्च दृश्यत्वान्न स्वाभासानि तथा मनोऽपि प्रत्येतव्यम्। न चाग्निरत्र दृष्टान्तः। न ह्यग्निरात्मस्वरूपप्रकाशं प्रकाशयति। प्रकाशश्चायं प्रकाश्यप्रकाशकसंयोगे दृष्टः। न च स्वरूपमात्रेऽस्ति संयोगः। किं च स्वाभासं चित्तमित्यग्राह्यमेव कस्यचिदिति शब्दार्थः। तद्यथा स्वात्मप्रतिष्ठमाकाशं न परप्रतिष्ठमित्यर्थः। स्वबुद्धिप्रचारप्रतिसंवेदनात्सत्त्वानां प्रवृत्तिर्दृश्यते क्रुद्धोऽहं भीतोऽहममुत्र मे रागोऽमुत्र मे क्रोध इति। एतत्स्वबुद्धेरग्रहणे न युक्तमिति।

.**भोजवृत्ति**—तच्चित्तं स्वाभासं स्वप्रकाशकं न भवति पुरुषवेद्यं भवतीति यावत् कुतः दृश्यत्वात् यत्किल दृश्यं तद्द्रष्टृवेद्यं दृष्टं यथा घटादि दृश्यं च चित्तं तस्मान्न स्वाभासम्।

एकसमये चोभयानवधारणम् ॥20॥

ekasamaye cobhayānavadhāraṇam

[*ubhaya-anavadhāraṇam*] One cannot have two cognitions (cognition of self and cognition of material object) [*eka-samaye*] at one time. When a person realizes the self, he/she cannot have cognition of material objects and when he/she has cognition of material objects, he/she cannot have self-realization.

व्यासभाष्य—न चैकस्मिन्क्षणे स्वपररूपावधारणं युक्तं क्षणिकवादिनो यद्भवनं सैव क्रिया तदेव च कारकमित्यभ्युपगमः। स्यान्मतिः स्वरसनिरुद्धं चित्तं चित्तान्तरेण समनन्तरेण गृह्यत इति

.**भोजवृत्ति**—अर्थस्य संवित्तिरिदंतया व्यवहारयोग्यतापादनमयमर्थः सुखहेतुर्दुःखहेतुर्वेति। बुद्धेश्च संविदहमित्येवमाकारेण सुखदुःखरूपतया व्यवहारक्षमतापादनम्। एवं विधं च व्यापारद्वयमर्थप्रत्यक्षताकाले न युगपत्कर्तुं शक्यं विरोधात् न हि विरुद्धयोर्व्यापारयोर्युगपत्संभवोऽस्ति। अतः एकस्मिन्काल उभयस्य स्वरूपस्यार्थस्य चावधारयितुमशक्यत्वान्न चित्तं स्वप्रकाशमित्युक्तं भवति। किं चैवंविधव्यापारद्वयनिष्पाद्यस्य फलद्वयस्यासंवेदनाद्बहिर्मुखतयैवार्थनिष्ठत्वेन चित्तस्य संवेदनार्थनिष्ठमेव फलं न स्वनिष्ठमित्यर्थः। ननु मा भूद्बुद्धेः स्वयं ग्रहणं बुद्ध्यन्तरेण भविष्यतीत्याशङ्क्याऽऽह-

चित्तान्तरदृश्येबुद्धिबुद्धेरतिप्रसङ्गः स्मृतिसङ्करश्च ॥21॥

cittāntaradṛśye buddhibuddheratiprasaṅgaḥ
smṛtisaṅkaraśca

[*cittāntara*] If cognition of one mind by another mind [*dṛśye*] be postulated, [*atiprasaṅgaḥ*] there will be no end to the chain of [*buddheḥ*] cognition of one mind by [*buddhi*] another mind [*cha*] and [*smṛti-saṅkaraḥ*] the memories of all minds will mix up.

Note: The above sūtra says that minds are different per individual. There is no concept of uniform mind.

व्यासभाष्य—अथ चित्तं चेच्चित्तान्तरेण गृह्येत बुद्धिः केन गृह्यते साऽप्यन्यया साऽन्यन्ययेत्यतिप्रसङ्गः। स्मृतिसंकरश्च। यावन्तो बुद्धिबुद्धीनामनुभवास्तावत्यः स्मृतयः प्राप्नुवन्ति। तत्संकराच्चैकस्मृत्यनवधारणं च स्यादित्येवं बुद्धिप्रतिसंवेदिनं पुरुषमपलपद्भिर्वैनाशिकैः सर्वमेवाऽऽकुलीकृतम्। ते तु भोक्तृस्वरूपं यत्र क्वचन कल्पयन्तो न न्यायेन संगच्छन्ते। केचित्तु सत्त्वमात्रमपि परिकल्प्यास्ति स सत्त्वो य एतान्पञ्च स्कन्धान्निक्षिप्यान्यांश्च प्रतिसंदधातीत्युक्त्वा तत एव पुनर्ध्वस्यन्ति। तथा स्कन्धानां महानिर्वेदाय चिरागायानुत्पादाय प्रशान्तये गुरोरन्तिके ब्रह्मचर्यं चरिष्यामीत्युक्त्वा सत्त्वस्य पुनः सत्त्वमेवाहुवते। सांख्ययोगादयस्तु प्रवादाः स्वशब्देन पुरुषमेव स्वामिनं चित्तस्य भोक्तारमुपयन्तीति। कथम्

भोजवृत्ति—यदि हि बुद्धिर्बुद्ध्यन्तरेण वेद्यते तदा साऽपि बुद्धिः स्वयमबुद्धा बुद्ध्यन्तरं प्रकाशयितुमसमर्थेति तस्या बोधकं बुद्ध्यन्तरं कल्पनीयं तस्याप्यन्यदित्यनवस्थानात्पुरुषायुषेणाप्यर्थप्रतीतिर्न स्यात्। न हि प्रतीतावप्रतीतायामर्थः प्रतीतो भवति। स्मृतिसंकरश्च प्राप्नोति रूपे रसे वा समुत्पन्नायां बुद्धौ तद्ग्राहिकाणामनन्तानां बुद्धीनां समुत्पत्तेबुद्धिजनितैः संस्कारैः यदा युगपद्द्वह्यः स्मृतयः क्रियन्ते तदा बुद्धेरपर्यवसानाद्बुद्धिस्मृतीनां च बह्वीनां युगपदुत्पत्तेः कस्मिन्नर्थे स्मृतिरियमुत्पन्नेति ज्ञातुमशक्यत्वात्स्मृतीनां संकरः स्यात्। इयं रूपस्मृतिरियं रसस्मृतिरिति न ज्ञायेत। ननु बुद्धेः स्वप्रकाशत्वाभावे बुद्ध्यन्तरेण चासंवेदने कथमयं विषयसंवेदनरूपो व्यवहार इत्याशङ्क्य स्वसिद्धान्तमाह

चितेरप्रतिसंक्रमायास्तदाकारापत्तौ स्वबुद्धिसंवेदनम् ॥22॥

citerapratisaṃkramāyāstadākārāpattau
svabuddhisaṃvedanam

When [*apratisaṃkramāyāḥ*] unaffected [*citeḥ*] soul [*āpattau*] identifies itself [*tadākārā*] with the (nature of) mind, this is called *svabuddhi-saṃvedanam* (soul's identifying itself with the mind).

This all happens due to avidyā (soul's identification with material body). Sometimes persons identify themselves with the body and sometimes with the mind or the thought process.

व्यासभाष्य—अपरिणामिनी हि भोक्तृशक्तिरप्रतिसंक्रमा च परिणामिन्यर्थे प्रतिसंक्रान्तेव तद्वृत्तिमनुपतति । तस्याश्च प्राप्तचैतन्योपग्रहस्वरूपाया बुद्धिवृत्तेरनुकारमात्रतया बुद्धिवृत्यविशिष्टा हि ज्ञानवृत्तिराख्यायते । तथा चोक्तम्

न पातालं न च विवरं गिरीणां नैवान्धकारं कुक्षयो नोदधीनाम् ।

गुहा यस्यां निहितं ब्रह्म शाश्वतं

बुद्धिवृत्तिमविशिष्टां कवयो वेदयन्ते । ।इति । ।22 । ।

अतश्चैतदभ्युपगम्यते

भोजवृत्ति—पुरुषश्चिद्रूपत्वाच्चितिः साऽप्रतिसंक्रमा न विद्यते प्रतिसंक्रमोऽन्यत्र गमनं यस्याः सा तथोक्ता अन्येनासंकीर्णेति यावत् । यथा गुणा अङ्गाङ्गिभावलक्षणे परिणामेऽङ्गिनं गुणं संक्रामन्ति तद्रूपतामिवाऽऽपद्यन्ते यथा वा लोके परमाणवः प्रसरन्तो विषयमारूपयन्ति नैवं चितिशक्तिस्तस्याः सर्वदैकरूपतया स्वप्रतिष्ठितत्वेन व्यवस्थितत्वात् । अतस्तत्संनिधाने यदा बुद्धिस्तदाकारतामापद्यते चेतनेवोपजायते बुद्धिवृत्तिप्रतिसंक्रान्ता च यदा चिच्छक्तिर्बुद्धिवृत्तिविशिष्टतया संवेद्यते तदा बुद्धेः स्वस्याऽऽत्मनो वेदनं भवतीत्यर्थः । इत्थं स्वसंविदितं चित्तं सर्वार्थग्रहणसामर्थ्येन सकलव्यवहारनिर्वाहक्षमं भवतीत्याह

द्रष्टृदृश्योपरक्तं चित्तं सर्वार्थम् ॥23॥
draṣṭṛdṛśyoparaktaṁ cittaṁ sarvārtham

[*Chitta*] The mind [*uparaktaṁ*] coloured/modified by [*dṛṣṭṛ*] soul and [*dṛśya*] the material world [*sarva-artham*] appears respectively to be of the nature of chetana (consciousness or sentient beings) and jaḍa (insentient matter).

व्यासभाष्य—मनो हि मन्तव्येनार्थेनोपरक्तं । ततः स्वयं च विषयत्वाद्विषयिणा पुरुषेणाऽऽत्मीयया वृत्त्याभिसंबद्धं तदेतच्चित्तमेव द्रष्टृदृश्योपरक्तं विषयविषयिनिर्भासं चेतनाचेतनस्वरूपापन्नं विषयात्मकमप्यविषयात्मकमिवाचेतनं चेतनमिव स्फटिकमणिकल्पं सर्वार्थमित्युच्यते । तदनेन चित्तसारूप्येण भ्रान्ताः केचित्तदेव चेतनमित्याहुः । अपरे चित्तमात्रमेवेदं सर्वं नास्ति खल्वयं गवादिर्घटादिश्च सकारणो लोक इति अनुकम्पनीयास्ते । कस्मात् अस्ति हि तेषां भ्रान्तिबीजं सर्वरूपाकारनिर्भासं चित्तमिति । समाधिप्रज्ञायां प्रज्ञेयोऽर्थ प्रतिबिम्बीभूतस्तस्याऽऽलम्बनीभूतत्वादन्यः । स चेदर्थश्चित्तमात्रं स्यात्कथं प्रज्ञयैव प्रज्ञारूपमवधार्येत ।

तस्मात्प्रतिबिम्बीभूतोऽर्थः प्रज्ञायां येनावधार्यते स पुरुष इति । एवं
ग्रहीतृग्रहणग्राह्यस्वरूपचित्तभेदात्रयमप्येतज्जातितः प्रविभजन्ते ते सम्यग्दर्शिनस्तैरधिगतः पुरुषः ।
कुतश्चैतत्

.भोजवृत्तिः—द्रष्टा पुरुषस्तेनोपरक्तं तत्सन्निधानेन तद्रूपतामिव प्राप्तं दृश्योपरक्तं विषयोपरक्तं
गृहीतविषयाकारपरिणामं यदा भवति तदा तदेव चित्तं सर्वार्थग्रहणसमर्थं भवति । यथा निर्मलं
स्फटिकदर्पणादेव प्रतिबिम्बग्रहणसमर्थमेवं रजस्तमोभ्यानभिभूतं सत्त्वं
शुद्धत्वाच्छिच्छायाग्रहणासमर्थं भवति न पुनरशुद्धत्वाद्रजस्तमसी । तत् तदा
न्यग्भूतरजस्तमोरूपमञ्जितया सत्त्वं निश्चलप्रदीपशिखाकारं सदैवैकरूपतया परिणममानं
चिच्छायाग्रहणसामर्थ्यादा मोक्षप्राप्तेरवतिष्ठते । यथाऽयकान्तसन्निधाने लोहस्य चलनमाविर्भवति एवं
चिद्रूप पुरुषसन्निधाने सत्त्वस्याभिव्यङ्ग्यमभिव्यज्यते चैतन्यम् । अत एवास्मिन्दर्शने द्वे चिच्छक्ती
नित्योदिताऽभिव्यङ्ग्या च नित्योदिता चिच्छक्तिः पुरुषस्तत्सन्निधानादभिव्यक्तमभिव्यङ्ग्यचैतन्यं
सत्त्वमाभिव्यङ्ग्या चिच्छक्तिः । तदत्यन्तसन्निहितत्वादन्तरङ्गं पुरुषस्य भोग्यतां प्रतिपद्यते । तदेव
शान्तब्रह्मवादिभिः सांख्यैः पुरुषस्य परमात्मनोऽधिष्ठेयं कर्मानुरूपं सुखदुःखभोक्तृतया व्यपदिश्यते ।
यत्त्वनुद्रिक्तत्वादेकस्यापि गुणस्य कदाचित्कस्यचिदङ्गित्वात्रिगुणं प्रतिक्षणं परिणममानं
सुखदुःखमोहात्मकनिर्मलं तत्तस्मिन्कर्मानुरूपे शुद्धे सत्त्वे स्वाकारसमर्पणद्वारेण संवेद्यतामापादयति
तच्छुद्धमाद्यं चित्तसत्त्वमेकतः प्रतिसंक्रान्तचिच्छायमन्यतोगृहीतविषयाकारेण चित्तेनोपढौकितस्वाकारं
चित्सक्रान्तिबलाच्चेतनायमानं वास्तवचैतन्याभावेऽपि सुखदुःखभोगमनुभवति । स एव
भोगोऽत्यन्तसन्निधानेन विवेकाग्रहणाभोक्तुरपि पुरुषस्य भोग इति व्यपदिश्यते । अनेनैवाभिप्रायेण
विन्ध्यवासिनोक्तं सत्त्वतप्त्वमेव पुरुषतप्त्वम् इति । अन्यत्रापि प्रतिबिम्बे
प्रतिबिम्बमानच्छायासदृशच्छायोद्धवः प्रतिबिम्बशब्देनोच्यते । एवं सत्त्वेऽपि
पौरुषेयचिच्छायासदृशचिदभिव्यक्तिः प्रतिसंक्रान्तिशब्दार्थः । ननु प्रतिबिम्बं नाम निर्मलस्य
नियतपरिणामस्य निर्मले दृष्टं यथा मुखस्य दर्पणे । अत्यन्तनिर्मलस्य व्यापकस्यापरिणामिनः पुरुषस्य
तस्मादत्यन्तनिर्मलात्पुरुषादनिर्मले सत्त्वे कथं प्रतिबिम्बनमुपपद्यते । उच्यते प्रतिबिम्बनस्य
स्वरूपमनवगच्छता भवतेदमभ्यधायि । यैव सत्त्वगताया अभिव्यङ्ग्यायाश्चिच्छक्तेः पुरुषस्य
सांनिध्यादभिव्यक्तिः सैव प्रतिबिम्बनमुच्यते । यादृशी पुरुषगता चिच्छक्तिस्तच्छाया
तथाऽऽविर्भवति । यदप्युक्तमत्यन्तनिर्मलः पुरुषः कथमनिर्मले सत्त्वे प्रतिसंक्रामतीति
तदप्यनैकान्तिकं नैर्मल्यादपकृष्टेऽपि जलादावादित्यादयः प्रतिसंक्रान्ताः समुपलभ्यन्ते ।
यदप्युक्तमनवच्छिन्नस्य नास्ति प्रतिसंक्रान्तिरिति तदप्युक्तं व्यापकस्याप्याकाशस्य दर्पणादौ
प्रतिसंक्रान्तिदर्शनात् । एवं सति न काचिदनुपपत्तिः प्रतिबिम्बदर्शनस्य । ननु सात्त्विकपरिणामरूपे
बुद्धिसत्त्वे पुरुषसन्निधानादभिव्यङ्ग्यायाश्चिच्छक्तेर्बाह्यार्थाकारसंक्रान्तौ पुरुषस्य सुखदुःखरूपो भोग
इत्युक्तं तदनुपपन्नम् । तदेव चित्तसत्त्वं प्रकृतावपरिणतायां कथं संभवति किमर्थश्च तस्याः परिणामः
अथोच्येत पुरुषस्यार्थोपभोगसंपादनं तया कर्तव्यम् अतः पुरुषार्थकर्तव्यतया तस्या युक्त एव
परिणामः । तच्चानुपपन्नं पुरुषार्थकर्तव्यताया एवानुपपत्ते पुरुषार्थो मया कर्तव्य
इत्येवंविधोऽध्यवसायः पुरुषार्थकर्तव्यतोच्यते । जड़ायाश्च प्रकृतेः कथं प्रथममेवैवंविधोऽध्यवसायः ।
अस्ति चेदध्यवसायः कथं जड़त्वम् । अत्रोच्यते अनुलोमप्रतिलोमलक्षणपरिणामद्वये सहजं
शक्तिद्वयमस्ति तदेव पुरुषार्थकर्तव्यतोच्यते । सा च शक्तिरचेतनाया अपि प्रकृतेः सहजैव । पत्र
महदादिमहाभूतपर्यन्तोऽस्या बहिर्मुखतयाऽनुलोमः परिणामः । पुनः
स्वकारणानुप्रवेशद्वारेणास्मितान्तः परिणामः प्रतिलोमः । इत्थं पुरुषस्याऽऽभोगपरिसमाप्तेः

सहजशक्तिद्वयक्षयात्कृतार्था प्रकृतिर्न पुनः परिणाममारभते । एवंविधायां च पुरुषार्थकर्तव्यतायां जड़ाया अपि प्रकृतेर्न काचिदनुपपत्तिः । ननु यदीदृशी शक्तिः सहजैव प्रधानस्यास्ति तत्किमर्थं मोक्षार्थिभिर्मोक्षाय यत्नः क्रियते मोक्षस्य चानर्थनीयत्वे तदुपदेशकशास्त्रस्याऽनर्थक्यं स्यात् । उच्यते योऽयं प्रकृतिपुरुषयोरनादिभोग्यभोक्तृत्वलक्षणः संबन्धस्तस्मिन्सति व्यक्तचेतनायाः प्रकृतेः कर्तृत्वाभिमानाद्दुःखानुभवे सति कथमियं दुःखनिवृत्तिरात्यन्तिकी मम स्यादिति भवत्येवाध्यवसायः अतो दुःखनिवृत्त्युपायोपदेशकशास्त्रोपदेशापेक्षाऽस्त्येव प्रधानस्य । तथाभूतमेव च कर्मानुरूपं बुद्धिसत्त्वं शास्त्रोपदेशश्च विषयः । दर्शनान्तरेष्वप्येवंविध एवाविद्यास्वभावः शास्त्रेऽधिक्रियते । स च मोक्षाय प्रयतमान एवंविधमेव शास्त्रोपदेशं सहकारिणपेक्ष्य मोक्षाख्यं फलमासादयति । सर्वाण्येव कार्याणि प्राप्तायां सामग्र्यामात्मानं लभन्ते । अस्य च प्रतिलोमपरिणामद्वारेणैवोत्पाद्यस्य मोक्षाख्यस्य कार्यस्येदृश्येव सामग्री प्रमाणेन निश्चिता प्रकारान्तरेणानुपपत्तेः । अतस्तां विना कथं भवितुमर्हति । अत्रः स्थितमेतत् संक्रान्तविषयोपरागमभिव्यक्तचिच्छायं बुद्धिसत्त्वं विषयनिश्चयद्वारेण समग्रां लोकयात्रां निर्वाहयतीति । एवंविधमैव चित्तं पश्यन्तो भ्रान्ताः स्वसंवेदनं चित्तं चित्तमात्रं च जगदित्येवं ब्रुवाणाः प्रतिबोधिता भवन्ति । ननु यद्येवंविधादेव चित्तात्सकलव्यवहारनिष्पत्तिः कथं प्रमाणशून्यो द्रष्टाभ्युपगम्यत इत्याशङ्क्य द्रष्टुः प्रमाणमाह

तदसंख्येयवासनाभिश्चित्रमपि परार्थं संहत्यकारित्वात् ॥24॥

tadasaṃkhyeyavāsanābhiścitramapi parārtham
saṃhatyakāritvāt

Though [*tadā*] the mind [*saṅhatyakāritvāt*] is the product of matter being caused by sāttvika ahaṅkāra and [*chitram*] coloured/modified by [*asaṅkhyeya*] innumerable [*vāsanābhiḥ*] sanskāras of the visible world, yet [*parārtham*] it serves the purpose of soul (self-realization and realization of Brahman).

Here the difference between self-realization and realization of Brahman must be understood.

When sanskāras of the material world are completely erased from the mind, a soul is able to identify its true nature, this is called self-realization. In the state of self-realization, the mind is free from all sanskāras of the mundane world, but it has the sanskāra of 'aham'. Sanskāra of 'aham' is received by the mind during its origin from ahaṅkāra (individuality). In fact, ahaṅkāra is the second evolute of Prakṛti followed by mahat-tattva (intelligence) when unification of its three guṇas is disturbed. Due to this aham, the mind maintains its individual identity. But in Asamprajñāta samādhi, the sanskāra of 'aham' is also erased and a yogī completely merges with Brahman. This is called realization of Brahman. So, self-realization and realization of Brahman are two different things. The state of self-realization is known as the state of Jivan-mukti or living-liberation. A yogī takes birth but he lives a liberated life. Such yogīs are called Avatāras, like Rāma and Kṛṣṇa. After realization of Brahman, a yogī attains final Mokṣa called as Videha Mukti, i.e. attaining mokṣa after death.

व्यासभाष्य—तदेतच्चित्तमसंख्येयाभिर्वासनाभिरेव चित्रीकृतमपि परार्थं परस्य भोगापवर्गार्थं न स्वार्थं संहत्यकारित्वाद्गृहवत् । संहत्यकारिणा चित्तेन न स्वार्थेन भवितव्यं न सुखंचित्तं सुखार्थं न ज्ञानं ज्ञानार्थमुभयमप्येतत्परार्थम् । यश्च भोगेनापवर्गेण चार्थेनार्थवान्पुरुषः स एव परो न परः सामान्यमात्रम् । यत्तु किंचित्परं सामान्यमात्रं स्वरूपेणोदाहरेद्वैनाशिकस्तत्सर्वं संहत्यकारित्वात्परार्थमेव स्यात् । यस्त्वसौ परो विशेषः स न संहत्यकारी पुरुष इति ।

भोजवृत्ति—तदेव चित्तं संख्यातुमशक्याभिर्वासनाभिश्चित्रमपि नानारूपमपि परार्थं परस्य स्वामिनो भोक्तुर्भोगापवर्गलक्षणमर्थं साधयतीति कुतः संहत्यकारित्वात् संहत्य संभूय मिलित्वार्थक्रियाकारित्वात् । यच्च संहत्यार्थक्रियाकारि तत्परार्थं दृष्टं यथा शयनासनादि । सत्त्वरजस्तमांसि च चित्तलक्षणपरिणामभाञ्जि संहत्यकारीणि चातः परार्थानि । यः परः स पुरुषः । ननु यादृश्येन शयनासनादीना परेण शरीरवता पारार्थ्यमुपलब्धं तद्दृष्टान्तबलेन तादृश एव परः सिध्यति । यादृशश्च भवता परोऽसंहतरूपोऽभिप्रेतस्तद्विपरीतस्य सिद्धेरयमिष्टविघातकृद्धेतुः । उच्यते यद्यपि सामान्येन परार्थमात्रत्वेन व्यासिगृहीता तथापि सत्त्वादिविलक्षणधर्मिपर्यालोचनया तद्विलक्षण एव भोक्ता परः सिध्यति । यथा चन्दनवनावृते शिखरिणि विलक्षणाद्धूमाद्वह्निरनुमीयमान इतरवह्निविलक्षणश्चन्दनप्रभव एव प्रतीयते एवमिहापि विलक्षणस्य सत्त्वाख्यस्य भोग्यस्य पारार्थ्वेऽनुमीयमाने तथाविध एव भोक्ताऽधिष्ठाता परच्छिन्नमात्ररूपोऽसंहतः सिध्यति । यदि च तस्य परत्वं सर्वोत्कृष्टत्वमेव प्रतीयते तथापि तामसेभ्यो विषयेभ्यः प्रकृष्यते शरीरं प्रकाशरूपेन्द्रियाश्रयत्वात् तस्मादपि प्रकृष्यन्त इन्द्रियाणि ततोऽपि प्रकृष्टं सत्त्वं प्रकाशरूपं तस्यापि यः प्रकाशकः प्रकाश्यविलक्षणः स चिद्रूप एव भवतीति कुतस्तस्य संहतत्वम् । इदानीं शास्त्रफलं कैवल्यं निर्णेतुं दशभिः सूत्रैरुपक्रमते

विशेषदर्शिन आत्मभावभावनाविनिवृत्तिः ॥25॥

viśeṣadarśina ātmabhāvabhāvanāvinivṛttiḥ

[*Viśeṣadarśina*] Those who are able to realize the

distinction between mind and soul, [*nivṛtti*] they cease to be [*bhāvanā*] curious [*ātmabhāva*] about their individual identity.

व्यासभाष्य—यथा प्रावृषि तृणाङ्कुरस्योद्धेदेन तद्बीजसत्ताऽनुमीयते तथा मोक्षमार्गश्रवणेन यस्य रोमहर्षाश्रुपातौ दृश्येते तत्राप्यस्ति विशेषदर्शनबीजमपवर्गभागीयं कर्माभिनिर्वर्तितमित्यनुमीयते । तस्याऽऽत्मभावभावना स्वाभाविकी प्रवर्तते । यस्याभावादिदमुक्तं स्वभावं मुक्त्वा दोषाद्येषां पूर्वपक्षे रुचिर्भवत्यरुचिश्च निर्णये भवति । तत्राऽऽत्मभावभावना कोऽहमासं कथमहमासं किंस्विदिदं कथंस्विदिदं के भविष्यामः कथं वा भविष्याम इति । सा तु विशेषदर्शिनो निवर्तते । कुतः चित्तस्यैवैष विचित्रः परिणामः पुरुषस्त्वसत्यामविद्यायां शुद्धश्चित्तधर्मैरपरामृष्ट इति । ततोऽस्याऽऽत्मभावभावना कुशलस्य निवर्तत इति ।

भोजवृत्ति—एवं सत्त्वपुरुषयोरन्यत्वे साधिते यस्तयोर्विशेषं पश्यति अहमस्मादन्य इत्येवंरूपं तस्य विज्ञातचित्तस्वरूपस्य चित्ते याऽऽत्मभावभावना सा निवर्तते चित्तमेव कर्तृज्ञातृभोक्तृ इत्यभिमानो निवर्तते । तस्मिन्सति किं भवतीत्याह

तदा विवेकनिम्नं कैवल्यप्राग्भारं चित्तम् ॥26॥
tadā vivekanimnaṃ kaivalyaprāgbhāraṃ cittam

[*Tadā*] After realization of distinction between mind and soul [*chittam*] the seeker [*viveka-nimnam*] becomes able to move on the path of Mokṣa and [*kaivalya-prāgbhāram*] and is poised toward Mokṣa.

व्यासभाष्य—तदानीं यदस्य चित्तं विषयप्राग्भारमज्ञाननिम्नमासीत्तदस्यान्यथा भवति कैवल्यप्राग्भारं विवेकजज्ञाननिम्नमिति ।

भोजवृत्ति—यदस्याज्ञाननिम्नपथं बहिर्मुखं विषयोपभोगफलं चित्तमासीत्तदिदानीं विवेकनिम्नं विवेक मार्गमान्तर्मुखं कैवल्यप्राग्भारं कैवल्यफलं कैवल्यप्रारम्भं वा संपद्यत इति । अस्मिंश्च विवेकवाहिनि चित्ते येऽन्तरायाः प्रादुर्भवन्ति तेषां हेतुप्रतिपादनद्वारेण त्यागोपायमाह

तच्छिद्रेषु प्रत्ययान्तराणि संस्कारेभ्यः ॥27॥
tacchidreṣu pratyayāntarāṇi saṃskārebhyaḥ

[*Tacchidreṣu*] In the intervals [*pratyayāntarāṇi*] arise thoughts of the visible world [*saṃskārebhyaḥ*] by force of sanskāras.

व्यासभाष्य—प्रत्ययविवेकनिम्नस्य सत्त्वपुरुषान्यताख्यातिमात्रप्रवाहरोहिणश्चित्तस्य तच्छिद्रेषु प्रत्ययान्तराण्यस्मीति वा ममेति वा जानामीति वा न जानामीति वा । कुतः क्षीयमाणबीजेभ्यः पूर्वसंस्कारेभ्यः इति ।

भोजवृत्ति—तस्मिन्समाधौ स्थितस्य तच्छिद्रेष्वन्तरालेषु यानि प्रत्ययान्तराणि व्युत्थानरूपाणि ज्ञानानि तानि प्राग्भूतेभ्यो व्युत्थानानुभवजेभ्यः संस्कारेभ्योऽहं ममेत्येवंरूपाणि क्षीयमाणेभ्योऽपि प्रभवन्ति अन्तःकरणोच्छित्तिद्वारेण तेषां हानं कर्तव्यमित्युक्तं भवति । हानोपायश्च पूर्वमेवोक्त इत्याह

हानमेषां क्लेशवदुक्तम् ॥28॥
hānameṣāṃ kleśavaduktam

[*Hānam*] The elimination [*eṣām*] of these sanskāras of the visible world is [*uktam*] described [*kleśavad*] like that of the elimination of kleśas (afflictions). That is, when kleśas are eliminated, they cannot develop again, similarly when sanskāras are eliminated, their immediate rise is not possible.

व्यासभाष्य—यथा क्लेशा दग्धबीजभावा न प्ररोह समर्था भवन्ति यथा ज्ञानाग्निना दग्धबीजभावः पूर्वसंस्कारो न प्रत्ययप्रसूर्भवति । ज्ञानसंस्कारास्तु चित्ताधिकारसमासिमनुशेरत इति न चिन्त्यन्ते ।

भोजवृत्ति—यथा क्लेशानामविद्यादीनां हानं पूर्वमुक्तं तथा संस्काराणामपि कर्तव्यम्। यथा ते ज्ञानाग्निना प्लुष्टा दग्धबीजकल्पा न पुनश्चित्तभूमौ प्ररोहं लभन्ते तथा संस्काराऽपि। एवं प्रत्ययान्तरानुदयेन स्थिरीभूते समाधौ याद्दशाऽस्य योगिनः समाधिप्रकर्षप्राप्तिर्भवति तथाविधमुपायमाह-

प्रसंख्यानेऽप्यकुसीदस्य सर्वथा विवेकख्यातेर्धर्ममेघः समाधिः ॥29॥
prasaṃkhyāne'pyakusīdasya sarvathā vivekakhyāter
dharmameghaḥ samādhiḥ

When a yogī is able to [*prasaṅkhyāne*] realize the distinction between mind and soul and [*akusidasya*] becomes free from the allurements of divine powers attained by him/her during the course of samādhi; his/her [*viveka-khyāte*] viveka-khyāti (sense of distinction between mind and soul) is strengthened and he/she enters into the stage of [*dharma-megha*] Dharma-Megha Samādhi (which is the highest stage of Samprajñāta Samādhi). Dharma-Megha Samādhi means that which irrigate (clears) the path of Dharma (Mokṣa).

व्यासभाष्य—यदायं ब्राह्मणः प्रसंख्यानेऽप्यकुसीदस्ततोऽपि न किञ्चित्प्रार्थयते। तत्रापि विरक्तस्य सर्वथा विवेकख्यातिरेव भवतीति संस्कारबीजक्षयान्नास्य प्रत्ययान्तराण्युत्पद्यन्ते। तदाऽस्य धर्ममेघो नाम समाधिर्भवति।

.**भोजवृत्ति.**—प्रसंख्यानं यावतां तत्त्वानां यथाक्रमं व्यवस्थितानां परस्परविलक्षणस्वरूपविभावनं तस्मिन्सत्यप्यकुसीदस्य फलमलिप्सोः प्रत्ययान्तराणामनुदयात्सर्वप्रकारविवेख्यातेः परिशेषाद्धर्ममेघः समाधिर्भवति। प्रकृष्टमशुक्लकृष्णं धर्मं परमपुरुषार्थसाधकं मेहति सिञ्चतीति धर्ममेघः। अनेन प्रकृष्टधर्मस्यैव ज्ञानहेतुत्वमित्युपपादितं भवति। तस्माद्धर्ममेघात्किं भवतीत्यत आह

ततः क्लेशकर्मनिवृत्तिः ॥30॥

tataḥ kleśakarmanivṛttiḥ

[*Tataḥ*] From that (Dharma-megha Samādhi) all [*kleśa*] afflictions and [*karma*] sanskāras are eliminated.

व्यासभाष्य—तल्लाभादविद्यादयः क्लेशाः समूलकाषं कषिता भवन्ति। कुशलाकुशलाश्च कर्माशयाः समूलघातं हता भवन्ति। क्लेशकर्मनिवृत्तौ जीवन्नेव विद्वान्विमुक्तो भवति। कस्मात् यस्माद्विपर्ययो भवस्य कारणम्। न हि क्षीणक्लेशविपर्ययः कश्चित्केनचित्क्वचिज्जातो दृश्यत इति।

.**भोजवृत्ति.**—क्लेशानामविद्यादीनामभिनिवेशान्तानां कर्मणां च शुक्लादिभेदेन त्रिविधानां ज्ञानोदयात्पूर्वपूर्वकारणनिवृत्त्या निवृत्तिर्भवति। तेषु निवृत्तेषु किं भवतीत्यत आह

तदा सर्वावरणमलापेतस्य ज्ञानस्यानन्त्याज्ज्ञेयमल्पम् ॥31॥

tadā sarvāvaraṇamalāpetasya jñānasyānantyājjñeyamalpam

[*Tadā*] After elimination of afflictions and sanskāras [*sarvāvaraṇa-malāpetasya*] all impurities of mind come to an end, [*ānantyāt*] consequently there is abundance [*jñānasya*] of knowledge and [*alpam*] very less remains [*jñeyam*] to be known.

व्यासभाष्य—सर्वैः क्लेशकर्मावरणैर्विमुक्तस्य ज्ञानस्याऽऽनन्त्यं भवति। तमसाभिभूतमावृतम् ज्ञानसत्त्वम् क्वचिदेव रजसा प्रवर्तितमुद्घाटितं ग्रहणसमर्थं भवति। यत्र यदा सर्वैरावरणमलैरपगतमलं भवति तदा भवत्यस्याऽऽनन्त्यम्। ज्ञानस्याऽऽनन्त्याज्ज्ञेयमल्पं संपद्यते। यथाऽऽकाशे खद्योतः। यत्रेदमुक्तम्

अन्धो मणिमविध्यत्तमनङ्गुलिरावयत्।
अग्रीवस्तं प्रत्यमुञ्चत्तमजिह्वोभ्यपूजयत्।।इति।।31।।

.**भोजवृत्ति.**—आत्रियते चित्तमेभिरित्यावरणानि क्लेशास्त एव मलास्तेभ्योऽपेतस्य तद्विरहितस्य ज्ञानस्य शरद्गगननिभस्याऽऽनन्त्यादनवच्छेदात् ज्ञेयमल्पं गणनास्पदं न भवत्यक्लेशेनैव सर्वं ज्ञेयं जानातीत्यर्थः। ततः किमित्यत आह

तततः कृतार्थानां परिणामक्रमसमाप्तिर्गुणानाम् ॥32॥

tataḥ kṛtārthānāṃ pariṇāmakramasamāptirguṇānām

[*Tataḥ*] When the perfection in Dharma-medha Samādhi is attained, [*guṇānām*] the objective of the guṇas [*kṛtārthānām*] having been fulfilled, [*samāptiḥ*] there is an end to [*pariṇāmakrama*] the successive results or role of sattva, rajas and tamas guṇas (into birth cycle).

व्यासभाष्य—तस्य धर्ममेघस्योदयात्कृतार्थानां गुणानां परिणामक्रमः परिसमाप्यते । न हि कृतभोगापवर्गाः परिसमाप्तक्रमाः क्षणमप्यवस्थातुमुत्सहन्ते । अथ कोऽयं क्रमो नामेति

भोजवृत्ति—कृतो निष्पादितो भोगापवर्गलक्षणः पुरुषार्थः प्रयोजनं यैस्ते कृतार्ता गुणाः सत्त्वरजस्तमांसि तेषां परिणाम आ पुरुषार्थसमाप्तेरानुलोम्येन प्रातिलोम्येन चाङ्गाङ्गिभाव स्थितिलक्षणस्तस्य योऽसौ क्रमो वक्ष्यमाणस्तस्य परिसमाप्तिर्निष्ठा न पुनरुद्भव इत्यर्थः । क्रमस्योक्तस्य लक्षणमाह

What is this succession? The same is defined in the ensuing sūtra.

क्षणप्रतियोगी परिणामापरान्तनिर्ग्राह्यः क्रमः ॥33॥

kṣaṇapratiyogī pariṇāmāparāntanirgrāhyaḥ
kramaḥ

[*Kramaḥ*] Succession is [*kṣaṇa pratiyogī*] relative to kṣaṇa (time taken in the displacement of an atom or time taken by an atom moving from one place to another place) [*nigrāhyaḥ*] known [*aparānta*] at the end of [*pariṇām*] conclusion of series.

Note: Succession of guṇas here means progressing from the lover level, that is tamoguṇa and ending with sattvaguṇa. After sattvaguṇa is obtained, the guṇas are left behind and a yogī starts the journey of self-realization.

व्यासभाष्य—क्षणानन्तर्यात्मा परिणामस्यापरान्तेनावसानिन गृह्यते क्रमः । न ह्यननुभूतक्रमक्षणा पुराणता वस्त्रस्यान्ते भवति । नित्येषु च क्रमो दृष्टः ।

द्वयी चेयं नित्यता कूटस्थनित्यता परिणामिनित्यता च । तत्र कूटस्थनित्यता पुरुषस्य ।
परिणामिनित्यता गुणानाम् । यस्मिन्परिणम्यमाने तत्त्वं न विहन्यते तन्नित्यम् । उभयस्य च
तत्त्वानभिघातान्नित्यत्वम् । तत्र गुणधर्मेषु बुद्ध्यादिषु परिणामापरान्तनिर्ग्राह्यः क्रमो लब्धपर्यवसानो
नित्येषु धर्मिषु गुणेष्वलब्धपर्यवसानः । कूटस्थनित्येषु स्वरूपमात्रप्रतिष्ठेषु मुक्तपुरुषेषु स्वरूपास्तिता
क्रमेणैवानुभूयत इति तत्राप्यलब्धपर्यवसानः शब्दपृष्ठेनास्तिक्रियामुपादाय कल्पित इति ।

अथास्य संसारस्य स्थित्या गत्या च गुणेषु वर्तमानस्यास्ति क्रमसमाप्तिर्न वेति ।
अवचनीयमेतत् । कथम् । अस्ति प्रश्न एकान्तवचनीयः सर्वो जातो मरिष्यति मृत्वा जनिष्यत इति ।
ओ3म् भो इति ।

अथ सर्वो जातो मरिष्यतीति मृत्वा जनिष्यत इति । विभज्यवचनीयमेतत् । प्रत्युदितख्यातिः
क्षीणतृष्णः कुशलो न जनिष्यत इतरस्तु जनिष्यते । तथा मनुष्यजातिः श्रेयसी न वा श्रेयसीत्येवं
परिपृष्टे विभज्य वचनीयः प्रश्नः पशूनधिकृत्य श्रेयसी देवानृषींश्चाधिकृत्य नेति । अयं त्वचनीयः प्रश्नः
संसारोऽयमन्तवानथानन्त इति । कुशलस्यान्ति संसारक्रमपरिसमाप्तिर्नेतरस्येति अन्यतरावधारणे
दोषः । तस्माद्व्याकरणीय एवायं प्रश्न इति ।

गुणाधिकारक्रमसमाप्ता कवल्यमुक्त । तत्स्वरूपमवधार्यते

.भोजवृत्ति.—क्षणोऽल्पीयान्कालस्तस्य योऽसौ प्रतियोगी क्षणविलक्षणः
परिणामापरान्तनिर्ग्राह्योऽनुभूतेषु क्षणेषु पश्चात्संकलनबुद्ध्यै व यो गृह्यते स क्षणानां क्रम उच्यते न
ह्यननुभूतेषु क्षणेषु क्रमः परिज्ञातुं शक्य । इदानीं फलभूतस्य कैवल्यस्यासाधारणं स्वरूपमाह

पुरुषार्थशून्यानां गुणानां प्रतिप्रसवः कैवल्यं स्वरूपप्रतिष्ठा वा
चितिशक्तिरिति ॥34॥

puruṣārthaśūnyānāṃ guṇānāṃ pratiprasavaḥ kaivalyam
svarūpapratiṣṭhā vā citiśaktiriti

When Dharma-megha samādhi is attained, [*guṇānāṃ*]
the sattva, rajas and tamas-guṇas become [*puruṣārtha-śunyānāṃ*] purposeless for the embodiment of soul,
(because now the soul is not getting a body[5]). [*vā*] and
[*svarūpa-pratiṣṭhā chiti śaktiḥ*] the soul is established into
its true form by realising its true nature. This is called
Kaivalya.

व्यासभाष्य—कृतभोगापवर्गाणां पुरुषार्थशून्यानां यः प्रतिप्रसवः कार्यकारणात्मकानां गुणानां
तत्कैवल्यं स्वरूपप्रतिष्ठा पुनर्बुद्धिसत्त्वानभिसंबन्धात्पुरुषस्य चितिशक्तिरेव केवला तस्याः सदा

---

5 Role of guṇas is limited to the extent of soul's geting a body

तथैवावस्थानं कैवल्यमिति ।

इति श्रीपातञ्जले सांख्यप्रवचने योगशास्त्रे श्रीमद्व्यासभाष्ये चतुर्थः कैवल्यपादः ।।4।।

.भोजवृत्तिः.—समाप्तभोगापवर्गलक्षणपुरुषार्थानां गुणानां यः प्रतिप्रसवः प्रतिलोमस्य परिणामस्य समाप्तौ विकारानुद्भवः यदि वा चितिशक्तेर्वृत्तिसारूप्यनिवृत्तौ स्वरूपमात्रेऽवस्थानं तत्कैवल्यमुच्यते ।

न केवलमस्मद्दर्शने क्षेत्रज्ञः कैवल्यावस्थायामेवंविधश्छिद्रूपो यावद्दर्शनान्तरेष्वपि विमृश्यमाण एवंरूपोऽवतिष्ठते । तथाहि संसारदशायामात्मा कर्तृत्वभोक्तृत्वानुसंधातृत्वमयः प्रतीयतेऽन्यथा यद्ययमेकः क्षेत्रज्ञस्तथाविधो न स्यात्तदा ज्ञानलक्षणानामेव पूर्वापरानुसंधातृशून्यानामात्मभावे नियतः कर्मफलसंबन्धो न स्यात्कृतहाना कृताभ्यागमप्रसङ्गश्च । यदि येनैव शास्त्रोपदिष्टमनुष्ठितं कर्म तस्यैव भोक्तृत्वं भवेत्तदा हिताहितप्राप्तिपरिहाराय सर्वस्य प्रवृत्तिघटित सर्वस्यैव व्यवहारस्य हानोपादानलक्षणस्यानुसंधानेनैव व्याप्तत्वाज्ज्ञानक्षणानां परस्परभेदेनानुसंधानशून्यत्वात्तदनुसंधानाभावे कस्यचिदपि व्यवहारस्यानुपपत्तेः कर्ता भोक्ताऽनुसंघाता यः स आत्मेति व्यवस्थाप्यते । मोक्षदशायां तु सकलग्राह्यग्राहकलक्षणव्यवहाराभावाच्चैतन्यमात्रमेव तस्यावशिष्यते । तच्चैतन्यं चितिमात्रत्वेनैवोपपद्यते न पुनरात्मसंवेदनेन । यस्माद्विषयग्रहणसमर्थत्वमेव चिते रूपं नाऽऽत्मग्राहकत्वम् । तथाहि अर्थीश्रित्या गृह्यमाणोऽयमिति गृह्यते स्वरूपं गृह्यमाणमहमिति न पुनर्युगपद्बहिर्मुखतान्तर्मुखतालक्षणव्यापारद्वयं परस्परविरुद्धं कर्तुं शक्यम् । अत एकस्मिन्समये व्यापारद्वयस्य कर्तुमशक्यत्वाच्चिद्रूपतैवावशिष्यते अतो मोक्षावस्थायां निवृत्ताधिकारेषु गुणेषु चिन्मात्ररूप एवाऽऽत्माऽवतिष्ठत इत्येवं युक्तम् । संसारदशायां त्वेवंभूतस्यैव कर्तृत्वं भोक्तृत्वमनुसंधातृत्वं च सर्वमुपपद्यते । तथाहि योऽयं प्रकृत्या सहानादिनैसर्गिकोऽस्य भोग्यभोक्तृत्वलक्षणः संबन्धोऽविवेकख्यातिमूलस्तस्मिन्सति पुरुषार्थकर्तव्यतारूपशक्तिद्वयसद्भावे या महदादिभावेन परिणतिस्तस्यां संयोगे सति यदात्मनोऽदिष्टातृत्वं चिच्छायासमर्पणसामर्थ्यं बुद्धिसत्त्वस्य च संक्रान्तचिच्छायाग्रहणसामर्थ्यं चिदवष्टब्धायाश्च बुद्धेर्योऽयं कर्तृत्वभोक्तृत्वाध्यवसायस्तत एव सर्वस्यानुसंधानपूर्वकस्य व्यवहारस्य निष्पत्तेः किमन्यैः फल्मुभिः कल्पनाजल्पैः । यदि पुनरेवंभूतमार्गव्यतिरेकेण पारमार्थिकमात्मानः कर्तृत्वाद्यङ्गी क्रियेत तदाऽस्य परिणामित्वप्रसङ्गः । परिणामित्वाच्चानित्यत्वे तस्याऽऽत्मत्वमेव न स्यात् । न ह्येकस्मिन्नेव समये एकेनैव रूपेण परस्परविरुद्धावस्थानुभवः संभवति । तथाहि यस्यामवस्थायामात्मसमवेते सुखे समुत्पन्ने तस्यानुभवितृत्वं न तस्यामेवावस्थायां दुःखानुभवितृत्वम् । अतोऽवस्थानां नानात्वात् तदभिन्नस्यावस्थावतोऽपि नानात्वं नानात्वेन च परिणामित्वान्नाऽऽत्मत्वम् । नापि नित्यत्वम् । अत एव शान्तब्रह्मवादिभिः सांख्यैरात्मनः सदैव संसारदशायां मोक्षदशायां चैकरूपत्वमङ्गीक्रियते ।

ये तु वेदान्तवादिनश्चिदानन्दमयत्वमात्मनो मोक्षे मन्यन्ते तेषां न युक्तः पक्षः । तथाहि आनन्दस्य सुखरूपत्वात्सुखस्य च सदैव संवेद्यमानतयैव प्रतिभासात्संवेद्यमानत्वं च संवेदनव्यतिरेकेणानुपपन्नमिति संवेद्यसंवेदनयोरभ्युपगमादद्वैतहानिः । अथ सुखात्मकत्वमेव तस्योच्येत तद्विरुद्धधर्माध्यासादनुपपन्नम् । न हि संवेदनं संवेद्यं चैकं भवितुमर्हति । किंचाद्वैतवादिभिः कर्मात्मपरमात्मभेदेनाऽऽत्मा द्विविधः स्वीकृतः । इत्थं च तत्र येनैव रूपेण सुखदुःखभोक्तृत्वं कर्मात्मनस्तेनैव रूपेण यदि परमात्मानः स्यात्तदा कर्मात्मत्वपरमात्मनः परिणामित्वमविद्यास्वभावत्वं

च स्यात्। अथ न तस्य साक्षाद्धोक्तृत्वं किंतु तदुपधौकितमुदासीनतयाऽधिष्ठातृत्वेन स्वी करोति तदाऽस्मद्दर्शनानुप्रवेशः आनन्दरूपता च पूर्वमेव निराकृता। किं चाविद्यास्वभावत्वे निःस्वभावत्वात्कर्मात्मनः कः शास्त्राधिकारी। न तावन्नित्यनिर्मुक्तत्वात्परमात्मा नापि अविद्यास्वभावत्वात्कर्मात्मा। ततश्च सकलशास्त्रवैयर्थ्यप्रसङ्ग। अविद्यामयत्वे च जगतोऽङ्गीक्रियमाणे कस्याविद्येति विचार्यते। न तावत्परमात्मनो नित्यमुक्तत्वाद्विद्यारूपत्वाच्च कर्मात्मनोऽपि परमार्थतो निःस्वभावतया शशविषाणप्रख्यत्वे कथमविद्यासंबन्धः अथोच्यते एतदेवाविद्याया अविद्यात्वं यदविचाररमणीयत्वं नाम। यैव हि विचारेण दिनकरस्पृष्टनीहारवद्विलयमुपयाति साऽविद्येत्युच्यते। मैवं यद्वस्तु किंचित्कार्यं करोति तदवश्यं कुतश्चिद्भिन्नमभिन्नं वा वक्तव्यम्। अविद्यायाश्च संसारलक्षणकार्यकर्तृत्वम् अवश्यमङ्गीकर्तव्यम्। तस्मिन्सत्यपि यद्यनिर्वाच्यत्वमुच्यते तदा कस्यचिदपि वाच्यत्वं न स्यात्। ब्रह्मणोऽप्यवाच्यत्वप्रसक्तिः। तस्मादधिष्ठातृतारूपव्यतिरेकेण नान्यदात्मनो रूपमुपपद्यते। अधिष्ठातृत्वं च चिद्रूपमेव तद्व्यतिरिक्तस्य धर्मस्य कस्यचित्प्रमाणानुपपत्तेः।

यैरपि नैयायिकादिभिरात्मा चेतनायोगाच्चेतन इत्युच्यते। चेतनाऽपि तस्य मनःसंयोगजा। तथाहि इच्छाज्ञानप्रयत्नादयो गुणास्तस्य व्यवहारदशायामात्ममनः संयोगादुत्पद्यन्ते। तैरेव च गुणैः स्वयं ज्ञाता कर्ता भोक्तेति व्यपदिश्यते। मोक्षदशायां तु मिथ्याज्ञाननिवृत्तौ तन्मूलानां दोषाणामपि निवृत्तेस्तेषां बुद्ध्यादीनां विशेषगुणानामत्यन्तोच्छित्तेः स्वरूपमात्रप्रतिष्ठत्वमात्मनोऽङ्गीकृतं तेषामयुक्तः पक्षः यतस्तस्यां दशायां नित्यत्वव्यापकत्वादयो गुणा आकाशादीनामपि सन्ति अतस्तद्वैलक्षण्येनाऽऽत्मनश्चिद्रूपत्वमवश्यमङ्गीकार्यम्। आत्मत्वलक्षणजातियोग इति चेत। न सर्वस्यैव हि तज्जातियोगः संभवति अतो जातिभ्यो वैलक्षण्यमात्मनोऽवश्यमङ्गीकर्तव्यम्। तच्चाधिष्ठातृत्वं तच्च चिद्रूपतयैव घटते नान्यथा।

यैरपि मीमांसकैः कर्मकर्तृरूप आत्माऽङ्गी क्रियते तेषामपि न युक्तः पक्षः। तथाहि अहंप्रत्ययग्राह्यः आत्मेति तेषां प्रतिज्ञा। अहंप्रत्यये च कर्तृत्वं कर्मत्वं चाऽऽत्मन एव। न चैतद्विरुद्धत्वादुपपद्यते। कर्तृत्वं प्रमातृत्वं कर्मत्वं च प्रमेयत्वम्। न चैतद्विरुद्धधर्माध्यासो युगपदेकस्य घटते। यद्विरुद्धधर्माध्यस्तं न तदेकं यथा भावाभावौ विरुद्धे च कर्तृत्वकर्मत्वे। अथोच्यते न कर्तृत्वमकर्मत्वयोर्विरोधः किंतु कर्तृत्वकरणतयोः। कैनेतदुक्तं विरुद्धधर्माध्यासस्य तुल्यत्वात्कर्तृत्वकरणत्वयोरेव विरोधो न कर्तृत्वकर्मत्वयोः इति। तस्मादहंप्रत्ययग्राह्यत्वं परिहृत्याऽऽत्मनोऽधिष्ठातृत्वमेवोपपन्नम् तच्च चेतनत्वमेव।

यैरपि द्रव्यबोधपर्यायभेदेनाऽऽत्मनोऽव्यापकस्य शरीरपरिमाणस्य परिणामित्वमिष्यते तेषामुत्थानपराहत एव पक्षः। परिणामित्वे चिद्रूपताहानिश्चिद्रूपताभावे किमात्मन आत्मत्वम्। तस्मादात्मन आत्मत्वमिच्छता चिद्रूपत्वमेवाङ्गीकर्तव्यम्। तच्चाधिष्ठातृत्वमेव।

केचित्कर्तृरूपमेवाऽऽत्मनमिच्छन्ति। तथा हि विषयसांनिध्ये या ज्ञानलक्षणा क्रिया समुत्पन्ना तस्या विषयसंवित्तिः फलं तस्यां च फलरूपायां संवित्तौ स्वरूपं प्रकाशरूपतया प्रतिभासते विषयश्च ग्राह्यतया आत्मा च ग्राहकतया घटमहं जानामीत्याकारेण तस्याः समुत्पत्तेः। क्रियायाश्च कारणं कर्तैव भवतीत्यतः कर्तृत्वं भोक्तृत्वं चाऽऽत्मनो रूपमिति। तदनुपपन्नं यस्मात्तासां संवित्तीनां स किं कर्तृत्वं युगपत्प्रतिपद्यते क्रमेण वा। युगपत्कर्तृत्वे क्षणान्तरे तस्य कर्तृत्वं न स्यात्। अथ क्रमेण कर्तृत्वं तदेकरूपस्य न घटते एकेन रूपेण चेत्तस्य कर्तृत्वं तदैकस्य रूपस्य सदैव संनिहितत्वात्सर्व

फलमेकरूपं स्यात्। अथ नानारूपतया तस्य कर्तृत्वं तदा परिणामित्वं परिणामित्वाच्च न चिद्रूपत्वम्। अतश्चिद्रूपत्वमेवाऽऽत्मन इच्छद्भिर्न साक्षात्कर्तृत्वमङ्गीकर्तव्यम्। याद‍ृशमस्माभिः कर्तृत्वमात्मनः प्रतिपादितं कूटस्थस्य नित्यस्य चिद्रूपस्य तदेवोपपन्नम्।

एतेन स्वप्रकाशस्याऽऽत्मनो विषयसंवित्तिद्वारेण ग्राहकत्वमभिव्यजत इति ये वदन्ति तेऽपि अनेनैव निराकृताः।

केचिद्विमर्शात्मकत्वेनाऽऽत्मनश्चिन्मयत्वमिच्छन्ति। ते ह्याहुर्न विमर्शव्यतिरेकेण चिद्रूपत्वमात्मनो निरूपयितुं शक्यम्, जड़ाद्वैलक्षण्यमेव चिद्रूपत्वमुच्यते तच्च विमर्शव्यतिरेकेण निरूप्यमाणं नान्यथाऽवतिष्ठते। तदनुपपन्नम्। इदमित्थमेवंरूपमिति यो विचारः स विमर्श इत्युच्यते। स चास्मिताव्यतिरेकेण नोत्थानमेव लभते। तथाहि आत्मन्युपजायमानो विमर्शोऽहमेवंभूत इत्येनाऽऽकारेण संवेद्यते। तताश्चाहंशब्दसंभिन्नस्याऽऽत्मलक्षणस्यार्थस्य तत्र स्फुरणान्न विकल्परूपतातिक्रमः विकल्पश्चाध्यवसायात्मा बुद्धिधर्मो न चिद्धर्मः। कूटस्थनित्यत्वेन चितेः सदैकरूपत्वान्नाहंकारानुप्रवेशः। तदनेन सविमर्शत्वमात्मानः प्रतिपादयता बुद्धिरेवाऽऽत्मत्वेन भ्रान्त्या प्रतिपादिता न प्रकाशात्मनः परस्य पुरुषस्य स्वरूपमवगतमिति।

इत्थं सर्वेष्वपि दर्शनेष्वधिष्ठातृत्वं विहाय नान्यदात्मनो रूपमुपपद्यते। अधिष्ठातृत्वं च चिद्रूपत्वम्। तच्च जड़ाद्वैलक्षण्यमेव। चिद्रूपतया यदधितिष्ठति तदेव भोग्यतां नयति। यच्च चेतनाधिष्ठितं तदेव सकलव्यापारयोग्यं भवति। एष च सति कृतकृत्यत्वात् प्रधानस्य व्यापारनिवृत्तौ यदात्मनः कैवल्यमस्माभिरुक्तं तद्विहाय दर्शनान्तराणामपि नान्या गतिः। तस्मादिदमेव युक्तमुक्तं वृत्तिसारूप्यपरिहारेण स्वरूपे प्रतिष्ठा चितिशक्तेः कैवल्यम्।

तदेव सिद्ध्यन्तरेभ्यो विलक्षणां सर्वसिद्धिमूलभूतां समाधिसिद्धिमभिधाय जात्यन्तरपरिणामलक्षणस्य च सिद्धिविशेषस्य प्रकृत्यापूरणमेव कारणमित्युपपाद्य धर्मादीनां प्रतिबन्धकनिवृत्तिमात्र एक सामर्थ्यमिति प्रदर्श्य निर्माणचित्तानामस्मितामात्रादुद्भव इत्युक्त्वा तेषां च योगिचित्तमेवाधिष्ठापकमिति प्रदर्श्य योगिचित्तस्य चित्तान्तरवैलक्षण्यमभिधाय तत्कर्मणामलौकिकत्वं चोपपाद्य विपाकानुगुणानां च वासनानामभिव्यक्तिसामर्थ्ये कार्यकारणयोश्चैक्यप्रतिपादनेन व्यवहितानामपि वासनानामानन्तर्यमुपपाद्य तासामानन्त्येऽपि हेतुफलादिद्वारेण हानमुपदर्श्यातीतादिष्वध्वसु धर्माणां सद्भावमुपपाद्य विज्ञानवादं निराकृत्य साकारवादं च प्रतिष्ठाप्य पुरुषष्य ज्ञातृत्वमुक्त्वा चित्तद्वारेण सकलव्यवहारनिष्पत्तिमुपपाद्य पुरुषसत्त्वे प्रमाणमुपदर्श्य कैवल्यनिर्णयाय दशभिः सूत्रैः क्रमेणोपयोगिनोऽर्थानभिधाय शास्त्रान्तरेऽप्येतदेव कैवल्यमित्युपपाद्य कैवल्यस्वरूपं निर्णीतमिति व्याकृतः कैवल्यपादः।

इति श्रीभोजदेवविरचितायां पातञ्जलयोगशास्त्रसूत्रवृत्तौ चतुर्थः कैवल्यपादः।।4।।

॥ इति पतञ्जलि-विरचिते योग-सूत्रे चतुर्थः कैवल्य-पादः ॥

iti patañjali-viracite yoga-sūtre caturthaḥ kaivalya-pādaḥ

॥ इति श्री पातञ्जल-योग-सूत्राणि ॥

|| iti Śrī Pātañjala-yoga-sūtrāṇi ||

References

Colebrooke H.T. (1827). *Transactions of the Royal Asiatic Society of Britain and Ireland*, Vol. 1, PARBURY, ALLEN, & Co, London.

Count Bjornstjerna (1844). *Theogony of Hindus*, John Muray, London

Davies John (1907). *Hindu Philosophy The Bhagvad Gita*, Kegan Paul, London

Enfield William (1791). *The History of Philosophy*, Vol.1, J. Johnson, London

Hunter W.W. (1881). *The Imperial Gazetteer of India*, First Edition, 9 Vols. London, Tubner & Co.

Manning (Mrs.) (1869). *Ancient and Mediaeval India,* 3 vols. London, Wm. H. Allen & Co.

Max Müller (1859): *History of Ancient Sanskrit Literature, Williams and Norgate, London.*

Max Müller (1866). *Science of Language*: Lectures Delivered at the Royal Institution of Great Britain in April, May, & June 1861. *Longmans, Green*

Olcott, H.S. (1885). Theosophy, Religion and Occult Science, London, George Redway, York Street, Convent Garden.

Praphulla Chandra Ray (1902). *A History of Hindu Chemistry*, Vol.1, Williams & Norgate, London

Sarda, Diwan Bahadur Harbilas (2007). Ed. Ravi Prakash Arya, *Hindu Superiority*, Indian Foundation for Vedic Science, India.

Schlegel Friedrich (1818). *Lectures on History of Literature,*

Ancient and Modern. Vol.1, Edinburgh, London

Weber Albrecht (1878). *History of Indian Literature*, London, Trubner & Co. Ltd.

Williams, Monier (1879): '*Modern India and Indians*, Third Edition, Tubner and Co. London.

Wilson H.H (1845). *History of British India* by James Mill, 5th Edition, Vol. 1, London, James Madden

Wilson H.H, (1861): *Essays and lectures on the Religion of Hindus*, Vol. 1, Trubner & Co. London.

Wilson H.H (1864) *The Vishnu Puran*, Tubner & Co. London.

Foundation's Publications

1. Engineering and Technology in Ancient India
2. New Discoveries About Vedic Sarasvati
3. Dhanurveda: The Vedic Military Science
4. Vedic Concordance (Four Vols.)
5. Vedic and Classical Sanskrit - A Contrastive Analysis of Phonological and Morphological Features
6. Vedic Meteorology: The Ancient Indian Science of Rainmaking
7. Vedic Theory of Origin of Speech
8. Researches into Vedic and Linguistic Studies.
9. Bhāratīya Kālaganaṇā Kā Vaijñānika eva' Vaiśvika Svarūpa
10. Jesus, the Christ was a Hindu
11. History and Origin of Mathematics
12. Indian Origin of Greece and Ancient world
13. India the Civiliser of the World
14. Yuga yugin Trigarta (Trigarta through Ages)
15. Vedic Microbiology
16. Revisiting the Roots of Judeo-Christianity
17. Tributes to Renaissance Rishi
18. Rishi Dayananda in the Eyes of the West
19. Yogavāsiṭha Mahārāmāyaṇa, edited with English translation: 4 vols.
20. Vālmīki Rāmāyaṇa, edited with English Translation: 4 vols.
21. Ṛgveda, edited with English Translation: 4 vols.
22. Sāmaveda, edited with English Translation
23. Yajurveda, edited with English Translation
24. Nature of Vedic Science and Technology
25. Science of Vedic Meters and Musical notes
26. Science and Technology in Mahabharata
27. Reviving the Age-old Historical Tradition of India

28. Vedic Farming

29. Psychology in Yoga Darshan

30. Rainmaking With the help of Yajna

31. Stepping into the 52nd Century

32. Weather Forecast in Vedic Times

33. Sanskrit the Original Source of English

34. An Introduction to Bhāratīya Kālaganana

35. Somayāga: Vedic Process of Rainformation

36. Agniṣomīya Paśuyāga: Vedic Operation for Rainmaking.

37. Concordance of Vedic Mantras as per Ṛṣis and Devatās. (Two vols.)

38. Concordance of Vedic Mantras as per Devatas and Risis. (Two vols.)

39. Vedic Concordance of a quarter part of a mantra (The revised, re-edited, and updated Devanāgarī version of Bloomfield's Vedic Concordance) 4 Vols

40. Concordance of Vedic Rishis and Devatas

41. Concordance of Vedic Devatā and Ṛṣis

42. Indian Chronology to Indian History

43. 7000 years old Calendar of various Indian Eras

44. 7000 years' Calendar of Lunar Phases (8 Vols)

45. Śrimad Bhagvad Gītā: A Vedic Scientific Scripture of Liberation

46. Bible in India: Indian Origin of Hebrew and Christian Revelations

47. Introduction to the Vedas

48. The Ṛgveda Saṁhita: A Spiritual, Scientific and Socio-political Commentary. Vol. 1

49. Signatures of Time: A Collection of 231 Letters of Swami Dayanand Sarasvati written in 19th Century India

50. Vedika Svāsthya Vijñāna

51. Indic Studies and Western Hermeneutics

52. Lost Scientific Literature of Bharat

Vedic Science

A Quarterly Journal of Indian Foundation for Vedic Science dedicated to the Vedic Sciences and Scientific Interpretation of Vedas and Allied Literature

World Vedic Calendar

World Vedic Calendar is a Sāyana Pañcāṅga (updated according to precession). First time in the history of Indian calendars the details of Vedic solar months and lunar months have been given. This calendar cites Indian Festivals as astronomical according to Sāyana Pañcāṅga and as historical according to Niryana Pañcāṅga.